"This book is for every teacher leader, coach, and educational practitioner who seeks to interrupt educational inequities. Elena shares her vulnerability and insights, embraces the power of emotions, and deepens our understanding so we can expand our skillsets—helping us to put relationship before task and keep equity at the core."

> —*Tamisha Williams, Dean of Adult Equity & Inclusion, Lick-Wilmerding High School*

"Coaching for Equity is an extremely accessible and terrifically useful book for educators at all levels. Elena's authentic and caring voice comes through as she combines personal narrative seamlessly with concrete strategy to help all readers develop their conversational skills around issues of inequity. I recommend her books again and again."

> —*Jennifer Abrams, Communications Consultant and author of* Having Hard Conversations and Swimming in the Deep End

"Finally! – a unique and deeply needed guide to creating equity and shifting hearts, minds, and classrooms using tools of compassion and curiosity instead of tools of force, superiority, and judgment."

> —laura brewer, *How To Make Love*

"Elena insightfully offers leaders the essential mindsets, practice frameworks, and explicit tools to create equitable school conditions for every student, every day. This book should be essential reading for all school leaders committed to ensuring students reach their full potential and schools deliver on their promise to disrupt barriers that disproportionately and negatively impact the academic and socio-emotional experiences of black and brown students."

> —*Alexandrea Creer Kahn, former Chief Academic Officer at Leadership Public Schools and co-author of* Identity Safe Classrooms: Pathways to Belonging and Learning

"*Coaching for Equity: Conversations that Change Practice* takes the courageous step of explicitly naming and addressing the social, political, and historical nature of white supremacy and colonialism in American schooling. I've had the privilege of learning from Elena over the last eight years and her brilliance in coaching radiates in person and on the pages. Read and study this text to develop your praxis and your commitment to justice and liberatory education."

> —*Javier Cabra Walteros, Chief Academic Officer at Envision Education*

"Finally! Elena Aguilar's *Coaching for Equity* is an accessible guidebook that pushes us beyond platitudes of equity to the essential ground of creating complex learning environments that demonstrate—*every day*—what it takes for all children to receive the educational experiences they deserve. *Coaching for Equity* is for all of us who have been hungry for guidance about how to gather our people, get past our fragility, and "journey towards justice and liberation" as we work in service to all children."

>—*Kimberly N. Parker, Ph.D., Shady Hill School and co-founder of #DisruptTexts*

"Elena Aguilar, once again, delivers an illuminating resource for educators. Through personal experiences, a historical perspective, proven educational methods, and clear direction—teacher leaders will gain tools and strategies necessary for doing the challenging yet essential work of transforming their schools into welcoming, inclusive and equitable environments for learning. I certainly did."

>—*Ellen Shulman, Principal, Minneapolis Public Schools*

"Elena Aguilar writes, leads and coaches from compassion, curiosity and a deep commitment to honest conversations about systemic inequities. In this book, Aguilar provides clear, actionable and compassionate tools and resources to ensure that every single child has access to an equitable education."

>—*Kendra Lee, Director of Diversity and Inclusion Learning for Comcast*

"Elena Aguilar writes with a humility and power that pulls you in like a warm, engrossing fire. She has a way of unapologetically telling the truth while also meeting you where you are with profound respect for your journey as an educator at any point in your career and as a complete human being. *Coaching for Equity: Conversations that Change Practice* is a book of wisdom that can only be birthed after decades of firsthand experience and deep reflections on making the unconscious conscious in order to have educational equity for every child, every day."

>—*Daisy Han, CEO of Embracing Equity*

"I believe a majority of people want to create and contribute to a more equitable society, and we are too often frozen in our good intentions because we cannot address inequities we do not see, we don't know how to address the inequities we do see, we fear the pain of the process, and we fear the potential to do more harm. Elena Aguilar offers us a road map to activate our agency and begin the work of dismantling the systems of oppression that hurt us all. She offers a set of tools to begin building the healing human connections we crave."

—*Grace Losada, EdD, leadership coach and former vice president of*
 Fusion Education

"Elena has a brilliant approach to providing practical tools, methods, and strategies to examine the behaviors of educators that contribute to creating and sustaining an equitable educational experience that every student, regardless of identity and lifestyle, deserves. As teachers and educational leaders look to refine our practices to best meet the needs of **all** our students, we will benefit from *Coaching for Equity* by thinking about things in ways that we should have all along."

—*Dr. Trina Moore-Southall, Director of Equity and Inclusion, Brentwood*
 School, Los Angeles

"Elena Aguilar has built a compelling equity-coaching model. Her transformational approach evolves from her core values and 30 years of coaching and experience with diverse cultures. Through story telling she presents strategies that support systemic change; she offers implementation guidelines, and tools. Coaching for Equity is a timely, professional resource that supports an invaluable approach."

—*Virginia McHugh Goodwin-Wildflower Foundation Coach*

"As we long to re-imagine schooling during our time of worldwide trauma, Elena Aguilar brings her expertise about emotional resilience and helps us craft the skillful conversations needed to create equitable classrooms, schools, and districts that honor the needs of all the learners, both children and adults. This book will refill your reservoir of hope; it will provide you with the blueprint for building an environment where compassion and academic excellence go hand-in-hand."

—*Cheryl Beeson, retired school and district administrator*

Coaching for Equity

Coaching for Equity

Conversations that Change Practice

Elena Aguilar

JB JOSSEY-BASS™

A Wiley Brand

Jossey-Bass
A Wiley Imprint
111 River St., Hoboken, NJ 07030
www.josseybass.com

Jossey-Bass books and products are available through most bookstores. To contact Jossey-Bass directly, call our Customer Care Department within the U.S. at 800–956–7739, outside the U.S. at +1 317 572 3986, or fax +1 317 572 4002.

Wiley also publishes its books in a variety of electronic formats and by print-on-demand. Some material included with standard print versions of this book may not be included in e-books or in print-on-demand. If this book refers to media such as a CD or DVD that is not included in the version you purchased, you may download this material at http://booksupport.wiley.com. For more information about Wiley products, visit www.wiley.com.

Library of Congress Cataloging-in-Publication Data

Names: Aguilar, Elena, 1969- author.
Title: Coaching for equity : conversations that change practice / Elena
    Aguilar.
Description: First edition. | Hoboken, NJ : Jossey-Bass, [2020] | Includes
    bibliographical references and index.
Identifiers: LCCN 2020023661 (print) | LCCN 2020023662 (ebook) | ISBN
    9781119592273 (paperback) | ISBN 9781119592334 (adobe pdf) | ISBN
    9781119592341 (epub)
Subjects: LCSH: Educational equalization. | Communication in education. |
    Educational leadership. | Mentoring in education.
Classification: LCC LC213 .A38 2020 (print) | LCC LC213 (ebook) | DDC
    379.2/6—dc23
LC record available at https://lccn.loc.gov/2020023661
LC ebook record available at https://lccn.loc.gov/2020023662

Cover Design: Wiley
Cover Image: © Deejpilot/Getty Images

Printed in the United States of America

FIRST EDITION

PB Printing SKY10026765_050321

For:

Harriet
Medgar
Paulo Freire
Adelia y Azarías
Yochewet and Tsyvia
Luevinia and George Washington Goodwin
Bessie and Prentis Sr.
Brenda, Rocio, Huber,
and all my former students
Dennis, Sharon, and Hannah
Jeff, Larry, and Louie
and for
Gilbert, my father
Linda, my mother
Stacey, my heart
and Orion, my life

Love is the bridge between you and everything.

RUMI

CONTENTS

ABOUT THE AUTHOR

Elena Aguilar is the author of *The Art of Coaching, The Art of Coaching Teams, Onward: Cultivating Emotional Resilience in Educators, The Onward Workbook* and *The Art of Coaching Workbook.* She was a longtime contributor to *Edutopia* and *EdWeek,* and frequently publishes articles in *Educational Leadership.* Elena is the founder and president of Bright Morning Consulting, an educational consulting group that works to transform education. Bright Morning offers in-person and virtual workshops and online courses based on Elena's books. Elena is also a highly sought-after keynote speaker and hosts The Bright Morning Podcast. You can learn more about Bright Morning at http://brightmorningteam.com.

Elena lives in Oakland, California, with her husband and son. She also writes fiction, essays, and memoirs, which you can read on http://elenaaguilar.com. When she's not writing, coaching, or teaching, she enjoys being in nature, reading fiction, making art, and traveling abroad.

ACKNOWLEDGMENTS

Where to start when there are so many people who contributed to this book? Perhaps with Jessie Cordova, who played a critical role in getting this book going; she provided a much-needed kick that catapulted me into writing this. Charlotte Larsen provided vital encouragement at a time when I had spiraled down into self-doubt. Lori Cohen read the first draft and gave me validation that I didn't know I needed and that propelled me onward. laura brewer's repeated offerings of support and her willingness to listen to whatever I needed to express carried me through some rough patches. I'm also grateful to her for her insights into the distinctions between justice and liberation. Finally, some years ago, Laurelin Whitfield helped me organize a messy jumble of ideas into the Transformational Coaching Rubric 2.0 and provided critical support to help me expand my offerings.

We all have moments when someone says or does something that from their perspective might seem minimal or insignificant, but that arrives in precisely the right way, in the right time, and that fills a gaping need. During the course of writing this book, the following people contributed in that way for me: Raiza Lisboa, Angie Brice Thomas, Marika Beck, Shannon Carey, Andrey Castro, Kathy Eisenhower, Lizzie Salzfass, and Chiara Kupiec. I feel shy about thanking them over and over, because they'll say, "It was nothing," but I am most grateful for their contributions. In addition, Maia Heyck-Merlin's friendship sustained me across significant ups and downs while writing this book. And I am so lucky to have the compassionate guidance of Eloiza Jorge, my coach. Coaches need coaches.

I have the deepest gratitude for my team at Bright Morning: Janet Baird, LesLee Bickford, Rebecca Blackmer, Patrick Britton, Lori Cohen, Noelle Apostol Colin, Jessie Cordova, and Debbie Daly. They are a phenomenally committed, thoughtful, creative group of people, and they're a lot of fun: I'm forever grateful for the laughter in a game of Telestrations with them. Their commitment to our mission and ability to lean on each other allowed me to have long periods of focused writing time for this book—a luxury I've never had. I finished this manuscript in mid-March 2020, as the coronavirus changed our world. I wouldn't have finished this book on time had my team not been supremely agile and creative. This group of people affirms my belief every day that we can transform our schools and organizations.

The following friends and colleagues gave me invaluable feedback on drafts of this book: Michele Reinhart, Erin Davis, Lindsey Dixon, laura brewer, Jessie Cordova, and Lori Cohen. Each of these readers offered insight and comments that made this book so much better than what it would have been without their feedback; they challenged and pushed me, shared their own experiences and reflections, and offered encouragement and nudges. Lori also provided much needed support in the final stage on the recommended readings, references, and more. Caitlin Schwarzman read the chapters of this book over and over, thinking about everything from the big ideas and graphic representations to the commas and adverbs. She's provided this kind of content-editing on three of my books now, and I'm endlessly grateful for her fearless feedback.

My dear friend and colleague, Carol Owala, contributed to this book in a multitude of ways. She is my *dada*, a word that means sister in Swahili—and having never had a sister, I'm learning that this means endless encouragement and boundaryless love. She is also my colleague, my comrade, in the larger effort to transform our world, and I am a better educator and leader because of what I've learned from her. I'm forever grateful that our paths crossed and for the joy and beauty she's brought into my life.

I couldn't ask for anything more from Amy Fandrei, Pete Gaughan, and Mackenzie Thompson, the amazing team at Jossey-Bass. I am grateful for their trust, professionalism, and support of me at every step of the writing process.

The following educators have taught me a tremendous amount specifically around how to build equitable schools: Elia Bustamante, Cheryl Lana, Javier Cabra, Tina Hernandez, Larissa Adam, Angela Parker, Michael Scott, Steve Sexton, Yanira Canizalez, Drea Beale, Alex Creer Khan, and Crystal Land. Your vulnerability, courage, and commitment to children and to racial equity continue to inspire me and I'm immeasurably grateful to have worked with you. And also to "Khai" and "Stephanie" and all the other educators I've coached whose identity I won't reveal: I have only gratitude. You were my teachers.

On the home front: my father, Gilbert, and my aunt, Jeanne, continue to support me with unconditional love. My mother's legacy and teachings are elemental to who I am and to what I create: she raised me amid a joyful, diverse community that was committed to justice. Although my mother passed away in 2000, she has influenced every day of my life and every word I've written. My son, Orion, reminds me that every child deserves to be seen for who they truly are. It has been the greatest joy of my life to watch him become the person he wants to be.

I have adored my husband, Stacey Goodman, since 1997, but his support on this book further deepened my appreciation for him. He read every chapter with refined attention to detail, tone, structure, organization, and anecdotes. Day after day, and month after month, he helped me sort through the morass of ideas and emotions that arose in the process of writing this book. He challenged me when I swerved from my commitment to curiosity and compassion, and he insisted that I keep my eyes on the prize of liberation. He is a tremendously compassionate and wise person with a remarkable moral integrity. He is an inspiration to me to live a life of beauty and kindness.

INTRODUCTION

Jabari was the first student I covertly followed as part of a project to better understand the inequities at the middle school where I was a coach. Our student achievement data, particularly for African American students, had raised red flags in our district and our school's leaders were asked to do something about it. At our Instructional Leadership Team (ILT) meeting, I mused over what we could learn by shadowing a student for a day. Jabari was nominated as a candidate for this inquiry because he was a "pretty good kid." We wanted to understand the experience of average students to start with—not the outliers or those who were really struggling, but the average kids—who should have been doing much better than they were.

I lurked outside our school on a chilly January morning, and when I saw Jabari's mom drop him off, I commenced my project. Wearing jeans and a fleece, carrying a backpack, and only about 5 feet tall, I easily blended in with students. I don't think Jabari ever noticed that I was following him as he went to his classes and lunch, and then got on the city bus after dismissal. What I observed that day will never leave me.

Using the Teacher-to-Student Interaction Tracker (which you'll find in Chapter 11), I noted every exchange an adult had with Jabari. Of the interactions that I noted, 68 percent were in the negative category, 20 percent were neutral, and 12 percent were positive. Here's a sample of what I heard (devoid of tone of voice, but the words alone are revealing):

- "Take your hoodie off, young man."
- "Hands by your side as you walk these halls."
- "Sit up straight, please."
- "Two minutes is enough time for you to take out your math book."
- "I asked for an inside voice."

- "Hoodie down."
- "We walk in these halls."
- "Your eyes should be tracking me."

The overwhelming majority of comments that were made to Jabari by an adult focused on his body and behavior. Jabari didn't seem bothered by the comments—he often did what he was asked, although when the dean told him to walk in the halls, he said, "I am!" (which he was). The dean then responded with, "And don't talk back to me, young man, or you'll be in the office." Jabari just rolled his eyes and kept walking. Of the 14 different adults who interacted with Jabari that day, only one expressed care: "Nice to see you today, Jabari," she said. Very little was said about his thinking, writing, reading, or anything related to his academics. He was never called on or praised. By the end of the day, I was on the verge of attacking the next adult who made a critical, unkind comment to Jabari.

At the next ILT meeting, I presented the transcript of what I'd heard. Team members were surprised and defensive. Some tried to dismiss the data with statements like: "This was just one day. It's not representative of what our students experience." I pushed back and argued that even if it was "just one day," it was problematic, and I asked how much data like this I'd need to collect before we accepted that the culture at our school was unwelcoming and hostile to kids. One teacher felt like this data validated what staff had been asked to do when students were walking in the halls. "I thought we were supposed to say these kinds of things to kids," she said. I got frustrated and accused everyone of perpetuating racism and contributing to the high dropout rates in our district. "No wonder black boys hate school," I said. I wish I'd had more refined communication skills to share what I'd observed.

A couple years later, in 2012, I was coaching at another school where staff was concerned by the slow academic progress of English Language Learners. I proposed that I shadow a student, and when the staff agreed to let me do this, I followed Marilu for 3 days. Marilu had immigrated from Mexico a few years earlier, and although she was chatty outside of class, she was a quiet student. After observing Marilu for 3 days, I recorded only two interactions on the Teacher-to-Student Interaction Tool. Marilu had been addressed twice: "Good morning, take a seat"; and "You can put that [homework] right there." More alarming, however, was the fact that while she was in class, she had not spoken *at all*, not even once—not to another student and not to a teacher. Not once in 3 days. There were a few times when teachers asked students to engage in an activity with others when they were supposed to speak—but each time, Marilu had opted out, and no one had held her accountable. It was no surprise that her test scores for spoken English were low and that she was failing or barely passing most of her classes.

When I debriefed this data with the English Department chair, who had brought this concern to me, I had more refined coaching skills than what I'd had at the previous school, having participated in some coaching professional development and having reflected a great deal on myself as a coach. I facilitated a reflection into the root causes of what we were seeing in Marilu's data, of broader trends across the school for the achievement of English Language Learners, and of possible next steps. The English Department chair (who was one of Marilu's teachers) was devastated by the data and her own complicity. Although she was a relatively new teacher (in her third year) and led a department with strong personalities, we came up with some action steps that would, within a couple of years, result in significant changes in the experiences and outcomes for English Language Learners. The Leadership Team in this school adopted the practice of shadowing kids and employed it as a schoolwide practice to gain insight into the experiences of several groups of students who were struggling academically and socially.

There were key differences between these two inquiry explorations. First, the conditions for learning—both for adults and kids—in the two schools were significantly different. In the first, where I shadowed Jabari, the staff was far from being able to engage in a conversation about equity in a meaningful way. This doesn't mean that they *couldn't*—but at that point, I didn't scaffold us into a conversation about equity because I didn't know how. This staff had very few conversations about equity or even about their own teaching practices—although they did talk a great deal about student (mis)behavior and their administrators.

In the second school, the staff regularly engaged in conversations about racial equity and their own instructional practices. Finally, my skill set as a coach for equity had developed a great deal, and I could guide the team to reflect on the data I'd collected.

There are three key points that I hope you'll glean from these opening anecdotes:

- We can learn a lot by following students. I've facilitated this inquiry experiment across the country, in urban, suburban, and rural schools and in public and private schools with educators who are seeking to better understand the outcomes and experiences for a group of students. Every time, we've learned something new, and something that we can act on. When it comes to interrupting inequities, there are many factors that are outside of our control or perhaps influence as educators—*and* there's a great deal that is within our control, including how we talk to kids every day and what we ask them to do while they're in our classrooms.

- Attending to context and conditions is critical as we work to create equitable schools. The better we can understand the context in which teachers and leaders work, the more effective we can be as coaches. Understanding context allows us to meet people where they're at and strategically guide them in a learning journey. We must attend to conditions—it's another domain in which we have a great deal of influence.
- Who we are matters tremendously in our ability to coach and lead for equity. How we show up is a critical variable in our ability to transform schools. And how we show up is most closely within our sphere of control, which is why it's worth focusing on if we aspire to contribute to equity in schools.

In this book, I focus on this third point—your skill set as a coach and leader—while also guiding you to create the conditions in which we can build equitable schools. We'll stay focused on the things that are within our influence and control. Thank you for being here.

A Couple of Notes

Terminology and grammar: In this book, I use the traditional pronouns *he* and *she*, and in recognition of nonbinary gender identification, I also use *they*. Additionally, I use *Latinx* as a gender-neutral or nonbinary alternative to Latino or Latina.

Confidentiality: For the sake of protecting the people I coached, I've modified markers that would reveal their identity. I've changed the obvious things like the grades and content, and I've modified some of what they said. To do this, but to still preserve integrity, I've created composite clients because otherwise, in some cases, it would be too easy to guess some people's identities.

On Bridge-Building

Human beings are challenged by a paradox: we are social animals wired for connection to other humans, *and* we are wired to sort people into categories, withdraw into our groups, and fear what seems different from us. We ache to be seen in our full humanity, *and* fear of what we don't understand pulls us back from seeing the complex humanity of other people. This tension exists within each one of us and within our communities—a tension between the desire to come together and the fear, and other forces, that propel us apart. Contending with this paradox lies at the core of our efforts to build equitable schools, and therefore must be acknowledged.

In recent years, social, political, and economic divisions in the United States, and elsewhere, have become even more glaringly apparent. We see where people can't listen to each other, haven't built the skill and ability to learn from each other, lack empathy for each other, and are failing to achieve their goals and visions for peace. And yet, there are many who believe, myself included, that the desire for connection, freedom, and healing is stronger than the desire to hurt, dominate, and oppress. In spite of what has been recorded in some versions of history, I believe the human desire for belonging and healthy community is paramount to all others, although I also recognize that some people's actions have not always aligned to this intention.

In my work in schools over the last 25 years, I've seen educators who declare a commitment to equity, but whose practices fall short of achieving equitable outcomes for students. There's a gap between what they believe (or think they believe) and what they do (or are able to do). I've also worked with many teachers and leaders who aspire to create classrooms and schools where every child thrives, but who did not know how to do so.

Bridging the gap between where we are and where we want—or need—to be requires us to learn together and to talk to each other: conversations close these chasms. I've learned how to have conversations that heal deep wounds, align intentions, and prompt effective action. I consider myself to be an architect of connection.

The bridge offers an evocative metaphor for a process of change. Building a bridge requires sophisticated skills and knowledge, planning, collaboration, imagination, vision, coordination, patience, courage, and love—we'll need all of these attributes as we engage in conversations that cross gaps and as we create equitable schools.

Interconnectedness is a biological, environmental, sociological, emotional, and perhaps spiritual truth. We yearn for connection because we know that we are all connected. We know that to feel whole within ourselves, we must be whole and connected with others. My deepest intention in this book is to bring individuals and communities together. Conversations are the way we'll get there. My intention is that when you finish this book, you'll feel hopeful that healing is possible, and you'll see how we can transform schools into places of liberation through conversations.

Defining Equity

Equity has become a word that's far too easily and loosely used—so let's get to defining it. (For commonly used words, see Appendix G.)

Every Child, Every Day

Educational equity means that every child receives whatever she/he/they need to develop to her/his/their full academic and social potential and to thrive, every day. By *thrive*, I mean *academically as well as social-emotionally*. Every child has a right to feel loved and cared for and to feel that they belong to a community. Emotional well-being is as important as academic success in this definition of educational equity.

Educational equity means there is no predictability of success or failure that correlates with any social or cultural factor—a child's educational experiences or outcomes are not predictable because of their race, ethnicity, linguistic background, economic class, religion, gender, sexual orientation, physical and cognitive ability, or any other socio-political identity marker. Here are some examples of educational equity:

- A Latinx child who enters kindergarten speaking only Spanish performs as well on reading assessments in third grade as their native English-speaking counterparts.
- An African American teen is just as likely as their white or Asian classmates to enroll and thrive in an engineering program in high school.
- Girls are equally represented in advanced math courses—and are equally as successful as their male classmates.
- A Latinx male with a learning difference in Oakland, California, or in the Bronx in New York City, is just as likely to graduate from high school on time as his white counterparts and is prepared to pursue the career or college path of his choice.
- There's proportionality in the demographics of kids sent to the office: if a district's African American population is 20 percent, then at most, 20 percent of office referrals are for African American students.

Beyond the predictability of success and failure, educational equity means that every child is seen for who they truly are, and their unique interests and gifts are surfaced and cultivated. For every child to cultivate their unique gifts, they need access to an extensive range of learning opportunities, activities, and material. This means that when Prentis Jr. discovers in first grade that his love and skill for drawing surmounts all others, he has the opportunity and encouragement to pursue this passion. This means that in fourth grade, when Thui's verbal abilities are recognized, her public speaking skills are developed. Education is a vehicle to self-realization and freedom.

Educational equity means *every* child, *every* day. Period.

And yes, this is a high bar: *Every child.*

And it is an attainable goal.

I wonder how I would have reacted as a new teacher, 25 years ago, if I'd read the preceding description of equity. I suspect I would have listed all of the structural and systemic factors that would make attaining equity impossible. *Every kid?!* I might have scoffed. Not with the education budget being what it was, not with the amount of trauma in the communities I worked in, not with the astronomical turnover of teachers in our schools, not with 42 students in my second-grade class, not without books or paper or chalk. I might have slammed this book shut.

I might not have realized that my response had to do with my own intense emotions. This included the doubt I had in *my abilities* as a teacher; I feared that I would never have the skills and knowledge to meet the needs of every child, and I felt ashamed of my shortcomings. I was also incensed about what I saw in schools, about the suffering that children experienced. I despaired that change would ever happen; I feared that I wouldn't be able to meaningfully contribute. I was frustrated and felt hampered by what I could do, and I was very sad as I looked at the state of education and as I learned about the suffering my students experienced. These emotions were overwhelming, and if someone had told me that meeting the needs of every single child was an attainable goal, I might have reacted with anger.

I know our schools are under-resourced, that there's trauma in many communities, and that teacher turnover is an obstacle to meeting the needs of children. The complexity of the external factors that impede us from realizing this vision of equity are more sharply visible to me than they've ever been. And yet, I still hold this as an attainable goal: every child, every day. I have seen classrooms and schools come very, very close to meeting this goal. When I acknowledge my fear, grief, doubt, and anger, I can hold this goal and move toward it. Your fear, grief, doubt, anger—and all your emotions—can be a part of this journey. Bring them along if you'd like, and let's keep our eyes on the prize: every child, every day.

White Supremacy

Racism, as we know it today, wouldn't exist without white supremacy. Racism is based on the ideology that "white people" are superior. When I use the term *white supremacy* in this book, which I do a lot, I mean the mindset and belief system of white superiority that has become institutionalized in policy. White supremacy is further explained in Chapter 3.

Racial Equity and Intersectionality

This book focuses on racial equity. Race is a social construct that has no bearings in science. The concept of race, and then racial superiority, and then white supremacy, was created to justify the genocide of indigenous peoples, the enslavement of millions of Africans, and an exploitative economic system. Notions of white supremacy were developed hand in hand with the expansion of colonization and capitalism (Kendi, 2016).

For centuries in the United States, whiteness granted individuals freedom, allowed them to vote, own property, run for office, live in the suburbs, get a loan, attend certain schools and universities, drink from certain water fountains, sit in the front of the bus, and learn to read. Today, an individual's race is what might get them a job interview (or not), what might allow them to feel safe when camping in a rural area, what might get them pulled over for speeding (or for no reason at all) or thrown in jail, or what might provoke a police officer to shoot an unarmed teenager—and then to be acquitted of that murder. In the United States today, race is the ultimate determinant of a person's livelihood, health, financial success, home ownership, and even life expectancy. In Oakland, California, where I live, a black man has a life expectancy of 71 years—whereas a white man can expect to live some 87 years (*East Bay Times*, 2009).

Almost every corner of this world we live in has been polluted by white supremacy. It manifests in our institutions, systems, and actions, and in our mindsets. White supremacy shows up in our schools and classrooms every day—in public and private classrooms, in classrooms taught by white people and people of color, and in homogeneous and diverse classrooms. It is a dangerous force, in part because it is often invisible. Furthermore, white supremacy has been harmful to people of color and people of European decent; everyone will benefit from dismantling white supremacy.

We'll also explore the intersections between race and gender, race and class, and race and gender and class. *Intersectionality*, a concept coined by professor Kimberlé Crenshaw, is a concept to describe the prejudice stemming from the intersections of racists ideas and other forms of bigotry such as sexism, classism, ethnocentrism, and homophobia. Identity markers intersect and create unique experiences of marginalization.

Here are some statistics that validate why we need to focus on race in schools:

- The U.S. Census Bureau projects that by the middle of 2020, the majority of the nation's children will be nonwhite (U.S. Census Bureau, 2018).

- In 2015–2016, about 80 percent of public school teachers were white (National Center for Education). Research has shown that white teachers have lower expectations of students of color, which affects student success (Gershenson and Papageorge, 2018).
- Seventy-five percent of white Americans do not have friends of a different race (Cox, Navarro-Rivera, and Jones, 2016). Most white teachers get information about people of color from external sources—movies, news, social media, etc.

These numbers validate the urgency with which we need to discuss race, identity, and how racism manifests in schools.

Finally, this book focuses on the experiences of "black and brown" children. While acknowledging the complexity of racial identity, there's a great deal of research on how the experience of say, a Japanese-American child will be different from (and perhaps better than) the experience of a Lakota child in North Dakota, or a Native Hawaiian in Honolulu, or an African American child in the southside of Chicago. "Black and brown" refers to people who are descendants of the African diaspora (which may include Haitians or Jamaicans, for example) as well as to recent immigrants and refugees from Africa. I alternate referring to students as "African American," and "black" to acknowledge those different groups and cultural roots. Finally, "black and brown" also refers to First Nation/ Indigenous/ Native American/American Indian peoples, to Latinx people, and to a range of others who are "brown" (and perceived as non-western) including Palestinian, Polynesian, Cambodian, and Pakistani people.

Every Conversation Is a Conversation About Equity

Every conversation I have in and about schools is a conversation about equity— regardless of the demographics of the school. Every time I set foot in a school or speak to an administrator or a coach or a teacher, everything I see and hear is filtered through an equity lens. I think about who is thriving, who is sitting where, who is raising their hand, who is being yelled at, who is reading what, who is playing with whom, who is in the front office waiting for the principal, who the principal is, who the teachers are, what the teachers are doing in professional development (PD), how teachers redirect off-task students, how the teachers explain a concept, how the teachers check for understanding, what teachers assign for reading, how students are grouped, how students are instructed to walk in the hallways, who is praised, who gets feedback, and so much more. I filter each observation and wondering through an equity lens. I look for patterns and trends, and I look for outliers. I process what I see through my understandings of sexism, classism, institutional racism, and other forms of bigotry and discrimination.

There is no distinction between a conversation in which I am coaching for equity and any other. Equity issues are present in every situation—that's the nature of living in a society in which systems of oppression (including white supremacy and patriarchy) are embedded in our mindsets, behaviors, and institutions. We often don't recognize the prevalence of systemic oppression, because that's precisely how it works—by becoming invisible, by seeming to be "normal," and by being just a part of how things are, how we think, and how we feel.

What Is in This Book

To coach for equity, we must see inequities and know what to do about them. We must recognize how racism and white supremacy manifest in the classroom, and we must have an idea about what equity looks like—what we're trying to coach someone toward. In this book, you'll find a few key resources to help you build your knowledge and understanding of this content: there's the Equity Rubric (Appendix B), which is a comprehensive attempt at outlining and describing the indicators of equitable inputs in a school. In Chapter 3, and interspersed throughout the book, you'll find descriptions of many key terms and concepts you need to understand. Those concepts are foundational to recognizing inequity in schools.

In order to coach for equity, there is an expansive set of abilities that you need. These abilities include a set of knowledge. Amongst other things, you need to know how to work with adult learners, how to recognize inequities in the classroom, and how to understand emotions. You also need a set of skills including how to use a wide array of Transformational Coaching tools, how to coach around beliefs, and how to coach using the four Phases of Transformational Coaching. You also need will: a deep commitment to interrupting inequities and a profound sense of purpose. Capacity is necessary to coach for equity—time and resources. You need cultural competence: a set of skills and knowledge to understand your own identity and the identities of others, and to navigate difference. Finally, you need emotional intelligence: self-awareness, the ability to navigate your own emotions, as well as an ability to recognize the emotions of others and to navigate their emotions. These abilities are outlined in Table 1 Abilities Required to Coach for Equity, and you can see which chapter or chapters specifically support the development of those abilities.

Table 1   Abilities Required to Coach for Equity

Area	Element	Chapter in *Coaching for Equity*
Knowledge	Of coaching	1 and Appendix C
	Of racism & white supremacy	3 and Appendix B
	Of adult learners	5
	Of emotions	7
	Of identity	8
	Of teaching and education	Appendix B
Skill	How to implement Transformational Coaching	All
	How to coach behaviors, beliefs, and ways of being	All
	How to move through the Phases of Transformational Coaching	1, 2, 4, 5, 6, 7, 9, 10, 11, 12 and Appendix A
	How to coach for system change	1, 3, and Appendix D
	How to create the conditions in which adults can learn	All
Will	A commitment to interrupt inequities	All
	A deep sense of purpose	All
	Courage	All
	To learn and reflect on one's own practices	All
Capacity	Time to learn, practice, reflect, and attend to self Funds for books, professional development, and a coach and/ or therapist	NA

(Continued)

Table 1 (Continued)

Area	Element	Chapter in *Coaching for Equity*
Cultural Competence	Awareness of one's own identity markers	2 and 8
	An understanding of power dynamics through a lens of identity and systemic oppression	All
	Ability to navigate racial differences in coaching relationships	8
	Experience with people who hold different identity markers than your own	NA
Emotional Intelligence	Refined self-awareness, ability to navigate one's own emotions, and cultivate resilience	All
	Ability to navigate the emotions of others	2, 4, 7
	Compassion and curiosity	All
	Ability to build trusting relationships	All

Structural Features to Anticipate

There are some features in this book that I hope will help you understand and reflect on the content and incorporate it into your work. These features include the following:

- "Interludes": At the end of each chapter, you'll find an opportunity to reflect on one of the *Principles of Transformational Coaching*. You'll learn about these *principles* in Chapter 1, and be introduced to them at the end of the Introduction.
- At the end of each chapter, there's a section called "Before You Go." Here you'll find prompts to help you dig deeper into and reflect on the content of the chapter. I'll also suggest a few actions that you can take right away.

Additional Resources

My new workbook, *The Art of Coaching Workbook: Tools to Make Every Conversation Count* (2020) is an invaluable companion to this book. The exercises and resources in it will guide you to become an effective Transformational Coach.

On my website, http://brightmorningteam.com, you'll find the two massive rubrics that are in this book's appendices, and you'll also find additional resources and tools related to the content of this book including:

- The Coaching Lenses
- The Consultancy Protocol
- Planning for an Equity-Focused Conversation
- Reflecting on My Own Biases
- The Classroom Visit Tool

Who You Are—The Readers

This book is for leaders who are committed to justice and freedom. While this book focuses on leaders in schools, it could be useful for leaders in any organization who use coaching as a means to help people learn. And this book is for those who identify as white as well as those who identify as people of color.

For Leaders

Author and researcher Brené Brown defines a leader as anyone who takes responsibility for finding the potential in people and processes (Brown, 2018). Coaches and teachers are leaders in schools—if they choose to see themselves that way. So yes, this book is for all kinds of coaches—instructional coaches, data coaches, curriculum coaches, technology integration coaches, and so on. This book is also for mentors, department chairs, superintendents, principals, and anyone in a formal leadership position. To clarify: This book is for educators who accept responsibility for interrupting inequities in schools—regardless of position. If you see inequities and are committed to doing something about them—you want more resources, tools, and strategies; and you want to have effective conversations about equity—then this book is for you.

If you're not sure if there's a racial equity problem in the United States and in many areas of the world (or if you disagree with this fact), this book may not be

a teacher of English as a Second Language, and her adult students were often at our house cooking, singing, and telling stories. In England, we were poor—occasionally "on the dole" (welfare) and sometimes unable to pay for heat, but everyone in our community was poor.

In 1980, my mother, younger brother, and I moved to the United States. My parents had divorced—my father returned to Costa Rica, and my mother wanted to be near her mother, who had retired to a wealthy beach community in Southern California. I started fifth grade wearing secondhand clothes from the Salvation Army and new sneakers. From the first days in school, I was teased relentlessly about my hand-me-downs and "K-Mart crappies." Kids chased me on the yard shouting, "Go back to Mexico!" This initially confused me, although I also knew what they referred to—I was not white. In my high school of 1,600 students, I was one of four Latinx students. There was one African American family in this town and a handful of Jewish families. Everyone else seemed to be of northern European descent. Teachers took one look at my name, my phenotype, and my single mother rolling up in her old car, and they placed me in remedial classes. I was a shy and quiet C-average student, and I was ignored most of the time.

My little brother had epilepsy and other physical and behavioral challenges. When we moved to California, he was bullied viciously. He'd fall on the ground at the bus stop, convulsing, and kids would kick him and shout "seizure boy!" Teachers didn't seem to like him and didn't know what to do with him. On the day he turned 16, he quit school. My brother did overcome some of these adversities: He eventually got his diploma, went to college, and now works in the medical field. But his experience made me become a teacher who walked into a classroom and looked for the boy-child who was most struggling, who was socially ostracized, and who was in pain. I would hone in on that child and heap all the love and attention I could on him. As a teacher, my attention focused on the struggling boys, and the quiet, ignored girls.

My mother was a fierce advocate for my brother and me. She talked to me about politics and literature, and when I had writing assignments, she'd give me feedback on draft after draft. My teachers told me I couldn't write because I couldn't spell; my mother questioned me on my ideas, challenged me to dig deeper into my beliefs, guided me to articulate my thoughts, and showed me how to craft compelling paragraphs. My mother taught me to write.

As for my racial identity, because of my phenotype and name, people often assume I'm Latina, but sometimes perceive racial ambiguity. I've been asked, more times than I can count, "What are you?" I dislike the phrase "I'm half this and half that" because it connotes incompleteness. I consider myself to be 100% Jewish and

100% Latina. While this is my internal experience, externally I'm generally perceived as being Latina.

In my professional life, my perceived identity has often been viewed pragmatically—as a way to fulfill a quota. For decades, I suspect I was only hired because either a person of color was needed to diversify a group, or because I was Latina. I once interviewed for a teaching position for which I was a good fit, and at the interview, the principal said, "I'm concerned because you don't have experience teaching this grade level, but we serve a primarily Latino community and we don't have any Latinos on staff." I entered that position thinking, *I'm going to prove that I'm worthy, that I deserve to be here.* To be clear: I'm all for affirmative action and diversity, but for many years, in many roles, I was not recognized for who I am and what I can do. I didn't feel seen or valued. I still suspect that at times I'm invited to speak or present at a conference because the organizers want a Latina to round out the diversity of their panels—not because of the merits of my work or my presentation skills. It takes diligent awareness to shake the imposter syndrome that lurks around my confidence.

There's one more identity marker that affects who I am as an educator and the content of this book. My husband is African American—he grew up in a working class family in Memphis and is the first generation in his family that did not have to pick cotton. We've been together since 1997 and have one child—a son, who at the time of writing this is in high school. Our son is an easy-going kid who is obsessed with astronomy and classical music and is determined to work for NASA. In both the public and private schools that he's attended, we've experienced a steady current of implicit bias. In kindergarten, he was described as "spacey and distractible," his first-grade teacher recommended testing him for Attention Deficit Disorder (ADD), and his fifth-grade teacher labeled him "defiant" and believed he had learning disabilities. Our son attended a middle school that during the time he was there, fell apart. Amidst organizational chaos, biases of all kinds can take the reins, and it seemed as if every time he stood up, sat down, walked a hall or turned a corner, he was seen as acting out or being disrespectful. Until he entered high school, it felt like we needed to advocate for him every 15 minutes—to direct teachers to see his strengths and skills, to unpack their biased assumptions, to insist that he be seen in his full humanity. Over and over, concerns about his behavior superseded interest in his intellect. Remember, also, that we live in the San Francisco Bay Area, one of the supposedly most progressive regions of the United States.

While I've never doubted the extent of the inequities in our schools, being the mother of an African American boy has been a daily reminder of how far we have to go. Throughout our journey of advocating for him, I've been keenly aware of the privilege I have: I speak and write fluent English, I have financial resources, I have a flexible work schedule, I have a spouse to partner with, I deeply understand the education system, and I have social and cultural capital that I can leverage when talking to educators. And even with all of this privilege, my son did not receive the education he deserved for many years, because of the way that educators responded to his racial and gender identity markers, and because of the racism that permeates our world.

I am also learning a great deal from my son's experience in high school, a school that has made significant strides toward true equity and inclusion, and in which he is receiving a meaningful education. His high school has also affirmed a core belief I hold, which is that *it is possible* to provide students with an equitable education; the pervasive racism in our country can be mediated. I have seen how the policies and practices at his school are fulfilling this commitment as well as how individual educators respond to feedback. Sometimes I want to cry in relief and gratitude over what my son is finally receiving, and then I also want to cry in grief and anger over what every black boy, and every child, deserves but is not getting.

And so, if at any point you wonder why I'm so focused on black boys in this book, know that it's because the two people I love the most in this world are black men.

I want to be very clear about something: My experience of loving these two black men does not mean that I know what it's like to be African American. I do not write from that knowledge. Nor does this mean that the white supremacy that I've internalized has been voided through a marriage certificate. I'm still excavating my blind spots and biases. I don't present my marriage and motherhood in an effort to expand my credentials as an enlightened warrior for justice. Knowing, marrying, or mothering someone of a different race or ethnicity doesn't mean you are woke.

What I know is this: I know what it's like to be a cisgendered, able-bodied, neurotypical, heterosexual woman of color who is married to an African American man who can afford to send our son to private school. I also know what it's like to be new to this country, to be perceived as a second class citizen, to be pigeonholed because of my race and class, and to be ignored because of my race and gender. I know what it's like to constantly question your experience of things: to wonder whether your son really is a shmuck at times (like a typical teenager) or whether teachers are reacting to his gender and ethnicity; to get defensive and go on the attack and accuse people of racism—and then to feel guilty and remorseful and self-doubting. I know enough about how my gender and racial identity affect my life to fill another book. Ultimately, I know what it's like to see and experience the world, every day, through a lens of power, privilege, and race. I know what it's like to get tired of holding this lens, and I also know what it's like to unearth profound reserves of energy and commitment.

This is who I am. I can only write what I know. I can only tell the stories I've lived.

How to Get the Most from this Book

Here are some tips for getting the most out of this book that range from the technical sphere to the emotional, social, and perhaps even spiritual spheres.

Technical Suggestions

First, read this book sequentially. There are stories that run through several chapters, and the ideas build on each other. Take time to respond to the reflection questions at the end of each chapter. Your learning will deepen exponentially. Also, if you haven't read *The Art of Coaching*, you might want to have it handy. *The Art of Coaching Workbook* (2020) will also be a useful resource (until I have time to write *The Coaching for Equity Workbook!)* Finally, the most powerful learning happens in community. I hope that you'll discuss this book with others, using the questions at the end of each chapter. In addition, I offer workshops on this content. Information about those is also available on my website.

When I Disappoint You

As you read, you might think, "I wish she talked more about issues that immigrants face," or "What about inequities for _____?" You may wish I'd spoken to the issues that are closest to your heart or house or history. I wrote what's closest to my heart and home and history. I wrote what I know and what I've seen. I wrote my stories. This is all I can share with you. If you feel that stories and chapters are missing in this book, I hope you'll write those. We need all the storytellers we can get in this effort to build equitable schools.

As you read these stories, you might disagree with how I managed the conversation and think, *I can't believe that she said (or didn't say) . . . I think she should have . . .* And that's OK. There are lots of ways to have these conversations, and I'll reveal my thinking so that you can understand why I made the choices I did. I don't necessarily have the "right" way—although I have figured out some strategies that work when the goal is to honor the humanity of the person in front of me and also provide students with what they need in order to thrive and be successful in school every day.

Finally, I ask that you forgive me if in any way I cause you harm with the content of this book. I am aware that I have limitations and blind spots, I continue to learn every day about ways in which I perpetuate inequities and oppressive ideologies, and I am committed to transforming those mindsets and practices. I know that I cannot wait until I've reached some unattainable level of perfection, and so I must share what I know now, which is imperfect and limited. I anticipate that after this is published, after I've learned more and heard your feedback, I'll wish I could modify sections or change my mind about things I've written; and then, perhaps there'll be another book. Right now, I'm not allowing this anticipation or fear restrain me from sharing these stories. I hope you will email me or approach me if we meet, and share your feedback, and I hope you will forgive me when I fall short.

Feel, Heal, and Witness

I anticipate that at times, this book may be challenging and painful. White educators may feel uncomfortable as we explore issues of race and privilege. For many people of color, this book may bring to the surface past and present traumas related to their educational and professional experiences.

As I've learned about equity, there have been countless times when I've recalled something I did as a teacher and felt guilt, shame, and grief as I realize that I perpetuated white supremacy. I can see how I may have created unsafe learning environments, how I may have taught history in a way that was disempowering or dehumanizing to some groups of people, and how my own biases got in the way of reaching and teaching every child. This doesn't feel good.

Here are four things I tell myself when those feelings come up:

1. *Feel all the feelings.* Explore them. Be with them. Don't get paralyzed or consumed by them. Emotions are messengers who want to give us information: listen to them.
2. *Know better, do better.* Practice self-compassion and commit to learning and doing better.
3. *Do this work with others.* Listen and learn from others, seek out their input, collaborate, and create alliances. It is only in learning from and collaborating with people who hold different identity markers than mine that I'll make the most significant learning leaps.
4. *Slow down.* Many of my regrets happened because I was pressed for time, when I wasn't prepared and hadn't solicited feedback. I said things when I was tired and impatient. Slowing down allows me to clarify my intentions and anticipate the potential impact of my actions.

Truth be told: I intend for readers to experience cognitive dissonance and have big feelings. I intend for you to feel sad, angry, confused, and hopeful. See what happens if you embrace the discomfort. Discomfort won't kill you, and every time you go through an uncomfortable phase, you'll be more prepared and resilient the next time discomfort shows up. Only by feeling our emotions will we sort through the mess of our history and find a way through.

Remember: *It's not your fault that things are the way they are, but it is your responsibility to do something about them.*

Key to reading this book will be to hone your ability to recognize what activates strong emotional reactions for you. Emotions offer important messages. When they make an appearance, learn from them. My books, *Onward: Cultivating Emotional Resilience in Educators* and *The Onward Workbook*, are resources for learning about emotions.

We're on a journey toward justice and liberation. This journey includes healing from the pain of our individual and collective history. Racism and other systems of oppression have hurt everyone. Healing can be a long process, and we can face setbacks, but engaging our emotions is a key part of healing. We *can* heal from the trauma of our history, and I know that we yearn for healing because human beings crave connection and we ache to have healthy relationships with each other. I have seen and heard this in every conversation I've ever had within and outside of schools.

In moments of discomfort, I urge you to bear witness. The concept of bearing witness comes from psychology and some spiritual traditions. It's what you do when a friend shares a painful story and you listen openly and empathetically, taking it all in without feeling like you need to offer solutions or fix their problems. We can bear witness to others whom we'll never meet when we read their books, listen to their poetry, take in their art, music, and movies. When you bear witness, you suspend habitual thinking and analysis and you acknowledge the existence of pain or suffering. You connect with a deep place of empathy and see a web of causes and conditions that create suffering—and then you might be poised to take action to stop that suffering. In bearing witness, you experience the interconnectedness of all beings; you sense how your pain and suffering are connected to someone else. In order to heal the wounds of humanity, we'll need to witness each other's pain and suffering. This is not an optional part of the journey—it is a critical part of how healing happens. Elie Wiesel, a Holocaust survivor and the author of *Night*, eloquently wrote, "For the dead and the living, we must bear witness."

Bearing witness takes courage, and there may be times when you are called to witness unbearable suffering—your own and other's. In these pages, in your pursuit of justice and liberation for all, allow yourself to be changed by what you witness—in yourself, in others, and in your community. Witnessing can be excruciating and cathartic, and it is part of the process toward connection, healing, and wholeness. Keep your eye on the prize—to create equitable schools—and hold space for your emotions.

And finally: turn to each other. Reach out and strengthen connections with others—yes, this also takes courage. Our collective traumas happened in relationship to each other—our collective body as a species was traumatized in the last 500 years. Our healing needs to happen in community. Reach for each other.

Before You Go . . .

Reflect

- Why are you reading this book?
- What are your fears about reading this book?
- What do you hope to get from this book? How do you hope you'll feel after you've read it? What do you hope you'll be able to do after you've read it?
- How might the content of this book make your life more meaningful, rewarding, joyful, and satisfying?
- What kind of world would you like to live in? What would be different?

Interlude: Compassion

Principles of Transformational Coaching

- **Compassion**
- Curiosity
- Connection
- Courage
- Purpose

Compassion: We relentlessly strive to center the humanity of others. We preserve people's honor and dignity above all. We know that kindness is our greatest power. We practice self-compassion which includes taking care of ourselves. We know that the journey towards liberation will be long, so we rest and attend to our minds, bodies, hearts, and spirits.

Ours is not the task of fixing the entire world all at once, but of stretching out to mend the part of the world that is within our reach. Any small, calm thing that one soul can do to help another soul, to assist some portion of this poor suffering world, will help immensely.

—*Clarissa Pinkola Estes*

- Which part of the world is within your reach for you to mend?
- What kinds of small, calm things have you done and can you continue to do to help others?
- How could you stretch just a few inches more to mend another part of the world?

[M]any White people experience themselves as powerless, even in the face of privilege. But the fact is that we all have a sphere of influence . . . The task for each of us, White and of color, is to identify what our own sphere of influence is (however large or small) and to consider how it might be used to interrupt the cycle of racism.

—Dr. Beverly Daniel Tatum

- How do you define your sphere of influence when it comes to dismantling racism, white supremacy, and other systems of oppression?
- What leads you to define your sphere in this way?
- How have you seen your sphere of influence expand? How could you continue to expand it?

IDEAL
REALITY

CURRENT REALITY

1 Resilience

2 Teams

3 Equity

4 Leadership

5 Instruction

CHAPTER 1

Transformational Coaching: A Model for Change

The difficult I'll do right now. The impossible will take a little while.
—BILLIE HOLIDAY

When you fly over it, the Golden Gate Bridge appears to be an impossible feat of engineering suspended over the Pacific Ocean. If you take a boat beneath it, you'll see the extensive sets of cables, the planks of the deck, the guard rails, the steel joints—the many components that make up the system. You'll also appreciate the strength of the pillars that emerge from the ocean to support the structure. You'll gain a deeper appreciation for the complexity of the bridge. Without a structure, a bridge cannot span a chasm.

This chapter provides an overview of the model of Transformational Coaching and of how to coach for equity within this model. If you learn better by looking first at the parts, by reading an example, and then coming back to the whole, as it's explained here, consider reading Chapters 2, 3, and 4 first.

Structures to Span Chasms

My transition from teaching into my first coaching role was abrupt. Six months in, I begged my principal for a change in assignment. "I can't do this," I wailed after leading a series of professional development (PD) sessions in which I'd felt constant pushback.

My primary thought for the first several years that I coached was, *What am I supposed to be doing?* When I asked my administrators for direction, I was told to "support teachers." *How?*, I wondered. *Toward what end?* Teachers would ask, "What is it you do?" When I pushed back on making photocopies or putting up a bulletin board for a teacher, I'd hear, "But you're a coach." I'd want to say, *A coach isn't an assistant.* And then I'd think, *But what IS a coach!?* I didn't have an answer. There was no shared definition of coaching or of the work of a coach, and there was no agreement on the purpose of my role, or how I was expected to show up, or what I was working toward.

My school held a vague commitment to educational equity—but what that meant for coaching and PD was undefined. This meant that when I sat down for a coaching session with teachers, I didn't feel empowered to direct the conversation toward issues of equity. It meant that when teachers blamed students for their academic struggles, I felt that all I could respond with was my opinion—which made our conversation feel like a debate. I felt isolated, confused, and disempowered. And I was ineffective.

In my second year as a coach, the old house I rented had plumbing problems. Strange noises came from the pipes. The water pressure dropped dramatically. Then no water came from the faucet. I called a plumber—20 minutes later, he'd figured out the problem, and within a few hours, it was fixed. I watched in awe as the plumber worked. "How did you know what was wrong?" I asked in amazement. He described a simple, straightforward diagnostic process to identify the problem, and then a sequence to repair the problems. To me, the situation had seemed overwhelmingly complex and possibly insurmountable. But the plumber had a process. What was the equivalent, I thought, for me as a coach? How could I go into a teacher's classroom with a sequence to guide what to do? Teachers are not pipes, of course, and classrooms aren't usually old houses—a technical fix won't work in schools. But I knew that had the plumber randomly looked at pipes in my house, it would have taken a very long time to solve the problem.

For the last 10 years, as I've consulted on coaching programs, the primary obstacle I see to effective coaching is a lack of structures. I've seen organizations that have resources, will, and PD for coaches—but almost no organization I've worked with has in place an explicit, articulated coaching model. A coaching model lays out the mechanisms along which we'll get somewhere—it outlines a process; it lowers risk; it provides common language; and it assures that although we are suspended above a beautiful and frightening thing like the ocean, we will go somewhere together. Without structure, we cannot span a chasm.

Imagine now that we are standing on one side of a chasm where the ways of doing school are currently practiced. This is the side where Jabari, the student I described in the Introduction, attends school. It's the side where black and brown kids are suspended for rolling their eyes, where security guards patrol the halls, where teachers say, "These kids can't . . ." On this side, Jabari will rarely see his experiences reflected in the curriculum, many teachers will have low expectations of him, and it's unlikely that he'll have access to advanced math and science classes, or after-school programs, or project-based learning. On this side, school is an instrument of oppression. It serves to reproduce the status quo, which grants access and privilege to some groups (white, middle- and upper-class, English-speaking) while other groups are further marginalized.

Perhaps your own children attend schools on this side. Some children from dominant cultures are more or less served on this side—meaning, they have decent experiences in school and graduate ready for college or career. But be honest: The quality of education on this side of the chasm has much to be desired. There's still too much bullying, kids and adults are far too stressed, and lectures, textbooks, and testing consume much of everyone's time. We can try to reform bits and pieces or grit our teeth and make the best of it, or we can look across the chasm where a different reality can exist.

On the other side of this chasm, schools can be places of healing and liberation. They can be a microcosm for a more just and equitable society, a place where adults and children learn to be together in healthy community, a place where we learn about ourselves and others. On that side, Jabari is in classes where he engages in critical thinking about complex ideas, where he has access to means of creative expression, and where he collaborates to generate novel approaches to addressing the social, economic, political, and environmental challenges that our planet faces. On that side, Jabari encounters kindness and understanding from the adults he meets; it is a place where he, and every child, thrives. It is a place he loves to be in, where his full humanity is embraced.

There are two reasons why these schools don't exist in very many places: They are hard to imagine—or we are afraid to imagine them—and even when we do hold this vision, we don't know how to get there. I believe in the power of our imagination. It might need to be loosened up, it might need to be deconditioned from a lifetime of habitual thinking so that it can be freed of the toxins of systems of oppression, and it might need to tone its weak muscles. But I know we've got imagination—and I know that in the company of others, with commitment, it can grow. We humans are brilliantly creative, imaginative creatures.

I believe that you want to cross this chasm between where we are now and a place characterized by kindness, justice, freedom, and learning. I believe you want this for yourself, for the young people you love, and for the students you serve. Look across this divide and you will see a bridge. This bridge is Transformational Coaching. This is a model for change—a model that can be used by teachers, coaches, principals, and superintendents, and by any team or organizational leader. Transformation will only happen if we learn. It will not happen by law or mandate. Coaching is a structure that supports learning. Transformational Coaching can take us from where we are now to where we want to be.

Let me be your guide right now to show you the key features of this bridge. First, you'll see multiple lanes on the deck of the bridge—these will take us from our current reality to our ideal reality. One lane is all about emotional resilience. When you walk or drive along that lane, you coach for emotional resilience. In another lane, you coach teams—creating healthy and productive groups of people. And in another lane, you coach for equity. You interrupt the practices, beliefs, and systems that are inequitable. Another lane focuses on leaders, and when you're in that lane, you coach toward leadership development. There's also a lane for traditional coaching of instructional practices—designing lessons or assessments, for example.

We'll travel in each of these lanes as we create a new reality—sometimes spending more time in one lane than another, sometimes crossing back and forth within one conversation. Maybe while analyzing student work and discussing how to support English Language Learners, the teacher you're coaching will express emotional exhaustion and you'll shift into coaching for resilience. Or perhaps as you coach for equity, it becomes apparent that decisions made in the grade-level team make it difficult to implement equitable practices—perhaps curriculum or scheduling decisions—and then you shift to developing leadership skills and to coaching teams.

Along the edge of the bridge, you'll see guardrails. One of them represents the need for you to take care of yourself. You'll need to know yourself, and to attend to your own emotions and learning needs to cross this bridge. The other guardrail represents the need to develop a trusting relationship with your clients. To cross this chasm, we need refined emotional intelligence—we need to be highly skilled at understanding our own emotions and navigating them, as well as understanding and navigating the emotions of others. That's what these two guardrails remind us of.

The bridge of Transformational Coaching crosses the water and is supported by five pillars. These pillars are the principles of Transformational Coaching. You'll read about those in this chapter, but now I just want you to see that the entire structure is held up by these principles—these values.

In this book, I'll be leading you along the lane of coaching for equity. I'll show you the key tools and skills you'll need to guide others along the bridge—the folks you coach and lead. In my other books, I've offered additional resources for the other lanes. I hope you'll reach out for those as you make this journey across the bridge. Please know that the approaches in this book, these tools to coach for equity, won't work well if lifted out of a Transformational Coaching model. However, without explicitly addressing coaching for equity, without engaging with the tools in this book, we won't cross the chasm to transformed, liberated schools.

Walk with me along this bridge of Transformational Coaching. I'll share conversations about emotions, equity, identity, children, history, and a whole lot more. There'll be moments of discomfort, times when the fog will roll in and we'll feel a little confused, and then we'll hear the laughter, tears, connection, and courage. And on the other side is a place where we'll all feel much happier and much freer.

This chapter is an overview of the Transformational Coaching model that I've created and a close look at the lane of coaching for equity, which can only be truly implemented within a Transformational Coaching approach.

Assumptions behind Transformational Coaching

These are the assumptions behind Transformational Coaching. These are beliefs about education, about education and equity within American society, about the role and responsibility of teachers, and about schooling. By making assumptions known, we create transparency. Transparency builds trust, creates opportunities for buy-in, and reveals the ideological blueprints of a structure.

Assumptions about Education
- Learning is a basic human need, and the purpose of education is to provide students with skills and knowledge so that they become critical thinkers, compassionate leaders, and self-actualized people who contribute to the healing and transformation of this world. It is possible to create classrooms and schools that provide equitable and rigorous learning experiences for children and that result in equitable outcomes for students. Classrooms and schools can be a microcosm of what is possible.

Assumptions about the Problem

- Educational inequities are pervasive: racism plays out in schools in a myriad of ways. African American, Latinx, and other marginalized students are more likely to have limited access to high-quality curriculum, to be subject to harsher discipline, to encounter multiple forms of structural and interpersonal racism, and to attend schools in neighborhoods that have been systematically under-resourced (Carter, Skiba, Arredondo, & Pollock, 2014; Losen & Skiba, 2010). Racism has permeated how white people and people of color respond to student behavior, select curriculum, hire and promote staff, and partner with parents—among many things.

- Unjust structures and institutions are the problem—not the kids, not their parents, not their families, and not their communities. Educational inequity has sometimes been viewed as a problem of "achievement gaps" or teacher quality, but there is no "achievement gap." Structural racism is at the root of educational inequities (Trujillo et al., 2017). People created inequitable systems and, intentionally and unintentionally, we perpetuate unjust systems. Inequitable systems were constructed by ruling powers to subjugate large populations and keep people enslaved, disempowered, disenfranchised, and marginalized. *Educational inequity is the result of intentional design.*

- The problem we face is a problem of change, and problems of change are problems of learning. We must consider the conditions in which learning happens, how learning is organized and structured, who facilitates learning, how the learning facilitators learn, and how we design, guide, and measure learning.

Assumptions about the People

- Every child can learn and self-actualize. *Every single child.* Children who are born in poverty, who don't speak English, who have learning differences or physical challenges, who may not be raised by their birth parents, who have experienced trauma, who did not come to school knowing numbers or letters—all children can learn. In addition, all children come to school with their own knowledge, insight, experiences, passions, and ideas; they are not repositories for us to fill with our ideas and opinions (Freire, 1968).

- Educators exist to serve children. Students deserve educators who are skilled and knowledgeable about teaching and learning, and who are self-aware and resilient. In addition, educators need the support of leaders in their school buildings, districts, and local, state, and federal governments. For us to truly transform schools into equitable places where every child learns, stakeholders need to align on the root causes of the problem and on solutions: The task of building equitable schools can't fall entirely on the backs of teachers. While we face a real lack of resource in schools, we also have extensive internal resources including our creativity, will, commitment, resourcefulness, perseverance, compassion, patience, and courage. When we engage our internal resources, we'll be more resilient and able to build equitable schools.

- Coaches working in education were excellent teachers who acquired skills to guide adult learning and lead change. Coaches require ongoing opportunities for their own learning so they can master the skills listed in Appendix C: Transformational Coaching Rubric 2.0.
- Supervisors and administrators can use Transformational Coaching strategies to guide staff to grow and to transform schools.

Assumptions about the Process

- We find time and money for what we prioritize. Resources are limited in many schools—however, *if we prioritize dismantling systemic oppression, if we prioritize the needs of our most marginalized students, we can find the time, support, money, and resources that we need.* Claiming a lack of resources as a reason to not address equity is a poor excuse that preserves the interests and privileges of those who have been in power for hundreds of years.
- Coaching must be holistic and must address an educator's behaviors, beliefs, and ways of being. Coaching that relies heavily on technical strategies is transactional and replicates inequitable power dynamics. Educators need prescriptive coaching that focuses on instruction, and they need coaching that attends to the emotional experiences of our work. Especially while exploring issues of equity, educators will experience strong emotions including anger, grief, and shame. And in organizations that have a commitment to hiring and retaining educators from marginalized communities, this emotional experience will likely be more intense. Furthermore, coaching must address underlying mental models and the biases we hold, because without awareness of those, we risk reproducing inequitable schools. An effective coach can guide a teacher to explore biases and also design a rigorous lesson and use data to drive instruction.
- Human beings have emotions, and it's our right to experience them, engage with them, and learn from them on the journey of change. At times, emotions may be unpleasant, but they are part of the process. We are stronger and wiser when we attend to them. Avoiding emotions or getting stuck in them can be counterproductive to equity, but we don't need to suppress or repress emotions. Transformational, sustained change happens when we integrate emotions into learning.

- Everyone has suffered under white supremacy—every individual and every ethnic and cultural group. By acknowledging our common suffering, we find ways to heal. *And:* The genocide and attempted cultural erasure of the Native people of the continents we call North and South America, and the enslavement of African peoples, are the original sins and festering wounds in the United States and in most developed nations in the world. Without reconciling with this history, we will struggle to come together as a nation. Without reparations, there can be no justice (Coates, 2014). Without justice, there can be no healing. Our journey must include opportunities for healing—for healing from the collective trauma that is our nation's (and our world's) recent history. Healing happens through individual processes and in community (Menakem, 2017). Educators need opportunities to process and heal together.
- Healing requires an ability to have conversations. If we learn to have powerful conversations, we can have powerful learning experiences. If we have powerful learning experiences, we can change our teaching practices. If we change our teaching practices, we can create equitable schools. If we create equitable schools, we'll take great strides toward justice—and toward healing. *Conversations are bridges to justice, healing, and liberation, and we can make every conversation count towards creating a just and liberated world.*

Transformational Coaching

Before we explore Transformational Coaching, let's take a step back to create a shared understanding of what coaching is, and what a coach does.

The title *coach* has been loosely and widely applied in the field of education. New teachers are sometimes assigned a coach who might be a mentor and confidant, or simply someone who stops in every other week to fill out paperwork for compliance purposes. Many mandated curricula initiatives deploy "coaches" to enforce fidelity. Some schools have "data coaches" who gather and analyze data, prepare reports, meet with teachers to discuss the results, and suggest actions to take. Some organizations assign a coach to an underperforming veteran teacher as a step in the termination process. Some districts have "school improvement coaches" for schools that have low test scores. This is why it's critical to define what coaching is, and what a coach does. Let's start with what coaching isn't. Coaching *is not*:

- A way to enforce a program. Coaches should never be used as enforcers, reporters, or evaluators. This approach demeans the field of coaching and makes teachers rightfully suspicious of coaches.

- A mechanism to fix people. Coaching is not something to do to ineffective teachers. It is not a box to be checked so that a district can move toward disciplinary measures. Coaching should be optional—we can't force people to learn.
- Therapy. A coach does not probe into someone's psyche or childhood. Emotions arise in coaching—and a coach can acknowledge emotions and help someone process them—but a coach also knows the line between what she can and should do for a client and the role of a mental health professional.
- Consulting. A coach is not necessarily an expert who trains others in a way of doing something; a coach helps build the capacity of others by facilitating their learning.

Coaching is professional development. It's a structure through which we can reflect, grow, and refine our practices; it's a way we can learn to use new tools and to incorporate new approaches; it's a method for improving teacher and leader practices and improving student outcomes. Coaching is one way that educators can engage in professional development, one form that is ideally complemented by other experiences which could include Professional Learning Communities, critical friends, weekly PD sessions, and an occasional conference.

Coaching is effective because it is job-embedded, it is ongoing, it's one-on-one, and it can be differentiated to meet the needs of an individual learner. Being job-embedded, ongoing, and differentiated are three top criteria for effective professional development. Research has found that coaching is the most effective form of PD for teachers: when teachers engage in infrequent and decontextualized trainings, less than 20% of new practices were implemented in the classroom; *when coaching is combined with training, implementation of those new practices rises to between 80 percent and 90 percent* (Joyce and Showers, 1982).

Coaching is a vehicle through which we can reflect on our practice, understand ourselves better, surface and shift our own beliefs, and build new habits, because coaching is just a way to learn and grow—everyone deserves a coach for as long as they want. Life is a learning journey, and the only thing we can count on is change. Educators can benefit from working with a coach throughout the entirety of their career.

Traditional approaches for coaching teachers emphasize addressing instructional practices, curriculum, assessment, and pedagogy. As a new coach, I used these approaches. I gave teachers heaps of resources and lots of feedback, I told them to do certain things differently, I directed them to see what wasn't working in their classroom, and I modeled new practices. Some of this coaching worked in the sense that teachers tried new things and saw different results. Much of this coaching didn't work. Teachers pushed back, or implemented the strategies with limited impact, or they complied while I was around and then returned to their old ways when I was out of sight. Some teachers engaged with this coaching, but after a year or two, claiming burnout, they quit. Traditional approaches to coaching didn't transform teaching and learning.

The Three Components of Transformational Coaching

These are the three components that a Transformational Coach must attend to:

- *The Coach: With an emphasis on the coach's attention to their own learning.* A Transformational Coach attends to their own behaviors, beliefs, and ways of being.
- *The Client: With a holistic approach to working with a client.* Transformational Coaching addresses a client's behaviors, beliefs, and ways of being.
- *The Systems: With a commitment to transform systems and the individuals within them:* A Transformational Coach identifies and understands the larger systems in which we live and work and takes action to transform them. This element makes Transformational Coaching unique as a model to address equity—we work with individuals while surfacing the often-invisible and often-inequitable systems in which they work. Models that focus only on individuals have limited impact and run the risk of reproducing inequitable systems.

Let's explore the skills of a Transformational Coach.

The Coach: Starting with Ourselves

A Transformational Coach has an extensive set of abilities that include specific coaching skills and knowledge of instructional strategies, pedagogy, specific content areas, and educational equity. What makes Transformational Coaching more comprehensive than other forms of instructional coaching is the emphasis on *beliefs* and *ways of being*—the client's and the coach's. A *way of being* includes high emotional intelligence, an ability to form trusting relationships, refined identity awareness, and deep will and commitment. An effective Transformational Coach is self-aware and reflective, is anchored in a set of ways of being (which we'll look at soon), and is regularly engaged in his own learning. A Transformational Coach is clear on his beliefs about himself, about racism and justice and freedom, about his role and responsibility as a coach, and about how change happens. Finally, a Transformational Coach has deep knowledge of instructional and leadership practices and of educational equity.

When I was getting started as a coach, my coach, Leslie Plettner, offered an invaluable lesson when she said, "No one can learn from you if you think that they suck." My mind was blown as I realized that I'd been coaching from a place where I did indeed believe that everyone around me sucked. I felt disdain for the teachers I coached. I did not believe in their potential to be effective teachers. I believed that these teachers wanted to harm the black and brown children in our school. When I showed up to coach these teachers, I was angry at them, I didn't trust them, I didn't like them, and I didn't even want to be near them. You can't learn from someone who feels this way about you.

Even after I stopped coaching from a place of disdain, some of my coaching conversations were successful and others flopped. One week, a client would have meaningful insights into their teaching, and I'd feel good about my coaching. And then the next week, with the same client, the conversation would limp along, and my questions didn't result in insights. Initially, out of frustration, I'd externalize responsibility and blame the client—*it was because of how they were showing up that day,* I'd think. While not every single conversation we have will result in immediately visible transformation, I sensed there was more I could do to ensure we were on the right trajectory.

After a while, I noticed that the success of coaching conversations had everything to do with how *I* was feeling, with *my* attitude, and with how *I* was showing up. When I was tired, irritated, despairing, hopeless, and so on, the conversation did not go very well. When I was open, curious, compassionate, humble, and so on, the conversation went well. I'd noticed this same dynamic when I was a teacher. It was what the Israeli educator Haim Ginott referenced in this quote: "I've come to the frightening conclusion that I am the decisive element in the classroom. It's my daily mood that makes the weather."

Around the time that I had that realization, I began coaching other coaches. I would listen to their coaching conversations and observe them with their clients. My emerging theory was validated over and over: It was the coach's disposition— the coach's attitude and emotional state, *the coach's way of being*—that made the difference between a powerful and a weak conversation, between a transformational conversation and one that may or may not impact kids. I scrutinized the variables in a conversation—the quality of the coach's questions, the coach's knowledge of the teacher's content, the coach's plans for the conversation, and the teacher's mood and disposition—and over and over, I came to the same conclusion: The key factor was the coach's way of being. How the coach showed up, how they engaged with their own emotions, and how they communicated made all the difference.

Through reflecting on my practice and observing other coaches I've landed on six key dispositions or ways of being of a Transformational Coach. When working from these ways of being, we are primed to coach for equity. Transformational Coaches are compassionate and curious, have trust in the coaching process, are oriented toward learning, embody humility and mutuality, and are courageous. I'll describe these in Chapter 6, but as you read the stories about coaching for equity, I hope you'll keep an eye out for where you saw me demonstrating them.

The Client: Coaching Behaviors, Beliefs, and Ways of Being

If we aspire to create sustained, transformational change, and if we aspire to coach for justice and liberation, then we must coach our client on their behaviors (designing lessons, delivering instruction, analyzing data, creating assessments, and so on) as well as on their thoughts and beliefs, and also around their way of being (their emotions, identity, and will). Transformational Coaching is a holistic method because it attends to these three domains of who we are—to our behaviors, beliefs, and ways of being—"The Three Bs." You can read an overview of this model in Table 1.1: What Are the Three Bs?

In Figure 1.1: The Three Components of Transformational Coaching, the pyramid represents the idea that behaviors emerge from beliefs, and beliefs emerge from ways of being. However, the boundaries between beliefs and ways of being,

Table 1.1 What Are the Three Bs?

	What it is	How we see it
Behavior	What we do. In schools: ability to design lessons, deliver instruction, create a productive learning environment, analyze data, etc. What can be captured on video.	Evident in our skill set.
Beliefs	What we think and believe. Comes from what we know and from our experiences.	Reflected in our decision-making, the assumptions and conclusions we make; our behaviors emerge from beliefs.
Ways of being	Who we are—how we show up and how we are experienced. A blend of our dispositions, will, and sense of identity.	Manifests in our emotions, communication, and levels of resilience.

Figure 1.1 The Three Components of Transformational Coaching

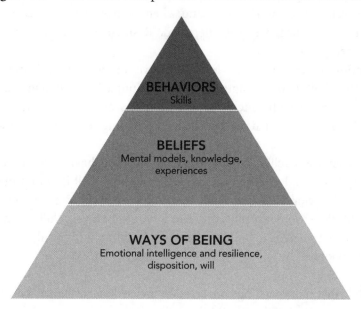

and between beliefs and behaviors are porous. Addressing *only* behaviors without surfacing, evaluating, and shifting the underlying beliefs and ways of being will not result in transformation or even in sustained change.

Coaching the Three Bs is a holistic method that in and of itself is an affront to systems of oppression. Systems of oppression strive to disconnect action from our hearts, minds, spirits, and bodies, while Transformational Coaching invites connection between realms of existence. Transformational Coaching is a response to industrialist, efficiency-obsessed systems that focus on and prioritize changing actions and behaviors. When you acknowledge emotions in a coaching conversation at work, you destabilize a larger system of oppression.

The Three Goals in a Transformational Coaching Conversation

In any coaching conversation, there are three goals: to increase the client's emotional resilience, to strengthen the client's reflective abilities, and to build the client's skills. Let's look at the connection between these goals in a conversation and the larger commitment to coach behaviors, beliefs, and ways of being.

- **Resilience**: When we coach to build resilience, we coach a way of being. Resilience increases when we acknowledge and explore our emotions; when we deepen self-knowledge and self-awareness; when we tap into positive emotions including hope, purpose, curiosity, and empathy; when we are focused on our sphere of influence and control; and when we feel like we're learning. When we build resilience, we feel energized. Resilience shifts and expands our way of being.

- **Reflection**: When we coach to build reflective abilities, we coach around beliefs. Reflective abilities are strengthened when we unpack our thoughts, understand the processes through which we make decisions, and recognize the underlying mental models that form our beliefs. Strengthening reflective abilities can shift our beliefs.
- **Skill**: When we coach to build skill, we create new behaviors. Skill is built when learning is scaffolded, when the desired or needed skill is within our Zone of Proximal Development, and when the skill we're building is the right size and the right piece. Sometimes in order to buy into building skill, we need to see evidence that we need to build that skill set. Building skills results in more effective behaviors.

It is possible that in a coaching conversation focused on resilience, you guide your client to develop new skills to build their own resilience, or you might guide them into deeper understanding of how their mental models undermine their resilience. In another conversation, you might focus on beliefs about students, which will likely raise emotions and therefore provide an opportunity to coach around resilience. Sometimes we might provide what seems like straightforward instructional coaching that builds skill, and we might wonder how we're coaching around resilience. If we close that conversation with an opportunity for the client to name what they've learned and how they feel at the end of the conversation—and they say, "I'm excited to try this tomorrow with my students!"—then they bring a moment of awareness to the positive emotions that come up from learning, and they've increased their resilience. The art of coaching is the ability to weave together coaching of behaviors, beliefs, and ways of being in a way that doesn't feel contrived.

The Systems: Transforming Systems

To practice Transformational Coaching, you need to understand systems and explore how to change systems. A first step is to know the systems to which we belong and have some understanding of them. By recognizing the broader institutions, structures, and organizations in which we work, we can evaluate our spheres of influence and control, identify entry points for making change in those larger systems, and appreciate the interconnectedness of all things.

What happens in a classroom is affected by what happens in the larger organizations in which it is embedded and by what happens in the larger socio-political and economic levels. Let's consider an example. The civil war in Myanmar (Burma) has displaced tens of thousands of people. Between 2002 and 2019, the United States accepted about 178,000 Burmese refugees. In California (and other states) where refugees were resettled, resources were allocated to meet the refugees' needs, including their educational needs. In some school districts, interpreters were hired, classes for Newcomers and English Language Learners were expanded or created, and counseling services for traumatized children were provided. Teachers and staff were hired, trained, or re-trained to understand and meet the needs of their Burmese refugee students, as well as to communicate with their parents. Teachers and staff expanded their cultural competence and ability to work with English Language Learners.

Oakland, California, where I've lived and worked for over 25 years, has large numbers of immigrants including hundreds of Burmese refugees. Some years ago, I coached Alison, the teacher of a self-contained, middle-school class of Newcomer students. Alison had experience teaching English Language Learners, but in PE, the teacher didn't have this experience. In PE, the Newcomer students didn't understand the teacher's instructions, they had never experienced basketball or running around a track, and they were fearful of the way the PE teacher shouted. As a result, they couldn't access the learning and often asked to be excused from PE. Alison raised this situation when she asked if I could coach the PE teacher. I responded by asking her if PE was the only place where her students experienced difficulty. She explained that they experienced fear and frustration in many spaces in the school and community including when they went to the cafeteria for lunch and when they were stopped by the security guards. I invited Alison to assert her leadership and take action.

Alison saw the layers of systemic issues and decided to address them. First, she led a couple sessions with the whole staff (including the cafeteria workers and the security guards) on strategies for communicating with English Language Learners and Newcomers. She shared the backgrounds of a couple of students who had lived most of their lives in refugee camps in Thailand and for whom shouting activated the trauma they'd experienced. In response to this, the PE teacher shared that he felt terrible that he'd frightened the students. "I was just trying to make sure they could hear and understand me," he said. Alison shared simple strategies to ensure that her students could understand directions, and the staff were grateful and receptive. As the staff practiced these new strategies, Alison also invited them to surface and name their beliefs about working with immigrants. This conversation allowed a staff that was primarily people of color to unearth some biases about immigrants, which became a powerful conversation about the different kinds of privileges that we hold.

During these sessions, Alison also heard teachers expressing a desire to communicate with her students' parents. She reached out to a refugee resettlement center to engage the services of translators for parent-teacher conferences. The principal of the school had heard that there were tensions in the neighborhood between the Burmese immigrants and their Mexican and Guatemalan neighbors, and organized an event to bring families together to learn about each other. By doing so, the principal addressed social systems on the level of the city and neighborhood.

A Transformational Coach who holds an awareness of systems and the interconnectedness of events can help a frustrated or struggling teacher engage resources and outside partners, and take actions that support students. A coach can also help a teacher recognize what is outside of their sphere of control, which can bring comfort and an ability to prioritize. Holding a systems-thinking approach helps a coach empower the client to transform systems and their own practices.

> In the next section, I'll reference Appendix C: the Transformational Coaching Rubric 2.0. This rubric is more detailed, concrete, and explicit about equity practices and emotional intelligence than the one published in *The Art of Coaching*. It's most useful to guide reflection and learning. Although it's massive, when digested one domain at a time, it is invaluable for coaches. You can also download it from my website, http://brightmorningteam.com.

The Four Phases of Transformational Coaching

There are four phases in a Transformational Coaching model, as shown in Figure 1.2. These phases are more or less sequential, although at any moment, we may draw strategies from other phases. These four phases describe the process regardless of what lane of Transformational Coaching we're in—whether we're coaching teams, coaching for emotional resilience, focusing on coaching for equity, or providing prescriptive instructional coaching. Here's an overview of the phases:

- **Phase 1: Surface**. We surface the state of affairs in a classroom, school, or organization by seeking understanding of the teacher or leader, students, community,

Figure 1.2 The Phases of Transformational Coaching

THE PHASES OF TRANSFORMATIONAL COACHING

ATTEND TO SELF

1 SURFACE
surface current reality

2 RECOGNIZE
recognize impact

4 CREATE
create new practices

3 EXPLORE
explore emotions

BUILD RELATIONSHIP WITH CLIENT

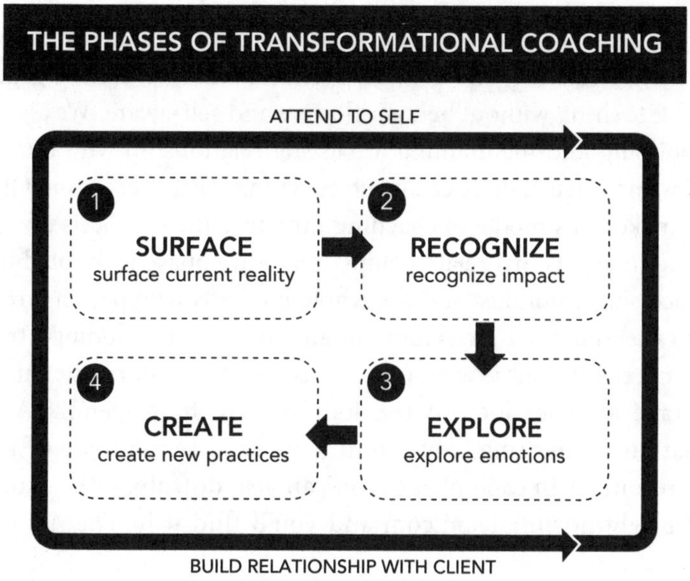

institutional history, and current reality. We learn about what's going on, the problems, and the challenges.

- **Phase 2: Recognize**. We guide a client to unpack the root causes of the challenges they're facing and explore the underlying mental models that contribute to the problems. We guide the client to identify and reflect on how those problems impact students, their communities, and themselves.
- **Phase 3: Explore**. We coach our client to acknowledge, name, accept, and understand emotions. This allows the client to release emotions and access deeper levels of courage, commitment, and confidence.
- **Phase 4: Create.** We coach to create new beliefs and ways of being, which in turn create new behaviors.

While these four phases characterize the overarching arc of the coaching process, we continue to hold three goals in each conversation: to build resilience, reflective abilities, and skills. It's by staying focused on these goals that we ensure that we're coaching behaviors, beliefs, and ways of being. Sometimes strategies overlap. In Phase 2, we engage strategies to unpack beliefs. When we're in Phase 3, we emphasize resilience-building strategies. When we're in Phase 4, we draw heavily on strategies to build skill. In this book, you'll read a couple of stories, each of which spans several chapters, to see how a Transformational Coach moves through these phases.

Throughout this process, coaches must constantly attend to our own needs—to our emotions, learning, and growth. We know that we can't engage in Transformational Coaching without being reflective and self-aware. We also constantly attend to building and maintaining a trusting relationship with our clients. We know that "without trust, there can be no coaching" (Echeverría and Olalla, 1993).

What makes this model of coaching unique is the emphasis on attending to emotions and interpersonal relationships. An entire phase is devoted to considering and processing emotions, and the whole model is wrapped in a reminder for the coach to attend to their own emotions and to attend to building a trusting relationship with a client. This is what makes this model transformational.

Let's take a closer look at the four phases. In Appendix A: Phases of Transformational Coaching, you'll find a guide to remind you of the key elements and resources in each phase (you can also download this from my website, http://brightmorningteam.com and you'll find it in *The Art of Coaching Workbook*).

Phase 1: Surface Current Reality

In this first phase, we aim to understand the lay of the land, the client's current reality including challenges, strengths, and opportunities. We need to clearly see the client's teaching or leadership practice, beliefs, way of being, and organizational context. A coach seeks to understand who the client is, why they got into education, their vision for themselves as an educator, and their strengths. A coach draws on masterful listening and questioning strategies.

In this phase, the coach observes the client in action (teaching or leading). The coach also listens for and identifies mental models that originate in oppressive ideologies and that result in inequitable experiences, access, and outcomes for students. The coach draws on their knowledge of racism and white supremacy and of how systems of oppression manifest in our classrooms. Without this knowledge base, the coach might not see inequities in a classroom. (This knowledge base is discussed in Chapter 3).

It's critical that the coach attend to their learning and emotional needs in this phase. A coach needs support to process their observations and stay grounded in a Transformational Coach's way of being. In this phase, a coach engages skills in Domains 2 and 3 of the Transformational Coaching Rubric, 2.0. In this first phase, a coach builds a foundation for coaching by building a strong relationship with a client based on a solid understanding of who they are.

Phase 2: Recognize Impact

In the Recognize Phase, the coach helps the client see how their behaviors, beliefs, and ways of being perpetuate systemic oppression. The coach gathers data that reveals the impact of the client's practice on students and that deepens the client's willingness to make changes in their practice. It's important that the coach gathers a variety of data—including observations, student survey/voices, and video. The purpose of the data is not to shame the client: it is to help them see the impact on students. The coach helps the client confront discrepancies between their vision for themselves and the impact of their actions.

In this phase, the coach guides the client to increased awareness of their underlying mental models. The coach can offer the client resources to learn more about racial and gender identity development and white supremacy, and how these manifest in our systems, beliefs, and practices. It's essential to explore how dehumanizing ideologies harm everyone—including the client.

The coach must continue cultivating awareness of their thoughts and feelings during this phase and recognizing when they need support from others. During this phase, clients often push back and seem resistant. A coach can feel stretched in their coaching skills, understanding of the situation, and capacity to respond to their own emotions and their clients' emotions. This can impact the coach's ability to stay in relationship with the client, and the coach may unintentionally undermine trust. The coach might also have new insights about the ways in which they have perpetuated white supremacy and systemic oppression and may need coaching to reflect on their own behaviors, beliefs, and ways of being.

Phase 3: Explore Emotions

In the Explore Phase, we engage emotions to help the client solidify a commitment to changing their practices. We coach to surface, acknowledge, accept, explore, understand, process, and release emotions.

Strong emotions can surface in this phase in both the client and coach. It's common for clients to experience grief as they recognize aspects of their identity that they need to transform. Clients may also experience remorse, shame, and anger as they come to new insights about themselves and their practices. The coach provides space and time and creates the conditions for the client to come to these insights.

It's critical that the coach has a strong knowledge of emotions and how to coach emotions—this is a knowledge base that is discussed in Chapter 6. The coach must also recognize the boundary between coaching emotions and the work of a mental health professional: a coach doesn't probe into the origins of the emotions in the client's childhood. In addition, a coach needs to know the indicators of depression and anxiety, and when to encourage a client to seek professional medical or psychological help.

In the Explore Phase, the coach consistently communicates an acceptance of emotions and a belief that wisdom and resilience can be accessed by experiencing emotions. The coach recognizes that this phase is critical to healing and liberation.

Phase 4: Create New Practices

In the Create Phase, we coach the client to enact new practices. By the end of this phase, the client demonstrates different behaviors from what they were before the coaching—behaviors that create an equitable classroom.

In this phase, a broad set of coaching strategies are used, many of which are those we commonly think of as coaching strategies: We co-plan, observe and offer feedback, analyze student work together, and so on. While engaging in these activities, we guide the client to make connections between their new behaviors and instructional practices, and their new or expanding beliefs and ways of being. This allows the client to strengthen their ability to recognize the mental models from which their behaviors emerge, and to identify which mental models perpetuate white supremacy and systems of oppression and which lead to healing and transformation. We strive to heighten the client's awareness so that when we're not around, they can recognize when they are perpetuating inequitable practices and shift their behaviors.

The Role of Relationships: The Guardrails

A Transformational Coach pays close attention to the quality of the relationship between themselves and their clients. In a space where a trusting relationship is valued, clients can take risks. Courage is required for us to traverse a chasm and create something new.

Running parallel to the lanes on the bridge are guardrails. The first guardrail represents attending to ourselves—to building a healthy relationship with ourselves as we guide others on the journey across the bridge. To take care of ourselves, we create and insist on time to learn, to collaborate with others, to process our thoughts and feelings, to understand our identity markers, to develop our skills, to unpack our beliefs, to cultivate new ways of being, and to heal from pain and suffering. We know that we can't do this work, we can't guide people in a journey, unless we're attending to ourselves. Doing so sets us up to be in healthy relationship with ourselves.

The second guardrail represents the relationships that we build with others on this journey: with our clients and colleagues. Those relationships need to be characterized by trust. Coaches and leaders build trusting relationships and then maintain them, repairing them when they are weakened or damaged. In order to build trust, we draw on our understanding of the role that identity plays in emotions and building trust along and across lines of difference—racial, gender, age, and other differences.

The trust that is built with ourselves and with our clients—trust that's infused with an understanding of race, racism, identity, and emotions—is a guardrail on the tracks to transformation.

The Five Principles of Transformational Coaching

The vertical support structure that's used, in part, to hold up a bridge is called a *pile* in engineering terms. Made of wood, concrete, or steel, the piles, or pillars, are hammered into the soil beneath a bridge until the ends reach the hard sublayer of compacted soil or rock below. Piles hammered to this depth leverage the grip and friction of the soil surrounding it to support the load of the bridge deck.

Principles are statements reflecting values, vision, theory, and belief; principles inform and direct the actions we take. Principles are the pillars that extend from the depths of the earth that rise up through the water and support the bridge. They uphold the integrity of the structure; they enable the bridge to remain intact regardless of the weight that crosses the deck. These are the five principles of Transformational Coaching:

- **Compassion**: We relentlessly strive to center the humanity of others. We preserve people's honor and dignity above all. We know that kindness is our greatest power. We practice self-compassion, which includes taking care of ourselves. We know that the journey toward liberation will be long, so we rest and attend to our minds, bodies, hearts, and spirits.
- **Curiosity**: As we suspend our judgments and opinions, we seek deep understanding of other people, of ourselves, and of the situations we're in. Our curiosity expands through our willingness to be changed by what we hear.
- **Connection**: We never lose sight of the connections between all living things. We know that the hope for our world lies in our ability to see ourselves in all living things, and to see all living things in ourselves. We refrain from binary thinking.

- **Courage**: We draw on deep sources of courage, we face our fears, and we act with courage every day. We don't wait until we know everything, or have every detail worked out to do something. We take action and course-correct when necessary. We act with healthy urgency. We know that just as people created inequitable systems and just as we have adopted the mindsets from those systems, people can create new systems and can adopt new mindsets. This gives us the energy to take risks.
- **Purpose**: Our purpose is to create a world characterized by justice, equity, and liberation. The journey is the destination. We can fulfill our purpose when we act with compassion, curiosity, connection, and courage.

To cross the chasm from our current reality to a place where schools are equitable places of learning requires that we are anchored in these five principles. We act on these in a coaching conversation, when we're making decisions about how to coach, when we're designing a coaching program, when we're leading teams, when we're facilitating professional development, when we're managing coaches, and so on. Whenever there are decisions to make about how we'll cross the bridge, we act on these principles. They keep the structure from collapsing under heavy weights or in storms.

Next, we'll dive into a story to explore coaching for equity. It's time to see what these ideas look like in action.

Before You Go . . .

Read the following prompts and select two or three that feel most valuable to you based on where you are in your learning journey. Spend meaningful time considering your reflection before moving on.

REFLECT ON THIS CHAPTER

- Which components of Transformational Coaching do you already practice? Which elements of Transformational Coaching are not a part of the way you coach?
- Which phases of Transformational Coaching do you feel prepared for? Which phases feel like they'll be most challenging?

REFLECT ON YOUR PRACTICE

- If you've ever received coaching, how would you describe it? What domain (behavior, beliefs, or ways of being) did it focus on? Is there a domain that you would have liked the coach to pay more attention to?
- How would you describe the coaching you do? Which domain do you focus on? What impact could you have on your clients, organization, and students if you coached in all three domains?
- What do you feel is blocking you (if anything) from coaching behaviors, beliefs, and ways of being? What would need to happen so that you could coach the Three Bs?
- What do you think your coaching, teaching, and leadership might be like if you had a coach who practiced Transformational Coaching?
- How might your experience as a child have been different had your teachers worked in a system that used this model of coaching for equity?

Interlude: Curiosity

Principles of Transformational Coaching

- Compassion
- **Curiosity**
- Connection
- Courage
- Purpose

Curiosity: As we suspend our judgments and opinions, we seek deep understanding of other people, of ourselves, and of the situations we're in. Our curiosity expands through our willingness to be changed by what we hear.

"Don't think about why you question, simply don't stop questioning. Don't worry about what you can't answer, and don't try to explain what you can't know. Curiosity is its own reason . . . Have holy curiosity."

—Albert Einstein

- What would it be like for you to have "holy curiosity"?
- What does your body feel like when it's curious?
- What makes it hard for you to feel curious?
- What did this chapter make you more curious about?
- Which of your behaviors, beliefs, and ways of being are you willing to change?

CHAPTER 2

Jumping into Coaching for Equity

*For me, forgiveness and compassion are always linked:
how do we hold people accountable for wrongdoing and yet
at the same time remain in touch with their humanity
enough to believe in their capacity to be transformed?*
—BELL HOOKS, WRITER AND ACTIVIST

Stephanie would cry so much when we met that I worried she'd become dehydrated. She'd apologize for crying, assure me that she wasn't depressed, and express gratitude for coaching. But week after week, she'd sob for almost the entire hour that we'd meet. At first, I'd responded to her distress by acknowledging her emotions and consoling her. She was a new teacher, and teaching is stressful. I took her tears as a sign of emotional release and appreciated that she trusted me.

After a while, I found myself feeling frustrated, and then angry, that she cried so much. Whenever I'd try to move into the glaring equity issues in her classroom, her crying became more intense. Her tears started to feel like a way to keep the conversations that needed to happen at bay, a barrier between me and her. I felt like if I didn't attend to her sorrow, I was being cruel and unsympathetic. And yet, I was getting tired of it. And the kids in her classroom weren't learning. And it was my responsibility—*because as a coach, I am responsible for the learning of children*—to do something. I just wasn't sure what.

Stephanie is a white woman, and I've coached many white women. She was also a new teacher, and I've also coached many new teachers. I'm sharing this story with you because it was representative of many coaching situations that I found myself in, and because it's complicated. As you read about Stephanie, you might think: *She's struggling with all the things that new teachers struggle with—what does this have to do with equity?* I hope to present the messy overlap between the challenges that most new teachers face and the struggles of a new teacher who doesn't have much knowledge or experience working with racially and socioeconomically diverse students, who has internalized messages of white supremacy and unconsciously acts on those, and whose emotional intelligence is low.

This chapter illustrates the first phase of Transformational Coaching, when our goal is to surface the client's current reality. We need to understand what they do, how they think and feel, and the organizational context in which they work. As we do this, we identify the aspects of their practice that are inequitable, or that lead to inequitable outcomes for students. All along, we must attend to building trust with our client—and to successfully do that, we also need to attend to ourselves. As you'll read, however, we also draw from other phases when necessary—to explore emotions, or create a new practice, to take into account the impact of an action. Transformational Coaching is dynamic and fluid, while also contained within a macro system (see Figure 2.1: The Phases of Transformational Coaching).

Figure 2.1   The Phases of Transformational Coaching

THE PHASES OF TRANSFORMATIONAL COACHING

ATTEND TO SELF

1 **SURFACE** surface current reality

2 **RECOGNIZE** recognize impact

4 **CREATE** create new practices

3 **EXPLORE** explore emotions

BUILD RELATIONSHIP WITH CLIENT

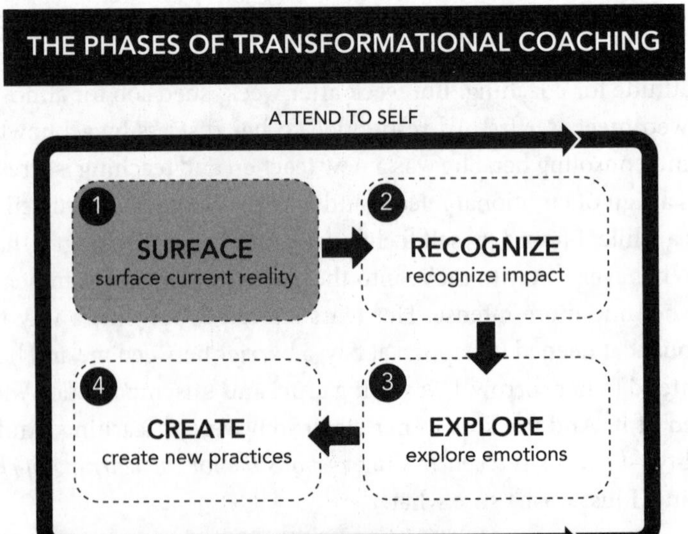

> **Phase 1: Surface**
>
> Goals in this phase:
>
> - Understand the client's teaching—their behaviors, beliefs, and ways of being.
> - Explore the client's underlying mental models.
> - Understand the client's organizational context.
> - Recognize inequitable practices and beliefs.
> - Build a trusting relationship.

As you read this chapter, it's possible you'll recall some of your own experiences in the classroom and might have feelings, including guilt and regret, about what you did or didn't do. As a person of color who was an unprepared new teacher, I still feel the sting of hindsight as I regret things that I did or didn't do, or said or didn't say—in my classroom, with my colleagues, to my principal. If we are reflective, we're likely to have feelings, and we're also likely to grow. So, recognize, name, and accept your feelings when they make an appearance, and see what you can learn from them. We can't do better until we know better; we can't know better until we reflect and learn from our emotions.

Building Relationships and Surfacing Strengths

Stephanie and I met a week before school started. She was a late hire, assigned to teach ninth-grade English. She was eager and enthusiastic about teaching, having moved to Oakland, California, from a small town near St. Louis, Missouri, because her best friend from college lived in San Francisco. Stephanie had attended a traditional teacher-preparation program and had student-taught in a suburban sixthgrade classroom under the guidance of a 30-year veteran. "She was a great teacher," Stephanie said, "but she was also very traditional. I want at-risk students to see me as a role model, I want to get to know them and be their friend. I know I can help them make something of themselves, help them get on a good path." Stephanie talked about her "Hispanic" students and told me that she loved everyone the same and didn't "see color."

Red flags peppered this first conversation. The high school Stephanie worked in was diverse: About 30% of students were Latinx, another 30% were African American, 20% were Southeast Asian, about 10% were white, and the remaining 10% were

Yemenese and Palestinian. Around 80% of students received free or reduced lunch. I was concerned about the role Stephanie saw herself playing as a teacher (students don't need a teacher to be their friend) and her self-perception as someone who would "help" (I wondered if she wanted to say "save") "at-risk" children in the "inner city." These terms—*help* and *at-risk*—reflect deficit thinking, reflect a mindset that students in this community didn't have resources or skill sets, and that what they needed was an outsider, perhaps an educated white person, to guide them. I was aware that Stephanie didn't have strong background knowledge for the cultural context of our students. And I was concerned about her reference to "not seeing color."

Although in the initial phase of Transformational Coaching we focus on understanding a client and building our relationship, this doesn't mean that we can't also be instructive and provide missing knowledge or information. In that first conversation, after Stephanie had used the phrase "at-risk children" a few times, I said, "Stephanie, I know that the label 'at-risk' is used widely, but it's problematic." I briefly shared some of the reasons why it's not an empowering term, and then I offered her a couple of alternatives—*underserved students* and *marginalized communities*—and defined those terms. She appreciated the information and quickly incorporated them into her vocabulary. (Chapter 3 will discuss the language we use in more detail.)

Looking for Strengths

In our first conversation, I'd reminded myself to search out Stephanie's strengths and skills. This is something I'd had to learn—it didn't come automatically to me. As a new coach, some five years prior to working with Stephanie, I'd been consumed by a teacher's shortcomings, unable to see their abilities and positive attributes, which left me feeling hopeless and angry. As I learned about coaching—through my own trials and errors, in reading about neuroscience and the science of behavioral change, and from reflecting on the mental models that promoted focusing on the negative—my coaching skills expanded. When we see someone's strengths, we have a more balanced picture (because everyone has strengths) and we can build on those strengths.

Stephanie did have strengths. Underlying her comments about wanting to "help at-risk children" was a desire to serve others. She'd wanted to be a teacher since she was 15, when she'd tutored second graders who were struggling to read. She spoke passionately about her desire to contribute meaningfully to the world, and shared stories of her grandmother and great-grandmother who had been farmers and teachers and who had instilled in her a sense of responsibility to serve. She was coming from a place of care and from a set of values that resonated with me.

Stephanie was a hard worker. She described how she prepared lessons, created PowerPoint presentations, sought out resources and materials, and assessed student work. As she described her process, I could see that she knew something about teaching and learning. I'd worked with many teachers who hadn't been through a teacher preparation program, but Stephanie had a solid foundation for teaching.

I appreciated Stephanie's desire to improve. "I want to hear everything you have to say," she told me in that first meeting. "Don't hold back, OK?"

I've learned that while someone may say they want feedback, their intention for asking doesn't always mean they truly want it or can hear it. We know that it's admirable to ask for feedback, especially when we're new to a role, but we may not be clear about how we want to get that feedback, or when, or what might make us able to hear it.

I responded to Stephanie's invitation for feedback with one of my favorite coaching stems: "Tell me more about where this [question/comment] is coming from."

Stephanie hesitated, and then responded with a little laugh: "I want to be an excellent teacher. I don't want to waste time getting better. I've been told that I'm sensitive, so I'm trying to improve at receiving feedback, and I think I'll do that if I just get a lot of it. I'll get desensitized."

I took this opportunity to speak about how I coach and explain what coaching is:

"If I just give you directive feedback, then I'm robbing you of the opportunity to come to your own insights. Coaching is a way to look in a mirror so that you can see what you're doing. I want to help you become a more reflective practitioner. I will give you directive feedback sometimes, but I'll also help you learn how to think through what you're doing so that you can be sure that your teaching is reaching every student."

Stephanie nodded, although her expression looked uncertain. "OK," she said, "could you observe me during the first week of class and tell me what you think? I don't want to wait until halfway through the year for you to tell me I'm not doing well!"

"I'm happy to come in during the first week," I said, "and to give you feedback." I reminded myself that we were just building trust—that I needed to build her trust in me and in the in coaching process. So, I asked her: "What kind of feedback specifically would you like? Can you give me an example of the kind of feedback you might hope for?"

Stephanie thought for a moment. "I guess just whatever you see. What you think I can improve on. If you see any problems, I should know right away."

"How about if next week, we just look at routines and procedures?" I asked. I wanted to focus feedback on something tangible that she could make progress in quickly—and I'd learned that routines and procedures are not only key to how smoothly a class runs but are also fairly easy to quickly course-correct.

"Sure," Stephanie said, "and anything else you see, too!"

"I appreciate your enthusiasm to work on your teaching, Stephanie, I really do." And although I still saw the red flags, I meant it. You can see red flags and you can see strengths, skills, and positive attributes at the same time. In fact, to be a strong coach for equity, it's essential that you do.

Low Expectations and a Deficit Mindset

The first time I observed Stephanie in the classroom, it took all of my self-control not to intervene. It was the first week of school, Stephanie was a first-year English teacher, and she was teaching ninth graders, so I really wanted to believe that what I was seeing could be attributed to the newness of it all. But I also knew, without a doubt, that the first week is an indicator of what will come—it's critical that during that week, we establish our presence as a person in charge, build relationships, articulate expectations, and set the tone for the year.

The Observation

Here's what I observed: Stephanie, a petite white woman in her early 20s, wearing a black pencil skirt, a simple blouse, and low heels, nervously trying to get the class's attention. Her voice was thin and wispy, an octave too high for ninth graders—a vocal register more appropriate for primary age students. She fidgeted with her hands, alternating between fiddling with the chain around her neck and perching them on her hips. "We need to quiet down now," she said, her voice barely audible from where I stood in the back of the crowded room. "Um, class, um, it's time to get started." Her voice lilted up at the end of the sentence, as if she was asking a question, not giving directions. Most students tend to follow directions at the beginning of the year—they so badly want to learn and do well—and the kids more or less settled down.

Stephanie proceeded to give instructions about the activity that students would do. They were writing their biography as readers, but the directions were confusing. One young man called out: "Hey, teacher. What are we supposed to do first? I don't get it." Others echoed his confusion. Stephanie tried again, but she seemed unclear about the steps in the process. She rushed through slides that had way too much text on them and provided far too many directions all at once. We were 18 minutes into a 55-minute period, and more and more students had disengaged from Stephanie's explanation and had started having conversations with each other.

"OK, for today, students, you don't have to do this assignment," Stephanie said wiping her perspiring face. "I'm sorry, I think it is too hard, you're right. Today, why don't you just do this part—the drawing part—and sketch a scene from one of your favorite novels?"

"Are we in kindergarten again?" asked a girl sitting in the front row. I could tell that Stephanie had heard, but she feigned otherwise.

Stephanie circulated through the classroom, making awkward conversation. She spoke to her students as if she was speaking to third graders—her syntax and vocabulary were simplistic, and her tone of voice was forced: "Oh, Sandra, that's a pretty flower!" "Jessica, I like the way you drew that house." "Alex, that's such a cute dog. Do you have a dog? I like dogs." Many students drew, a handful talked to each other, one put on headphones and did math homework, and a couple put their heads down on their desk and went to sleep. When Stephanie passed those who were off task, she just ignored them.

A boy in front of me leaned forward and in a loud whisper, in Spanish, said to his friend, "She looks hot in that skirt, right?" I generally don't intervene or say anything to students when observing a class, especially not at the beginning, but I couldn't let that go. I stood up and moved into his line of sight. I glared at him—my refined teacher-look as fierce as ever. He turned red, lowered his eyes, and in Spanish said, "I'm sorry, I'm sorry."

The period was ending. "Do we turn these in?" shouted one student.

"No, that's OK," Stephanie said. "You can keep them. You've all done great work today."

Alex crumpled up his paper and tossed it into the trashcan. "Why'd we do that if you don't even want it?" he asked.

Stephanie's face was plastered in a nervous smile. "There's no homework tonight, students," Stephanie said. "Good work today," she said as the bell rang and kids bolted from their seats.

Stephanie and I were scheduled to meet after school. I was glad I'd have a few hours to think about how to debrief this observation. There was so much to discuss and so much Stephanie needed to work on—from her ability to design a rigorous lesson to her ability to interact with this age group appropriately. She seemed to know little about what ninth graders are like, and she hadn't designed a lesson that would engage or challenge them. She seemed excruciatingly uncomfortable around her students, a discomfort I suspected had to do with her lack of experience or exposure to the demographic she was teaching. I drove back to my office to write up my notes and prepare questions for the debrief.

Debriefing the Observation and Exploring Discomfort

"I can't wait to hear what you thought," Stephanie said as I settled into a student desk after school. "I mean, it's just the first week, so we're still getting into things, but what did you think?" She was smiling, but her eyes looked anxious. A long time ago, I learned that the eyes reveal whether the smile is genuine or not.

"Stephanie," I said, "if you want to improve as a teacher, you'll need to reflect on your lessons every day. That's what I'm going to support you in. So, what did *you* think?"

"Well," she said, "I mean, the kids were pretty good today. That period has some rascals, but maybe because you were there, they were well behaved. And they followed instructions." I couldn't read her tone of voice—I felt an incongruity between her words and demeanor. She didn't look like she believed her words.

I nodded. I was jotting down the phrases she was using. "What did your students learn today?" I asked.

"Oh gosh," she said, her voice cracking. She covered her mouth with her hand as the tears started rolling down her cheeks. I wasn't sure why she was crying and immediately felt guilty for having said or done something to upset her.

"What's coming up for you right now?" I asked Stephanie.

She pulled a tissue out of the box on her desk and wiped her face before trying to explain. "Oh, I'm sorry. I'm so sorry. I mean, I know it's just the first week of school, but I guess you're right." Stephanie blew her nose. "They should have learned something. My objective was that they'd begin brainstorming their history as a reader, but they didn't really do that, did they? I mean, the drawing was supposed to be part of it, but they didn't learn anything." Her crying intensified, and I spent the rest of that session consoling her. I helped her name her emotions— she felt sad that the lesson had gone so poorly; afraid that she wouldn't be a good teacher; ashamed that I'd witnessed this lesson; and angry at herself for not being prepared to explain the instructions. I felt optimistic about her reflection, hopeful that she'd be able to make changes for the next lesson based on these insights. She recognized, for example, that her slides had too much text, that she needed to scaffold lessons, and that she needed to "ask students to do something more important," as she said.

But here were the questions—printed out and taped into my coaching notebook—that I'd intended to ask in the debrief:

- Tell me about how you decided on this lesson. What did you hope students would learn in this lesson? What standard is it based on?
- What did you hear and notice about how students engaged with the lesson? What do you think they thought of the lesson?
- When students went home, what do you think they said to a parent or older sibling about English class?
- If you could do it over again, what would you do the same and differently?
- What questions do you have about your students? What do you want to learn about them?

Although I'd been eager to ask these questions, and a part of me whined: *But I was so prepared and these are good questions!* I also recognized I needed to let them go. It's invaluable to plan and prepare for conversations—those plans often make all the difference—but you also need to be unattached to plans. Staying flexible and responsive to a client's needs is a key skill for a coach. And yes, sometimes we'll feel disappointed, frustrated, or sad when we don't get to implement our plans—all valid feelings—and in those moments we might be consoled by staying unattached to outcome. I have come to tell myself to *trust the coaching process*, as I've learned that just because a conversation doesn't go the way I want it to go, it doesn't mean that coaching won't be powerful. It just might happen in a different way, or on a different timeline.

Stephanie and I agreed that the next time we met, she'd bring a lesson plan for me to give her feedback on. I'd hold off on observing her until she felt more confident, and we'd focus on planning.

When There's a Deficit Mindset Spill

Stephanie's mood would swing from chipper and cheery to despondent in minutes, and I came to see that the chipper was inauthentic, a mask of anxiety. The next time we met, after skimming through the lesson plan she'd brought, I asked, "I am most interested in your thinking behind the planning. Can you start by sharing how you determined this lesson?" And Stephanie started crying.

She apologized through her tears. "It's just that the only time I can let down my guard is when I see you," she said.

"Who do you feel like you're on guard in front of?" I asked.

"Everyone!" She blew her nose. "My students, other teachers, my principal. I can't be myself with them. They have to see me as strong and competent and together."

"Do you think they see you that way now?" I asked.

"Oh yes! I'm so careful when I'm with them. I never cry in front of them."

I wondered, however, if others truly did perceive Stephanie as strong and competent, or if they picked up on her inauthenticity.

"When you and I meet, I feel like I can just relax and be myself," she said.

"Well, I'm glad to hear that," I laughed. "I guess I'll take that as a compliment."

Stephanie talked about how hard teaching was, how she'd never realized it would be this hard. How every day she got to school by 7:00 a.m. and didn't leave until after 6:00 p.m., although with the days getting shorter, and it being almost dark at 7:00 a.m., she felt "unsafe driving through the neighborhood" in the morning and in the evening. She was still settling into her apartment, sorting out the logistics of living in a new area, and she was lonely for home.

With shaky conviction in her voice, Stephanie said, "But I know that this is where I'm meant to be. I truly feel a calling to help these kids. They've just been through so much, it's really unfair. All the violence and poverty in their neighborhood." Stephanie looked at me. "You've seen it around here—so much trash dumped on the streets and the crack addicts wandering around all day. And the broken homes—so many of them have dads in prison. Or their dads are in Mexico, or they've never even met them." She paused. "I can't imagine growing up without a dad. I mean, they're growing up without role models, practically orphans. My heart aches for them."

Her tears hadn't stopped.

Discomfort is part of this journey for all of us—for Stephanie, for me, and for you, reader. Stay in the discomfort. It won't kill us.

If You Could Have Heard My Thoughts

I'd been nodding, taking in what Stephanie was saying, and jotting down notes as I always do, but I was getting increasingly uncomfortable. I noticed that my head had stopped moving. I did not want her to think I agreed with her. But then I worried that she'd notice I'd stopped nodding and would take this as criticism. I felt self-conscious and awkward.

At first, I thought I'd heard her express empathy for students, but empathy is when you walk *in* someone's shoes. You feel their feelings. I sensed she was feeling pity for her students—and pity is when you see someone's suffering from a distance; pity protects the viewer and creates a barrier between people. Empathy closes the gap between the other person and you. Empathy connects us, because even when someone's situation is very different from our own, even when we've never been in it, we connect with another person's humanity—we recognize the common needs, desires, and emotions that are part of being a human being.

What also bothered me was that Stephanie saw her students and their communities as monolithically broken, damaged, victims. And there's a lot of danger in such a perception. First, it positions the holder of the perception—in this case, the teacher—as the natural savior, poised on the front line. This savior, then, is imbued with tremendous power, while the students and their communities are robbed of their agency, disempowered, and perceived as vessels to be filled, saved, and rescued. Seeing yourself as a savior is reflective of what's known as a "colonist" mindset. We explore this in Chapter 3.

More problematic, however, is that this assumption of a broken community is false. Every community has resilience and has figured out how to survive and thrive and bounce back after adversity. Stephanie wasn't seeing the skill or resilience or the beauty in her students, and that perception dehumanized them.

All of this historical and sociopolitical context served as a backdrop in my mind as Stephanie talked about her students. I was getting angry. I could feel warmth spreading across my face. I mulled over the questions I could ask Stephanie that might disrupt the deficit mindset she was stuck in. I thought about asking, "What are the strengths you see in your students?" But I worried that she wouldn't be able to answer—because she couldn't see those strengths. That had happened before with teachers who demonstrated a deficit mindset: I'd ask them to find strengths in their students, and they couldn't name any, or named superficial ones. And then the problem magnified.

So, was the problem that Stephanie didn't *know* her students? That she didn't have enough information about them? Or that she couldn't see or hear or recognize strengths, even if she was exposed to them?

A deficit mindset is like an oil spill—it coats every organism, it obscures beauty, it does great harm to the environment, and it's tedious to clean up.

I'd lost track of what Stephanie was saying as my mind meandered through these thoughts. The last words I'd registered her saying were, "They're growing up without role models, practically orphans. My heart aches for them."

I'm embarrassed to tell you what happened next, and yet it's what happened: I said I needed to go to the bathroom. I came back saying that the principal urgently needed me and that we'd need to continue our conversation at another point. I left.

Sometimes it's okay to check out, remove yourself from a situation, hit pause, or take a break. Sometimes it gets to be too much. And it's far better to do something like what I did with Stephanie, than to do what I'd done previously with other teachers when I'd discharged my anger and grief and damaged those relationships. I was learning how to engage with my emotions at this point, and leaving the conversation felt like a way to attend to myself.

My strategies at that time for dealing with my emotions were limited. I vented to a colleague. I distracted myself with finishing past-due monthly reports. And then I ruminated over the conversation, thinking about what I wish I'd said and what I could say next time. I read and wrote. This helped me gain some mental clarity, but I wasn't really feeling my feelings. Ironically, the conclusion I'd arrived at about how to coach Stephanie was that I needed to have a conversation with her that directly explored her emotions.

The Undulating Landscape of Emotions

Two weeks after my meeting with Stephanie, during which I'd felt like I got a clear picture of the deficitmindset she held about her students, we met again. In the first five minutes during the "check-in" section of our conversation, Stephanie launched into a story about a drive-by shooting in the neighborhood. She started crying. I interrupted her story. "Stephanie, can you identify the emotions you're experiencing right now?"

"I'm so sorry I keep crying," she said, blowing her nose. Then with a forced laugh, she added, "I told you I was sensitive."

"There's nothing wrong with crying," I said. "Which emotions are the tears reflecting?" I asked.

"I guess I'm just overwhelmed," she said. "It's all so much."

I nodded. "Being overwhelmed is an intense feeling," I said. "Can you unpack it a little? Being overwhelmed usually involves a number of feelings. What's in there?"

Stephanie cried harder. "I guess sadness," she said. "I am sad." She nodded.

I made an "uh huh" sound of validation. "What else?"

"My heart breaks for them," she said.

"So, more sadness?" I asked.

"Yes, and I feel scared that I won't be able to help them. That I won't do a good job."

Now we're getting somewhere, I thought. "So, you feel uncertain about your abilities, worried that you won't do what you're committed to doing."

"Yeah," she said. "I want to be a good teacher. I really do."

My heart softened at that moment, which helped me realize that it had been tightening up. I'd been feeling irritated with Stephanie—because she cried so much, because she seemed to have little awareness of what she was saying, because she knew so little—but I heard her genuine desire to serve, and I could connect with that. I reminded myself that if I was to be an effective coach with her, my empathy needed to be present, always.

"Sadness and fear are normal, Stephanie," I said. "Which doesn't mean that you'll always feel sad and afraid. Can you recall other times in your life when you experienced a big change and felt sad and afraid?"

Stephanie thought for a moment. "I guess when I went to college," she said. "That was hard. My classes were challenging and I had to work my butt off, but it wasn't as hard as this. My college was a few hours from home, so I went back almost every weekend."

"It sounds like a big difference was that you had more support in college—that you were close to your family."

Stephanie's crying picked up. "Yes," she said, "I did."

"So it sounds like you're lonely," I said.

She nodded. Her eyes were red and puffy. I too have felt very lonely in my life, and I've been far from home without a support system. Part of me wanted to hug her and feed her soup and brainstorm how she could develop community. But I restrained from moving into "fix-it" mode or emotional consolation. If I'd done either of those things, I would have been robbing her of the potential to work on her own problems, to engage her own agency and power to think through her situation.

"Stephanie," I said, "if your best friend was going through what you're going through, what would you say to her?" I took a long, audible breath—doing so can unconsciously cue others to take a deep breath also.

"I'd say that she can do this, that she's stronger than she thinks," Stephanie said. "I'd say that she needed to make sure to get enough sleep and to eat healthier." Stephanie smiled.

"How much sleep have you been getting?" I asked.

"Not much. I work late, and then I have trouble falling asleep, and I wake up around 3:00 or 4:00 a.m. because I'm anxious. But then I go to the gym and that helps a bit."

"I'm glad to hear you're getting exercise," I said, "and I do know that sleep really helps. Do you have any thoughts about how you might address the sleep issue? Because it sounds like you want to."

"I should probably stop working earlier. Then I could take a bath and read a novel, and I'd probably fall asleep easier. I tend to sleep for most of the weekend, so I know I need more sleep."

"And if you weren't so exhausted on the weekend, you'd have more energy to develop your community in the Bay Area."

"Definitely," she nodded. She'd stopped sobbing and her breathing had normalized.

"How are you feeling, right now?" I asked.

"A little better, I guess," she said. "I know what I'd tell my best friend if she was in my shoes, so that helps to think about it that way. I'd also remind her that this is her life's dream—to teach—and to remember that."

"Let me ask a direct question, Stephanie. Do you think you can improve as a teacher? Do you feel confident in your ability to learn?"

She looked surprised. "Yes, I do," she said with conviction in her voice. "I had a hard time my first year of college. I didn't do well in the first semester. It was so much harder than my high school. I thought I was going to flunk out. But I caught up and graduated on time."

"So you've struggled before—and that's great—that can help you feel confident that you can learn what you need to learn to be a good teacher," I said.

"But this is so much harder," Stephanie said. "I mean this is a different universe of hard."

I nodded. "Learning is learning," I said, "and you've done a lot of it. My job is to help you see how you can transfer your skill at being able to learn to this challenge, now. But your first assignment, if I can give you one, is to get more sleep. OK?"

Stephanie nodded in agreement.

I continued asking her questions: "Was there anything in this session that was helpful, Stephanie? Any questions I asked or insights you got?"

"Oh, definitely," Stephanie said. "It was super helpful to think about what I'd say to my best friend. I pride myself on being a good friend, so that felt easy."

"If that reminder helps you gain insight, maybe it would be useful to write that question on a piece of paper and post it near your desk, or put it somewhere you'll see it regularly."

Stephanie smiled. "I'll do both of those things—and I'll write it on sticky notes and put it everywhere. I can be a good friend. That feels like something I know how to do."

"Great," I said. "Let's keep recognizing the things you know how to do and explore how to transfer those skills."

When I left Stephanie's classroom that afternoon, Alfredo, a ninth-grade math teacher, and also a new teacher, stopped me in the hall. "Is she doing OK?," he asked. "I've been asking her if she needs help," he said. "I know she's having a rough time of it." I appreciated him for reaching out and asked how his year was going. "It's good," he said, "I mean, I have no life and I never eat lunch, but it's all good." Alfredo looked like he was barely older than his students, in spite of the neat white button-up shirt he wore and his polished black shoes. I knew he was from Oakland, that he spoke Spanish, and that he aspired to be a lawyer. Although I didn't coach him, I'd peeked into his classroom a few times and had seen obvious indicators that learning was happening.

As we said goodbye, Alfredo said, "You know, she just doesn't know these kids," waving his hand toward Stephanie's room.

"I know," I said.

"And *they know* she doesn't know them," he added.

"I know," I said.

I wanted to ask Alfredo for his advice; I wanted to say things that I shouldn't have said; I wanted to scream: *How do we get more teachers like you, who do know these kids?* But I wasn't sure what to say. Being tongue-tied and doubting myself seemed to be a common experience for me as a coach. I also didn't want Alfredo to feel like he had to take care of his struggling colleague, but I could see that he felt responsible for his students.

"I appreciate your kindness, Alfredo," I said. "Maybe one of these days I can bring Stephanie in to observe you teach and to see how you relate to our students. I think she could learn a lot."

"Yeah, of course," he said. "But she might think she can't do what I do because she's not from here."

"I hear you," I said. This was a common response from teachers when they observed other teachers and an important consideration for a coach when taking a teacher to observe someone. Coaches need to set up observations to guide their clients to observe behaviors, and then to get curious about the beliefs and ways of being that are underneath those behaviors. Alfredo had a valid concern. I was grateful he was teaching and told him so.

When the Problems Feel Overwhelming

I went back to my office. I was daunted by how many issues were at play and unsure about where to start. *What's the problem?* I asked myself. I've found it helps tremendously to sit, reflect, and write out everything that comes up for me and then make connections or identify patterns. If this isn't your typical go-to, give it a try. Here is the list I generated in response:

The problem is . . .

- She just doesn't know these kids.
- She's a new teacher who is unprepared for teaching, who doesn't know how to relate to ninth graders, who doesn't know how to design a meaningful, rigorous lesson.
- She defines the role of a teacher as being to "help" children. Therefore, she's got all of the knowledge and she assumes she needs to pour it into these empty, or flawed, vessels.
- Her definition of a teacher in this marginalized community is to save the children. She sees herself as the hero and as her students as damaged, hurt, needy.
- Her understanding of her students is limited, narrow, and distorted by racism. She's a white woman who has never lived in a diverse community.
- She's getting attached to these ways of thinking about her role, her students, their capacities, their communities and her identity.
- Her emotional intelligence is low—she recognizes the emotions she's having but doesn't have strategies to navigate them. Without those strategies, she may not recognize the impact her emotions have on others—on her students—and she may not effectively respond to their strong emotions.
- She has perfectionist tendencies that exacerbate her emotional distress and undermine her ability to learn.

As I identified her areas for growth, specifically in her instructional practices, I recognized that Stephanie had many. For example, when I asked Stephanie about her decision-making around determining learning targets for lessons, her responses were limited. I didn't know if her decisions were based on low expectations for her students, and therefore her lessons and learning targets lacked rigor, or were a reflection of being an inexperienced teacher and not knowing what was developmentally appropriate. In addition, Stephanie was also adjusting to life in a new region, she didn't have a support system, and she was physically stretched by all of these conditions. I imagined Stephanie would have struggled as a new teacher anywhere—even in her own backyard, teaching sixth graders. However, Stephanie was teaching students in a marginalized community, students whose needs in school had not been met for many years, students who had already had many teachers like

Stephanie—teachers who lacked cultural competence and basic skills as a teacher. Stephanie had options and choices in life; her students had fewer—the stakes were high for them in ninth grade.

In Transformational Coaching, we'll be faced with a dilemma: When a client has many areas for growth, where do we start? I felt compelled to jump right in and explicitly address Stephanie's lack of cultural competence and the deficit view she held of her students. But at this point, this compulsion emerged from anger: I wanted her to recognize that she was an unprepared and crappy teacher. I wanted her to feel ashamed of taking on the role.

But what purpose would it serve to make her feel guilty for teaching in Oakland? I definitely didn't want her to quit. In Oakland, during most of the 19 years I worked in the district, we struggled to attract, hire, and retain teachers. In many schools, we lost half of all teachers every three years. We often had to hire unprepared teachers from other parts of the country so that we wouldn't have vacancies. I could wish that there were legions of culturally competent, highly skilled teachers seeking jobs in our under-resourced district, but there weren't. As my colleague, Jenn would say, "You dance with whoever shows up to the party." I felt stuck and unsure how to proceed with Stephanie. Eventually, we would have a conversation about cultural competence and a deficit mindset, but it couldn't be a means to punish or humiliate her.

The following day, I took a hike in the redwood forest with my husband. I wrapped up a long rant about Stephanie saying, "I just don't know what to do." My husband's initial response irritated me even more—he expressed empathy for Stephanie. I'd wanted him to validate all my complaints about her and to join me in trashing her. But he recalled his own experiences as a teacher working in a community that he didn't understand, and his experiences teaching high school students and struggling through the first months in the classroom. I got mad at him and said I needed more empathy.

"Ah," he said. "What else are you feeling? You're good at naming *her* low emotional intelligence, but you're not clear about your own feelings. And now you're going to take out your anger on me for not saying the right thing. So, what are *you* feeling?"

It's hard to see your own blind spots. This was a lesson I thought I knew: When you're stuck, go back to yourself—start with who you are—and feel your feelings. But I'd forgotten that lesson. My husband is a good listener and a kind and empathetic person, and by the end of our hike, I felt grounded and prepared to coach Stephanie.

Turning Inward

Throughout the process of coaching for equity, coaches must attend to themselves. Attending to yourself implies that you know yourself, and that you stay anchored in who you are. There are three key components to who we are: Our emotions, our identity markers, and our sense of purpose. Our emotions are central to how we experience the world—knowing our emotions and understanding how to engage with them in a healthy and meaningful way is a critical way to attend to ourselves. Our racial identity, and other identity markers, are also central components of who we are and how we experience the world. Finally, our sense of purpose in life is essential to our sense of self and deserves attention. Let's unpack these three components of who we are and consider how we can attend to them while we coach for equity.

Starting with Emotions

When I coached Stephanie, initially my emotions emerged from my commitment to justice: It wasn't fair or right that students in Oakland didn't have highly skilled, culturally competent teachers. I acknowledged my fatigue in having to have "this conversation" again—a conversation about deficit thinking and race. I recognized my anger at white supremacy—at how it has affected my life and the lives of people I love, and how it has damaged our world.

Transformational Coaching requires that you recognize your emotions and tend to them. I felt angry at Stephanie, but I knew that it wasn't her fault that she held distorted notions of her students. I also believed that it was her responsibility to surface and shift those notions. I reminded myself that I too held distorted notions about others—that I was not better than her, and that it was my responsibility to skillfully, compassionately coach her toward equity. If I stewed in my own righteous anger, I'd erect a barrier between us, one that was just as impermeable as the tears that Stephanie shed as a shield.

Recognizing your emotions can be hard at first. Emotions need a safe enough space to come out. Emotions such as sadness and fear may not reveal themselves when we sense they won't be accepted, and then they masquerade as other emotions. Sadness and fear often show up as anger. Anger can feel more comfortable than sadness or fear because it has more energy than the flat, hopelessness of sadness. We can learn how to be present with anger and acknowledge the underlying fear and grief, and also to coach from a place of compassion and curiosity.

If you want to learn to recognize your emotions, you need to spend time with them—write about them, talk about them, reflect on them as you walk, run, or sit. Visualize having a conversation with your emotions and listen to what they have to say. Sense how your emotions manifest in your body, noticing where you feel their presence. As you spend time with them, communicate acceptance. Emotions hide if you believe that it's not okay to have them, or if you want them to quickly go away. If you allow emotions to exist, if you recognize and name them, they'll likely shift and become less intense or uncomfortable. Emotions can be our teachers and can allow us to access internal wisdom and strength. Appendix E: The Core Emotions can help you identify what you're feeling—I highly recommend that you print the table in that appendix for your own use and to use with clients.

It's been a process for me to learn to acknowledge my feelings. It takes daily practice to stay anchored in the emotions of compassion and curiosity. I occasionally question whether there's another, faster way of causing change, whether I could just bypass all of this compassion stuff and call someone out on their racist habits, but this question comes from fatigue or frustration—not from genuine curiosity. When I notice myself aching for a faster way, I acknowledge my fatigue and frustration. Fatigue, impatience, and sadness arise, but those feelings don't get to run the show—or to be at the source of the questions that I ask a client. With awareness, you can act with intentionality. When strong emotions arise, you'll be prepared for them and they won't throw you off your game. We'll continue exploring emotions in Chapter 7.

Exploring Identity

Your racial identity is among many other identity markers—such as your gender, class background, and sexual orientation—that profoundly affect how you see the world and operate in it. With awareness, you'll be more able to connect your emotional responses to your experiences in these identities, and you'll often feel a sense of relief and clarity at making those connections.

Upon reflecting on the conversation with Stephanie in which I heard her deficit mindset and walked out, I recognized that I was triggered by her statements: "I can't imagine growing up without a dad. I mean, they're just growing up without role models, practically orphans. My heart aches for them."

I grew up without a dad. However, I wasn't practically an orphan, I did have role models, and I didn't need anyone to save me. I recognized that some of the feelings that arose in me while coaching Stephanie—the anger and sadness—were unhealed wounds from my childhood experiences in school. As I tended to those wounds, I was more effective coaching Stephanie. *Coaching for equity reveals areas in which we need and deserve healing.*

Exploring your identity markers is a worthy journey, one that is best done individually and in a healthy community. The first step is to get clearer about your identity markers and the role they play in your life.

Here's an activity to get you started. List your most prominent identity markers including your race, ethnicity, socio-economic status, religion, gender, sexual orientation, spoken languages, nationality, political affiliations, physical abilities, citizenship status, income, educational background, and age. Now, think and write about these questions:

- Which of these identity markers do you prioritize when sharing about yourself?
- Which ones do you think others typically notice about you?
- Which ones do you tend to not really think about?
- Name your top three identity markers. Which specific life experiences made those so prominent?
- Do your closest friends share aspects of your identity? How so?

Cultivating a positive racial identity is a critical step to healing from racism. When you have a positive racial identity, you are aware of the history of your racial group and you are secure in your racial identity (Neville & Cross, 2017). A positive racial identity is possible when you have learned about who you are as a racial being—both the privileges and disadvantages it affords you—and how your racial identity affects your experience with others and the world. On my website, you can find additional resources to support this exploration. I also highly recommend Dr. Annaliese Singh's *The Racial Healing Handbook*. This is an outstanding resource and a perfect companion to this book. We'll continue exploring identity in Chapter 8.

Anchoring in Purpose

To coach for equity, you must be grounded in a deep sense of purpose. Acting from our purpose boosts our hope, optimism, and confidence. (In my book *Onward*, and the accompanying *Onward Workbook*, you'll find exercises to reflect on purpose.)

My purpose in life is to contribute to healing and transformation in the world. I am committed to compassion, justice, and community as the vehicles through which transformation will occur. This commitment has guided me as a coach for equity. I reflect regularly on how I work with compassion, when and with whom my compassion is fragile, and how to cultivate more self-compassion. I interrogate my notions of justice—what does justice look and sound like when it's deeply imbued with compassion? How can I work for justice, while not deviating from my commitment to compassion? How do we build just, resilient communities? How do I unconsciously perpetuate systems of oppression in the communities I belong to? What is the relationship between justice and liberation? Exploring my purpose keeps me humble and focused.

Staying connected to my emotions helps me stay anchored in my purpose. When anger or sadness surges, I consider whether I've strayed from my purpose. We're also likely to have a strong emotional response when we see others acting in conflict with what we hold as our purpose. When we recognize our own emotions and listen to them, we can gain deeper insight into who we are.

In difficult coaching moments, including some when I coached Stephanie, I chose to act on my purpose—which meant that I coached from compassion, curiosity, and a commitment to community. To do this, I had to engage with my emotions and as I processed my frustration and sadness, I accessed deeper reserves of love and confidence.

A Conversation about Crying

Two months into the school year, I carefully planned for a conversation with Stephanie about her tears. It began with me saying, "Stephanie, today I want to start with talking about the crying—your crying." Then I paused, watching her face for how she'd react. The late afternoon, autumn sunlight was filling her classroom, and today I'd chosen to sit across from her, rather than next to her as I usually did. I wanted to signify that I would take a more directive stance. I intended to be compassionately confrontational—to push her to examine her behavior, beliefs, and ways of being.

"I'm so embarrassed that I'm always crying with you," she said.

I replied in a kind but firm tone: "You've shared that. And as I've said before, there's nothing wrong with crying. It's human. We all do it. But I'm not sure how to make sense of it. Sometimes I think you're releasing emotions, which is healthy. Other times I wonder if you might be depressed."

I watched her take this in. She nodded slightly. I continued: "And sometimes I wonder if the tears prevent us from having meaningful conversations about your teaching and our students." I had decided to be transparent—I really was wondering about these things.

"I guess there's some truth to that," Stephanie said, her voice softened. She took a slow breath. "I can see how we've spent a lot of time talking about my feelings and you've been super sweet and caring." Her eyes welled with tears. I was grateful to hear that she'd experienced me in this way. "It's just that it's been such a hard transition," she said.

"Take another deep breath, Stephanie." She did and her breathing became more regular. "Here's what I'm wondering: have our conversations about your feelings helped you become a better teacher?"

"Oh yes, definitely!" she said. Her voice was firmer and the tears had receded. "Those really helped." She paused before continuing: "In my family and back home, we don't talk about feelings. I mean, I know we have them, but we don't talk about them. And now I see how that made them bigger and more intense—not in a good way. You're the first person who has said it is ok to have and talk about feelings."

I nodded and continued: "As I've said, Stephanie, we are human beings, and human beings have feelings, and we deserve to recognize and talk about them in all spheres of our lives. I'm glad you've appreciated that. And I want you to have space to include them our conversations. I'm also wondering how we can spend more time talking about instruction and building a positive classroom community."

Stephanie shifted in her chair. "I think when my health insurance kicks in, I might want to get a therapist," she said.

"That sounds wise," I responded. "I think everyone can benefit from therapy. And you're still welcome to discuss your feelings in our meetings."

"I really do want to be a good teacher," Stephanie said. "I will try to stop crying so much when we meet, OK?"

"The tears aren't a problem, Stephanie," I said. "I think I often feel the need to address the tears and emotions. I'm wondering what might happen if when your strong emotions come up, we don't diverge from talking about teaching? Does that make sense?"

"Yes, it does." She nodded.

"It'll be hard for me to stay out of a consoling coaching mode—and so I guess I'm needing your permission to refrain from doing that so much." Sometimes being honest is a way to stay anchored in integrity and get someone's buy-in to what you're proposing to do.

Stephanie smiled. "You've got it," she said. "Permission to push through the conversation when I'm crying."

"Thank you," I said. "I'm still learning to be a coach—I'm sure I'll always be learning—and so I am excited to try different strategies. And I really welcome your feedback at any time. My commitment is the same as it's always been: to help you become the teacher you want to be—one who has a huge, positive impact on her students, on every single student."

"So what do you think we need to talk about?" Stephanie asked. "I feel like there's so many things that I need to improve in, where do you think we should start?"

I paused. I was nervous about saying what I wanted to say, what I knew I had to say. I was grateful for Stephanie's trust—in the past, I'd failed many times to gain a client's trust. I took a deep breath and looked down at my hands. Then I made eye contact and said, "I think we need to talk about your identity as a white woman teaching in a community of color. We need to talk about how your identity markers affect how you understand your students and how you teach." My tone was neutral and my voice clear and strong.

Stephanie's eyes widened. She sat very still. After a few long seconds, she said, "OK."

"I know, that's a big topic," I said. "And it probably sounds kind of scary."

"Um, terrifying, actually," she said. "I'd be more comfortable talking about my sex life!" She laughed self-consciously.

"I know," I said, "race feels like a taboo topic. Which is why it's so important that we talk about it."

Stephanie nodded. "We don't talk about that back home either. But here it's like the elephant in the room."

"I'm glad to hear you're onboard with this conversation," I said.

"Could we talk about it next time?" Stephanie asked. "Or do you think we need to talk about it now?"

I thought for a moment. Was she trying to postpone the conversation? Was she imagining it would be a one-and-done conversation? Was there another pressing issue she wanted to talk about?

I responded: "Stephanie, I think all of our conversations are about race and class and gender identity. Or perhaps, an awareness of our identity needs to be included in every conversation. So we don't need to have a big conversation about identity and race today—although I'd like to give you some homework so that we can start talking explicitly about it next time—and I want to think about how we can integrate reflections on identity into every conversation. Make sense?"

"It does, I guess." Stephanie said. "What's my homework?"

"Start reflecting on your identity," I said. "When you became aware of racial difference, which aspects of your identity feel most important to you, when and how you learned about people of other races, and what you learned. How does that sound?"

"I can do that," Stephanie said. And she looked confident. And I registered that this was the longest conversation we'd ever had without tears.

"Do You Think I'm Racist?"

I had planned a conversation in which I would lead Stephanie through a reflection on how her identity as a white, middle-class woman from the Midwest impacted how she taught and related to students. I had a list of provocative and reflective questions to help her reach new insights about her low expectations, deficit mindset, and lack of cultural competence. I'd practiced this conversation with a colleague and processed the emotions that were surfacing in me, and I felt grounded in my values. I was ready.

I also knew that we needed to have this conversation now, because according to a growing set of data, Stephanie's students were not succeeding in her class. On the latest reading assessments, 85 percent of Stephanie's students read below grade level; and on the mid-fall progress reports, the majority of students received grades of C or lower. When I observed the classroom instruction, I could see why. Stephanie's tenuous authority in the classroom was slipping. Students wandered the room and were not held to classroom rules and agreements. Assignments were low rigor and irrelevant. Tasks had little value or purpose, students got away with a whole lot, and they weren't learning. I needed to do something—I, too, was responsible for these children.

It was a quiet Friday afternoon when I walked into Stephanie's class, prepared for the conversation about race. I could tell that Stephanie had been crying. I noticed a twinge of irritation rise in myself, and then allowed that emotion to pass. I thought about how much she wanted to serve our community and how hard she was trying. I quickly envisioned her as a young child—a gimmick that activates my empathy for someone—and I noticed how that helped me feel settled. Empathy feels good.

"What's going on, Stephanie?" I asked. "It looks like you've been crying."

"I really don't want to cry," she said.

"Have you tried deep breathing?" I asked, as this was a strategy she'd been practicing to help her navigate strong emotions. She nodded.

"I'm OK. Let's do this," Stephanie said, her voice devoid of enthusiasm.

"What do you hope might come from this conversation?" I asked Stephanie. I wanted her to visualize a positive outcome and to connect with a purpose for engaging in the conversation. I noticed how confident I felt.

The tears started streaming down Stephanie's face. "I just don't want you to think badly of me," she said. "I'm so afraid you'll think I'm racist. Do you think I'm racist?"

"I will answer that," I said, "but I want you to know that I'm confident that this conversation will be meaningful and helpful for you. I know it'll help you learn and become the teacher you are committed to being."

I was ready for Stephanie's question—and I will tell you exactly what happened. It was a memorable conversation, and very much like many conversations I'd had previously and afterwards. But in order for a coach to have a conversation about what it means to be racist, you need knowledge. You need an understanding of what racism is, where it came from, and how it works. So I'm going to pause in this story about Stephanie for a bit of direct instruction on this topic.

Before You Go . . .

Read the following prompts and select two or three that feel most valuable to you based on where you are in your learning journey. Spend meaningful time considering your reflection before moving on.

REFLECT ON THIS CHAPTER

How do you think that your background, experiences, and identity markers (especially your race and gender) affected how you felt when reading this chapter?

- What connections can you make to Stephanie's experiences and feelings? When have you experienced any of the feelings she did?
- In phase one of Transformational Coaching, we focus on surfacing the client's current reality. We want to understand who they are as a teacher and what they think, feel, and believe. We also need to see and identify inequities. What do you see that Stephanie is doing (or not doing) that may lead to inequitable outcomes for students? What beliefs about her students do you imagine are lurking below the surface of her behaviors? How would you describe her way of being?

- Review the first section and identify the questions that helped me surface Stephanie's current reality. As you do so, consider what you're learning about her current reality and which questions you're having. Also note your emotions.
- How would you describe the way Stephanie was experiencing and responding to her emotions? What did you learn about her emotional landscape?
- Review the Transformational Coach Dispositions (found in Appendix C: Transformational Coaching Rubric 2.0). Which ways of being did you see me demonstrating with Stephanie? Which do you think I could have more effectively demonstrated?

REFLECT ON YOUR PRACTICE

Review Domains 2 and 3 of the Transformational Coaching Rubric 2.0. Which of those areas do you feel skillful in? If you had to pick one area to concentrate on, which would that be and why?

- How do you feel when someone cries a lot? How is your response different based on your relationship to that person and based on what they are crying about?
- What are your fears about having conversations about race and identity?

TO DO

Next time you are coaching, ask yourself: What am I feeling? Where do I sense these emotions in my body? What do they want to tell me? Jot them down right now in your coaching notebook, or on a sticky note, so that you'll remember.

What could you read to help you learn about people whose identity experiences are different from yours? Create a list, right now, of books you'd like to read. If you need some suggestions, consult Appendix F: Resources for Further Learning.

Interlude: Connection

Connection: We never lose sight of the connections between all living things. We know that the hope for our world lies in our ability to see ourselves in all living things, and to see all living things in ourselves. We refrain from binary thinking.

> *We are each other's business; we are each other's harvest; we are each other's magnitude and bond.*

Gwendolyn Brooks, poet

- What would it mean if we lived in a world where this was true? How might your life be different than it is now?
- What would it take for us to live together in a way where we are each other's business, harvest, magnitude and bond?

> *If you have come to help me, you are wasting your time, but if you have come because your liberation is bound up with mine, then let us work together.*

Lila Watson, Indigenous Australian artist, activist, and academic

Think about a group of people in another part of the country or world who belong to a racial/ethnic or cultural group about which you know very little.

- What does it mean to you to see yourself in them?
- Which feelings come up when you think about your interconnectedness?

Now, think about your own community.

- Which groups of people in your community are marginalized or othered?
- In which ways are you connected to them?
- How is your liberation bound up with theirs?

CHAPTER 3

How to Understand Race, Racism, and White Supremacy

*Not everything that is faced can be changed, but nothing
can be changed until it is faced.*
—JAMES BALDWIN

As a person of color, learning about the impact that white supremacy has had on my life has given me an intellectual framework to talk about racism and has made me feel more empowered. I've acquired language to describe what I've experienced and seen in schools for decades. This learning has also opened my eyes to moments when I contributed to perpetuating white supremacy. Whether because I'd internalized the messages of white supremacy, or because I wasn't aware of what I was doing, learning has allowed me to see places and times when I became complicit in oppressing others. This has been (and continues to be) a painful experience—but one that is ultimately liberating. As I know better, I do better. Learning about white supremacy and racism has been a stepping stone to healing.

If you're committed to coaching for equity, then when you observe a teacher, or lead a department in creating policies, or when you are in conversation with colleagues about students, you'll need to know what racial inequities look and sound like and how to talk about them. Beyond a professional commitment, we all need to learn more about white supremacy and racism—whether because we are committed to leading equitable organizations, or to heal from the damage of white supremacy, or to live a morally aligned life in which we recognize the interconnectedness of all beings. White supremacy affects people all over this planet—whether or not you live or work around people of color. We need to understand what this means, how it affects everyone, and how this came to be. This learning will allow us to construct and traverse bridges of authentic connection.

Depending on our identity markers and life experiences, we also have different things to learn. Learning about white supremacy and racism will be a lifelong commitment for all of us. There's no level of "wokeness" at which we graduate or retire. We may need to take a sabbatical from learning—cognitive understanding needs to be balanced with psycho-social/spiritual healing or else we risk physical and emotional exhaustion and malaise. People of color live racism and white supremacy every day and may feel like we have less to learn and need more breaks—at least this is true for me. And then after a break, we'll return to learning—to reading and listening and deeper levels of understanding.

In this chapter, I'll explain how the idea of "whiteness" came to be, how white supremacy was established, and how it's affected our country and education system. I'll also define racism. I've tried to keep this chapter succinct and hope that it can be used as a shared text for discussion. If this had existed when I coached Stephanie, I might have given her sections to read—such as the section called "What Is Racism?" or the section on the power of language in this chapter. I hope the content of this chapter generates interest in a deeper exploration of these concepts and history. In Appendix F: Resources for Further Learning, you'll find suggestions to continue learning.

Pause and Process

Before you read this chapter, take a few minutes to acknowledge any feelings that are arising. Name them. Notice how your body feels as you name and gently explore those emotions. See if you can sense the feelings and questions that are hiding on the edges of your consciousness—the ones you aren't ready to name or admit. Can you invite them out to be seen?

Given your identity markers, how do you think this chapter might impact you? What comes up for you when engaging in this kind of learning?

What do you hope to get in this chapter? What do you hope to learn?

For most of you, I anticipate this chapter will stir up strong feelings and be a hard read. Plan now for how you can take care of yourself after you finish. Can you plan to take a walk? To talk with a friend? To do something that nourishes your spirit?

What Is White Supremacy?

Let's start with a foundational concept: Racism wouldn't exist without white supremacy. *White supremacy* is the ideology that white people are superior. This ideology began with the transatlantic slave trade and has been institutionalized for over 500 years in the United States and in white settler societies including in Canada, Australia and New Zealand, and South Africa. It manifests in a myriad of forms and affects the lives of everyone in the world in innumerable ways. In many countries, white supremacy manifests in the legal system, in who owns property, in what we see on TV, in who has access to higher paying jobs and good medical care, in who and what we find beautiful, in who lives where, in the words that we use, in which schools receive more funds, in how teachers "manage" students, and in much more. You can't understand racism without understanding white supremacy, so let's deconstruct it.

Where Did "White People" Come From?

Human beings have long categorized ourselves and others into groups based on religion, tribe, and even clothing. But categorizations based on complexion are relatively recent. It's hard to imagine that someone coined the term "white" because the concept is now one that is so fundamental to how we see the world—but the term and concept have been in use for less than 500 years. In 1619, when the first Africans were abducted and taken to Virginia as slaves, there were no "white" people. It wasn't until the 1680s that this term was used in colonial records. It was, however, during those first decades in the new colonies that the concept of *white people* was established—as a way to describe the superiority of Europeans, and people of European decent, over Africans.

"White" came to mean anything that was not African and anyone who was not of European origin. By the early twentieth century, in some states in the United States, just one drop of "black blood" made someone "colored." But whiteness has had shifting boundaries. For many years, Irish, Italian, and Jewish people were not considered "white" by other Europeans, and they faced discrimination because of their perceived racial status. Some Europeans and mixed-race people chose to identify as white so that they could receive the privileges of being white. My maternal grandfather, a Jew from Eastern Europe, was born with the name Solomon Skolnik. Because of the anti-Semitism he experienced, he changed his name in the 1930s to Frank Carlson. While this didn't completely eliminate the discrimination he experienced, it did reduce it. This was a privilege available to him—the privilege of skin color.

Just to be sure we're clear on one fact: *There are no racially-based biological differences between human beings.* There is no gene or cluster of genes common to all blacks or all whites. Classifying people into "races" has no scientific basis. *Race is a social construct.* A small group of men who sought wealth and power created the categorization of people into races as a way to elevate their superiority. They based this categorization on the amount of melanin in skin, so that they could dehumanize Africans, enslave them, and exploit their labor. Race is not real; whiteness is a creation. Racism, however, is very real.

Using the categories of "white people" and "people of color" is problematic because identity is very complicated. However, these terms are shorthand for conveying the general meaning of who has power and who does not. They are limited as categories and deserve more exploration. Often the intersections of our identities help us gain a much richer understanding of our privileges and of the discrimination, biases, and oppression we experience. For example, you may have racial privilege (if you are of European decent) but you may lack other privilege based on other identities (if you are female-identified, and disabled, and from a low-income background). These intersections, and the experiences of all groups of marginalized people, deserve attention. In this book, I focus on racial equity—with some acknowledgment of experiences that intersect with other identity experiences.

Author Paul Kivel offers useful insight on whiteness:

> It is critical to remember that racism doesn't exist without white supremacy, and white supremacy doesn't exist without the concept of whiteness. Racism is based on the concept of whiteness—a powerful fiction enforced by power and violence. Whiteness is a constantly shifting boundary separating those who are entitled to have certain privileges from those whose exploitation and vulnerability to violence is justified by their not being white. (1996, p. 19)

A Brief History of the Origins of White Supremacy

As we study history, we will learn that race is a social and political construct designed so that a small group could amass a lot of wealth. Understanding history is empowering. Here's a brief timeline of the mess that's brought us to where we're at now (for more of this history, see Zinn, 1980, and Kendi, 2016):

- In the fourth century BCE, Aristotle created theories justifying Greek slave-holding and superiority. The Romans and early Christians adopted these beliefs. In the ancient world, ethnic, religious, and color prejudice existed, but *races* such as White Europeans and Black Africans did not.

- In 1377, the Muslim historian, Ibn Khaldun, wrote extensively about the inferiority of the "Negro nations" (and the Slavs—the origin of the word "slave") and argued for their enslavement.

- In 1415, Portuguese royalty gained control over trade routes into Sub-Saharan Africa. They subsequently published the first European book that justified the enslavement of Africans based on racist ideas.

- In 1444, the first Portuguese ships carrying enslaved Africans arrived in Europe. Slave-trading was defended as a Christian missionary expedition.

- In the 1400s, the Portuguese wrote extensive denigrating narratives about Africans, describing them as animals and as savages who desperately needed religious and civil salvation. Portuguese explorers, agents, and slave traders circulated these writings extensively. Meanwhile, the Portuguese royalty's profits skyrocketed as the exploitation of African land and people increased. Remember this: European royalty got very, very rich from enslaving Africans.

- In 1481, the Portuguese built Elmina, a massive fort on the coast of Ghana, which became West Africa's largest slave-trading post.

- In 1492, Columbus landed in the West Indies. Right from the start, Spanish colonists transferred their racist perceptions of Africans onto the indigenous people they encountered. The enslavement, exploitation, and genocide of the indigenous people of the continent known as America began.

- Spanish colonists wanted to mine gold and to plant and process sugar in the "new world," but they required laborers. Millions of indigenous people died from disease, resistance, and brutality. Spanish capitalists and religious leaders argued for the enslavement of Africans.

- Simultaneously, Europeans traveling in Africa disseminated stories about uncivilized, sexualized, animalistic African people. These narratives circulated widely in Europe as the slave trade picked up.

- In 1619, the first African slaves were taken to Virginia. The Virginians employed racist ideas to legalize and codify slavery. In the 1630s, the Puritans in New England followed suit.

- In the 1680s, "White," as a language of race, appeared in the lexicon of those of European descent living in Virginia, and then appeared for the first time in Virginia law in 1691. Wealthy Virginian landowners legislated "the whites" as a new class of people into existence. They gave whites certain rights and took other rights from blacks.

> *Racism is the need to ascribe bone-deep features to people and then humiliate, reduce, and destroy them.*
>
> —Ta-Nehisi Coates

Colonization

Colonization played a monumental role in the creation of a system of white supremacy and its legacy lives on: it's another key concept to define.

Colonization is a system of power that's based on beliefs of one group's superiority over another. In the last 600 years, colonization has been based on the notion that people of European origin had the right to dominate other lands and cultures because as white people, they were smarter, more "civilized," and more deserving. This continued a legacy that began perhaps a thousand years prior and that had been justified with Christianity. The Celts of the British Isles and western Europe were colonized by Christians. Beginning in the 1500s, European colonizers destroyed cultural practices of indigenous people (in the Americas, Africa, Australia and New Zealand, and parts of Asia and the South Pacific) including their languages and religious/spiritual practices, and forced them to adopt the colonizer's religion and language, and provide their labor—for free. Over time, many of the colonized internalized the beliefs and practices of the colonizer, and the brutality of the system became obscured.

In the United States, we rarely remember that we are on stolen lands, lands that were taken through blankets intentionally infected with smallpox, through broken treaties, and through outright genocide. These lands were taken when the people who had been here for thousands of years were removed, forcibly marched across the country, and corralled into "reservations." Our lack of memory, and the intentional distortion of truth, has led to the macabre. Take Thanksgiving, for example, a holiday supposedly based on a feast that white Plymouth settlers shared with Native American people after their first harvest. This is typically celebrated with a big meal and family gathering. However, while there's little evidence that this historical feast actually occurred, there is plenty of evidence of the massacres that the white settlers perpetrated on the native peoples of the Plymouth region, and of the decimation of the indigenous people of this hemisphere. History has been sanitized, and the brutality of colonialism has been erased. This perpetuates the power of white supremacy.

Remember Resistance

Here's something else that those in power have not wanted us to know or remember: people have *always* resisted oppression and dehumanization and white supremacy. Always. From the moment that Columbus set foot on the island of Cuba and that Spanish exploiters began enslaving the natives, the Taínos resisted, as did the indigenous inhabitants of Jamaica and Mexico and Peru and Florida and across the Americas; indigenous resistance to colonialism continues to this very day. Africans fought back when they were captured in their villages, as they were forcibly marched to the west coast of Africa, on ships on the Atlantic, in the field and the house, and in more ways than we'll ever be able to catalogue.

In modern history, resistance has taken myriad forms and has been unceasing. Some of this history we know, some we don't, because as the African proverb reminds us, until the lions have their own historians, the history of the hunt will always glorify the hunter. It has served white supremacy to repress these stories and to keep them from us. But you don't have to look very far, even in traditional history narratives, to find the stories of those who resisted and refused to internalize messages of inferiority. You can find them in history books, in memoirs, and in the stories of train porters and strawberry pickers and church goers. We can, and must, look to these people for inspiration and courage. Just because their stories aren't taught in eighth grade standards doesn't mean they didn't exist.

Perhaps people are color *are* more "defiant"—perhaps we should proudly wear this label; our ancestors resisted annihilation and subjugation, and perhaps when we are called "defiant," we should stand taller. Perhaps defiance is an assertion of our rights and existence, a healthy challenge to white, patriarchal, capitalist authority—a cause for celebration and appreciation, not grounds for suspension. The history of our resistance has been intentionally obscured from people of color and from people of European decent as well—from those who also resisted and from those who were passive. Our journey to justice and liberation will require that we excavate those stories and celebrate them. The knowledge of our resistance can fuel our courage and commitment.

Pause and Process

- Which feelings are coming up in this reading? Are they different from the ones that you noticed in the beginning of the chapter?
- How, and from whom, have you learned about racism?
- What has this learning journey been like?
- What might you gain from continuing this learning journey?

What Is Racism?

A definition of racism is what Stephanie wanted when she asked me, "Do you think I'm racist?" Defining racism, and a racist person, is essential to transforming schools and building a more just society. For so long, our image of a racist has been of a cross-burning, cloaked Klansman. Or of a skinhead with a swastika tattooed on his forehead. By defining racism in these ways, a lot of us have been relieved from taking responsibility for the racism that we consciously and unconsciously act on.

The Short Definition

While there's debate about how to best define racism, there's also general agreement about the following:

- Racism is a system of oppression that emerges from beliefs that one race is superior to another based on biological characteristics.
- The only racist system that has ever existed is one based on the ideology of white supremacy; this system is designed to benefit and privilege whiteness by every economic and social measure.
- Racism is prejudice plus power: in the United States (and in many places in the world), institutional power is held by white people.
- A racist is someone who consciously or unconsciously upholds a system and culture of white supremacy.

Based on this definition, there is no such thing as "reverse racism." While people of color can show prejudice against white people, this form of discrimination doesn't come with systemic privilege. It's not institutionalized.

Let's explore a couple of ways to further define and understand racism: Racism as a policy and practice and racism as a toxic pollutant.

Racism as Policy and Practice

The dominant narrative about racism has long been that racist *ideas* produced racist *policies*. A *racist idea* is believing that African or Black people are inferior, uncivilized, fit for hard labor, and so on; a *racist policy* is slavery or segregation. According to this interpretation of history, beliefs about racial difference preceded slavery. White people feared African people and looked down on them, and essentially said: "Enslaving you is justified because you're almost an animal, you're very strong, and you're built for work. Also, we'll give you Christianity, which will at least save your soul."

In his book, *Stamped from the Beginning* (2016), Ibram X. Kendi turns this notion on its head. Kendi critiques what he calls the "popular folktale of racism: that ignorant and hateful people had produced racist ideas, and that these racist people had instituted racist policies (p. 9)." Kendi makes a brilliant 600-page case for how America's history of race relations began with racial discriminatory policies, which led to racist ideas, which led to ignorance and hate. Sequencing racism in this way is essential to how we understand and dismantle it.

Kendi continues this exploration in his moving and thought-provoking *How to Be an Anti-Racist* (2019). In this book, he proposes that we stop thinking of "racist" as a pejorative and start thinking of it as a simple description. You are either racist or you're anti-racist, Kendi argues; you are either upholding white supremacy, or you're actively participating in taking it apart. He urges us to focus exclusively on policy, arguing that the solution to racism will start with policies, not ideas. He suggests that antiracist ideologies will emerge once we are bold enough to enact an antiracist agenda that would include criminal-justice reform, more money for black schools and black teachers, and a program to fight residential segregation.

When I reflect on research about the positive impact on black children from having just one black teacher, I'm convinced by Kendi's arguments. I also know that the outcomes for black and brown children would be different in schools if there were clear and concrete policies around who is sent to the office for what (for example, "defiance" should not be criteria for an office referral), for how children are tested for learning differences, and for what literature is assigned in eighth grade. Different educational policies would make a tremendous difference in the lives of black and brown kids in school.

Then I reflect on the way teachers (black, white, and of color) have spoken to my black son, how their perception of his defiance distorted the relationship they built with him, and how that impacted his sense of belonging and psychological safety. While perhaps some policies could have buffered him from the impact of these beliefs, I also know that we must address the thinking, feeling, and believing of anyone who works in a school if we intend to change the experience and outcomes for children of color.

I'm also troubled by Kendi's proclamations of binaries and absolutism. Binaries are dangerous and lead to righteousness. Thinking in binary ways has gotten us into the mess we're in today because we can't and haven't acknowledged the interconnectedness of all things, the gray zones and the both/and. The path out of the situation we're in now requires that we avoid the emotional comforts of a simplification of history or humanity or thinking. That's what binaries provide, and the world is too complex.

We need policies that buffer us from the impact of white supremacy *and we need more*. We need to recognize how racism has affected our hearts, minds, bodies, and relationships as well as the social fabric of our communities, and we need to attend to this harm and heal from it. Policy can't do that. Kendi's arguments are rational and logical, and they are a great contribution toward justice, but we are thinking-feeling-physical beings. As Patrisse Cullors, one of the founders of Black Lives Matter, says, "We can't policy our way out of racism" (OnBeing, 2017).

Racism as a Toxic Pollutant

Dr. Beverly Tatum, author of *Why Are All the Black Kids Sitting Together in the Cafeteria?* offers a useful analogy for racism. She writes:

> [Racism] is like smog in the air. Sometimes it is so thick it is visible, other times
> it is less apparent, but always, day in and day out, we are breathing it in . . . if
> we live in a smoggy place, how can we avoid breathing in the air? (1999, p. 6)

Expanding on Tatum's analogy, I equate racism with a toxic substance that's not only in the air but has also seeped into the soil in which we plant crops and into the water system from which we drink. It's virtually impossible to avoid ingesting it, and we've been doing so since we were born. Our parents and grandparents breathed in these poisons and drank water and ate food that was putrid with racism. Racism coats our arteries; it is etched into our neural pathways, distorting our thoughts. Our physical, emotional, and social bodies are toxic with the poison of racism. And by "we" I mean all of us—people of color and white people. Some people of color unwittingly internalize notions of white supremacy despite the fact that doing so contributes to our own marginalization. Everyone learns explicit and implicit stereotyped messages in families, schools, and communities. We learn these stereotypes, and we act on them consciously and unconsciously.

But we have choice. Choice is the ultimate freedom afforded by human consciousness. Just like we have choices about what we eat, drink, and breathe, we have choices about the mental and emotional toxins that we ingest. When the air is smoggy, we can wear a mask—and we can find clearer air. We can choose food that is less toxic; we can purify our water; we can take supplements that cleanse our system of toxins.

As we attend to our individual well-being and health, we must address the root cause—we must understand who is contaminating the air, soil, and water; we must warn others of the contamination; and we must demand change. It may not be our fault that we live in toxic systems, although some people do seem to make an active choice to live in a toxic environment. However, it is our responsibility to call attention to when our friends and loved ones ingest these poisons and when we see them spreading the poison to others; it is our responsibility to clean them up. We have a choice about where we live, what we breathe, and how we respond to the toxins in our world.

Let's return to this fact: Race and ethnicity are social constructs—elements of a system developed by humans to categorize people who "appear" to share common features. The amount of melanin that you have in your skin signals something to the world about the societal norms that will be applied to your presumed race. Race is an inaccurate social construction to describe who you really are, but your perceived race and the race you perceive of others matters a lot in society because of white supremacy. Racism is the construction of "races" from particular biological characteristics that people have, and the use of this construction to lift up certain groups in society into a dominant class and keep other groups in an oppressed class.

Racism is embedded into structures including schools, government, social programs, and the legal system. If we intend to permanently rid our individual systems of the toxins of racism, we'll need to transform those structures as well. The foundations and walls of those structures are saturated with toxic mold spores. Our individual mindsets and behaviors will never be truly rid of the toxicity of racism if we're in poisonous environments. That's not to say that you can't purge yourself of a lot of toxicity—you can become acutely aware of when you are ingesting racist poison and when you're acting on it and contaminating others. But it takes daily practice to examine your own mind, heart, and behaviors for white supremacy. Ultimately, we'll only be healthy, whole, and free if we dismantle the systems in which white supremacy is lodged. It took 600 years for us to get where we are today—it might take a while to dismantle corrupted systems and to rid our minds of contaminants. This doesn't mean that we shouldn't take immediate action to start changing things; it means we're in for a long journey.

Repeat this over and over: *Greed* gave birth to racial categorization and white supremacy. Racial classification and white supremacy were created to justify the unfettered brutality required of slavery and colonialism. And in the last 500 years, the concept of race and white supremacy has served the social, political, and economic interests of dominant groups. We've been indoctrinated into a belief that racism is just the way things are. It'll take us a while to internalize that categorizing people into races was invented by fifteenth-century European royalty, explorers, and burgeoning capitalists in their quest for wealth.

It is a liberating concept to remember that human beings have not always been racist. Yes, human beings have a tendency to sort each other into categories, but sorting by the amount of melanin in a person's skin and by phenotypical features is a relatively modern practice. Racism has been perpetuated by normalizing it and suggesting that it's just something human beings do. Unless we remember that racism was created, it can seem like something humans are destined to do—but that's just not true. The way we think about what racism is creates the mental models in which we can get out of the mess we're in. If we recognize it as something we created, we can dismantle it and create something new.

Pause and Process

- Which ideas were familiar to you in this section on racism? Which ideas were new?
- What questions has this section left you with?
- How do you think your sense of your own racial identity affected how you read this section? How might someone from a different racial identity have experienced it?

How Racism Manifests in Schools

The education system in the United States (and in many developed countries) was not designed to serve all students well. In 1779, Thomas Jefferson proposed an educational system with different tracks for, in his words, "the laboring and the learned." Scholarships would allow a select few of the laboring class to advance by "raking a few geniuses from the rubbish."

The first public schools on the east coast of the United States existed to social-ize white male children in religion and morality. Children from wealthy families were educated at home by tutors, and later sent to boarding school, often in Europe. Missionary schools were established as a mechanism to convert Native children. After the Civil War, the Freedman's Bureau established schools in the South for black children.

Industrialization created the need for universal education in the United States (as it had in Europe), and in 1918, schooling became compulsory through elementary school. Schools focused on efficiency, results, and creating compli-ant future laborers. The architects of the education system described schools as factories, and children as "raw products" that "are to be shaped and fash-ioned into products to meet the various demands of life." (Cubberley, 1916). Our school calendar; the "cells and bells" that we find in just about every school; and the emphasis on testing, order, and control come from an educa-tion model designed to advance capitalism. Capitalism, remember, birthed the ideology that white people are superior and that people of color exist to serve their masters.

Education in the United States has never been a right included in the Consti-tution, and from the beginning, our education system sorted people by race, gender, and class. Remember, also, that the United States was not founded on principles of equity and justice—"We the People" only included *some* people. Access to oppor-tunity has never been equitable or fair. This is a difficult history we're contending with—and it's why our work can feel fundamentally conflicting and contradictory at its core. And we're not alone in this conflict—it's one confronting educators all over our world.

Grappling with this history raises the question of purpose. What do we see as the purpose of education? What is our ultimate goal as educators? The solution to educational inequity is not to help students navigate a dysfunctional system that was never designed for them. *We can't use the same structures and systems if we want different results.* And yet, changing those systems will take time. What can we do right now for our kids who are forced to endure "cells and bells," order and control, and standardized tests?

In order to create something new, we'll need to thoroughly deconstruct the systems we've been indoctrinated into—we'll need to unearth the mental models that we've worked from, and question everything. Yes, there have been education "reformers" and schools that attempted to interrupt the status quo—and some of those have been honorable and others have inadvertently replicated the status quo. We'll have to question how we do schooling and for what purpose.

As we construct a vision of education for liberation, and as we learn skills to provide our students with a more-equitable education tomorrow, we must do our own learning. We can start by identifying the ways that racism manifests in schools and classrooms. Table 3.1: The Manifestation of White Supremacy outlines a handful of indicators of white supremacy in schools. This is not intended to be a comprehensive description, but a resource to get us thinking. Appendix B: The Equity Rubric is a more expansive resource to describe what equity is, and isn't, in schools.

Table 3.1 The Manifestation of White Supremacy

In our society, the ideology of white supremacy manifests in:	In schools, the ideology of white supremacy manifests in:
Institutions, systems and policies including: • Social, political, economic, legal, and financial systems • Slavery, colonialism, Jim Crow segregation, and redlining	• Discipline policies • The school calendar • Graduation criteria • Curriculum • Textbooks that center the experience of white people and erase the brutality of white supremacy • Tracking • Uniforms • The strict regulation of children's bodies
Cognition, attitude, and emotional responses including: • Prejudice • Values of dominant culture • Implicit or unconscious bias • Deficit thinking • Internalized oppression • Stereotyping • "White fragility"	• These kids can't . . . • They need me to save them. • I'm afraid of those kids. • I need to not be like other immigrants. • Asians are just good at math. • Respect looks like a child making eye contact with an adult. • Those parents don't value education. • I feel like I'm being attacked when I get feedback on my communication.
Behaviors and actions including: • Genocide and violence • Bigotry and discrimination • Microaggressions	• The criminalization of student behavior • Insisting that only English be spoken • Incorrectly pronouncing names; giving students nicknames
Outcomes including: • Racism • Inequality, inequities, and disproportionality • White privilege	• School-to-prison pipeline • Graduation rates • College admissions • Access to opportunities

Racial disparities are evident in education in several categories: access to opportunities; criminalization of student behavior; and outcomes including test scores, grades, and graduation rates. What follows is not intended to be a comprehensive list of the inequities we can find in school but rather a big handful of data points that hopefully provoke reflection and further inquiry. Although African American and Latinx students are more likely to receive lower grades, score lower on standardized tests, and drop out of high school, and less likely to enter and complete college than their white counterparts, the data on student achievement is problematic. For that reason, I've chosen to provide you with some data on access to opportunities and the criminalization of student behavior as a way to gain greater understanding of the indicators of racial inequities in school.

Access to Opportunities

- Students of color are less likely to have qualified teachers—teachers who have been prepared to teach (Goldhaber et al., 2015).
- Black, Latinx, and Native American youth have less access to honors and advanced placement (AP) classes than white youth. They are less likely to enroll in advanced science and math classes, which can reduce their chances of being admitted to a four-year college, many of which require completion of at least one high-level math class for admission (Klopfenstein, 2004).
- Black and Latinx students are less likely to be identified as gifted and talented. Black and Latinx third-grade students are half as likely as whites to participate in gifted and talented programs. In contrast, children of color are more likely to be identified as requiring special education services by teachers (Grissom and Redding, 2016).

Criminalization of Student Behavior

Educators frequently notice misbehavior among black students while ignoring the same behavior in white students. Black students are seen as troublemakers and disciplined more harshly than their white counterparts who are granted leniency.

- Black preschool students are more likely to be suspended than students of other races and are more likely to be suspended for minor disruptions and misbehaviors including wetting their pants, kicking off their shoes, and crying. Black students make up just 18 percent of children in preschool but represent nearly half of preschool children suspended (Smith and Harper, 2015).
- At five years old, black boys are perceived as being threatening. A 2016 study showed that white people begin to perceive black boys as threatening at five years

old, associating them with adjectives such as "violent," "dangerous," "hostile," and "aggressive" (Todd, 2016).

- Black students are three times more likely to be suspended or expelled than their white peers (U.S. Department of Education Office for Civil Rights, 2014). This is even more pronounced in 13 states in the U.S. South, where 55 percent of the 1.2 million suspensions involving black students nationwide occurred (Smith and Harper, 2015).

- Black girls are more likely than all other female students and some groups of boys to be suspended or expelled (U.S. Department of Education Office for Civil Rights, 2014).

- Students of color are more likely to attend schools with a greater police presence, increasing the odds that they will enter the criminal justice system. The presence of law enforcement on school campuses also increases the risk of such students being exposed to police violence (Javdani, 2019).

- Overt and unconscious biases against black and brown children lead to high suspension rates and excessive absences; to not reading at grade level by third grade and falling behind academically; to the "achievement gap" and eventually to dropping out of school (Bowman, 2018).

The Power of Words and the Language of Oppression

Let's return to the term *at-risk* that Stephanie used to describe her students—and let's examine the language we use. When used as an adjective for people, "at-risk" is problematic and inaccurate. Every person and every community has strengths, resources, and resilience, and this label is stigmatizing. Although many of us have used the term "at-risk," it's time to adopt new language.

An alternative to "at-risk" might be the term *historically underserved*. This phrase acknowledges external forces that have not served an individual student or population well. Many children of color in our schools have been "underserved"— they don't receive the services and support that they deserve, that their white counterparts receive. They are not "underachieving"—they haven't been given access to the same experiences and quality of education as children who are "achieving." Although I sometimes use this term, it also feels vague and abstract, and it doesn't point the finger directly at those who are responsible for exploiting communities, or at those who created the conditions in which people were underserved.

The term *underserved* can sound like an accident or an error of omission—and there was nothing accidental about what happened to communities that have been "underserved." I've stopped using this term because it obscures historical truths.

We can also talk about groups of people as being *disenfranchised*, which means to be denied rights or privileges. Traditionally, disenfranchisement means being stripped of the right to vote, but it can be used to describe the experience of not belonging or feeling powerless. I use this word when I'm sure that those I'm speaking to understand the definition.

The term *marginalized communities* is perhaps a better way to refer to groups that have been underserved or disenfranchised. Marginalized groups are denied full access to rights, opportunities, and resources that are normally available to members of a different group. Marginalization prevents people from participating fully in social, political, and economic life, and can block them from human rights.

Another useful term is *othered*. Othering encompasses many expressions of prejudice on the basis of group identity. When we "other" someone, we dehumanize them—we say they are fundamentally different from us. People are othered because of the groups to which they belong. When people "belong," they are socially positioned in way that gives them access to power and resources; this belonging is usually to a group-based identity. To be "othered" is to be perceived as "not belonging."

How Words Lead to Liberation

Words convey tremendous power. Examine the words you use about yourself and others. Are the words disparaging, dehumanizing, narrow, and constricted? Do they focus on the negative, the deficits, the missing holes? When a word points to a problem, where is the blame placed? On the child or their family or community? On their school? Or on white supremacy, colonization, and capitalism? Which words and phrases place responsibility on broader socio-political institutions and on the historical events that resulted in the suffering of some communities? These words lead to justice. Which words direct us to envision a transformed world, a beloved community? These words lead to liberation.

Systems of oppression maintain their power by intentionally teaching misinformation. Misinformation is communicated through the language we've been taught and that we use. If we want to transform systems of oppression, we need to scrutinize the language we use. It's going to be a dizzying journey to uproot the language that has divided and dehumanized us, and it's a necessary step on the path to justice and liberation. I know that sometimes examining language can feel trite, contrived, nit-picky, or exhausting. And it's necessary. The risks are high when we don't examine our language, as author and researcher, Brené Brown, reminds us: "Dehumanizing language is always the beginning of violence." Get comfortable with discomfort and strengthen your patience muscles: this will be a journey.

Effective communication relies on shared definitions. Words convey worlds of meaning. It's our responsibility when we use words to use them with wise intention. Here are some questions to explore when considering words:

- Who put the word or term out there? In what context did the word originate? What was the motivation and intention behind using that word?
- How has the term been used? Who has used it? If it's been used to describe a group of people, how do those people feel about that word? Do they use that word to describe themselves? How do they feel about other people using that word?
- How accurate is the word?
- Whose experience is centralized by using a term and whose experience is diminished?
- What is the relationship of institutionalized power to the word and who has been harmed by it?

I know you might be thinking: *These are a lot of dense questions to consider about words, and if I considered all of these, I'd be rendered speechless.* I hear you. However, white supremacy, capitalism, and patriarchy have shaped our language; the words we use reveal and create the way we think. If we want to think differently, and create a different reality, we need to examine and change our language.

Language helps us clarify problems and point at the people and systems that are responsible for suffering. And language is a means through which we can imagine and create alternatives to our current reality. Word choice broadens our imagination. Let's be intentional about our language, and let's use language that creates liberated minds, bodies, hearts, and communities. As Archbishop Desmond Tutu said: Language does not just describe reality. Language creates the reality it describes.

More Words to Eliminate

While we're examining problematic words that are commonly used in education, here are some more that should be removed from our vocabulary because they are inaccurate and dehumanizing: *disadvantaged kids, underachieving students, crime-ridden, ghetto, broken homes, drug-infested, juvenile delinquent,* and *drop-outs.*

These are all terms that have been slapped onto black and brown communities and that have perpetuated their representation as places of problems and as people who are fundamentally flawed. Labeling people or communities with these terms narrows our perceptions, reduces people to problems, and perpetuates systemic oppression. If you use these terms and you're not sure what's wrong with them, I encourage you to do some research (google: *What's wrong with using "ghetto"*) and talk to others to understand why they're problematic and to learn alternatives.

Let's also stop using "minorities" when talking about people of color. The term *minority* implies being not-white, which then centers whiteness as the norm. It's also an inaccurate term. People of color are the global majority, and according to census projections, by 2043, the majority of people in the United States will be people of color. White people are already less than 50 percent of the population in California and Texas (just as they were two hundred years ago, before these regions were colonized). *Minority* is imprecise and diminishing to people of the global majority—and I do like the term *global majority*. It's accurate and empowering. One last suggestion: There's a difference between saying, "People who live in poverty," and "poor people." The first describes conditions; the second describes people. Use the phrase *people who live in poverty*.

While we're talking about how to name people, there are some other terms to eliminate. Describing human beings as "illegal" is inaccurate and hurtful; it's also used by those arguing for xenophobic and racist immigration policies. *Actions* can be illegal—*people* are not illegal. In its place, use *undocumented immigrants*. Finally, "Hispanic" is an inaccurate term in the way it's usually used. *Hispanic* refers to people who speak Spanish and/or are descended from Spanish-speaking populations. *Latino*, *Latina*, and the gender-neutral term *Latinx* refer to people who are from or who descended from people from Latin America.

In education, we regularly use words that originate in an economic system (capitalism) whose goal it is to amass wealth and extract profit at any expense, a system that originated in mass exploitation and systematic violence. Words such as *asset*, *value-add*, *investment*, and *accountability*—all frequently used in schools— derive from capitalist economics. When we talk about *using* or *managing* people, we're engaging a transactional mindset, viewing people as objects and resources. Our intent may not be to think about people as objects, but subconsciously we reinforce that concept. We also use a lot of militarized language when talking about schools and education such as: *in the trenches, soldiering on, plan of attack, first line of defense, go to battle for, stand in the line of fire*, and *on the frontlines*. Schools are not armies; children are not soldiers. Language like this is also dangerous and objectifying.

Finally, a word used with astounding frequency and harm is *dark* when associated with something confusing, dangerous, upsetting, troubling, or anything negative, as in: "That was a dark period in my life," or "This movie uses dark humor." This is often used in contrast to "light," which is used to describe hope, clarity, healing, purity, and so on. A study was done through UC Berkeley of 11 million words that most people use over their lifetime. Some 40–50 percent of the time, they found that the word *black* was used to mean something negative (powell, 2015). While perhaps we've reduced how often we use the word *black* to mean something dangerous, illicit, or inferior (as in: "She was in a black mood: "He's the black sheep of the family"; and "I bought that on the black market"), we still use the word *dark* for the same purpose. Using language like this perpetuates negative associations of dark-skinned people. And no, there's nothing wrong with darkness per se—it is beautiful and mysterious—*but we don't talk about darkness in that way*. We use the word *dark* to mean danger. Then we're surprised that we've internalized so much unconscious bias about dark skinned people. Let's stop using it.

There are so many words that I feel irresponsible for not naming that need to be eliminated from our vocabulary including *lame, gypped, fag, thugs, gangbangers, delinquents, inner city,* and *retarded*. Words have created tremendous suffering in our world. It's time we scrutinize and scrub our language of the violence of oppression. It's time we begin using and teaching language of liberation. (And again, if you're not sure what's wrong with using these words, google it).

> When white Americans frankly peel back the layers of our commingled pasts, we are all marked by it. We . . . are marred either by our connections to the specific crimes and injuries of our fathers and their fathers. Or we are tainted by the failures of our fathers to fulfill their national credos when their courage was most needed. We are formed in molds twisted by the gifts we received at the expense of others. It is not our "fault." But it is undeniably our inheritance.
> —Douglas A. Blackmon, 2008, pp. 394–395

It's Time to Take Action

Racism has hurt and dehumanized everyone. People of color have opportunities limited by barriers, and our experiences and identities are marginalized. White people have also suffered from being a part of a racist system. In being grouped as "white" (and in identifying themselves as "white"), many white people have lost a connection to their ethnic group and may not know much about their cultural backgrounds and histories. Their identity is based on not being something—not being black, not being a person of color—and being superior to others because of their race. This has created a great deal of unconscious identity insecurity and confusion. Furthermore, white people participate in a system in which they gain advantages that, as individuals, they may not have earned—this can generate feelings of guilt and shame. I believe that many white people recognize the damage done to their integrity and morality by participating in and benefiting from white supremacy. They recognize that they cannot be whole until the injustices of the past and present are reckoned with and until they no longer reap unearned privileges as a result of the classification systems of past and present white supremacists.

Learning about racism allows us to see the false mental models that underlie our daily actions. White supremacy has maintained its power by integrating itself into the fabric of our culture, into our hearts and minds, and into all institutions, and by doing so, it has become invisible. White supremacy feels normal; we experience it as the "natural" way of things. In order to dismantle systems of oppression, including white supremacy, we need to see those systems for what they are—to see what they're made of and how they are made, and to see that they are constructed by people. Patriarchy is a construct. Heterosexuality is a construct. These are constructs to which people have attached meaning and values, but each of these are ideas. Things that have been constructed can be deconstructed. In learning about racism and how it was constructed, we'll see how we've all been hurt and how we've harmed others, and we'll see how we can transform our minds, relationships, schools, and world.

Finally, learning about racism is healing, and healing can lead to liberation. In order to heal, you must recognize the wounds in yourself—the ways in which you've been hurt by racism and white supremacy, and the ways you've hurt others. As you unlearn stereotyped racial messages you've internalized about yourself and others, you'll step deeper into a healing process. Learning about racism is a learning journey that will never end—there will always be more layers to understand and explore. And it will be painful. But it will be worth it.

A Note for White People

People of color are often leaned on to explain race and racism—and sometimes we're willing to do just that (often we have to), and sometimes it gets very tiring. Fortunately, there are an increasing number of excellent resources available to help you learn about race, racism, and white supremacy (see Appendix F: Resources for Further Learning for my recommendations). Know that people of color appreciate that you are learning, and also know that we're not going to give you awards for doing so. Do this learning for your own healing and liberation, for your community and your children, and for the global majority.

I imagine this chapter might have been hard to read. I hope you will now take a break from reading to tend to your body, heart, mind, and spirit. How could you replenish the reserves of energy that it took to read this chapter? What helps you reconnect with your courage? With joy? With hope? Who could you reach out to and talk to and be with?

A Note for People of Color

This chapter was hard for me to write. I experienced intense waves of rage and grief as I worked on it. I imagine it might have been hard to read. I hope that you will now take a break from reading to tend to your body, heart, mind, and spirit. How could you replenish the reserves of energy that it took to read this chapter? What helps you reconnect with your sense of power? With joy? With hope? Who could you reach out to and talk to and be with? How might you tap into the strength of your ancestors?

If we were sitting next to each other right now, know that I'd reach over and hold your hand. I wouldn't say anything, I wouldn't make eye contact. I'd just hold your hand and think: *I'm here with you. I'm here with you in this storm of emotion.* And in that moment, that would be what I could offer. My presence. For whatever it's worth: I'm here with you.

Before You Go . . .

Read the following prompts and select two or three that feel most valuable to you based on where you are in your learning journey. Spend meaningful time considering your reflection before moving on.

REFLECT ON THIS CHAPTER

- Which emotions were most present for you in this chapter? How did you engage with those feelings?
- At which points in this chapter did you experience cognitive dissonance (a conflict between what you hold to be true and new information)?
- How do you think your identity markers (including your race) affected how you read this chapter? What do you think it was like for someone of a different race to read this chapter?

TO DO

How could you start, continue, or deepen your learning about white supremacy and racism today? What could you read or do next (see Appendix F: Resources for Further Learning) to continue this learning? How might you determine what you need to learn more about? What learning are you avoiding? What learning might provide healing? Who could be a thought partner or critical friend for you as you make these decisions about what to learn next?

Interlude: Courage

Courage: We draw on deep sources of courage, and face our fears, and act with courage every day. We don't wait until we know everything, or have every detail worked out to do something. We take action and course-correct when necessary. We act with healthy urgency. We know that just as people created inequitable systems and just as we have adopted the mindsets from those systems, people can create new systems and can adopt new mindsets. This gives us the energy to take risks.

If you haven't read *Between the World and Me,* by Ta-Nehisi Coates, it's a must-read. In it, Coates writes:

> It does not matter that the "intentions" of individual educators were noble. Forget about intentions. What any institution, or its agents, "intend" for you is secondary. Our world is physical . . . A great number of educators spoke of "personal responsibility" in a country authored and sustained by a criminal irresponsibility. The point of this language of "intention" and "personal responsibility" is broad exoneration. Mistakes were made. Bodies were broken. People were enslaved. We meant well. We tried our best. "Good intention" is a hall pass through history, a sleeping pill that ensures the Dream.

Read that passage again. And again.

Now answer these questions:

- What kind of courage can you generate within yourself to look at the difference between your intentions and actions?
- How do you suspect your intentions have been received by others?
- When and where might your intentions have inadvertently contributed to harming others?

CHAPTER 4

How to Talk About Race

If you have come to help me, you are wasting your time,
but if you have come because your liberation is bound up with mine,
then let us work together.
—LILA WATSON, INDIGENOUS AUSTRALIAN ARTIST,
ACTIVIST AND ACADEMIC

With more background knowledge about race, racism, and white supremacy, we can get back to the conversation I had with Stephanie, the conversation I described in Chapter 2. Remember: Stephanie was a new ninth-grade English teacher, a white woman teaching black and brown students in Oakland, California. It was mid-November, Stephanie was overwhelmed and sad, and her students weren't learning much in her class. Once I tell you what happened, I'll unpack my decision-making, and then I'll share some thoughts about when and how to talk about race.

Let's first re-ground in the phases of Transformational Coaching. In the second phase, we aim to recognize the impact that white supremacy and a lack of cultural competence has on a teacher's or leader's practice, and we aim to guide the client to this recognition as well. We also strive to help our client identify the impact that their lack of knowledge and skill has on their students, as well as on themselves. We want to build their buy-in to change in this phase, and we need to do this without casting blame and judgment, but with helping the client see that their liberation and the liberation of those they serve is interconnected. We want to

Figure 4.1 The Phases of Transformational Coaching

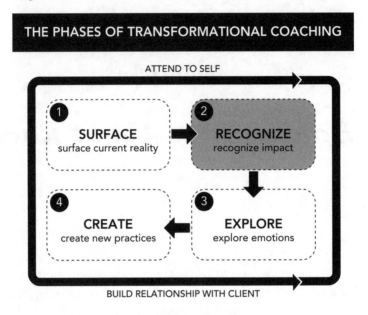

guide them to see that they can do better and that it will be worth the bumpy learning journey. And we want to guide them to recognize that they must do better—that recognizing and interrupting inequities is their responsibility as an educator. Often in this phase, we move into the *Explore Emotions* phase, and then back into *Recognize*—emotions usually surface as we recognize their impact, and it is imperative that we explore them (see Figure 4.1).

Phase 2: Recognize

Goals in this phase:

- Guide a client to recognize how white supremacy and systems of oppression manifest in their classroom, teaching (or leadership) practice, beliefs, and way of being.
- Help the client identify and reflect on how systemic oppression impacts students, their communities, and the teacher or leader themselves.

Recognizing What Is and What Could Be

"Do you think I'm racist?" Stephanie asked.

I paused and then asked her, "Stephanie, what are you most afraid of right now?" I made eye contact for a second longer than what felt comfortable.

"I'm afraid that you won't answer my question," she said.

"Hum." I paused again. "What will that mean, if I don't answer you? What fear does that bring up?" I asked.

"That you think I'm evil, and you won't want to coach me, and you'll talk about me behind my back." Stephanie slumped over.

"And so, what if I do, Stephanie?" I was thoughtful about the tone and volume of every word, and intentional to be neutral but warm. I wanted to push Stephanie to explore her fears.

"I guess I would feel hurt and rejected. I want you to be proud of me. I want you to like me."

I nodded. "Thanks for your honesty. That makes sense. I can relate," I said. Again, I paused for a moment. "Stephanie, I have a question. This might seem hard, but if you were sitting here, in my chair, and you were coaching someone like you, who just asked that question—*do you think I'm racist?*—how would you respond?"

Stephanie's eyes widened. "Oh gosh," she said, "I . . . I guess . . . I mean, I guess I would want to say no, that she's not racist, because I wouldn't want to hurt her feelings."

"Is that what you hope I'll say?" I asked.

Stephanie shifted in her seat. "No, Elena," she said, "I don't. Because I don't think that's true. I think I probably am racist or something. I guess I just don't know what to think or what I'm doing wrong in my classroom. Could you just be honest with me?"

"Yes," I said, my tone becoming subtly more authoritative. "Stephanie, I think you are operating from mindsets that are racist. I think that you, like most people in this country, have internalized beliefs about black and brown people that are faulty—beliefs that hold white people as superior and all others as inferior. And I think that many decisions you make in the classroom reflect those beliefs."

I stopped. Stephanie was sitting very still, staring at me, but she wasn't crying.

I continued: "I also think that you can unlearn these beliefs and change your practices. I think you could be a very effective teacher for black and brown kids."

I was being honest—I recognized many strengths in Stephanie. When she didn't plan lessons from a deficit mindset, she designed rigorous, meaningful, relevant lessons. She created assessments that were precise in revealing what her students struggled with, and she was able to differentiate instruction in response to what she learned about students' needs. I'd seen other teachers like her make tremendous growth, and I do believe that white-identifying teachers can be effective with students whose identity markers they don't share.

Stephanie was nodding slightly. "That's good to hear," she said. "I trust your judgment."

"I think that it's easier to assume that we're all racist, and that we all have learning to do," I said.

We sat together in silence for a moment before I asked her: "Are you ready to explore the ways you've unconsciously acted on racist beliefs?"

Stephanie flinched. I was being intentional about confronting her with this idea—that she was perpetuating racism. "Yes," she nodded.

"Why?" I asked. "Why are you ready to do this?" I wanted her to connect with her desire for engaging in this reflection, for changing. I didn't want her to engage in this conversation so that I'd like her or because she felt it was expected. I wanted her to tap into her will and commitment.

"Because I came here to help kids," she said.

"So, who do you want to be as a teacher?" I asked.

"What do you mean, 'who do I want to be?'" Stephanie asked me.

"I'm sorry if that question wasn't clear," I said. "We can show up in different ways for students—as someone who helps them, guides them, directs them, supports them; as a role model or mentor or leader. We can be a reflection of their potential." I paused. "That's what it means to 'be' someone for students."

"OK," Stephanie said, "I want to be . . ." She stopped and looked away. "I don't know," she said, her voice barely audible. "I don't know who I need to be here."

I smiled. "Stephanie, that's a great answer!" I said. "I love that answer." She looked confused, so I went on to explain: "It feels exactly right that you don't know. You don't know who your students need you to be, because you don't really know them. So how can you know who you want to be?"

Stephanie's brow furrowed. "I've always felt confident and self-assured. Coming here to teach has been the hardest thing I've ever done, and now I don't know who I am!"

"I know," I said. "I'm proud of you for taking these risks and for being in this uncertainty. It's uncomfortable. And I'm excited to see what you'll learn—about yourself and your students."

In that moment, Stephanie looked so lost that I just wanted to hug her. I knew that place of confusion—I'd been there, too. Not as a teacher, but in other moments in my life.

"Do you think it would be better for everyone if I just went back home and then these kids could have a teacher who understands them?" Stephanie asked. "A teacher who is like them?"

I replied: "To be honest, Stephanie, I wish we had more teachers who came from the same backgrounds as our students. But we don't. If you quit, it's unlikely that we'll find a fulltime replacement. They'd have subs all year. And you are here now. So how about if we start exploring what you might do to be the teacher your kids need?"

"OK," Stephanie said.

Turning over Decision-Making to a Client

When I'm at a crossroads in a conversation, as I was in this moment with Stephanie, I often visualize a flow chart that lays out the directions I could take. As you may remember, in Chapter 1, I explained that in any coaching conversation there are three goals: to increase the client's emotional resilience, to strengthen the client's reflective abilities, and to build the client's skills.

At this point in my conversation with Stephanie, I had some options for what I could do next:

- Help Stephanie build her knowledge about racism and white supremacy, defining a deficit mindset and how that spurs low expectations. (I'd draw on the knowledge base I described in Chapter 3.)
- Coach Stephanie to explore her own racial identity; help her see how her desire to "save" her students emerges from an ideology of white supremacy—and why that's so problematic (also drawing on the knowledge base in Chapter 3).
- Create a plan for how Stephanie could get to know her students better and build stronger relationships with them.
- Discuss specific instructional practices. Work on how she could increase engagement, student talk, and so on—things that could lead to greater equity for the students in her class.
- Provide directive coaching on teaching reading.
- Coach her around time management so that she might work more efficiently and perhaps get more rest in order to deal with the emotions that come up every day.

Any of these directions could have been meaningful and would have strengthened her reflective abilities and built skill. But recognizing how disempowered Stephanie was feeling, I decided I wanted to offer Stephanie an opportunity to make a decision in this conversation. Sometimes being able to make what seems like a tiny decision – like what to talk about in a conversation – can activate our sense of agency. I asked her, "What do you think would be most helpful for us to talk about now?"

Stephanie's response was: "I would like to talk about how to be sure my students know that I care about them, and how I can be a bit stricter so they'll learn."

Exploring the Origins of Beliefs

"That seems like a valuable conversation for us to have, Stephanie," I said. "Do you worry that if you're stricter, they won't think you care about them? That those two behaviors contradict each other?"

Stephanie thought for a moment. "No, I guess not. I just don't ever want to be a teacher who controls kids by screaming at them." Stephanie was referring to the teacher next door who boasted that she kept kids in line with public humiliation. We could often hear her yelling.

"So, you don't have any models for what it looks like to hold kids accountable to behavioral expectations in a way that is kind and caring?"

"No, I guess not," she said. "Or, I guess I don't know how to do that with these kids."

My heart skipped a beat as it always does when I hear the phrase *these kids*.

"What do you mean by 'these kids,' Stephanie?"

"My students. Kids who aren't like me. Who don't have my background."

This seemed like a good entry point to more deeply explore Stephanie's cultural competence. "Can you be more specific about what you mean when you say, 'background'?" I asked.

"I mean, kids from different races."

"And from a different socioeconomic class, right?" I added.

"Yes, kids who are different from me because of race and class," she repeated.

"I hear that you're saying that you don't know how to work with kids from different socioeconomic and racial groups—and that's honest. So, how do you think you've decided how to treat them?"

"I don't know," Stephanie said. "I mean, I think I understand what you're asking—if I don't know them, why have I done what I've done, right?" I nodded. "I guess, I don't know them, but I guess I have done things and treated them in a way that was based on what I thought I knew about people like them."

"Tell me more. What do you mean?"

Stephanie explained: "I guess I thought that kids who have a lot of instability in their life need to have a safe and calm place to go to. Their homes and neighborhoods are chaotic and so that's what I was trying to do."

"Is that what you've accomplished?" I asked.

"Not really, I guess. I don't yell at them, but I know my classroom isn't the definition of calm."

"And what other assumptions about black and brown kids do you think you've acted on?"

Stephanie thought for a moment and then said: "I think I know where you're going with this. I think you want me to see that I've underestimated what my kids can do." Stephanie took a deep breath. "I've believed that they can't follow instructions or rules, so I let them get away with things—things that I don't think I would have let white students get away with. And those beliefs are a part of racism because they are about how black and brown people aren't as capable as white people. Right? Is that what you want me to see?"

Attending to Trust

I experienced a moment of anxiety. It's never good for someone to feel like you're manipulating them in a conversation, that you're trying to "get them to see" something. But at that moment, I realized that *I was*—I wanted Stephanie to come to her own realization of how she was acting on white supremacy, acting on beliefs about black and brown people's abilities. This is a tension when you're using facilitative coaching strategies—these questioning strategies can feel manipulative at times. I needed to be transparent and ensure that Stephanie's trust wasn't slipping.

"I'm sorry, Stephanie, if it felt like I was leading you in that questioning. I guess I was. I could have probably said that better. And yes—I do want you to see how your behaviors are emerging from beliefs about people of color, beliefs that people of color are inferior, unable to be successful, that expectations need to be low for them." I paused and thought about the words I wanted to say, and then I continued: "I think what I want you to see is that you have been acting on these beliefs because you said you don't know how to teach kids who are from a different background. So, in the absence of that knowledge, you relied on your limited knowledge about black and brown people, knowledge that you probably acquired through the mass media, popular culture, and perhaps in your community back home."

I stopped, wanting to let that sink in, wondering if I was talking too much or getting too abstract. Then I went on: "I guess I also want you to see that you've been doing the best you can, and that you have the potential to make a lot of growth."

Stephanie nodded. Her face seemed unusually relaxed, and I noticed my appreciation for her growing. Again, I could see that she wanted to do right. "Are there other things you think I should know that you haven't told me?" she asked.

Linking Beliefs and Behavior

"Are you afraid of your students?" I asked.

Stephanie flinched. "Afraid of them? No, I don't think so. I mean, I . . . I think I don't understand them sometimes. So maybe I seem like I'm afraid, but it's because I don't understand them."

"OK, that makes sense," I said. "Sometimes you seem anxious around them. Uncertain. Especially around some of the young men."

Stephanie tried to express what she'd been feeling: "I suppose I feel uncertain around some of them. Some of the boys are really tall and the way they joke with each other and play sometimes. I mean, I don't think they'll hurt me—I don't, but I don't want to be in their way."

"Stephanie," I said, "When you give instructions, sometimes it seems like you're apprehensive about using a strong voice or asking for their full attention. You seem timid, I guess. I experience it as fear, but I don't know what you're feeling."

"I'm just uncertain," Stephanie said. "I feel like I don't know what I'm doing, ever. And clearly you can see that too. I guess the kids see that as well."

Stephanie was getting tired. I could read her fatigue in her eyes, and her shoulders were slowly hunching over. It's critical to note signs of fatigue and to shift a conversation when a client is getting too tired. One can only process and remember a handful of insights into themselves, and Stephanie had arrived at a number of deep insights. It's important to let those insights integrate into someone's mind.

Shifting to Skill Building

One of the three goals in a coaching conversation is to build the client's skills. Doing so actually boosts resilience as well because when we learn, and reflect on our learning, we tap into resilience.

"Stephanie," I said, my voice resonating with renewed energy. We still had about half an hour left of our meeting. "Let's spend the rest of our time together today practicing some new habits, OK? Let's explore how you can give directions and ensure that everyone is paying attention—and how you can do that in a caring way that holds every student to high expectations. How does that sound?"

Stephanie smiled, a relaxed and authentic smile. "Yes, that sounds great."

And that was what we did for the remaining 30 minutes of our meeting. We practiced how to give clear instructions and check for procedural understanding. We role-played—where she was the student who was off task or distracted, and I modeled how to clearly, strictly, and caringly redirect that student or get their attention. She wrote the scripts she would use for giving directions for the next day's lessons, and I coached her on how to make sure those scripts were sharp and short. Economy of language is a key teaching skill when giving directions. Stephanie may have still held some distorted notions about her black and brown students, and it would take time to fully rid her system of those beliefs, but in the meantime, she would be able to get students' attention and deliver a more rigorous lesson. In this case, I used *rigor* to mean engagement in instruction and material that is academically challenging in an empowering way to students. This is an example of a moment when I'd also moved into the fourth phase of Transformational Coaching—creating new practices. This was a new practice built on a new belief that her students needed her to be more "strict," as she'd called it, and to hold higher expectations for student behavior. Later we'd also unpack what she meant by "strict," as in far too many places, being "strict" comes out of a desire to control black and brown children. But as she practiced giving directions, I could see a shift in her stance, in her way of being: it was commanding, yet caring. She was figuring out who she wanted to be.

Closing the Conversation

As we wrapped up our meeting, I asked Stephanie if she could share two big insights she'd gained about herself through our conversation. It's useful to offer clients an opportunity to synthesize their takeaways, and it helps you hear what was most important. Here's what she said: "I guess the first is that this conversation wasn't as bad as I thought it would be. It wasn't comfortable, and I feel embarrassed by how I've been, but it wasn't the worst thing ever. And I guess the second thing is that I feel a little bit hopeful. I can see the general direction that I need to go in to be a better teacher. But it's more than that—to be a better person. I was so afraid you'd say that I was racist because I want to be a good person. So, I guess I feel like I can be better. And that's a relief."

As we said goodbye, Stephanie thanked me. "You're so patient with me," she said. "I feel like you're a good example of how I want to be with my students. You're calm and kind, but you also keep pushing me, and you won't let me get away with anything. It's kind of scary, to be honest, but also kind of exciting because I feel like what you're saying is that you know I can do this learning."

Stephanie paused. "I think I'd be more frustrated with me if I was my coach," she laughed.

I smiled, feeling genuine care for Stephanie. I hadn't felt very patient during the conversation, but I was glad that she'd experienced me as such. "Thank you, Stephanie. I appreciate your appreciation. And I really do believe you can learn. I'm honored to be a witness to your growth."

It is a gift to have a front row view into someone's learning. It's humbling. I'm truly grateful for Stephanie and the many clients I've had like her.

Take-Aways and Lessons

In this conversation, I was still working to understand Stephanie's mental models. I used probing questions to surface and explore her ways of thinking. I also coached Stephanie to reflect on how her mental models and beliefs manifested in her teaching practices—beliefs that originated in white supremacy. I wanted to also deconstruct these mental models, revealing them as a reflection of white supremacy. I wanted to coach Stephanie to take responsibility for how she'd been thinking and teaching—for own her actions—and also to see that she could change. I wanted Stephanie to tap into her will and reasons for changing, because I knew that what I was surfacing was that her entire identity needed to shift. I also wanted to help Stephanie build new practices—practices based on a shifting sense of identity and on beliefs that uplifted the capacities and potential of her students. I knew that as her sense of ability increased, she'd feel more confident about this whole process. Finally, I was intentional about keeping my eye on Stephanie's trust in me—I wanted to challenge and push her, but also make sure I wasn't pushing so hard that she shut down. And I wanted to celebrate the many little steps she was taking to unlearn her racist conditioning and become a teacher who would have an impact on black and brown kids in Oakland.

Attending to Myself

When I left Stephanie's school that day, I felt relieved and excited and also sad and nervous. The road ahead seemed long, there was so much for Stephanie to learn, and my mind spiraled out into all the systemic problems in our schools—like, why was it so hard to recruit, hire, and retain effective teachers of color? And then I'd rein in my mind and tell myself that I needed to focus (just for a little) on celebrating Stephanie's learning—and on celebrating my own growth as a coach.

Three Good Things

One of my favorite resilience-building strategies is called "Three Good Things." Each night, you write down three things that went well that day and why they went well. What's critical in that second part is that you identify what it was that *you did* that made that good thing happen. You need to see the connection between your own agency and the good thing—so that you don't feel like the good things just fall out of the sky. For example, I could say that one thing that went well today was that my most challenging class, right before lunch, was calm and we finished the lesson. I'd then recognize that it was calm because I greeted students at the door, I checked in for 20 seconds with Alfonso who often acts out, I had a compelling "Do-Now" projected, I had all my supplies organized, and so on. I'd be able to see how all my actions helped to create the good thing that had happened. (You'll find more about this strategy in another of my books, *Onward*.)

My Three Good Things from the day when I had the conversation with Stephanie that I've just related were:

- Stephanie didn't cry.
- Stephanie is starting to see her unconscious bias.
- I remembered my lunch.

When I pushed myself to articulate *why* these things happened, I wrote the following:

- I remembered my lunch because I left a note for myself to do so, because I'm committed to creating the conditions in which I'll be most successful—and that includes eating lunch.
- I am keeping my judgment at bay.
- I am digging deep within myself to find love and care for Stephanie—even when I'm triggered by what she says.
- I created the conditions in which she could bravely reflect on herself. I went slowly and thoughtfully enough to create a conversation where she could reflect.
- I am managing my urgency and trusting this coaching process—even though I still have doubts, I'm not letting those doubts obstruct how I'm being with her.

Talking to Yourself

As I reflected on the day, I noticed that I felt very tired—physically and emotionally. I felt drained and depleted. I coach myself, when I'm my only option—so I then had a conversation with myself. Here are snippets from that conversation:

MY-INNER-COACH: You're tired. That was a hard meeting and you did really well. What do you need right now?

ME: Netflix, probably. But just tell me this is worth it. Tell me that Stephanie will change; her students will learn to read and will graduate on time; Stephanie will stop talking about

	wanting to save her kids; and we'll get more culturally competent teachers in Oakland.
My-Inner-Coach:	I hear you. It sounds like you're feeling angry. Right? Anger is OK. And remember, it often masks other feelings.
Me:	Yes, I'm angry. And I'm sad because it's just so wrong that those kids don't get what the white, middle-class kids in that private school half a mile away get. It's wrong that our schools don't have books or toilet paper or air-conditioning when it's 95 degrees; that kids have to take stupid standardized tests; that we have all these security guards but no therapists; and that they were several grade levels behind by third grade. I just keep wondering: *Am I doing the right thing with my life?*
My-Inner-Coach:	Ah! Is that fear? Self-doubt?
Me:	I guess so. I'm always questioning myself, my choices, and whether I'm doing enough. I'm also so afraid of being hopeless and despairing.
My-Inner-Coach:	That *is* a scary emotion. Hopelessness. Despair. Do you want to explore those fears? Or the decisions you've made?
Me:	Not really. I'm tired.
My-Inner-Coach:	All of these feelings belong. Let them exist. They make you more tired when you push them to the side and try to ignore them. What would it be like to accept them?
Me:	I'm afraid to accept them. I feel like that would give them permanent license to live with me, and I don't like them.
My-Inner-Coach:	So, you're afraid of being afraid? That requires a lot of energy!
Me:	OK, I get what you're trying to tell me. If I acknowledged them, I might not feel so drained by them. [Pause] It just feels so unfair that I have to do this. I'm angry.
My-Inner-Coach:	I'm angry too.
Me:	It feels like as a person of color, coaching Stephanie is doubly hard. I have to be a good coach, and I also have to sort through the extra layer of emotions that come with being a person of color working at schools where other people of color are marginalized. Why can't there be more white people coaching each other on their racism?

MY-INNER-COACH:	I hear you on all of that. It is a double burden. I can hear your anger.
ME:	Also—I'm afraid that you're judging me. That you're frustrated with how often I get angry. That you don't think I'm learning fast enough.
MY-INNER-COACH:	It sounds like you don't trust me. You don't believe that I have your best interests at heart? That I don't care you about you? What's up with that?
ME:	I guess I have trust issues. Yeah—I don't trust you. Or me. But you are me, so what does that mean?
MY-INNER-COACH:	Maybe I'm you, and maybe I'm more than you. I don't know who I am! You made me. Who do you want me to be?
ME:	Be the one who trusts this process, who knows more than I can know right now, who has wisdom I can't access, who has insight and unbounded compassion.
MY-INNER-COACH:	Whoa, that's a lot of pressure! But hey—I can do it! I can do anything!

One way to attend to yourself and to listen to your emotions is to do what I've shared with you here—to engage in a dialogue with them, with different parts of yourself—with your tired and anxious self, or with your wise and knowledgeable self. Self-awareness and self-understanding are foundational when coaching for equity. You deserve the time and space for this exploration.

A Time of Growth

Since I became a mother, in 2003, I can't help but to ask myself every time I go into a classroom: *Would I want my son to be in this class?* My body often answers before my mind—my stomach will clench if my response is *No*. I'll experience a wave of nausea. Every child deserves to be in a classroom that I'd allow my own child to be in. While I'm skilled at recognizing the complexity of issues that are at play in a school and classroom, and that result in some spaces being unsafe or unhealthy learning environments, and while I'm skilled at empathizing with teachers and recognizing that they're all learning, I'm a mother. This identity often provides a baseline barometer for how I experience schools.

When I first observed Stephanie, I thought: *I'd never let my son be in this class, not for an hour.* After coaching Stephanie for two years, I thought: *If my son had to be in this class, it wouldn't be the worst thing in the world.* I wish I could tell you that Stephanie transformed within the two years I coached her—but she didn't. She made steady and strong progress in many areas, and she had a long way to go to become an excellent teacher with high cultural competence.

I'm not going to describe in depth the coaching I did with Stephanie that illustrates the final phase of Transformational Coaching—where we create new practices—in part because it looked and sounded like so much instructional coaching that I hope you've heard about and know how to practice. In sum: We did a lot of co-planning of lessons, I observed her and gave her feedback, I provided her with resources and took her to observe other teachers, I guided her to analyze student data and use what she learned to inform instruction, and I supported her to learn more about who her students were—about what they knew, liked, thought, felt, and could do—and more about their communities. She did this in an action research project and by reading.

Throughout this fourth phase of coaching, I included time for Stephanie to reflect on her expanding set of beliefs and on her evolving sense of identity. As she unpacked her socio-political, racial identity markers, she came to have a deeper understanding of her privilege and power. We examined, discussed, and reflected on everything from Stephanie's emotions, beliefs, and ways of being; to the instructional practices she used in the classroom; to the history of race and education. She rarely cried after the first semester of our work together, and she did get a therapist who helped her deal with her tendencies toward perfectionism.

Changing Systems

I had two critical learnings as a coach and leader from coaching Stephanie. First, I came to have a deeper appreciation for intersectionality and the complexity of identity. Stephanie was white (and we spent a lot of time exploring this identity), and she identified as a woman. There were several times when she expressed feeling unsafe as a woman in her classroom and school—she felt like some male students and male staff members looked at her in a way that made her feel uncomfortable, that their eyes scanned her body in a way that felt intrusive and offensive. She thought they made sexual references behind her back or in Spanish.

Initially, I wondered whether her implicit bias was seeping out—there's a long and dangerous history of white women perceiving black and brown men as being sexual predators. I wasn't sure if she was accurately assessing danger, but I also didn't want to dismiss her perceptions. Then there were occasions, like the first time I was in her class, when I witnessed male students talking about her body and making offensive sexual comments. She was only a little older than they were, and their minds and bodies were flooded with hormones—although what they were doing wasn't right. And it made Stephanie uncomfortable. Stephanie and I talked about how she could respond to the unwanted attention from students and staff, which required different kinds of responses. Stephanie did file a formal complaint about one security guard who routinely made inappropriate comments to her. With her students, she responded assertively that their comments were harassment and that she would call their parents and involve their principal if it continued.

Second, as a result of working with Stephanie, I took a bigger role in creating and leading change at the systems level in my district. At the time I worked with her, I was a part of a coach Professional Learning Community (PLC). We regularly used a Consultancy Protocol and Coaching Lenses (both of which you can download from my website, http://brightmorningteam.com) to deepen our conversations. This combination of tools is a powerful set of resources to gain a deep, thorough analysis and understanding of a situation.

In one consultancy with my PLC, I saw more clearly than ever the systemic problems that resulted in Stephanie's performance in the classroom. Amongst those, I saw the flaws in our district's hiring processes, I saw the shortcomings in how we onboarded new teachers, I saw the endless competing initiatives that reflected a lack of leadership and vision in our district, I saw how the absence of a teaching rubric that everyone bought into contributed to the struggles that Stephanie had, and I saw how the way professional development was designed and delivered at sites was limited and problematic. There were holes all over our system—and as a result, Stephanie struggled as a teacher, and her students didn't learn much. How much of this was her fault? Her responsibility? Why wasn't our district actively and intentionally recruiting prospective teachers from within our community? How could our district entice our own graduates to return to our district and teach there? How could we provide rigorous training in cultural competence for new teachers who came to teach in Oakland? What needed to happen so that this was the top priority for leaders? How could we partner with teacher-preparation programs to insist on more training in cultural competence? I had a lot of questions.

The approach our district was taking at the time to teacher development was one-on-one coaching, which was what I was doing. There are great benefits to this, of course, and there are limitations. In addition to individual coaching, Stephanie needed a lot more training—before she stepped into the classroom (in her credentialing program) as well as after. She needed support on-site, from administrators and from a PLC or department. At that time, in her school, departments only met to do compliance work, and Stephanie had no colleagues on-site with whom she regularly met.

There was a limit to what I could do with Stephanie. Change had to also be enacted on a systems level, which was what I began advocating for and working toward the year after I coached Stephanie. Several years later, after many meetings, presentations, and carefully crafted arguments, changes were enacted and policies were initiated that have helped to create the conditions in which new teachers can become more culturally competent, a little faster. We were on the right track, one that didn't leave the potential of change up to an individual coach and teacher. My transition into working at a systems level in response to the inequities I saw in Stephanie's classroom was a turning point for me as a coach and leader.

Refraining from Evaluating Impact

For a long time, I've told myself to refrain from judging the work I do, from evaluating whether or not it was successful or impactful. This is hard, and I want to look at what happened with Stephanie, for example, and say, "I didn't do a good enough job." And yet, I know this isn't true. I did what I could do given all of the limitations, and change did happen. It happened within the time I coached Stephanie—her lessons got much more rigorous, quickly; she observed other teachers and picked up some simple strategies for relating to students in a more appropriate way; we engaged in many difficult conversations about race; and her students came to enjoy her class and perform acceptably on assessments. I would have been OK with my son being in her class—not thrilled, but OK.

Stephanie taught in our district for three years, and then she returned to the Midwest. She emailed me just before the 2016 elections and shared that she'd been teaching in a small city, not far from where she grew up. The region she lived in had increasing numbers of immigrants and African Americans. "We now have a diversity committee at my school that I'm the head of," she wrote. "Almost everyone I work with is white—and we think that this is a problem and want to diversify our staff. We talk about what it means to be racist and how we can learn about our students, and we talk about our fears about talking about racism."

She offered words of appreciation about what she'd learned through our work together, and recounted a number of conversations we'd had that had created radical shifts in her thinking. "I must have been so hard to coach," she wrote, "but you never seemed impatient or angry with me. I felt like you cared about me, I felt safe talking to you, and I felt like every conversation helped me become a better person."

Her email brought back a flood of memories. Many of the conversations we'd had were challenging and required my skill, will, and emotional resilience—and many of them had an impact. Although I recalled things that I wish I'd done differently or felt lingering doubts about what I did, I also felt proud of the work I'd done with Stephanie. I did the best I could do, and I did have an impact.

Whether you are a coach, a teacher, a department chair, a team leader, a site administrator, or an organizational leader, you can strive to make every conversation one that dismantles white supremacy and systems of oppression. Every conversation can contribute to building a more just and equitable world, a world in which every person's full humanity is centered and seen, a world in which conversations are bridges to connection and healing.

The Path to Racial Healing

We need to talk about race—in schools, in families, in our country, and in our world. And talking about race feels scary for many of us. Before we talk about how to deal with other people's fear, let's start with our own. Then I'll offer 10 tips for talking about race.

Start with Yourself; Start with Your Fears

I have lots of fears when it comes to having conversations explicitly about race. I'm afraid that I'll do it wrong. I'm afraid that someone else—someone whom I respect—will listen or hear about it and tell me that I did it wrong, and that I'll agree with them. Or that I won't agree with them. I'm afraid that I won't be clear enough, and my message won't get through. I'm afraid that I won't be compassionate enough. I'm afraid that I'll be too compassionate, too understanding, and that by doing so, the other person won't see the harm they'd inflicted, the pain they've caused. I'm afraid of losing relationships. I'm afraid that people won't want to talk to me again. I'm afraid that I won't be ready, that I'll stumble and be inarticulate, and that I won't remember what I want and need to say. I'm afraid that I'll let down the people who need me to speak up and speak clearly. I'm afraid that I won't make a difference. I'm afraid that I'll become paralyzed. I'm afraid of my own anger. I'm afraid of other people's anger. I'm afraid that I'll check out and give up. I'm afraid that I'll start crying. I'm afraid of regrets. I'm afraid of being rejected. I'm afraid of failing.

What are you afraid of when you think about having conversations about race?

When I review my fears, I notice a surge of anger toward myself. How can I have so many fears? But I acknowledge the courage it takes to name fears, and the vulnerability it takes to recognize the rush of anger, and I acknowledge that underneath those emotions is a deep commitment to justice. I tell myself: *All of these feelings belong. It's powerful to recognize them.* And I notice how those thoughts help me feel calmer. I see my fears, and I soften my stance toward myself—I tell myself that I'm doing the best I can, that I'm good enough, and that I will continue to learn and stumble and learn and fail and learn and grow. I tell myself that I'll never feel completely ready, but that I have to have the conversation anyway. That if I don't, I'll feel much worse.

Sometimes conversations about race feel easier; sometimes they feel harder. I would like to say that with time, you'll get more comfortable—but I don't know if that's true. There are many variables that affect how these conversations feel, including our skill set, our disposition that day, our broader emotional state, the national context for the conversation, our relationship with the other person, our sense of safety in our role, and the specifics of the conversation. What has changed for me is my confidence that if a conversation doesn't go well, I can navigate whatever happens. I am clearer now on my triggers, and I have more coping mechanisms so that when those triggers are hit, I can make skillful choices in how I respond. What has also changed for me is my conviction that these conversations must happen.

Consider These to Be Healing Conversations

I don't call these "hard" or "difficult" conversations—such phrasing locks us into a mental model in which we expect them to be challenging. Sometimes I call these "conversations about race," and I don't use an adjective to describe what they'll be like. Lately I've been calling them "healing conversations." Often conversations about race and identity can be complicated and uncomfortable—for me and/or the other person. But even when they are, they also bring relief and closeness between two people, they can build community and strengthen relationships, they kindle our courage and commitment, and for these reasons, I find them to be healing conversations. Remember that physical and psychological healing doesn't happen quickly—it takes time, and it can be a painful process. But the *potential* in these conversations is of healing, so let's frame them through their potential.

I also acknowledge that for many people of color, these conversations are exhausting, especially when we have to have them over and over and over and over, often with the same people. For us, it often doesn't feel optional to have these conversations—not when we, and our students, and our children are suffering because of white supremacy. But also, I can't count the number of times when I've been in a professional situation where racial inequities have been hinted at or present and when it felt like all eyes turned to me—as the lone person of color in a group, or the person of color with more experience, tenure, or positional power—to speak up and say something. And although many times I spoke up, it gets tiring.

I appreciate when white colleagues speak up and say something about racial inequities. But to complicate things more: Sometimes I don't want white people to speak up and say something—not when it feels like they're saying something because they think that I won't be articulate in speaking up, not when it feels like they're speaking up to paternalistically care for me, and not when it feels like they're speaking up so that they'll get Brownie points for being a good white ally. But when that happens, if I have the energy, I'll describe how I'm experiencing their behavior in that moment. I'll remind them that intention and impact are different, and I'll nudge them to unpack their deepest intentions. And yes, this sometimes means things get more tense and uncomfortable.

If you're a white person, I know that this might be confusing, because I do want white people to speak up about racism. And now I'm saying that sometimes I don't want you to speak up. I hope that you'll still take risks to say something when you hear or see indicators of white supremacy, and that you'll do so with as much awareness of your deepest intentions possible. But more than that, I hope you'll speak up when I'm not in the room—when people of color aren't in the room. Most of the times that we need more white people to speak up about racism, people of color aren't in the room—not because they weren't necessarily invited, but because perhaps the Leadership Team is made up of five white leaders, and in a meeting, someone says something. In those moments when you don't want to feel uncomfortable, or you don't want to be "that person," and when there's no person of color in the room who would witness your silence—those are the moments when I hope you'll say something about racial inequities.

When things go well, interpersonal healing happens, perhaps in a conversation or later. But regardless of what happens, I can find opportunities for my own healing—even if someone got defensive or started crying. Whatever comes up for me when I'm doing work on equity, including my own fatigue, is a cue for me to attend to some part of myself, some part that is still sore, achy, and needs attention. And in spite of all the potential risks, exhaustion, and fears, we need to talk about race.

Ten Tips for Talking About Race

1. Normalize discussing race. Use the terms. Reference the ideas. The more you do so, the less uncomfortable it will feel to talk about race.

2. Find multiple entry points. Look for places where others will be somewhat willing to enter, where they have some skin in the game, and where they can see how they might personally benefit from the discussion. Remember that racism and white supremacy negatively affect everyone, and consider how you might help them see that as well.

3. Be humble. You're also a work-in-progress, and you've made mistakes in the past. You've been on your own journey. At some point in the future, you'll hopefully look back and see how much you didn't know at this point. We're all on this journey together.

4. Know what you're talking about. Prepare, practice. Don't be sloppy.

5. Be clear: offer sharp and clear definitions. Don't throw around terms that some-one else might not know—especially if you're throwing them as a way of leverag-ing power over someone. Check for understanding during the conversation—in a way that's not paternalistic.

6. Make a distinction between blame and responsibility. The way things are is not our fault, but it's our responsibility to clean up the mess we're in because many of us are benefiting from the privileges granted to us because of our race, class, gender, sexual orientation, abilities, and so on.

7. Be clear about purpose: Have conversations about race to help others grow and meet students' needs, to help others feel more whole, and to help our world heal—not so that you can feel righteous and powerful.

8. Build relationship. Build trust. If your purpose is to help someone grow and gain insight, then the space in which that conversation happens needs to be safe-*enough*. We don't need to aim for a "safe" space—that's a subjective evalu-ation around which there'll be disagreement. The purported lack of a "safe space" is also often used as an excuse for why we can't have conversations about race. Safe-enough doesn't mean comfortable.

9. Invite, accept, and acknowledge emotions—your own and those of others. There's no way we can (or should) have conversations about race without hav-ing any emotions. Emotions can be our partners, a resource, and our teachers. Tears are not the problem—it's how we respond to those tears that can be an issue—and we'll explore that in the section that follows about addressing fears about talking about race. But remember: Systems of oppression don't want you to have emotions, so if you reclaim and accept them, you're actively rebuking these systems.

10. Ask for feedback on any conversations that you facilitate around race, reflect on your facilitation and leadership, own any messy moments that you are responsible for, and commit to the process.

Why Calling People Out Doesn't Work

I'm often asked, "Why can't we just call people out on their racist behavior?" I flinch when I hear that phrase, *call someone out*, because it's an action of wielding power over someone, and it has undertones of intending to shame or humiliate someone; it's what we do when we don't know what else to do, when we're not prepared, and when we haven't processed our own emotions. I know this because I've done it— I've called people out and confronted them with their racism. *Calling people out doesn't work.* Shame is not an effective tool for transformation. It will not help us create a kind, compassionate, equitable world.

In the conversation I related earlier in this chapter that I'd had with Stephanie, I was acting on knowledge about the brain and identity, knowledge that offers alternatives to calling people out. Here's the key idea: When we experience cognitive dissonance (a conflict between what we hold to be true and new information), we are likely to experience fear, which causes our brain and mind to respond protectively in an attempt to preserve our psychological sense of self. So, if someone feels like you're attacking their beliefs, they'll armor up to protect those beliefs—especially if the beliefs are tied up with their sense of self and identity. Our mind experiences a threat to identity just like a threat to our body. Our neurological and physiological response to a perceived threat makes the belief get stronger and more entrenched. This is science: we can either fight it or work with it.

Our Brain

You can blame the amygdala for many problems we face. The *amygdala* is an ancient part of our brain structure that is always on the alert for threats. At the first sign of danger, the amygdala triggers biochemical messages through our bodies, telling us to panic—to fight, freeze, or flee. Our bodies flood with hormones, and our mind is consumed with thoughts of survival. Unless we regulate our response, the analytical, rational part of our brain shuts down.

Here's where this gets interesting and relevant to coaching for equity: Our mind perceives a threat to our identity like it perceives a threat to our physical existence. If we feel someone thinks that we might not be a good person, that we might be racist, we experience that as a threat to our identity. This perception triggers a biochemical response in our bodies that makes us feel defensive and want to fight back, or that makes us check out and disconnect, or that paralyzes us. If you tell me that I've perpetuated dehumanizing stereotypes about Muslims, my body will react as if you're about to physically attack me—because I believe that I am a good person and you're attacking my sense of self. My body will prepare to fight back, and my prefrontal cortex (where rational thinking happens) slows down.

As we understand and accept the social, biological, and psychological factors involved in having conversations about racism, we can sequence and prioritize coaching strategies. This neuroscience affirms why it's imperative to build a relationship with a client and create psychological safety. This is not a nice, fluffy, or optional stage in coaching—it's critical. This research validates a need to attend to emotions and have skills to coach emotions. We need to know how to respond to tears and anger and how to support a client to decrease anxiety when it surges—to use breathing strategies, for example, to regulate their body's response to fear.

We also need to know that our brain and mind can change. We can learn how to de-escalate our neurological responses to our perception of danger—especially when that danger is a perception that we're being told we're not a good person. We can learn to recognize when a situation doesn't merit fighting, fleeing, or freezing. We can change our brains and form new neural pathways that lead us to different action, that allow us to have more productive and more powerful conversations about race and systemic oppression. This is the promise and potential of the field of mindfulness, something I've written about (Aguilar, 2019) as have others (Magee, 2019). Mindfulness meditation is an invaluable method for us to slow down our cognition, so that we can become more aware of our biases and distorted thinking; we can regulate our biochemical response to fear; and we can learn, grow, and change our practices. It will take more than mindfulness to transform our schools—and I also know we won't be able to do it without mindfulness.

Our Moral Identity

Here's another knowledge piece you'll need to coach for equity: You'll need an understanding of the psychological concept of identity. An individual's identity is a collection of their values, personality, upbringing, communities, cultures, sociopolitical identities, religion, experiences, families, and education. We all have multiple identities that make us feel like who we are. One identity that most people hold is that of being *a good person*—this is called our *moral identity*.

As we go through life, we want others to see and acknowledge our multiple identities. If we feel like others aren't seeing us for who we are, we can feel threatened and stressed. We might get defensive, or fish for affirmations and center our own needs. For example: I believe I am a good person who is most of the time concerned about and kind to others. I want you to believe this about me without a doubt. If someone comments on my omission of equity issues for people who are disabled, I may experience that as a threat to my moral identity. I might share that my cousin is an international disability rights lawyer and activist; and that my brother had disabilities; and that as a teacher, I always made accommodations for kids with disabilities; and so on. I'll present you with a ton of evidence that shows that I'm a good person. It's a great quality—that we want to think of ourselves as good people—but in my efforts to protect my moral identity, I might not listen to what someone else says, and I might not learn.

Dolly Chugh (2019) proposes that we stop thinking of ourselves as people who are good or bad, racist or not, ethical or unethical, and that we think of ourselves as "good-ish" people. A good-ish person, Chugh says, is someone who is trying to be better, as opposed to allowing themselves to think that they are always a good person. It is a fallacy to think that a "good person" can exist. This notion of a fixed state of goodness, Chugh says, is a false binary that's seductive, but misleading and inaccurate. The truth is that we all do harmful things, but it's hard to see it in ourselves because we cling to an illusion that we are ethical and unbiased. What could be possible if we embraced the notion of being *a good-ish person*? If we committed to be a good-ish person as often as possible?

Stephanie saw herself as a good person. She cried buckets because she was afraid that I would think, feel, or say that she was a bad person because she didn't understand her students, because she didn't share their identity markers, and because she feared that all of this meant she was racist—which in her mind implied that she was evil. One aspect of her core identity felt like it was about to devoured by a saber-toothed tiger. Fear was a natural response. Stephanie's tears were a response to her amygdala being hijacked by thoughts that she would be exposed and shamed for being racist. Those tears became a barrier to the conversation, and they were a human response to fear. She wouldn't have become less afraid if I'd called her out on her racism or told her to stop being so fragile. I had to accept and work with her neurobiology, her thoughts, and her feelings. This is why in Phase 3 of Transformational Coaching, we explore emotions.

The Lengths We'll Go to Protect Our Beliefs

Once we have a belief (about ourselves or others), our mind does two things: It searches for information to confirm that belief (which is called *confirmation bias*), and then it protects that belief from harm. For example, let's say I'm a vegan and I believe that eating animals makes me a bad person. I will search for, interpret, favor, and recall information that affirms my belief. My belief may get stronger in the face of contrary evidence or other information, and I may be resistant to changing this belief because it would threaten my sense of identity.

Confirmation bias makes it hard for us to be open to a wide array of data—whether about diet or what we think low-income students of color are able to do. A teacher with confirmation bias will think that they are a good person who cares about kids and came to teach in Oakland because of a desire to help kids. They won't be aware that they've inhaled the smog of racism and white supremacy since they were born, and they may believe that their ninth graders are only capable of coloring. They'll create low-rigor lessons for students and give them a pass when they want to sleep in class. When a student mutters something about treating them like a kindergartener, that comment will be brushed aside and forgotten. When a coach shares data on how many kids were off task, the teacher will point at all the students who were on task. When the teacher observes their students in another class producing high-level analytical work, that'll be dismissed as something that only that other teacher can get out of them. This teacher with confirmation bias will do anything to protect their belief that they're a good person doing all they can and that they're seeing all that they can expect from their students. When this teacher is presented with information that doesn't match with what they believe, their brain instinctively protects those beliefs in what's called the *backfire effect*—they'll reject the new information and their belief gets stronger. If the information blindsides them, if someone tries to force them to see it, or if they're feeling afraid that their moral identity won't be acknowledged, their brain is even more protective and backfires more productively.

When we try to use facts to sway someone's opinion, we get nowhere. Beliefs get stronger. When people get defensive, they're protecting their core sense of self. Are you seeing how all of this research on the brain, cognition, and our neurobiological systems is applicable when coaching for equity?

This isn't a dismal situation we're in, however. There's hope. Humans are *prone* to choosing information and data that support our worldview while diminishing or dismissing evidence that contradicts it. But we can change the wiring of our brains, and change our beliefs, and take in new information *if we don't feel like our core identity will be crushed under the new information*. If we experience new data without our brain responding like it's being attacked, we can be receptive; if we don't feel like our identities will shatter in the face of new information, we can be receptive. Then beliefs and behaviors can change.

When you call someone out for being racist, their core identity of being a good person is threatened. This is why most of the time, this strategy won't work if your intention is to get them to change. This is why they'll appear resistant. I was able to engage Stephanie in conversations about race and white supremacy because I built a relationship with her. I saw a vast landscape of who she was, which included a recognition of her strengths and of her complexity as a person—and she knew that I saw that terrain. I deconstructed false binaries of good and bad, racist and not-racist, and created a learning space where falling, stumbling, and failing on a learning journey was OK. Stephanie was a good person, or perhaps more accurately, she was a *good-ish* person; my humility served to remind me that I, too, was a work-in-progress. We were both learning, and I regularly messaged this to Stephanie in many ways.

When coaching for equity, we need to accept our habitual neurobiological responses to feeling threatened, and our cognitive responses to feeling attacked. This doesn't mean that we can't change our responses and unlearn problematic racist practices. Accepting this information requires us to master and use coaching skills that are part of a Transformational Coach's toolset. In the next chapter, I'll continue to describe these and tell you how to change someone's mind.

Ten Ways to Respond to the Question, "Am I Racist?"

Here are 10 ways to respond when someone asks you if you think they are racist:

1. Tell me more about where that question is coming from.
2. Is this something you want to explore? What might you have to gain, or how would you benefit, from digging into this question?
3. What would it mean to you if you are racist?
4. What do you really want to know about yourself? What are you curious to discover?
5. What comes up for you when you contemplate that question and possible answers?
6. Let's unpack that concept first. What do you mean by racist? How do you define racism? What do racists think, feel, and do?
7. That may not be the most useful question to ask. Let's generate some other, more useful questions.
8. What do you know about racism? When and where did you first learn about racist people and racism?

9. How about if we shift the question to this one: On a scale of 1 to 10, how racist am I?

10. Yes, you probably are. To some degree, we all are.

There isn't really a "right" and a "wrong" thing to do when you're coaching—there's only what happens. Try something and reflect on the impact you had. Did your question or comment provoke deeper reflection? Did your question help your client gain new insights into themselves and their behaviors? Did your client respond by saying: "That's a good question," or "Huh—I've never thought of that," or "Let me think about that"? If so, you probably asked something that was meaningful. If the question or comment you made didn't seem to land well or didn't lead in the direction you were hoping for, try something else.

When coaching for equity, it's useful to start with a framework like the Phases of Transformational Coaching that gives you some direction on how to move through a coaching conversation. You'll also need to use your judgment. You'll need to be flexible and responsive to what arises in the moment. You'll need to meet someone where they're at and guide them along a learning journey. Tips and frameworks can be useful, as well as narratives of those who have traveled those paths before, but every journey is unique. I hope that you're finding guidance within the stories and strategies I'm offering, and I hope you're boldly exploring the trails in your woods.

Before You Go . . .

Read the following prompts and select two or three that feel most valuable to you based on where you are in your learning journey. Spend meaningful time considering your reflection before moving on.

REFLECT ON THIS CHAPTER

- What are your big learnings from the story about Stephanie? What is most relevant to your work?
- Of the "Ten Tips for Talking about Race," which ones feel easiest to you? Which feel most challenging?
- Of the "Ten Ways to Respond to the Question, 'Am I Racist?'," which one would you be most receptive to hearing if you asked your coach: "Am I racist?" How would you respond?

- Can you recall a time when someone accused you of something or said something about you that felt inaccurate, and that caused you to feel defensive? What part of your sense of self or of your identity felt like it was threatened? How did you respond?
- Can you recall a time when someone shared some feedback with you that was hard to hear? How did they do it? What was the impact? Was there anything you wish they'd done differently? Do any of the ideas in this chapter help you better understand how you responded or what they did?
- What happens in your body when you feel defensive? Which physical cues tell you that you're feeling attacked? How do you respond in those moments? How would you like to respond?

TO DO

- Have a coaching conversation with yourself beginning with the statement: "Am I racist?" Write what you hear yourself saying (as the coach) and asking (as the client). Where does this conversation take you?
- Review Domains 2 and 3 of the Transformational Coaching Rubric 2.0. Which of those areas do you feel skillful in? If you had to pick one area in which to develop, which would that be and why?
- Create a coaching PLC and use the Consultancy Protocol and the Coaching Lenses so that you can see the situations you're in with greater complexity, and so that you can begin to take action on the level of systems and structures.

Principles of Transformational Coaching

- Compassion
- Curiosity
- Connection
- Courage
- **Purpose**

Purpose: Our purpose is to create a world characterized by justice, equity, and liberation. The journey is the destination. We can fulfill our purpose when we act with compassion, curiosity, connection, and courage.

Our lives begin to end the day we become silent about things that matter.

—Dr. Martin Luther King Jr.

- What things matter to you? When and where do you speak up about them?
- When are you silent about things that matter?

CHAPTER 5

What You Need to Know about Adult Learners

Do the best you can until you know better.
Then when you know better, do better.
—MAYA ANGELOU

A Transformational Coach requires knowledge of many areas: of emotions; of race, racism, and identity; of systems and how to change them; and of teaching and education, among other areas. While some of these areas are specific to the field of education, many are true for work with adult learners in any field. In fact, an ability to coach can be explained as the ability to work with adult learners, so separating adult learning out from coaching doesn't really make sense.

I've written about the principles of adult learning in *The Art of Coaching* and *The Art of Coaching Teams.* When we focus on coaching adult learners for equity, there are a few specific tools that are invaluable. It makes sense for us to briefly examine the knowledge bucket of adult learning so that we can see how these tools apply to Coaching for Equity. In this short chapter, I'll share the framework I use most often when making decisions about how to guide adult learners. It's simple to apply and will further illuminate the coaching I did with Stephanie as well as the coaching you'll read about in later chapters in this book.

The Gaps between Current Ability
and Desired Ability

You want to play the saxophone or be a principal or teach Socratic seminars? There's a gap you'll need to close. Your manager wants you to lead better professional development sessions? There's a gap you'll need to close. In fact, there are most likely many gaps. When considering something we aspire to do—or that someone else wants us to do—we often face gaps between that goal and where we are right now. To close those gaps, we must first identify them.

Let's categorize those gaps, understand them, and look at some examples. Then we'll consider how to use this framework. I'll also suggest how to sequence learning after you've done a gap analysis. Finally, I'll use this framework of the gaps to group the abilities that a Transformational Coach must possess. This will be an opportunity for you to reflect on your own gaps and abilities, and to recognize your growth in the process of reading this book.

Which Kinds of Gaps Can We Have?

The framework that I call "Mind the Gap" organizes the gaps between our current abilities and our desired abilities into six groups: skill gaps, knowledge gaps, capacity gaps, will gaps, cultural competence gaps, and emotional intelligence gaps. Figure 5.1 depicts this concept, and Table 5.1 describes each gap and provides an example. (You can download Figure 5.1 from my website.)

The Interconnectedness of Gaps

We have a tendency to focus on skill and knowledge when we're addressing gaps. Sometimes we focus on will, trying to cultivate a sense of urgency or stoking the flames of mission and purpose. Capacity is often overlooked, as is evident any time district leaders roll out seven new initiatives in one year and then get frustrated that programs aren't implemented with fidelity when there just isn't the time to do so. The foundational domains—emotional intelligence and cultural competence—are most neglected. Teachers rarely attend training on how to deal with the first-grade student who can't stop crying every morning when her mom drops her off or how to navigate burnout and build resilience.

Cultural competence is especially essential in diverse educational settings, and also neglected. When the cultural competence of educators is addressed, it's usually in a one-day training. But many educational inequities wouldn't exist if schools committed to closing cultural competence gaps. Recall Stephanie, the

Figure 5.1   Mind the Gap

MIND THE GAP:
Identifying Learning Needs

ability to take
action, to do
what we need
to do

SKILL
The ability to execute the
technical elements of a
task. Can be the application
of knowledge.

KNOWLEDGE
The theoretical or practical
understanding of a subject.
Can also be information.

CAPACITY
The time and resources to do something.
Can also be emotional and physical
capacity.

WILL
Desire, intrinsic motivation, passion,
or commitment. Usually has an
emotional tone.

CULTURAL COMPETENCE
The ability to understand, appreciate and interact with
people from cultures or belief systems different from
one's own; the skill to navigate cross-cultural differences.

EMOTIONAL INTELLIGENCE
The ability to be aware of, manage, and express one's
emotions; the ability to recognize, empathize with, and
manage other people's emotions.

brightmorningteam.com

bright**morning**
every conversation counts

Table 5.1 The Gaps Defined

Gap	Description	Examples for a teacher
Skill	The ability to execute the technical elements of a task. Can be the application of knowledge.	• Frontloading vocabulary • Using discussion structures • Getting the whole class quiet • Breaking down the steps to solving complex equations • Identifying a doable learning target for a lesson
Knowledge	The theoretical or practical understanding of a subject. Can also be information.	• Understanding polynomials • Knowing students' names • Knowing how to redirect behavior
Capacity	The time and resources to do something. Can also be emotional and physical capacity.	• Having time to call students' parents/guardians • Having books to differentiate learning • Having the emotional wherewithal to manage an irate parent/guardian • Having the physical energy to attend evening and weekend school functions
Will	Desire, intrinsic motivation, passion, or commitment. Usually has an emotional tone.	• Loving the work • Wanting to serve a community • Feeling a calling to interrupt educational inequities • Holding a commitment to helping kids learn

Table 5.1 (Continued)

Gap	Description	Examples for a teacher
Cultural competence	The ability to understand, appreciate, and interact with people from cultures, identities, or belief systems different from one's own; the skill to navigate differences in identities.	• Recognizing assets in students who come from different cultural backgrounds • Understanding that eye contact has different meanings in different cultures • Validating students' background through selection of curriculum • Using the pronoun that someone asks you to use when talking about them
Emotional intelligence	The ability to be aware of, navigate, and express one's emotions; the ability to recognize, empathize with, and navigate other people's emotions.	• Awareness of feeling anxious when an administrator enters the class • Ability to draw boundaries around requests for help from colleagues • Ability to regulate one's irritation with a perpetually difficult student • Ability to connect with a difficult student • Ability to calm a distraught student

teacher I described in Chapters 2, 3 and 4, whose cultural competence gaps were extensive. If she had received training on cultural competence in her teacher preparation program and in her introduction to her school and district, she would have quickly closed many gaps. If Stephanie had been in a school that provided training on how to build relationships with students, some of her cultural competence gaps would have narrowed. Especially when we're looking through a lens of equity, we'll see many cultural competence gaps that overlap with skill and knowledge gaps.

In presenting this concept as a pyramid (Figure 5.1), I'm suggesting a hierarchy. We can understand theoretically that emotional intelligence (EI) and cultural competence are foundational, but it can be harder to really see how they operate. Let's see how that can play out with EI: a skill gap can create an EI gap, but if our EI isn't solid, then we can't truly close gaps in other areas. It's true that a will gap can blur with an EI gap. Will could be considered an emotion—but I've kept it separate because I think that too often, we ascribe a will gap to someone (a child or an adult) when actually, the person is experiencing an emotion such as fear or shame. If that person lacks strategies to deal with those feelings, the inability to do something appears as a will gap—but it really isn't. When we shift from assuming someone has a will gap to considering their gaps to be in the domain of EI, there are more options for action.

Areas for growth are always interconnected, and sometimes it's hard to know what's at the root of an inability to do something. Did Stephanie have "classroom management" struggles because she held a deficit mindset about her students and didn't hold them to high behavioral expectations (a gap in cultural competence)? Or because she was anxious about redirecting students (an EI gap)? Or because her expectations for her students were low, which could have been a knowledge gap about what high schoolers are capable of? What were Stephanie's gaps? Asking these questions and recognizing how gaps are interconnected can help us determine where to start when we coach someone.

Coaching Behaviors, Beliefs, and Being

Now I'm going to complicate this a bit more. Every action we take emerges from a belief. So, if you only coach at the level of behavior, and you don't surface and perhaps shift underlying beliefs, your coaching may not be sustained, it may not be transformational, and it may not interrupt inequitable practices at their root—in the land of ideology and white supremacy. This is why the Mind the Gap Framework is a tool that has to be used within a Transformational Coaching model. It must be used in conjunction with coaching that explores beliefs. In Chapter 6, we'll explore how behavioral and belief changes can happen hand in hand. The gaps are a useful tool for identifying behaviors to change—but you'll also need to know how to explore underlying beliefs to see transformational change.

How to Use This Framework

Let me be very clear: *Gaps are not deficits.* They are not fundamental flaws in who we are. Gaps are areas for growth. Conceptualizing these areas as gaps anchors us in a growth mindset when we're coaching. We *all* have gaps; we'll have gaps for as long as we live, because there's no person alive who has the ability to do everything. This framework is not about finding weaknesses; it's a tool to recognize potential and explore what lies in the way of fulfilling it.

When you are trying to figure out what someone's gaps are, use this framework both for reflection and as a shared tool for discovery. You have a role in identifying your client's gaps, but they know themselves very well—and engaging them as partners is a sign that you trust them, and you'll likely gain insight you wouldn't have otherwise.

Here's how I introduce this to clients. When Stephanie complained that her students didn't turn in homework, I explained the concept of the gaps and asked her which gaps she suspected her kids had. She quickly and accurately concluded that her students didn't have the skills to complete the homework she assigned. In contrast to the low rigor of instruction she delivered in the classroom, the homework she assigned asked student to use skills that they hadn't yet built.

When I asked Stephanie what *her gaps* were when it came to teaching, she was thoughtful. "I have so many gaps," she said. "It's kind of a relief to see it this way because I recognize how many areas for growth I have. But I do have will!"

I agreed with her, and I also said that I thought she *did* have some of the necessary skills and knowledge. "You are really good at lesson design," I said. "It's not rigorous in the way our students are ready for, but you can design lessons." She nodded in agreement. "And as for the content, English, you've got some solid knowledge there."

"But I have so many gaps!" Stephanie said. "Where should I start to close them?"

"That's the next question for us to figure out," I responded.

"Could we go through each of these areas and list everything I need to be a good teacher?" Stephanie asked. "We can list all of the skills I need, all of the knowledge, all of the emotional intelligence. Right?"

"This is one of your strengths, Stephanie," I said. "You are organized, you're a planner, and you were able to look at this and translate it into a schematic that would help you make growth." She smiled. We can categorize skills and knowledge into the six buckets of the gaps, and then we have a learning plan.

The framework of the gaps is a tool I frequently share with clients. I give them a copy of the graphic, I invite their reflections on their own gaps and their students, and I sometimes will reference my own gaps as a coach. Being transparent around this framework is a way to pull back the curtain on the process of learning, to normalize that we all have gaps, and to generate a commitment to growth.

When You See Gaps but Your Client Disagrees

There will be times when you recognize gaps in your client's abilities, but they disagree with your perception. Often, they'll point to one of two things: either they think there's another gap they need to work on that's more important, or they think that the problem is not their responsibility. For example, Greg, a new first-grade teacher, was frustrated about student behavior. When he asked what I thought he should do, I suggested that he work on building relationships with students. I believed I was seeing an EI and a cultural competence gap.

"No, that's not the problem," he said. "The problem is that I don't know how to manage first graders. I think I'm using strategies that are more appropriate for older students." He believed he had a knowledge gap. In this case, because we were still building trust and I wanted to get to know Greg better, I followed his lead. We visited two other first-grade teachers and observed their strategies for redirecting off-task behavior and for creating a focused classroom. As we reflected on the visits, I emphasized the observations I'd made of the relationships between the teachers and students. "OK, I see what you're saying about relationships," Greg said, "I don't know if I agree with you, but I see what you're pointing at." I left it at that for the time being. We later came to see how relationships and managing students were two sides of the same coin.

When I coached Maggie, a new sixth-grade history teacher who was struggling, I suggested that she work on procedures and routines. She knew the routines that could keep her class running smoothly, but she wasn't consistent in requiring students to use them. I believed Maggie had a skill gap. When I made this suggestion, she said, "The problem isn't that I'm not consistent. The problem is that these kids don't respect authority here." Maggie paused. "I shouldn't have to tell them over and over that they need to walk into class and start the Do-Now. Once is enough!"

This response revealed additional gaps and underlying beliefs, but it also helped me coach Maggie on her spheres of influence and control.

"Do you think there's anything that you can do to improve what's going on in your class?" I asked. I nudged Maggie to take responsibility for what she could do, and I also set about to gather data to help her see what I saw: that the way she explained routines was unclear, and that by not requiring students to use them, she was sending confusing messages. In Chapter 11, I'll describe how to incorporate data (including data captured on video) into coaching. One reason why data is so useful is that it helps to bridge an understanding between our own perception of our abilities and reality.

How to Sequence Adult Learning

When I first observed Stephanie, I was overwhelmed by the number of gaps I perceived. Sadly, this was not the first or last time when a teacher I was coaching had a great deal of growth to make in order to be effective. When faced with such a long list of areas for growth, I've wondered about the best sequence for coaching around closing gaps. Sometimes I've coached emotions first—when a teacher's temper flared every day and prevented him from delivering the strong lesson that he'd designed. But coaching emotions takes a lot of time, and change can be slow going in that area. Other times, when a teacher struggled to deliver a basic lesson and students were acting out, it seemed to make sense to focus on instructional delivery—at least then students might learn something. But if that same teacher hadn't developed a positive learning environment and she was sending throngs of kids to the office every day, then lesson planning didn't make sense as first the gap to focus on. Then it felt like creating a positive classroom environment was a better gap to start with—a gap that had to do with skill, knowledge, emotional intelligence, and cultural competence.

Where to Start

Here are some guidelines for where to start when coaching gaps:

- Notice where the client has energy or will to work. If they are excited about working on a skill or building a knowledge piece, go with that.
- Look for low-hanging fruit: a quick win can boost confidence in one's ability to learn and make growth.
- Look for skills that, if built, could have a big impact on students: a teacher's ability to get the whole class's attention, for example.
- Consider the way skills are sequenced to effectively teach.

Let's unpack that last item—the sequencing of teaching skills. Here's the sequence of reflections I consider when I go into a classroom where kids aren't learning. First, how does the teacher manage transitions, get students' attention, give instructions, and so on? This is a skill set that many new teachers don't have, and that results in serious breakdowns in a class. If routines and procedures aren't strong, that's where I start coaching.

Then I look at the relationship that the teacher has with students. Are interactions characterized by care and curiosity? Does the teacher see children's strengths, skills, and assets? Or does the teacher have a deficit mindset about his students? Is the teacher interacting with students in the 5:1 ratio of positive to negative interactions? (See Chapter 11 for an explanation of this). How does the teacher wield power in the classroom? Is it through holding power *over* students and controlling them with threats and consequences? Or is the teacher building mutually-respectful relationships with students? If the teacher's relationships with students aren't based on care and curiosity, and aren't culturally competent, that's the next place I coach.

Next, I pay attention to the relationships that students have with each other. This gives me insight into the levels of psychological and identity-safety that exist in the class. This is about how the class functions as a community of learners. A teacher is responsible for creating and cultivating a healthy, respectful student culture, so if this is an area of need, then I coach there.

I then scrutinize the quality of lessons: Are they rigorous? Relevant? Engaging? If students aren't learning, I start with examining the quality of lessons—starting with what the plans look like. Then I'll assess how well they're implemented—and if the breakdown in learning happens because of the teacher's gaps in being able to implement a lesson, then I coach there.

Finally, if students aren't learning, I'll pay attention to assessment practices. How does the teacher understand what students are learning? How often does the teacher assess students? And in which ways? What does the teacher do with the data that they gather on how students are doing? How does that data inform their instruction?

My recommendation is to follow this sequence when considering which gaps to close:

1. Routines and procedures (skill and knowledge)
2. Relationships with students (EI and cultural competence)
3. Relationships among students (EI and cultural competence)
4. Rigor and relevance of lessons (skill, knowledge, and cultural competence)
5. Assessment practices (skill and knowledge)

Yes, this sequence is probably simply what leads to "good teaching," and you could use it in any classroom, with any teacher. And there are many additional skills that a teacher needs in order to be an equity-conscious, culturally competent, effective teacher. Many of these attributes are included in Appendix B: The Equity Rubric. But even with a comprehensive list of abilities in our hands, we need direction on where to start.

Back to the Phases of Transformational Coaching

Perhaps you're wondering how the Mind the Gap Framework fits into the Phases of Transformational Coaching. The Phases describe the general process that we guide a client through. The gaps can be incorporated into every phase. As we begin coaching to *surface current reality*, we can use the concept of the gaps to gain insight into a teacher's abilities—to diagnose, in a sense, what we see in their classroom. We can also use it to encourage reflection on what they're struggling with in their classroom and to foster a commitment to growth. As we move through the Phases, we can continue to use the gaps to reflect on how the client is growing, where we need to specifically direct our coaching, and how we're selecting new practices to develop.

One of the reasons I use this concept so often is that it keeps my mind firmly within in a developmental, adult learning stance. When I see a problem in a classroom, or a teacher who is having a hard time, I ask myself: *What's the gap here?* This prevents me from tumbling into a place of judgment and frustration; in fact, just asking this question shifts my way of being toward curiosity. And as soon as I'm curious, I'm on the path to healthy action. In addition to the other strategies I've suggested, ask yourself over and over: *What's the gap here?* Ask that question about your client—and then ask that question about your own abilities: What are *my gaps* as a coach? Let's consider your gaps now.

The Coach as Learner

The Transformational Coaching Rubric 2.0 (Appendix C) is a comprehensive description of the abilities in which a Transformational Coach requires competence. I hope you'll spend time reflecting on your areas of strength and areas for growth, and on creating a plan for developing these abilities. To help you digest the Rubric, I've grouped abilities as they fall into the categories of the gaps. In Table 5.2: The Abilities of a Transformational Coach, you'll see the six gap areas, and the key elements in each gap.

As you review these areas and elements, where are your gaps? Where are your strengths? In which areas do you feel you've grown as a result of reading this book? What makes sense for you in terms of a sequence to follow to close your gaps?

Thinking about yourself as an adult learner will help you coach your clients. It will help you be humble and empathetic. Our journeys—our own learning journeys and those we make across the coaching bridges with our clients—will be easier and

Table 5.2   The Abilities of a Transformational Coach

Area of Transformational Coaching	Key elements
Knowledge	<ul><li>Of emotions</li><li>Of adult learners and coaching</li><li>Of race, racism, white supremacy, and systemic oppression</li><li>Of identity</li><li>Of systems</li><li>Of teaching and education</li></ul>
Skill	<ul><li>Transformational Coaching skills<ul><li>How to coach behaviors, beliefs, and ways of being</li><li>How to coach in the Phases of Transformational Coaching</li><li>How to coach for system change</li></ul></li><li>Ability to create the conditions in which adults can learn</li></ul>
Will	<ul><li>A commitment to interrupt inequities</li><li>A commitment to the Principles of Transformational Coaching: compassion, curiosity, connection, courage, and purpose</li></ul>
Capacity	<ul><li>Time to learn, practice, reflect, and attend to self</li><li>Funds for books, professional development, and a coach and/or therapist</li></ul>
Cultural competence	<ul><li>Awareness of one's own identity markers and the role they play in coaching</li><li>How to understand power dynamics through a lens of identity and systemic oppression</li><li>Ability to navigate racial differences in coaching relationships</li><li>Relationships with people who hold different identity markers than your own</li></ul>
Emotional intelligence (EI)	<ul><li>Refined self-awareness, ability to engage one's emotions and to cultivate resilience</li><li>Refined ability to recognize the emotions of others and to support them to explore those emotions</li><li>Embodiment of the coaching ways of being</li></ul>

more enjoyable if we stay curious and compassionate, if we remain connected to each other and grounded in our shared purpose to transform schools, and if we draw on our courage to traverse the chasm between where we are and where we want to be.

Before You Go . . .

Read the following prompts and select two or three that feel most valuable to you based on where you are in your learning journey. Spend meaningful time considering your reflection before moving on.

REFLECT ON THIS CHAPTER

- What insights did you get into the people you coach through the framework of the Gaps defined in Table 5.1?
- Recall a teacher whose behavior you perceived as being resistant, or who you thought had a will gap. Which other gaps do you think this teacher had?
- How could you get a clearer understanding of where your gaps as a coach are?

TO DO

- Identify a teacher with whom you might have a conversation about gaps— about their gaps and student gaps. Plan for that conversation and print out a copy of Mind the Gap to take with you.
- Spend some time reflecting on the Transformational Coaching Rubric 2.0. What insights can you get about your strengths and areas for growth from it?

Interlude: Compassion

Principles of Transformational Coaching

- **Compassion**
- Curiosity
- Connection
- Courage
- Purpose

Compassion: We relentlessly strive to center the humanity of others. We preserve people's honor and dignity above all. We know that kindness is our greatest power. We practice self-compassion, which includes taking care of ourselves. We know that the journey toward liberation will be long, so we rest and attend to our minds, bodies, hearts, and spirits.

Read the following three quotes a couple of times. What resonates? Which ideas are sparked? What questions surface for you?

> *"Here's what we have to say to all of America's men and women falling in the grips of hatred and white supremacy: Come back. It's not too late. You have neighbors and loved ones waiting, holding space for you. And we will love you back."*
> —Alexandria Ocasio-Cortez, politician and activist

> *"What actually sustains us, what is fundamentally beautiful, is compassion—for yourself and for those around you. That kind of beauty inflames the heart and enchants the soul."*
> —Lupita Nyong'o, actress and activist

> *"If we could read the secret history of those we would like to punish, we would find in each life a sorrow and suffering enough to disarm all our hostility."*
> —Henry Wadsworth Longfellow, writer

CHAPTER 6

How to Change Someone's Mind

The key here is not the kind of instruction but the attitude underlying it. When teachers do not understand the potential of the students they teach, they will underteach them no matter what the methodology.

—LISA DELPIT

When Margaret, a teacher I coached said, "What do you expect? These parents don't care about their kids," I was flabbergasted. I couldn't find words to respond. I was a new coach, and I'd never heard a teacher speak so bluntly. Margaret had proclaimed this as truth, as doctrine, her voice laden with disdain. And she was a woman of color. I went to an experienced colleague and asked her how she would have responded. She wrote a list of questions or responses I could use.

A week later, another teacher said, "The reason that our black male students aren't successful is because they don't have role models. What can we do about that?" I went back to my colleague and asked her for another list.

These were not isolated comments. An 8th grade reading intervention teacher pushed back against my coaching. "I can't teach these kids," she said, her voice thick with hostility. "Why don't you coach their elementary school teachers? They're the ones who need coaching. It's not my fault they're so far behind."

A math teacher said, "I don't send them to the 'time out chair,' I send them to 'isolation,' because *these kids* get that reference. They know about prisons, so I make it simple for them to understand my discipline system."

"She'll end up pregnant at 15," said the science teacher. "That's how those Mexicans are. I'm not wasting my time teaching her chemistry."

And another (young female) teacher said, "Can you come to the conference I have to have with Abdul's dad? I'm afraid to be alone with him. Middle Eastern men have no boundaries."

I collected lists of things I could say in response to each situation. And yet each time I heard something that was overtly or unconsciously racist (or sexist or classist or ableist or homophobic—I heard it all), I felt at a loss for how to respond. I felt that it I was obligated, as a coach and as a human being, to open a conversation, explore the underlying thinking, and stay in relationship with whomever made these comments. Even though I kept adding to my list of responses, I often didn't have sentence stems to use for whatever specific situation happened that day.

These racist statements expressed *beliefs*, and we can figure out how to act in response when we remember that *a belief is just a strongly held opinion*. A belief is not the truth—even if it feels like it is. In order to respond to these statements I was hearing from teachers, I needed to understand how beliefs were created and how they could be shifted. I needed to understand how to build trust.

In this chapter, we'll dive into how to surface, explore and shift beliefs that don't serve the full humanity of every child. We'll also dig into how to build trust. At the end, I've included a list of responses you can use when teachers you coach say racist things such as the statements that opened this chapter—because there *are* things that we can say.

Addressing Beliefs and Behavior at the Same Time

Bias can be overt, as it was in the statements that I just shared, and bias is also often expressed unconsciously. When you become aware that someone is expressing a racial bias—perhaps because they say something, or because their responses to the behaviors of one group of students are consistently more severe—you'll probably wonder where you should start. Do you start by addressing the underlying belief, or do you start by trying to shift the behaviors it produces?

The Chicken and the Egg

Mr. Glasser, a white man who grew up in Texas, was a seasoned middle-school science teacher. His relationship with students was respectful, he commanded a calm and focused classroom, and he never sent anyone to the office. Every day, he lectured to a silent class of students who sat in rows and took notes. But while students were sitting quietly, they weren't mastering the concepts, and, as you can imagine, they didn't like his class. Fortunately, Mr. Glasser's school had a new principal who was committed to ensuring that students had opportunities every day to talk to each other and to use academic language.

On a visit to his classroom, the principal (a young Latina) asked me whether I thought he was "just an ineffective teacher," or whether there were equity issues at play. "Do you think he has some biases about our students?" the principal asked me.

"Probably," I said.

The principal thought for a moment and then said: "I guess it doesn't matter whether he's ineffective or biased. The way he's teaching will result in inequities for our students. If they don't have equitable access to this content, they'll be disadvantaged when they go to high school."

She asked me to coach Mr. Glasser.

I wondered whether to start by addressing Mr. Glasser's teaching practices or the underlying beliefs that drove his actions. I wondered: *If our actions emerge from beliefs—to create sustainable, transformational change that gets at the root cause of the problem—shouldn't we start with those beliefs? Shouldn't coaching for equity begin by surfacing and shifting beliefs that are rooted in white supremacy, and then work on changing behaviors?*

The problem is that it will take a long time to excavate the ideology that fuels implicit bias and results in inequitable practices. I'm not willing to wait while my son's teachers unlearn decades of racist indoctrination so that they'll stop sending him to the office for "defiance." It wasn't right to ask Mr. Glasser's students to wait to get their hands into a science experiment; I couldn't ask them to sit in silence while we explored his beliefs. *Perhaps I should start with behaviors—on teaching him to do something different. Maybe*, I thought, *coaches should prioritize coaching on rigorous instruction, using varied assessment practices, and selecting literature that reflects the diversity of students. Maybe we should be heavily directive in our coaching, and perhaps administrators could issue a moratorium on suspending black and brown children.*

Here's the problem with that thinking: We might be able to instruct a teacher in new behaviors, but those will have limited impact. At some point, the teacher will get tired, and his underlying beliefs will percolate up and direct his behaviors, and reflexively, he'll send that black boy to the office for what he perceives as defiance. And at another point, there'll be a new situation for which we haven't trained him, and he'll resort to his default setting, resuming his habitual inequitable behaviors. *We can't teach every single behavior that a teacher must enact in order to be equitable with every single child and parent/guardian.* There are too many variables—too many daily decisions that a teacher needs to make about students, instruction, and assessment. Coaches must address beliefs.

The answer to this riddle of which comes first—behavior change or belief change—is simple: We must address both at the same time. However, given what we know about our brain and our inclination to protect our moral identity (discussed in Chapter 4), this exploration of beliefs and behaviors must happen within a context of trust. We can surface, explore, and shift a client's beliefs, while simultaneously engaging them in new behaviors. As they try different instructional practices, they'll see different results. Those different results can create new beliefs. Exploring beliefs deepens equitable practices; building equitable practices shifts beliefs.

Changing Practices and Shifting Beliefs

Mr. Glasser pushed back on my suggestion to incorporate group work. "That would be disastrous," he said. "They won't stay on task. LaKaya and José need tight structures and order or they can't control themselves. I wouldn't be able to manage the class. These kids can't handle group work."

I acknowledged these concerns, and then I persisted in encouraging Mr. Glasser to incorporate a group work activity into a lesson. "Let's just try it and see what happens," I said. "Just a 10-minute activity. What could happen? Just give it a shot—with all the experience you have in the classroom, it'll be OK!"

Sometimes the art of coaching is the art of nudging—without leaving bruises.

I co-planned the lesson with Mr. Glasser and insisted that he rehearse the instructions he'd give. I observed him when he delivered the lesson and offered on-the-spot coaching ("Check for procedural understanding; use proximity with José now; affirm that LaKaya is doing well . . ."). The group work was successful: LaKaya and José were on task, the exit ticket affirmed that every student accomplished the learning target, and Mr. Glasser admitted that it was fun.

When we debriefed, Mr. Glasser said, "That went better than I expected."

"What did you learn about your students? And about yourself?" I asked. Mr. Glasser observed that LaKaya and José were able to control themselves for a period of time, that group work wasn't as chaotic as he'd feared it would be, and that kids could learn by talking to each other. I was reminded that Mr. Glasser loved science and wanted his students to understand it and also love it.

After he reflected on the lesson, I said, "It sounds like *your beliefs* are changing—your beliefs about your students, about yourself, and about learning." Mr. Glasser nodded. "Can you tell me about how they are changing?" I asked.

Mr. Glasser explained that he had believed that kids needed a silent classroom so they could focus. He'd worried that if he changed his teaching methods, he'd be unsuccessful, and he'd thought he'd been doing what was best for his students. "I guess that's not true," he said with sadness in his voice, and then added, "But I guess an old dog can learn new tricks."

In a subsequent conversation with Mr. Glasser, I explored the origin of his shifting belief that kids couldn't handle group work. I asked why he'd thought that his students would struggle with group work. Where had that belief come from? What data was it based on? I asked how his belief had been informed by his own experiences.

Mr. Glasser described the classrooms that he'd attended as a child and in which he'd been successful. They were silent, and teachers were strict. "That's what it was like in Texas in the '50s," he said. And yes, many of us teach the way we were taught.

"I get that," I said. "Your experiences made you believe that good classrooms are quiet, structured, and adult-centered. These are also the values of our dominant culture." I paused, and then continued. "We live in a culture that enforces hierarchy and prioritizes individual success over the needs of a community."

I stopped so that I could think for a moment and then continued: "So, we've grown up in this dominant culture, and it's hard not to replicate it. But this culture hasn't served everyone. And it's dehumanized many people."

Mr. Glasser was making affirmative sounds and nodding his head.

I went on: "There *are* other ways that we can structure learning that would be effective and that wouldn't replicate systems of oppression. Would you be willing to continue exploring those?"

Mr. Glasser nodded. "I'll give it a try," he said.

He did not throw out all the lecture notes he'd compiled over the decades that he'd been teaching—but he was receptive to tweaking his approach, incorporating a 10-minute group activity into a lesson, or giving students a text to read and discuss in pairs. Change didn't happen overnight—but it did happen. Although we focused on instructional design and discussion structures, I included opportunities for him to reflect on how his beliefs were changing. He'd explain that he was coming to believe that students could learn in cooperative structures, that a classroom didn't have to be silent, that students would learn to love science if they did experiments. I wanted him to see that his beliefs were changing, and that when he needed to make instructional decisions, he could make them based on those evolving beliefs.

"If you believed that students could learn in cooperative structures," I'd say, "then what decision would you make about how to teach that concept?" Or: "If you believe that a classroom can be noisy and students still can learn, then how could you plan that lesson?" When Mr. Glasser worked from *updated beliefs*—beliefs that centered students and their needs and potential—he did different things, and more learning happened.

One of the last times I worked with him, Mr. Glasser seemed sad. "I've just been thinking," he said, "maybe as a kid, if I'd been taught in a way that allowed me to be a more active learner, and to build language skills and to think critically about science, maybe I could have been a scientist. I mean, I love teaching, but maybe I could have done something else, too."

I sensed his grief. He continued: "I always thought that the education I got was great, that it worked for me. But maybe it didn't."

"Maybe not," I said. "But you can create something different for your students tomorrow."

"Maybe," he said.

Coaching for equity raises many reflections, insights, and feelings. Sometimes there aren't easy answers.

Six Conditions in Which Beliefs Change

Coaches create conditions for growth, and there are six conditions that allow beliefs to change. Sometimes all of these conditions need to be in place in order for a belief to change and other times a belief can change if just a few conditions are in place. Beliefs change when:

- We feel safe enough.
- We understand how a belief was created.
- We encounter new information.
- Alternate beliefs exist.
- Our core identity is preserved.
- We see benefits to changing a belief.

Beliefs Change When We Feel Safe Enough

Letting go of beliefs entails loss and fear and, sometimes, sadness and anger as well. Regardless of which beliefs we're releasing, we deserve to have the support and guidance of someone who is kind, humble, and hopeful; someone who's both tuned into our needs and who encourages us to forge on through the discomfort. Feeling safe is an essential social and emotional condition that allows us to examine and shift beliefs. If a coach is judgmental, a client will be reluctant (or resistant) to unpacking mental models and flawed beliefs—especially about race and white supremacy.

For Stephanie to shift her beliefs about herself and about students, it was critical that I created a safe-enough space. Given all the emotions that surged in her as we explored her teaching and beliefs, she needed a space that was free of judgment, one that was challenging and yet hopeful.

When I reflect on the beliefs that I've let go of, especially distorted beliefs about other people, I'm flooded with feelings—including shame. Shame is a feeling that we experience as: *I'm wrong. I'm bad.* Guilt, in contrast, is experienced as: *I did something wrong.* Shame, say the experts, is not a productive or helpful emotion and can lead us to engage in unhealthy behaviors. When we experience shame, if we can talk about it—which is often hard to do—we can release it. A coach, therapist, or good friend can help us forgive ourselves and gain insight into what we did or believed that led to shame. This doesn't happen, however, if we don't feel safe enough with another person. This is why it's essential that we cultivate trust with the people we coach and lead (we'll explore this later in this chapter).

This first condition for beliefs to change is why in Phase 1 of Transformational Coaching we surface current reality, which includes developing an understanding of what our client needs in order to feel *safe enough*. It's also why we always attend to building a relationship with a client—this is one of the guardrails that keeps us safely on the bridge.

Beliefs Change When We Understand How a Belief Was Created

During Phase 1 of Transformational Coaching, we begin to explore the origins of our client's beliefs. Without this background, we're poorly informed about how to guide belief-change.

Ms. Russo insisted that her students speak only English when they were in her art class. "You *must* learn English!" she'd yell at her sixth graders, many of whom were recent immigrants. She would send kids to the office for speaking Spanish to each other. She'd tell me: "This is America! They need to speak English." She was in her early 60s, and had taught in the same school for almost 30 years. Kids were scared of her and hated art.

One day I asked Ms. Russo about her family's background. Her grandparents had come from Italy, she told me. Did she speak any Italian? No. She explained that when her family immigrated, they'd faced discrimination. "My grandparents decided not to speak to their children in Italian because they wanted them to have a better life," she explained. Her parents, aunts, and uncles had emphasized that English was the best language in the world, a currency to access jobs.

"That helps me understand why you have such a strong belief that our children should speak English," I said.

"Yes, I suppose so," she said as if she'd never made that connection.

I asked about her relationship with her grandparents. "They knew very little English, so I could hardly communicate with them," she said. I explained that our students also had grandparents and family members who only spoke Spanish—and that having relationships with family was important. She sighed and said: "I wish I'd been able to talk to my grandmother. She was kind and sweet. I missed out."

"I'm wondering if you'd be willing to unpack your beliefs about your students only speaking in English in class?" I asked. She agreed.

Ms. Russo was scary—I was even a little afraid of her. She was cantankerous. We had a short, intense conversation about her beliefs around English. When our conversation ended, I couldn't tell how she was thinking or whether any of her thoughts had shifted.

A week later, she asked me to observe one of her art classes—the class with the large group of newcomers. At the beginning of the class, she said: "Students, I need to apologize. I have been wrong in telling you to only speak English. You may speak in Spanish to each other as long as it's an appropriate time to talk. Elena, please translate that for me so I can be sure all of the students understand."

I was shocked. I translated and registered the surprise on the faces of some of the children. "You can go now," Ms. Russo said to me.

We often experience a belief as an untouchable, monolithic truth. But a belief is a strongly held opinion, and it can change when we understand where it came from. Ms. Russo's belief about speaking English shifted as she recognized the origins of her own beliefs about speaking English—and as she recognized that there were limitations and drawbacks to that belief. Mr. Glasser's beliefs changed as he recognized that he taught in the way in which he'd been taught—and that he may have missed out on opportunities because of the way he was taught.

It's empowering to recognize that our beliefs are built on specific information, often on data that is incomplete or even problematic. We can learn to recognize that we interpret information through our own experiences, social conditioning, family of origin, and so on, and thereby create a belief. In this process, we can acknowledge the origins of our beliefs and the context in which they were created, and also take responsibility for the impact the belief has had on our life and on the lives of others.

The Ladder of Inference, created by Chris Argyris and depicted in Figure 6.0, provides an invaluable tool for helping us see how our beliefs are formed and why we do what we do. This model describes how we unconsciously climb up a mental pathway of increasing abstraction that often produces misguided beliefs (Senge, 1994, p. 243). On the first rung of the Ladder, there's a tremendous amount of data and experiences that our brain is exposed to. Because we can't process it all, our mind selects certain data that fits with what we already know and understand—and so we ascend one rung. Now we have some filtered data onto which we add meaning. Meaning is often based on our own cultural backgrounds and experiences, and/or the culture of the organization in which we are working. From that rung, we ascend again and make assumptions and then come to conclusions. And then, almost at the top of the Ladder, a belief is crystalized, and that belief leads to actions (Figure 6.0).

Figure 6.0 The Ladder of Inference.

Here's an example. Angela wanted to implement stations with her first-grade students—something she'd been hesitant to try but was enticed into by the prospect of working with small reading groups. While with a group, she noticed the boys at a math station messing around. She noticed this, in part, because it's exactly what she was worried about (Angela already thought that many of her first-grade boys were too wiggly and distracted). The boys were building towers with the math manipulatives and talking loudly. She ascended the Ladder as she *interpreted* this to mean that they were off task. Ascending the Ladder again, Angela *assumed* that they were disrupting the learning of other students and that they wouldn't meet the day's objectives. She *concluded* that they just couldn't handle the freedom of being in stations, and then, almost at the top of the Ladder, she *arrived at a belief* that the only thing that works with first-grade students is whole-group instruction. She decided to scrap plans for stations and return to the way she'd taught—this was the action she took. Next time Angela noticed boys talking loudly, she'd focus on the pieces of data that reinforced her beliefs, starting the climb right back up the Ladder again. This is how her belief that *boys can't work collaboratively* was formed; this is how her classroom became teacher-centered; and this is why she reacted punitively when boys seemed distracted.

Our biases come in at the level of "selected data." If we've been unaware that we're breathing the smoggy air of racism and white supremacy all our lives, we'll select data that matches the biased beliefs we've absorbed. We will look at "observable data" and not see data that doesn't square with what we know. Our eyes will bypass the black and brown boys who are focused and quiet. We'll take one data point—one boy whom we perceive as being off task—and generalize it to mean that black and brown boys can't handle group work, and then we add layers of problematic interpretation and, finally, we end up with a problematic belief.

There are a few ways we can use the Ladder of Inference. First, it's a reminder that all beliefs emerge from data we encounter. When I'm confronted by actions such as those Ms. Russo was taking, the Ladder is a reminder to surface the data points at the roots of her belief. The Ladder also reminds me that new beliefs are constructed when we see, understand, and take in data points that are different from those we've fixated on. If Angela believes that boys can't handle group work, her beliefs will be challenged and might shift if she sees her own male students and others being successful in group work. The Ladder of Inference directs me to help clients broaden the data set from which they are making assumptions, to guide them to see more data, and then to explore different ways to interpret that data.

With Ms. Russo, I used the Ladder to construct questions that helped her reinterpret her students' desire to speak Spanish and to come to different conclusions. When I asked Ms. Russo about her family background and their attitudes about language and English, I intended to help her see how she'd arrived at her belief that only English should be spoken. As she did this, she recognized the limitations in her own beliefs and she uncovered a willingness to shift her practices.

We can use the Ladder with a client to help them see how they've arrived at beliefs and to help them create new beliefs. You can literally put the graphic in front of them and describe the process we go through and then ask them if they'd be interested in unpacking their beliefs. Inviting your clients into an exercise like this communicates your confidence in their intellect and willingness. You don't need to hide all your cards or strategies or tools—engage them as colleagues, and begin with an assumption that they want to learn, grow, and refine their teaching practices.

The Ladder of Inference Questioning Strategies described below correlate to each rung on the Ladder and help a client unpack their beliefs. Sometimes I show a client the Ladder and explain the concept, and then we try to take apart a belief, or sometimes I just ask the questions. You don't have to go in any specific order—sometimes it can help to start at the bottom and go up, and sometimes I jump to questions on one rung and then work up and down.

Sometimes, when using the Ladder of Inference, I've seen beliefs crumble in front of my eyes, and sometimes I've seen beliefs become unstable and then fall apart over time. The Ladder helps us to distance ourselves from our beliefs just a little bit—just enough so that we can muster the courage and will to examine them. When we explore beliefs, we open them up to being changed.

The Ladder of Inference Questioning Strategies

Actions:
- Can you identify the belief you hold that led to that behavior?
- What might be the consequences—intended and unintended—of acting out of this belief?
- What's possible if you act from this belief? What might be possible if you weren't holding this belief?

Beliefs:
- Which experiences might have led you to hold that belief?
- Which assumptions (or conclusions) might be holding up that belief?
- If this is the belief that you hold, how will that affect the actions you take?

(continued)

- Are there any other beliefs you might hold based on the meaning you've made and the assumptions you've drawn?

Conclusions:
- I hear that you've drawn a conclusion about [belief]. Can you identify the assumptions on which that's built?
- How do you think your culture and background have led you to the conclusion you've drawn?

Assumptions:
- Can you name the assumptions you're making?
- Can you identify any of the roots of that assumption? Where do you think it came from? Which experiences?
- Are there any other assumptions you might be able to come to based on this meaning?

Meaning:
- I'm hearing that you made meaning about [an experience you had/something you heard/something you saw]. Can you tell me about the meaning you made?
- Which elements of the meaning that you made are informed by your cultural and personal background?
- How do you think your cultural and personal background affected the meaning that you made [of that experience/what you heard/saw]?
- I hear that those specific data points caught your attention. What was the meaning that you made of them?
- I hear that you saw X, and the meaning you made was [paraphrase]. Does that seem accurate?
- Is there any other meaning you could make from this data?

Data:
- I hear that you saw/heard/experienced X. I want to make sure I heard this right—you're saying you saw/heard/experienced [paraphrase].
- Can you identify the data that you selected from the entire experience? If you imagine that your mind is a video camera recording everything, can you name the specific data points that you latched on to?

Beliefs Change When We Encounter New Information

Beliefs change when we're confronted with data that doesn't fit what we believe—when we experience what's called "cognitive dissonance"—*and* when that confrontation happens within a trusting relationship. When we're confronted with data that doesn't fit what we believe, without trust and psychological safety, we run the risk of the backfire effect (described in Chapter 4) and of strengthening a faulty belief.

Recall that the Ladder of Inference explains how beliefs are formed when we select data and attach meaning to it. Stephanie had beliefs about her students that were based on fragments of data—she knew little about them and the communities to which they belonged. This meant that the distorted, inaccurate, and racist beliefs about black and brown kids that circulate widely in our society became core data points for Stephanie—permeating her unconscious and resulting in actions that included low-rigor instruction.

As I recognized how little Stephanie actually knew her students, I constructed activities to help her learn more about them. This included walking around the neighborhood, shopping in the stores her students' families shopped in, doing home visits, listening to parents/guardians, reading about immigration to California, visiting the Oakland Library's history room, reading memoirs by black and brown people, reading about teaching black and brown kids, and more. As Stephanie acquired knowledge—firsthand knowledge about the community she served—she had more data from which to create beliefs. Sometimes, we just need more information.

There are many ways that coaches can help clients obtain new information. In addition to the approach I took with Stephanie, we can gather data through surveys, capture video of teachers and students, share observations, model instructional practices, observe effective teachers together, and provide books, articles, and additional resources. This is how coaching activities help change beliefs. You can learn more about coaching activities in my book *The Art of Coaching* (2013). What's critical is that as we engage clients in activities, we help them process and take stock of the new information they're acquiring. As they name these data points, we need to help them see how their beliefs are shifting.

The goal of Phase 2 of Transformational Coaching is to help clients see the impact of their behaviors. During this phase, they'll likely have a range of emotions, which we can help them process, and then we can guide them to create new behaviors. Those new behaviors are sustained when they are built on new beliefs.

Beliefs Change When Our Core Identity Is Preserved

Human beings are psychologically wired for self-preservation. We don't put ourselves—including our sense of self—in harm's way. Our sense of self includes a core identity as a "good person" (Chugh, 2018). Stephanie thought of herself as a good person who helped others—many of us in education think of ourselves this way. Defining racism, as I described in Chapter 4, was essential to help Stephanie preserve a sense of self. It allowed me to suggest that she could be a good person who acted in racist ways. Defining terms and understanding history is not just an intellectual activity—it's essential to allow ourselves to reflect on our core identities and feel like they will stay intact while we scrutinize our beliefs and actions.

You can't just smash someone's identity, or ask them to shatter it, and then leave them in pieces. You'll face resistance if this is your plan. Coaches can help clients to cultivate a new or expanded identity by supporting them to create a vision for themselves, to explore who they want to be, and to connect with what might be possible in an expanded sense of self (you'll read an example of how to do this in Chapter 10). When we use a Transformational Coaching model, and we coach around ways of being, this is what we're doing—we're inviting someone to reflect on who they want to be. Yes, we're wired for self-preservation, but we're also wired to crave learning and growth. When conditions are good, (when these six conditions in which beliefs change are present) we leap toward opportunities for growth.

In Transformational Coaching, we attend to a client's core identity when we are in Phase 2: Recognize Impact, and in Phase 3: Explore Emotions. These are prime moments to unpack what it means to be a good person, as well as to act on inequitable beliefs. As we learn together about racism—as well as classism, sexism, and all the ways in which groups have been othered—we must attend to the emotions that surface in ourselves and in others. We are human beings. Human beings have emotions. A Transformational Coach, a responsible, ethical coach acknowledges, accepts, and makes space for emotions—for their own and those of their clients.

Beliefs Change When We See the Benefits of Changing a Belief

For a while, I despaired about the school district I worked in. I often told my coach: "This district is so messed up. It's toxic and dysfunctional at its very core."

The first time I said this, she said, "Is that the truth or is it a belief?" Her question unnerved me—I thought I'd been sharing an objective truth.

After yet another rant about the hopelessness of my district, my coach said, "What do you gain from holding this belief?" In the moment, I responded defensively. I was confused by the question. I thought about it for a few weeks and realized that the belief allowed me to feel superior to others, it protected me from disappointment, and it allowed me to make excuses about the ways I behaved. I often went to meetings that felt like a tremendous waste of my time, where I was critical of the way the meeting was run, and of the leaders, and yet I didn't offer solutions. And then I'd complain to my coach about these meetings.

One day, my coach asked: "What would it be like if you went to one of those meetings open to the possibility that it could be useful?"

I admitted: "I guess I might feel better. Less tired. More engaged." I trusted her, but I didn't want to let go of my belief in the dysfunction of my district. It let me off the hook for being truly emotionally invested in my work; it kept me from disappointment and hurt.

My coach dangled the possibility of an alternate belief in front of me. "What if," she said, "you believed that it was possible for one of those meetings to be meaningful and useful?" She helped me see how tempting this belief could be to try on—just for one meeting. She helped me see how the new belief might align with my values. She pushed me to accept that I could be courageous and face disappointment and hurt again. She helped me connect to my integrity and my longing for hope.

I went to one of these meetings intent on being open to possibility, committed to dropping my belief that the district was deeply dysfunctional—just for that one meeting. This new belief felt like a costume—stiff and unfamiliar. And yet, I was curious about what might happen if I wore it. What happened in that meeting was that I felt a little bit better—during and after—and I had a meaningful conversation with a colleague. I expressed my ideas more clearly than I had before, and other people were receptive to them. My belief shifted—perhaps just an inch to the left of "this district is dysfunctional at its core," but it did shift.

We are willing to change our beliefs when we identify a self-serving reason to do so. And that is absolutely OK. We become open to change when we recognize how a belief has limited our ability to feel efficacious, to experience joy, to form relationships with others, or to do what we want to do—be that pursue to a dream job or to ensure that all of our students graduate. We're compelled to change a belief when we see how our life will be better if we do so. We're receptive to investigating beliefs when our willingness is genuine and we don't feel like anyone is forcing us to change them.

Beliefs provide us with a sense of security. They help us understand ourselves and the world around us. Giving up a belief can mean we lose a sense of security or of being grounded—so in order to change a belief, we need to recognize compelling reasons. We have to see how changing a belief might make our lives better. Although we're often fearful, when offered a glimpse of what might be possible, we'll take the risks to question our beliefs or behaviors.

In Transformational Coaching, there are multiple opportunities to guide clients to see the benefits of changing a belief. We invite them to see how changing a belief can help them manifest their vision of themselves as a teacher, feel emotionally better, and see different outcomes from their students. In Phase 2, as we guide clients to recognize the impact they are having in their classroom, they come to see the benefit of changing a belief. As we support clients to explore their emotions, we can point at the potential of shifting beliefs. In Phase 4, as we create new practices, we can again help clients connect to the potential in shifting, expanding, and changing beliefs.

Beliefs Change When We Recognize Alternate Beliefs

Our willingness to release beliefs is increased when we see a new belief to adopt. I let go of my belief that my district was "so dysfunctional" when I could substitute that belief with, "There are pockets of possibility and hope in this district."

For the first couple of years that George was a teacher, he struggled with kids who had learning differences. He felt ineffective with them, and he told colleagues: "Let's not put kids with IEPs [Individualized Education Programs] in my class. I suck at teaching them." With the support of his coach, George realized that he held a belief that he couldn't teach kids with IEPs. When they explored the impact of this belief, George recognized that it kept him from serving every child—which felt misaligned to his values. He also didn't like feeling that he had a limited skill set. He wanted to rid himself of his belief that he couldn't teach kids with IEPs, but he didn't know what that meant, or what would take its place. He came up with this: "I don't have the skills to be effective with students with IEPs, but I can learn them because I want to be effective with all students."

Adopting a growth mindset helps us identify alternate beliefs while we rid ourselves of the old. Angela, or any teacher who believes that kids can only learn if she's teaching the whole class at the same time, could say, "I believe that I can learn how to teach students in different ways," or "I believe that students want to be successful when working in stations." A teacher might decide that she no longer wants to believe that eye-rolling is a sign of disrespect—for one reason, she's getting in trouble for sending so many students to the office. So, she might tell herself, "I don't know what eye-rolling means right now, and I'm willing to stay open to find out." This statement of belief serves as a scaffold as she releases an old belief and adopts a new one.

This part of shifting beliefs is uncomfortable. It's why Phase 3 of Transformational Coaching is to explore emotions. As we become aware of old beliefs—beliefs that we recognize as having been harmful to others—we may experience sadness, guilt, and regret. Stephanie experienced a lot of intense emotions as she came to terms with the beliefs she held. It was my responsibility as a coach to hold space for her to process those, and it was a necessary part of coaching for equity.

This entire book is about how to change beliefs so that behaviors change. It's about exploring how our beliefs are influenced by our way of being—and how our beliefs create our way of being. And it's about how our way of being affects our behaviors. These six conditions are useful to understand because they point us to actions. Table 6.1 summarizes these conditions.

Table 6.1 Implications for Action

Beliefs change when	Implications for a coach
1. We feel safe enough.	• Build trust. • Cultivate a growth mindset. • Coach for emotional resilience. • Communicate confidence in the process and conviction that it's worth the discomfort.
2. We understand how the belief originated.	• Use the Ladder of Inference to help a client understand how beliefs are constructed. • Engage in conversations to excavate beliefs.
3. We encounter new information.	• Gather and share data, surveys, and video. • Read texts. • Listen to others.
4. Our core identity is preserved.	• Coach to affirm a more expansive sense of self. • Help the client connect with their purpose as an educator.
5. We see the benefits of changing a belief.	• Find a meaningful entry point to diminish resistance. • Help the client anchor in their purpose and legacy. • Raise awareness about the negative and unintended consequences of holding the belief. • Help the client see how releasing an emotion could feel liberating.
6. We recognize alternate beliefs.	• Scaffold the learning. • Offer alternate beliefs. • Help a client see a wider set of data.

How to Build Trust

Trust is perhaps more than anything else the critical element that allows Transformational Coaching to work. Building trust is essential to change beliefs—it's how you create the safety that I described in the first condition that allows beliefs to change. Here and there in this book, I've made nods to how you build trust, but I want to be more explicit about the key elements. (There's a lot more on how to build trust in my books *The Art of Coaching, The Art of Coaching Teams*, and *Onward*, and in an online course that you can find on my website, http://bright-morningteam.com).

Trust is *an emotion*—when we trust someone, we feel a certain way about them. We trust people who have our best interests at heart and who see our potential. We trust people who are humble and who refrain from judgment. We trust people who speak and act with integrity. When we trust someone, we believe they can do what they say they're going to do. If they agree to do something, we have confidence that they have the skills, abilities, and knowledge to keep their word.

If conversations are the bridges where we'll cross chasms, those bridges need to be trustworthy. If we, as coaches and leaders, are the architects and builders of bridges, it's imperative that we understand how to build trust and that we do it well. If we're going to invite people to walk across the Golden Gate Bridge–equivalent of conversations about race and white supremacy—which can be a beautiful walk in a beautiful place, albeit suspended far above a massive ocean—we need to know how to create structures that will support the weight of these conversations. Tried-and-true trust-building strategies can support this work. Let's unpack several high-leverage activities.

To Build Trust with Someone, Strengthen Your Own Emotional Intelligence

Emotional intelligence is the foundation of an effective leader (Goleman, 2001). It's our ability to understand ourselves as social and emotional beings and our ability to build healthy, trusting relationships with others. Our emotional intelligence allows us to understand ourselves and why we do things, to take responsibility for our actions and mistakes and to apologize. Building emotional intelligence is a lifelong process, as we are constantly changing and evolving. As you deepen your understanding of your emotions, you will see how your ability to build trusting relationships improves. My book, *Onward* (2018a) is a useful starting place for this learning.

Working with Stephanie pushed me to explore my own emotions, especially as they came up in response to her tears and naïveté. There were times when I felt pushed to the edge of my ability to navigate my emotions—like the time when I lied to get out of a conversation with her. I explored those emotions by talking to my husband about working with her, and in the conversation I had with myself. I also frequently reminded myself to name the feelings that were arising for me—be that anger, fear, doubt, or hope—and to accept those, as well as to remember that they would pass. Using my emotional intelligence allowed me to show up and coach Stephanie without reacting in the moment to what she said and did, and allowed me to not project my unprocessed emotions on to her.

To Build Trust with Someone, Be Transparent

If you're like me and most people I know, it will take practice to find the appropriate level of transparency when building relationships with clients. Too much transparency, and you may not be filtering your thoughts enough. Too much transparency can reveal all your own areas for growth and sometimes also your unhealed pain. But not enough transparency, and people wonder what you're really up to—what you're really thinking. I find it's especially important to be transparent about your agenda. When someone seems to be questioning it or when you get a sense that they think you are not speaking honestly, you can say:

> My intention in this conversation is to unpack beliefs about students and their communities. I'm nervous to talk about racism because it's still hard for me to talk about and I don't know everything, but my hope is that this is a conversation in which we both learn.

Make sure that in being transparent, the focus of the conversation doesn't shift on to you—this is not about you and you don't need to share too much.

When I told Stephanie that I wondered if her tears prevented us from having meaningful conversations about her teaching and students, I was being transparent. When I said I believed she could be a very effective teacher for black and brown kids, I was being transparent. When I said that I wished we had more teachers who came from the same background as our students, I was being transparent. Transparency is honesty blended with integrity. By revealing my thoughts and saying that I could see the elephant in the room, I built trust with Stephanie.

To Build Trust with Someone, Keep Your Word

Overpromising is a common mistake coaches make. We do this because we think it'll get us in good graces with others and we want to prove our value. Then we realize we've overcommitted and we break our promises. This erodes trust. Commit to only what you can really do well. Make sure that what you're offering *is* something that you have the skills and knowledge to do—and to do well. Learn time management skills so that you can keep your word. If you do overcommit, take responsibility for doing so—and then, especially if this is a pattern, figure out why you overcommit and what needs to happen so that you stop. Finally, keep your word about who you will talk to about the coaching you're doing. Trust can be irrevocably damaged if you breach confidentiality agreements.

To Build Trust with Someone, Know What You're Doing

We trust people who seem to know what they are doing. When they agree to take something on—to plan a meeting or take a group of kids on a field trip, we assume they are confident in their ability to do this thing. Don't agree to do things that you don't know how to do! This means you need to know your own skills well, you need to accurately evaluate your capacity, and you need to communicate clearly and with confidence what it is you can do. This is tricky because we distrust people who are arrogant—they can come off as overestimating their abilities. Finding the right tone takes some practice.

By the time Stephanie asked me, "Do you think I'm racist?" (at the end of Chapter 2), she trusted my abilities to have that conversation. When I told her that I was confident that the conversation we'd have would be meaningful and that it would help her grow, this affirmed her trust in me. I was reminding her that I knew what I was doing, that I wasn't going to get emotionally reactive myself and derail the conversation, and that like many conversations before, this one would be helpful. And in contrast to some coaching conversations I'd had in the past, I did know what I was doing. I'd done my homework and prepared and I was ready.

To Build Trust with Someone, Listen

Listening might be the most powerful tool for creating trusting relationships. We trust people who listen well—who listen without judgment, without interrupting us, without offering solutions. We trust people who communicate acceptance of what we say—even if they don't agree with us, they recognize what we're saying as our reality. We trust people who listen with empathy and with their full attention.

We trust people whom we can sense are listening with their heart. Learning to listen well is a remarkably challenging skill. It takes intention and time. And it's a skill that will make all the difference in the world to you in your interpersonal relationships—not just in your coaching. In each of my books and in multiple articles, I've written about how to refine your listening skills. I also teach listening skills in my in-person and online courses. Please check out these resources available on http://brightmorningteam.com.

To Build Trust with Someone, Be Unattached to Outcome

This is a somewhat paradoxical concept, because as a coach for equity, we are committed to children getting what they deserve—and I'm attached to that outcome. But there's no way I can be absolutely sure about *how* we'll reach that outcome. In coaching conversations, I hold my commitment to an outcome for each meeting lightly. I enter with goals and intentions for where the conversation will go, and I am flexible and responsive to what happens. I tell myself to be unattached to a specific outcome and see where things go. When I hold tightly to predetermined outcomes in a conversation, I can be experienced as passing judgment or holding an agenda. This undermines trust. I can plan for a coaching conversation and still be open to letting the conversation go where it needs to go. Taking this stance, I communicate confidence in my client's role in the conversation, trusting them to help guide the conversation in its most useful direction. Sometimes when conversations don't end up where I wanted them to go, I realize that they've ended up somewhere better—somewhere more powerful than what I'd imagined. When I'm unattached to specific outcomes, I hold my ego lightly—I recognize that I can't know everything, and I trust the process of coaching.

It's useful to think about trust less as a static state, and more as a dynamic experience that waxes and wanes. When trust feels fragile or even breaks, there's tremendous potential to make it stronger than ever through a repair process. And trust can be strengthened through this process of repair. As we coach for equity, we must always be attending to the quality and condition of trust.

What to Say When You Hear Racist Comments

I'm offering you the sentence stems and questions in Table 6.2 with the hope they'll help you consider a range of responses to use when you hear a client say something that's overtly or unconsciously racist.

Table 6.2 Possible Responses to Racist Comments.

What is said	Possible responses
What do you expect? These parents don't care about their kids.	<ul><li>Tell me more about how you came to hold that belief.</li><li>What does "caring" look like to you?</li><li>Would you be open to learning more about their parents?</li><li>It must be confusing to see parents who don't seem to care about their kids. Is this an assumption you'd like to unpack?</li></ul>
There's no way these kids can master all of the standards.	<ul><li>What are you getting from holding that belief? How do you benefit from that belief? What would be possible if you let it go?</li><li>What would have to be different for you to be able to say, "I know these kids can master all the standards"?</li></ul>
I can't do this. I just can't teach these kids.	<ul><li>If I could wave a magic wand and make that belief disappear, how would you act? How would you be?</li><li>If you believe that you can't teach these kids, what actions are available for you to take? What do you want to do?</li></ul>
The reason that our black male students aren't successful is because they don't have role models. What can we do about that?	<ul><li>What do you think our black male students need?</li><li>I wonder if that's what our black male students—and their families—think. Would you be willing to learn what they think?</li><li>What's within your sphere of influence then? What can you do to have a positive impact on our black male students?</li><li>What do you think we could do as a school to hire more black males who could serve as role models?</li></ul>

Table 6.2 (*Continued*)

What is said	Possible responses
I can't teach these kids. Why don't you coach their elementary school teachers? They're the ones who need coaching. It's not my fault they're so far behind.	• It sounds like you're feeling sad that our students are so far behind. And it's not your fault. So, what do you want to do to help them get on grade level? • All teachers need and deserve coaching. Which aspects of your teaching practice do you want to work on? • It sounds like you're feeling frustrated by the limits of your own abilities. What is it exactly that you feel like you can't do?
I don't send them to the "timeout chair," I send them to "isolation," because these kids get that reference. They know about prisons, so I make it easier for them to understand my discipline system.	• That language makes it seem like your classroom is a prison, and I doubt that's what you are intending to communicate. Can we explore your intentions? • It sounds like you've struggled to get kids to understand your approach to classroom management. Can we start there—with your management systems and approach—and then identify the language that's best to communicate it? • I don't think you're trying to prepare your students to be good inmates, right? What is your vision for your students? What do you imagine, and want, them to be doing when they're 23 years old?
She'll end up pregnant at 15. That's how those Mexicans are. I'm not wasting my time teaching her chemistry.	• I can hear that you're feeling uncertain about what will happen to that student—and every student in our school takes chemistry in eighth grade. So, let's figure out how you can be successful with her. • How have you arrived at this belief about Mexicans? Which of your experiences has led you to believe this? • Who deserves to learn chemistry?

(*continued*)

Table 6.2 *(Continued)*

What is said	Possible responses
Can you come to the conference I have to have with his dad? I'm afraid to be alone with him. Middle Eastern men have no boundaries.	• What are you concerned would happen? • What in your own cultural background do you think has led you to hold this belief about Middle Eastern men? • I'm willing to be there with you, and I can hear that you're still learning about our community, but you're also expressing some dehumanizing stereotypes about Middle Eastern men. Would you be willing to explore where those came from?
This is America. They should just speak English.	• I'm hearing fear. Can you help me understand what that's about? • Where did this belief you hold come from? • What might happen if they spoke Spanish in class? What's the worst-case scenario?
If we don't strictly enforce rules, they'll be out of control. These kids need tight structures and routines.	• What else do you think our students need to be successful in school—aside from routines and structure? • I think I'm hearing concern and care for your students. Is that right? Can we explore more of their needs—including what they need to feel loved and cared for in our community? • Can we explore where your fears about our students are coming from? • I'm aware that you don't share the racial or cultural background of our students, and I think it would be helpful if we explored how your identity shapes the way you see and understand our students. Would you be willing to do that?

Table 6.2 *(Continued)*

What is said	Possible responses
I'm letting her draw today because she's had such a hard week, and if I push her, then she has a meltdown and disrupts everyone's learning.	• Giving her permission to opt out of learning communicates a belief in what she's capable of doing. If your goal is that she learns, can we explore other options for how to help her manage her frustrations? • I wonder what her mother would want her daughter to be doing in class. Would it be helpful if we met with her and asked her this, and also asked her for insights into how to work with her child? • I hear your commitment to every child learning and that you're not sure what to do with one student. I hear that you've identified a learning area for yourself. Let's explore that.
He always sits alone, in the back of the classroom, because that's the only way he can stay focused and quiet.	• How do you want him to remember you, as his teacher? • How does this decision align to your core values? • What do you know about what he likes to do or what he's capable of doing? • It sounds like you're holding some beliefs about what he needs in order to be successful. Let's unpack those. • I wonder how he feels being isolated. I wonder what he tells his father about your class. • I've observed him in other classes and have seen him working well with groups. Would you be willing to explore what's happening in those other classes that enables him to be successful there? Could we observe him in other classes and talk to those teachers about what they do?

How you respond to statements such as those in the first column is informed by your role and purpose. If you are a coach, your purpose is to instigate reflection, insight, and learning. It's worth repeating this to yourself many times, because often when we hear the kinds of statements that I've listed, you might long to say something more direct, or something about your own feelings or experiences. That would be appropriate if you're speaking to a colleague, student teacher, supervisor, or someone with whom you don't have a coaching relationship.

If you are a positional leader, then you need to uphold your organization's vision and mission, especially its commitment to equity. If you have offered your staff opportunities to unlearn white supremacy and to create equitable classrooms, then you might say something like this:

> What you've just said is racist. Let's talk about how you can continue to learn about what you just expressed, because our school is committed to dismantling racism.

Or you might say something like this:

> The beliefs you expressed don't align to our mission. If you're willing to explore those and how they are harmful, then I'd love for you to continue being a member of our community. If you're open to it, you can start working with our coach to learn right away. If you're not willing to learn about how racism harms everyone, then you may not be a good fit for our school.

Of course, positional leaders can and should also use coaching strategies with those they supervise to help them grow, so it's also entirely appropriate to use any of the "Possible Responses to Racist Comments" in Table 6.2.

Although the following section describes what people of color experience, it is important for readers who are white to read this section as well in order to understand the realities that people of color face.

For People of Color Doing this Work

For many of us, reading the statements in the opening of Chapter 6 is uniquely and excruciatingly painful. We might be reminded of times when we were students and we experienced racism, or of incidents that happened yesterday or today when we were in schools, or of experiences that our own children, nieces, and nephews are facing. The words and actions that we witness land in our minds, bodies, hearts, and spirits in ways that wound. I know that we experience this work differently than our most committed and honorable white colleagues, and that we may need different medicine. Because of this, I feel compelled to share a handful of additional reflections on what it's been like for me to teach, coach, lead, and work in schools as a person of color who is committed to justice and liberation.

At times, this work has been exhausting—physically exhausting—to engage in the daily battles (big and small) of being a woman of color in this world, and then to walk through schools where I witness a never-ending stream of inequities, and then to fight for my son's right to dignity. It's been emotionally taxing to ride the waves of rage and grief, feeling resentful that so much responsibility for righting the wrongs of the past and present falls on my shoulders and on the shoulders of people of color. And this is just the tip of the resentment: it's just the professional resentment. That sits on top of a heap of resentment about white privilege. I've sat with so much anger about how my white friends and colleagues experience life, about the choices they've been able to make—to move anywhere in this country and feel comfortable and safe. To open children's books and find their images reflected back at them. To watch TV shows and not feel dehumanized. To go to a doctor and not suspect that they're giving you this medication or not giving you that one because of what they assume about you and your people. On top of anger at my colleagues who ascend professional ladders with more ease, get more exposure, and are paid more because of their identity markers. Who can send their sons to almost any school and be fairly confident that they'll get the education that they deserve. Their stomach isn't in a knot when their 14-year-old son walks to a 7-Eleven wearing a hoodie. They can walk around a department store in San Francisco and not have a security guard follow them. I'm tired of having what I know questioned and challenged—of being asked for the research that backs this and that idea—of having my intellect doubted. I'm tired of being told I'm "so articulate" and that I speak English so well. I'm tired of being asked if I'm a legal citizen. I'm tired of white people trying to prove how woke they are. And on and on and on. You know what I'm talking about, right? The experiences, the resentment, the exhaustion. The rage.

And then, because I choose to be a coach and a leader, because I choose the path I'm on, and because I won't let white supremacy and patriarchy deprive me of the inner peace that's *mine*, I am able to tend to my needs, anger, and grief and support others on their journey of becoming an equitable teacher and leader.

I've experienced compassion-fatigue listening to both people of color and white people talk about their experiences with racism. I've felt pressured to congratulate white people for the insights they make, for the biases they reveal, and for the awareness they gain of their own monumental privileges. I've felt depleted by the fatigue of coaching people who (between us) *take so fucking long to change*. My patience has been tested over and over and over, and my patience has grown in measures I never imagined it would. And that feels good. That insight brings me relief and satisfaction. My conviction that our country and our world can learn, understand, grow, and heal has grown. And that too brings relief. My sense of what's possible—for myself and for our world—has never felt greater. I feel more powerful than I've ever felt. I am more powerful than I've ever been.

Here's what helped: Acquiring language to describe my experiences, emotions, and thoughts. When I learned the term *microaggression*, I felt empowered to describe a daily experience—something I'd sensed but questioned because that's what we do when we experience a microaggression. We wonder: *Am I imagining that slight? Am I taking things too personally or reading into something? Am I crazy?* When we can name something, we have power. Learning the language to speak about systemic oppression has given me tools to respond to it.

Conversely, silence has also helped. Silence is a balm. Seclusion is frequently necessary for me. So is tending to my body. I withdraw, rest, and recharge on a daily basis and during and after moments of intense work. Meditation is one way I do this, reading fiction is another, and sometimes watching TV helps me recharge. Walking always boosts my mental, emotional, and physical well-being. Being in nature—amongst the redwoods or by the ocean—is incomparably restorative. My body responds to acupuncture, massage, and kale. I am not apologetic about taking time for myself, I don't make excuses or downplay my needs for self-care, and I allocate resources to my well-being. I reject the capitalist, patriarchal messages about how my body should be, what it should do, or how productive it should be. I let my body rest, find ease, and experience joy.

Understanding myself and my own shit has helped. Some of my shit is a result of the pain and suffering I've experienced from living as we all do in systems of oppression—and some of my shit has nothing to do with them. I've taken responsibility for who I am and how I show up in the world, for how I communicate and how I express my emotions. As I've done this, my sphere of control has expanded.

Understanding how I've perpetuated pain—how I've unintentionally contributed to the oppression of marginalized people—helps me stay humble and human. It helps me have empathy, and as I look at my own learning and growth, I'm more able to help others in their learning journeys. Recognizing the biases that I've acted on, and the resulting guilt and shame I've felt when I've become aware of them, has helped me stay committed to a learning process.

It helps me to remember that white women are not my enemy. That they, too, suffer from white supremacy and patriarchy, that their tears are not the problem, and that they can be our allies. We can acknowledge fragility and fears, and pass boxes of tissues, and continue conversations about race.

Meditation has helped tremendously. The meditation I practice (mindfulness from the Insight or *Vipassana* tradition) emphasizes cultivating nonjudgmental awareness and compassion—for ourselves and all living things. This practice, and the Buddhist teachings from which it emerges, offers me tranquility, equanimity, perspective, and compassion. I've learned how to be with others who experience distress and how to not become exhausted or depleted by it. I've learned how to be kind to myself.

My community helps. I'm selective about the people I spend time with. I've purged my social networks of people who are toxic or draining, or who aren't willing to examine their own biases. It's OK to draw boundaries, and to find people who nourish you, with whom you can learn and grow, and who listen to you. I need to be around people of color—and specifically, around people of color who are on their own journey of awareness and healing. And I am intentional about finding white allies—those who are on their own journey of learning and healing. I also have an extensive community of people who support me—but whom I've never met. They are writers, musicians, artists, filmmakers, designers, healers, leaders, and creators of all kinds, and folks from marginalized communities. When I read their words, play their music, or listen to them speak, I'm nourished through a sense of solidarity and I gain new insights. We live in an age when it's increasingly easy to find such a community via the Internet, and I'm grateful for that. My community also includes a handful of coaches, healers, therapists, and wise teachers who have been essential on my journey. Find your people. You need your people.

And finally, curse when you want to curse. Anticipate how your words might land, and where it might be better or not-so-wise to curse, and then say what you want to say—if it helps you release some of the suffering. This isn't permission to shit all over everyone everywhere, but it is permission to say, "This is fucked up"— if that's what your heart and mind want to say (because this situation we're in *is* fucked up—and you can quote me on that).

Here's what I've learned as a person of color doing the work of justice and liberation: You can be tired. And angry. And you can despair. Accept those waves of emotion and learn how to move through them. You can draw boundaries and say "No," and you can choose a different path if you want. Sometimes you might feel despair or discomfort, but settle into the discomfort—it will pass—and stay open to the lessons. Because this work can also bring you transformative hope and freedom. You'll find sisters and brothers all over the world and build a community that's strong and healthy and beautiful. You'll connect with your own resources and abilities, which are deeper than you ever suspected and that are unimaginably powerful. There is great joy to be found in our own internal power.

There is so much joy to be discovered.

I wish that we could continue this conversation in person, that we could sit together—perhaps on the beach or around a fire or at a table laden with delicious food—and share stories. We will heal in community.

Before You Go . . .

Read the following prompts and select two or three that feel most valuable to you based on where you are in your learning journey. Spend meaningful time considering your reflection before moving on.

REFLECT ON THIS CHAPTER

- How do the ideas in this chapter help you understand how Stephanie's beliefs changed?
- What insight did you get into working with the teachers you coach from this chapter?
- What did it feel like to read the statements in the first column of Table 6.2: Possible Responses to Racist Comments? What came up for you?
- How do you think your identity markers and your experience affected how you read the information in Table 6.2: Possible Responses to Racist Comments? What do you think it was like for someone who doesn't share your identity markers to read?

REFLECT ON YOUR PRACTICE

On Beliefs
- Can you identify a belief that you've held that has changed? Maybe a belief about what you could or couldn't do, or a belief about other people?
- Think about how that belief changed. Under which conditions did it change? What were the pivotal events or experiences that led to the belief changing? Which emotions came up in the process?

- Looking back, can you see how the belief was formed? What data or experiences did the belief emerge from?
- What did you lose from changing the belief? What did you gain from changing the belief?
- Some beliefs may have crumbled quickly whereas others slowly dissolved. Can you identify a belief that was instantly vaporized and another one that took a while to be deconstructed?
- At which points (if any) in this chapter did you feel your own beliefs being challenged? What is the belief you hold that felt challenged?

On Trust
- Call to mind someone from your professional life you really trust. How do you feel when you're with them? What is it about them that makes you feel this way?
- Call to mind someone from your professional world whom you don't trust. What do they say and do that makes you distrust them?
- Who do you think really trusts you? What is it that you do that results in them trusting you?

TO DO

- Identify three things you'll do differently in your coaching or leadership practice as a result of the content of this chapter.
- Select one of the ways of building trust that you'd like to do more intentionally and with more impact. Identify what it would take for you to do that.
- Identify how you might be able to use the "Possible Responses" in Table 6.2. This could mean that you'd use these responses, or this could mean that they provoke reflection on other aspects of your coaching.

Principles of Transformational Coaching

- Compassion
- **Curiosity**
- Connection
- Courage
- Purpose

Curiosity: As we suspend our judgments and opinions, we seek deep understanding of other people, of ourselves, and of the situations we're in. Our curiosity expands through our willingness to be changed by what we hear.

In her TED Talk, the writer, Chimamanda Ngozi Adichie, said:

The single story creates stereotypes, and the problem with stereotypes is not that they are untrue, but that they are incomplete. They make one story become the only story.

- Which are the single stories you might be carrying?
- Which of your beliefs are you curious about exploring?

In that same TED Talk, Chimamanda Ngozi Adichie also said:

Stories matter. Many stories matter. Stories have been used to dispossess and to malign. But stories can also be used to empower and to humanize. Stories can break the dignity of a people but stories can also repair that dignity.

- Whose stories are you willing to listen to?
- Whose stories are you willing to be changed by?

CHAPTER 7

What You Need to Know about Emotions

Transform yourself to transform the world
—GRACE LEE BOGGS

If you want to go straight to a story, you could skip this chapter for now. You could come back here after reading Chapters 9 through 12 to gain more understanding about the knowledge base of understanding emotions.

The most frequently asked question I get about coaching is: "How do you coach a resistant teacher?" This was also my question for many years, and resistance was never stronger in the people I coached than when I was attempting to address inequities. Let's get to the headline: *Resistance is an expression of strong emotions.* Learn how to coach emotions and you'll never encounter resistance again.

There's no way you can coach for equity and *not* encounter emotions. We are humans, and humans have emotions. And yet, for the most part, we're an emotionally illiterate society—we don't know what emotions are, we often don't recognize when we're having them, and we don't know how to talk about them. With a deeper understanding of emotions and how to engage with them, and with a greater appreciation for emotions, you'll be far more prepared to coach for equity. I rarely experience resistance when I'm coaching—there might be a tense moment here or there, but I really can't recall the last time I coached a truly resistant person. You might be reading my anecdotes and thinking: *She's making this up. It's not this easy.* I hear your doubt and fear, and I hope I can continue to pull back the curtain on my coaching to help you understand the knowledge and skill that informs how I coach.

When coaching for equity, I also draw on knowledge of identity, the skills to coach with an awareness of racial identity, and an awareness of coaching across lines of difference. I imagine holding knowledge of emotions in one hand, and knowledge of identity in the other. Each informs the other, and each is critical in Transformational Coaching. In part, this is because emotions are culturally constructed and socially conditioned. Depending on our identity markers, we're likely to have different understandings about how we can express emotions, and different values around emotions. Everyone experiences strong emotions, but it's the young white women I've coached who have cried the most, whereas older African American men rarely shed a tear. This has to do with the intersection between emotions, racial identity, gender, age, and systemic oppression. We'll explore this intersection in this chapter as well as in Chapter 8.

Toward an Appreciation of Emotions

How do you feel about emotions—your own and others'? That they are a bother? A messy and unpredictable thing to manage? An obstacle to coaching for equity? Your attitudes about emotions determine whether or not you will successfully coach for equity. This includes your feelings about the value of emotions and your willingness to learn about them and engage with them. What distinguishes Transformational Coaching from other approaches to change and school transformation, and from other coaching models, is that emotions are not only accepted and dealt with, but they are seen as the key that unlocks the pathway to equity, justice, and liberation.

Contextualizing Attitudes about Emotions

Accepting and embracing emotions is an act of political resistance. To do so is to reject systems of oppression that intentionally, by design, seek to dehumanize and subjugate us—they seek to severe the relationships we have with our bodies, minds, and hearts.

Some of the origins of contemporary patriarchy can be found in ancient Greece. Ancient Greece deeply influenced our political system in the United States and our social and cultural norms. Greek philosophers celebrated reason and the intellect while dismissing emotions, describing them as irrational forces that drive us to do harmful things and that threaten the fabric of the social order. Beliefs that many people hold today—that emotions are untrustworthy, childlike, and frivolous—were first described in this way in Greek, Roman, and early Christian writings. Emotions were believed to exist in the female domain, and expressing emotions was considered a sign of weakness—these values around emotions may sound familiar today. In ancient Greece, in order for someone to be successful, prosperous, politically powerful, and intellectually superior, emotions needed to be subdued, and controlled by reason. Things haven't changed much.

It's important that we have a basic understanding of this history because we almost take for granted that male domination is the natural order of things. History tells us that in pre-Hellenic Greece, and in other parts of the world, there were many cultures that were egalitarian. As patriarchal societies became dominant in Europe, many of these cultures were destroyed or repressed (Shlain, 1998; Miles, 1989).

In order for a system of oppression to effectively dominate, it must create and disseminate values that become invisible to those who are subjugated. It must be able to operate in every home, in every conversation, without military enforcement. The oppressed must unconsciously adopt these values, norms, and codes and act on them as if they are natural. We—the oppressed—must internalize the rules of the oppressors and believe them. We need to believe that boys shouldn't cry, that men should be stoic, that women can't show anger, that we shouldn't be afraid, and that girls should put on a happy face. We then regulate ourselves and uphold the system of oppression without being aware that's what we're doing. Patriarchy has maintained its power in part because it vilifies emotions; men and women have bought into this myth for thousands of years. When we reject and suppress emotions, we are cut off from what it means to be human.

Colonialism and capitalism are patriarchal systems: They flourish through violence, and they are maintained with violence. Men hold the political, economic, and social power in these systems in which women and everything in women's domains, including children and emotions, are inferior and need to be controlled. Messages about emotions have been refined, and new rules have been created—rules that define parameters for emotional experiences within identity markers.

These parameters become clearer when we think about what emotions we expect to see in people around us. What kind of emotional expression is acceptable from black women? From black men? From Asian men? From white women? From white men? What do we think and feel when someone from one of those groups expresses emotions in a way that is outside of what we consider acceptable? For example, part of the stereotype of blackness is that black people will be emotional; however, there are limits to how emotional black people can get, which emotions are OK to express, and where it's acceptable to express strong emotions. If black people violate those social norms on expressing emotions, the repercussions can be severe. Our intersectional bigotry affects how we perceive other people's emotions: if a black woman at work assertively advocates for her position, she may be seen as being pushy or angry. If a white woman does the same, she might be admired for "leaning in." Heteronormative white men are perhaps given the narrowest range of acceptable emotional expression: they are expected to be stoic and emotionless.

All of these norms mean one thing: we aren't allowed to authentically experience emotions. All emotions are mediated and regulated by systems of oppression: by patriarchy, capitalism, colonialism, and white supremacy. This has hurt men, women, and people in all economic classes and of all races and ethnicities. To understand why this is, you need to know what emotions are. Follow me on this exploration of emotions and identity.

What Is an Emotion?

An emotion is information. An emotion is a message that something matters. An emotion is the primary way that your body and mind send you signals about what you need. An emotion is a portal to wisdom. This is what systems of oppression have denied us access to: information and wisdom.

Emotions occur in our bodies and often have a mental or psychological component. Something happens and our bodies respond, and then our minds create meaning: A friend smiles at you and says, "Good morning," and your body produces dopamine (a feel-good hormone) and you think: *I'm glad to see her. I'm grateful for her friendship.* Or a seventh-grade student rolls her eyes at you, your body produces stress hormones, your heart beats a little faster, your breath gets shallow, and you think: *She's so disrespectful. I'm sick of teaching ungrateful kids.* This is what an emotion is: a cycle of mind-body experiences. How we respond in this experience, when it reaches the point of story-making, is what matters. And how we respond can take two directions: the path of liberation or the path of suffering.

Emotions are trying to give us information. The first monumental shift we could make in how we engage with emotions would be to see them as our friends. In so much of the Western world, we see the unknown as something scary, so we push it away. But what if we could welcome whatever emotion shows up? It would be a different world if we greeted an emotion warmly, invited it in for tea, and sat down with it and said: "Hi! I'm listening. What do you want to tell me?" To do that, we'll need to recognize *when* we're experiencing an emotion, and we'll need to hold a value that emotions are worthy. After that, we'll need resources for how to interpret what the emotion says and how to respond.

When emotions show up, our response can be found along a continuum. On one end, we experience emotions as a flood that sweeps us away. We can hurt people when we speak impulsively and lash out. In contrast, on the other end of this continuum, we suppress emotions. We ignore or avoid emotions, fearing that they will overwhelm us or could damage our relationships. We pretend they're not happening and try to work around them. Some people repress emotions indefinitely, or the emotions explode out. Emotions demand to be seen and heard, and they can come out unproductively in our words or in our silence, directed harmfully inward or outward.

For emotions to lead us down the path of liberation, we must welcome them, identify them, learn from them, and express them without blame or judgment. When we are open to emotions, we'll not only be more equipped to respond to uncomfortable or unpleasant emotions, but we'll be more responsive to the pleasant emotions. In shutting ourselves off from emotions, we're denying ourselves a whole lot of enjoyable emotions.

But what *is* the information that emotions are trying to give us? It is this information that makes them so dangerous—let's understand what emotions want to tell us.

Exploring and Embracing Our Needs

When an emotion comes knocking at your door, it's trying to tell you whether or not your needs are being met. When I get a message from a former student who fondly recalls being in my class, I feel joyful and grateful. These emotions show up to say: *Your need to matter, to make a contribution, and to live a purposeful life has been met.* When I recognize the feeling and the underlying need that's been met, I feel a sense of calm.

When my principal stops by my classroom and says, "Come to my office after school—we need to meet," I feel anxious and worried. These emotions show up to say: *Your need for clarity and peace of mind aren't being met.* When I recognize the feelings and the underlying needs that aren't being met, I can consider my options for how to respond to those feelings and unmet needs.

Emotions are information about whether our needs are being met. When our needs are met, we feel pleasant emotions. When our needs are unmet, we feel unpleasant emotions—and that's when we can be resistant.

Nonviolent Communication

When you think about human needs, you may recall Abraham Maslow, who presented the concept of needs in a hierarchy. His pyramid starts at the bottom with physiological needs, then safety needs, followed by needs for belonging, then for esteem, and finally at the top, needs for self-actualization. In the 1960s, psychologist Marshall Rosenberg built on Maslow's ideas and developed a conflict-resolution approach he called *nonviolent communication* (NVC). NVC is based on the assumption that all human beings have capacity for compassion, but people resort to violence or harmful behavior when they do not recognize more effective strategies for meeting needs. Rosenberg didn't believe in a hierarchy of needs but as constellations of needs. Figure 7.1 is a partial list of some human needs.

All of our needs matter, Rosenberg taught. It's this concept—and the strategies I've learned for how to respond to needs—that are the reason I don't experience resistance when I coach. I'm going to get back to that very soon, but first you need to understand this more—I draw on these ideas in every coaching conversation when emotions are present.

NVC teaches that we're all just doing our best to meet a need. Needs are *fundamental values* that drive our actions. They're what matter the most, the root reason for why we want what we want. Needs are universal and cross-cultural, and they are positive—as you read through the list in Figure 7.1, are there any that you don't appreciate? We all share the same needs, but we feel them with varying degrees of intensity, and we use different strategies to meet them. Some strategies are effective and skillful, others are less effective and less skillful. This is where emotions come in.

When Kids Roll Their Eyes

Let's go back to the seventh-grade student who rolls her eyes. When that happens, your body produces stress hormones, which causes your heart rate to accelerate. Then you tumble into thoughts that could include, *She's so disrespectful; I'm sick of teaching ungrateful kids*, and then into action—giving her a warning, writing a referral, and/or telling her that teachers must be respected.

This is a moment when you're experiencing anger. To be clear: She has not caused your anger—your anger is your own responsibility. But anger has shown up at your door and has a message for you—it wants you to listen to what it's communicating about your needs and values, which might be for respect, harmony, and cooperation. Here's what you can then say to yourself:

> *I value respect, harmony, and cooperation, which are worthy needs. I experience eye-rolling as disrespect. I wonder how I can communicate my needs to her? I wonder what she's feeling and what she needs that she's not getting? I wonder how I could hear what her needs are? I wonder if there's any other way I could interpret*

Figure 7.1   Universal human needs.

In the nonviolent communication model, universal human needs are often grouped into four categories: Subsistence and security, freedom, connection and meaning, and each has subcategories. This is not an exhaustive or definite list.

Subsistence and Security

Physical Sustenance
Air
Food
Health
Movement
Physical safety
Rest
Shelter
Touch
Water

Security
Consistency
Emotional safety
Order/Structure
Peace
Stability
Trusting

Freedom

Autonomy
Choice
Independence
Power
Responsibility

Relaxation
Humor
Joy
Play
Pleasure
Rejuvenation

Connection

Affection
Appreciation
Attention
Closeness
Companionship
Harmony
Love
Nurturing
Support
Sexual expression
Tenderness
Warmth

To Matter
Acceptance
Care
Compassion
Consideration
Empathy
Kindness
Mutual Recognition
Respect
To be heard and seen
To be known and
   understood
To be trusted
Understanding others

Community
Belonging
Communication
Cooperation
Equality
Inclusion
Mutuality
Participation
Partnership
Self-expression
Sharing

Figure 7.1 *(Continued)*

Meaning

Sense of Self
Authenticity
Competence
Creativity
Dignity
Growth
Healing
Honesty
Integrity
Self-acceptance

Self-care
Self-connection
Self-knowledge

Understanding
Awareness
Clarity
Discovery
Learning
Sense-making

Meaning
Aliveness
Challenge
Contribution
Effectiveness
Exploration
Integration
Purpose

Transcendence
Beauty
Celebration
Flow
Hope
Inspiration
Mourning
Peace (internal)
Presence

---

her eye-rolling—maybe she's not saying she disrespects me; maybe she's saying she's frustrated and doesn't know how to tell me that? I wonder if my racial identity—and her racial identity—play a role in how I interpret her behavior? I wonder if there are other places in my life where my need for respect, harmony, and cooperation aren't being met? I wonder if any other unmet needs are calling for my attention?

Here's what's possible next. You crouch down next to the student and you say, "Hey, can we check in for a minute after class? I'd like to understand what's going on for you."

After class, you stand in the doorway with the student and say, "When you roll your eyes, what are you feeling?"

She says, "I wasn't rolling my eyes."

You say, "OK," because you're not going to argue with her about whether she was or wasn't. "What were you feeling in class today?"

She says, "You're not fair. You're always picking on me."

You say, "OK, so you feel frustrated because you feel disrespected and singled out, and respect and belonging are really important—to everyone. When I asked you to throw away your gum and you rolled your eyes, I felt disrespected also."

I would like you to imagine the rest of this conversation—one in which the seventh-grade student acts age-appropriate and doesn't necessarily say everything we wish she'd say, and one in which you manage the conversation with skill and compassion. Within a few minutes, the student takes ownership for her behavior, which you appreciate, and she heads off to her next class. She does not end up in the office, and you feel calm, effective, and confident that you can respond to eye-rolling. The next time a student rolls their eyes, your body skips a beat and then you think: *I wonder if they're feeling afraid that they're being singled out—their need to feel like they belong is not being met.* And you say, "We have a school rule about gum. Please throw it out." And even if they roll their eyes, you don't experience it as disrespect.

Understanding Needs

In the NVC method, the word *need* is synonymous with *value* or *something that matters*. This doesn't mean that if we feel disrespected by a student, we turn to them and say, "I need you to respect me." This is mixing up what's meant by the word *need*. You could say: "I value respect, and I'm committed to respecting you also. If you are feeling angry, I'd like to ask that you share what you're feeling in words." This, of course, is assuming that the student has the emotional intelligence to recognize their feelings and communicate skillfully—which is why our students require social-emotional learning. Regardless of what the student says or does, we, however, can maintain equilibrium—we can listen to our own emotions and understand the messages they're trying to tell us about our own needs.

Recognizing our needs doesn't automatically mean they'll be met—sometimes they are, and sometimes they aren't. Sometimes our needs have more to do with something we need to change about our life, or we need internally, than something that another person can provide. We can learn how to express our needs to others and get more of them met—that's a great deal of what NVC teaches. But ultimately, freedom doesn't come from being able to control outcomes. It comes from knowing our values, developing ways to respond to the emotions that come up, and letting go. We can learn how to be at peace with some unmet needs.

Once I designed and facilitated an intensive learning experience for colleagues who were coming together from across the United States. I envisioned a collaborative experience that would be transformative, and I planned for a very long time, considering every little element. When the experience began, I welcomed my colleagues with tremendous excitement. But it didn't go the way I'd hoped. I received a constant stream of criticism, I was publicly embarrassed, and I heard that participants met in small groups to critique the professional development. People left feeling angry with me and disappointed in the learning experience. I felt angry and hurt. I berated myself, blamed them, and told myself: *I'll never do that again.*

Then I asked myself: *Which of my needs are not being met?* I read the list in Figure 7.1 and recognized that many of my needs for connection were not met—appreciation, communication, community, empathy, support, and trust. I appreciated the intrinsic beauty of these values. I acknowledged how hard I'd worked, and reached out to friends, who listened to me process and offered me empathy. When the anger and sadness dissipated a little, I felt a sense of calm. Then I began to ask myself other questions: *Which needs were unmet for the participants in this learning experience? Their unmet needs manifested in anger, frustration, fear, and criticism. Which needs were under these feelings?* As I contemplated this, I suspected that their needs for meaning weren't met. In fact, they kept saying: "We don't understand. We want more clarity." I'd experienced this as criticism or resistance. This insight allowed me to have a sense of warmth and care for those colleagues.

Marshall Rosenberg often said: "All violence is a tragic expression of unmet needs." When we recognize our own needs, and those of others, we tap into compassion. We see that everyone holds the same needs, and that words of anger and defensiveness are expressions of unmet needs. I wasn't able to come to a resolution with my colleagues after our learning experience, but I did come to a feeling of acceptance and peace within myself. My anger had been the gateway to that internal freedom. Because I accepted and listened to my anger as a messenger, I was able to find resolution within myself.

Think of a recent time when you experienced an unpleasant emotion. What did you want? What need wasn't met? Why was that value important? How did you respond when this need wasn't met? Did your response help you get that need met? Habitually asking such questions of ourselves can be revelatory. Learning to incorporate them into our coaching practice transforms our work.

Let's look at how such questions around needs and emotions transform our coaching. When someone I'm coaching demonstrates resistance (which shows up often as anger, fear, or doubt), I ask myself: *What do they need? What aren't they getting?* This settles my own emotional distress (I used to get angry at other people's resistance), and I can respond to what my client is expressing. Then the "resistance" vanishes. (I'll discuss more on this very soon.)

How to Work with Emotions and Needs

The first element that defines emotional intelligence is the ability to recognize when we're having an emotion. This is harder than it sounds. Many of us don't know how we feel, or feel numb, or feel things with great intensity. One of the first places that our emotions manifest is in our bodies—body-awareness is a starting point for understanding emotions. Again, this is harder than it sounds since many of us have been raised to disconnect from our bodies, to distrust our bodies, and to deny our bodies what they need. In order to control our minds, emotions, and bodies, systems of oppression need us to be distant from our bodies. It's not an accident that in our patriarchal, capitalist, racist societies, we're disconnected from our bodies. Reclaiming our right to an emotional life is deeply connected to reclaiming our right to live in our bodies. Our bodies sense emotions, express emotions, and generate emotions. As we gain skill in recognizing what's happening in our bodies, we get better at naming emotions.

We also need to cultivate awareness of what goes through our minds—of our thoughts. Our thoughts have tremendous power to exacerbate unpleasant emotions. The stories we tell about things that happen can send us spiraling into feelings that are uncomfortable. When my principal is curt when he passes me in the hallway, I tell myself that I must have done something wrong, that I'm in trouble now, which sends me into fear and anxiety. Perhaps on days when I'm feeling confident and rested, his response doesn't bother me. But if it's a day when I'm really low, and there's a lot of uncertainty at school, then maybe my need for consideration feels heightened. Sometimes that means I take action, action that can cause harm to others or myself. Maybe I'm distracted during my next class and my students don't get the full attention they deserve, maybe I doubt whether I should continue to teach here, maybe I question my competence, or maybe I project my frustration onto a student and get mad at them for eye-rolling.

I can learn, however, to intervene in the stories that my mind tells; I can learn to tune into my underlying needs that aren't being met—in this case, perhaps the need for mutual recognition, consideration, belonging, and appreciation—a need that wasn't met after my principal's curt comment in the hall. I can learn to be curious about my principal's needs: Maybe he values autonomy or kindness. Maybe he had a lot on his mind and was worried about something. Maybe he doesn't know how to give me feedback. As I learn how to listen to and respond to my emotions, I can also learn how to recognize, understand, and respond to the emotions that other people feel. My relationships can improve, my sense of power will expand, and my ability to coach toward transformation will be stronger than ever.

So how do we do this? If you want to understand emotions more, and to build skill with them, I have two suggestions for you. First, learn about the kinds of emotional intelligence I've been writing about in this chapter. Second, learn about and practice mindfulness. *Mindfulness* is the moment-to-moment cultivation of nonjudgmental awareness; it's an integration of kindness and awareness that allows us to make wise choices. Mindfulness helps us recognize when we're experiencing an emotion and helps us respond with intention and compassion. Mindfulness is a critical resource for building equitable schools—we'll need more than mindfulness to transform schools, but we also won't be able to create equitable, liberated transformed communities without it. For additional resources, see Appendix F: Resources for Further Learning.

Responding to Resistance

"When students talk over you when you're giving instructions, stop talking and wait until . . ." I was just beginning to describe how Mike could deal with this situation, but he cut me off. "I'm sick of hearing these suggestions," Mike said. "You're not the first one to tell me to do this—you know that, right? This is patronizing. I've been teaching for eight years, but it's only these kids who treat me like this." Mike crossed his arms over his chest, and then continued. "At my last school, in the suburbs, they didn't talk over me. These kids don't know how to respect authority. You need to do something about them, not tell me to do something different."

Mike's face was red. He was a tall, middle-aged white man.

Take a moment to visualize this situation. What would you have felt? How would you have responded?

When a client responds like Mike did in that moment, I can see two responses available to me. With one response, I *fight resistance*. With a second response, I *flow with resistance*. For many years when I began coaching, the only option I saw was to fight resistance. I wasn't very successful on that path, and in a moment, you'll read about what that sounded like. After learning about emotions and refining my coaching skills, I now understand how to flow with resistance. The second transcript you'll read is what actually happened when Mike said, "I'm sick of hearing these suggestions . . ." Let's start, however, with what I might have when I was still fighting resistance.

Fighting Resistance

When Mike said, "I'm sick of hearing these suggestions. . ." I geared up to fight his resistance. My stomach clenched, my palms perspired, I thought, *Oh yeah? Well, then, I'm going to roll up my sleeves and fight this thing out. Because I know I'm right and he's wrong and he needs to change and he's a racist pig and he's treating me like crap and I'm going to win this battle. Your resistance is futile, Mike.*

Here's how the conversation could have proceeded, if I'd fought his resistance:

ME: "It sounds like you're unwilling to do anything different, right?"
MIKE: "What do you mean by that? What are you insinuating?"

ME: "You're the teacher, Mike. It's your responsibility to change what you're doing. And your comment about 'these kids' —what do you mean by that?"

MIKE: "I'm supposed to change because they are disrespectful brats? This is why teachers don't stay at this school! Admin blames teachers for everything and doesn't enforce rules and coddles parents. I thought you were a coach. Why aren't you coaching me on English since that's what I teach?"

ME: "I am a coach, but we can't work on your English instruction if kids won't listen to you."

MIKE: "Which is exactly why we need to enforce rules about respect. They need to behave like civilized people."

ME: "When you talk about black and brown kids like that, it's racist."

MIKE: "Now you're calling me a racist? I'm done with coaching. In fact, I'm going to file a grievance with the union because this is an unsafe work environment."

I left the room shaking, afraid of what might happen, furious at Mike and at my principal for hiring him, and angry at the superintendent who didn't take a strong equity stance. Later I'd also realize that I was disappointed in myself—I wish I'd known what else I could have said; I wish I could have said something that he could have heard. And nothing changed for kids. Mike would still be the ineffective, biased teacher that he was—and he might be even more angry with his students.

Happily, that's not what happened.

Flowing with Resistance

Here's what our conversation actually sounded like. Watch for ways I flowed with resistance.

Mike's face was red. He crossed his arms over his chest.

I took a deep breath and exhaled slowly. "Mike," I said calmly, "I can hear that you're experiencing intense emotions." I was fully aware that saying these words to a male teacher felt awkward—and yet I said them anyway. I strove to make the tone of my voice sound authentic and confident. Mike's facial expression didn't change, which I took as a positive sign that my words hadn't intensified his irritation.

I continued: "What would be helpful for us to talk about right now?" I genuinely wanted to know where he was interested in taking the conversation. It sounded like he was feeling disempowered—when someone blames others for what's going on, and asks others to take care of the situation, that's what they're expressing.

Mike answered my question with this: "I told you. You—or admin—should do something about their behavior. It's not my fault that they are disrespectful."

I wondered: What need is Mike not getting met right now? Perhaps a need for order or a need to be understood?

"OK, I want to be sure I'm understanding you right," I said. "Are you feeling like you need help? Are you feeling anxious about your ability to deliver instruction?"

Mike's face took on a puzzled expression. "Why are you asking me about my feelings?" he asked. "I was clear: do something about the students."

I nodded. "I'm glad you asked why I'm asking about your feelings. You are having them, right?" I waited until he nodded. "Yeah, I mean I can see that you're experiencing emotions—which is normal. Humans experience feelings. And I can see that they're uncomfortable for you, right?" I waited.

Mike shrugged and said: "Look, this isn't about my feelings. I can deal with them. This is about student behavior." His pace had slowed just a little; the register of his tone of voice had dropped.

I pressed on in addressing his feelings. Feelings belong. We have them. We deserve to have them recognized and accepted at school. "Mike," I said, my voice still commanding authority. I knew he'd be comforted by my tone—it was a way I could convey that he'd be OK. I registered that underneath his anger and sense of disempowerment, he was afraid. I continued: "It's OK to ask for help. It's OK to feel stuck. I'm hearing that you want to be an effective English teacher here—for these kids, for *our* kids—and that you're not sure how to do that."

Mike stared at me with a blank expression. Blank was better than enraged, I thought.

"Does that feel accurate?" I asked. "That you want to be an effective teacher here?"

"I *am* an effective teacher," Mike said. "They just won't be quiet!"

"Yeah," I said. "It must be really frustrating to remember being in another school and feeling effective there, and not having that experience here."

"It's *not me*," Mike said. "It's the kids."

I responded: "I hear that you think it's the kids, Mike, I do. Wherever the problem is, it's frustrating. And sad. And disappointing. I'm just acknowledging those emotions. Those are uncomfortable. And when they flood our system, it means that the part of our brain that can think through things clearly is diminished."

"So now you're saying that my brain is diminished?" Mike said.

I smiled, in a way that I hoped wasn't mocking but instead brought a little levity. "No, Mike. I'm expressing empathy for you—those are uncomfortable feelings—and I'm sharing neuroscience about what happens in our systems when we experience those feelings."

I paused. "I want to help you figure this out, Mike. I know, from personal experience, how hard it can feel when you can't do what you showed up to do—and I know you're here because you want to teach our students English."

What you can't hear in these written words is my tone of voice. You can't see my body language. You can't gauge my intentions. It's essential that there's congruity between who you are being in a conversation like this and how your communication is expressed. This conversation I'm relating to you is the real one that happened—the first response is how I imagine I might have responded to Mike in another coaching model, or 10 years prior. What I felt in this real conversation was true empathy for Mike. He was suffering. He became a teacher because he wanted to serve children. And since he'd come to our school, he went to bed every night not having lived up to that internal commitment and desire. He was frustrated and angry and had used all of his resources to figure out what to do, and he still felt ineffective. He felt vulnerable and scared. And he was taking those emotions out on his students—which wasn't fair. But I felt empathy for him.

Mike exhaled and uncrossed his arms. He rested his hands on the table in front of us. "So what am I supposed to do?" he asked. "I just don't know what to do."

"I know," I said. "And not knowing is really scary. I hate it when I don't know what to do." I paused. We sat in silence for 15 or 20 seconds.

"I don't want to scream at them, because I know that's not cool," Mike said, "but it feels like if I just stop talking and wait for them, I'm giving them all the power."

"Right," I said. "So that's scary too! Can you see all the fear? I mean, just seeing it can feel like a relief."

"I wish you'd stop talking about my feelings and help me figure out what to do," Mike said.

I laughed. "OK, so now I hear that you're getting frustrated with me because you feel like I'm not responding to what you're asking for. Got it. I hear you—you want to move to action, right?"

"Yes, that's right."

"One last question about feelings, and then I promise I'll shift gears, OK?" I waited until Mike nodded. "How do you *want to feel* in your classroom?"

Mike exhaled again, this time loud and long. "I just want to feel like I'm doing a good job. I want to feel like kids learned. I want them to respect me. I want to feel appreciated. I want to not have to fight for attention every day. I want to feel calm and in control. I want to feel like I know what to do when they get off-task, like I don't have to come to you to get ideas."

"OK," said, "You want to feel calm and competent and effective." Mike nodded. "OK, so when kids talk over you, I want you to stop . . ."

The conversation I just described, up until this point, took about 8 minutes. I'd jotted that down in my notes. We spent the rest of the session exploring and practicing how to get students' attention. I also shared some strategies with Mike for how to recognize his emotions when they came up in the moment, and how to navigate those and respond to them in a way that didn't create further discord for anyone. I helped Mike anchor in his purpose for being a teacher. I helped Mike connect with his own agency and power. I raised a question about the role that Mike's identity markers played in how he experienced his students. I suggested we come back to talking about that next time. On my way out, Mike said, "I'm sorry I can be so difficult. Thanks for being patient with me." I told him I appreciated his honesty.

I left his classroom feeling energized, hopeful, and efficacious as a coach. When I visited Mike's classroom a week later, he was using the strategies we'd talked about, and there were longer and longer stretches when he was giving instructions and students were attentive.

Two weeks later, we had a conversation about Mike's racial identity and the assumptions he held about his students because of their identity markers.

Take-Aways from Two Paths

In both of these scenarios, (one fictional, the other real); Mike was the same person. The only difference was the coaching strategies I used. In the second scenario, I drew on my knowledge of emotions and human needs; I activated my compassion and curiosity, and I trusted the coaching process. I experienced his resistance as a maladaptive response to unpleasant emotions and unmet needs. I saw it as his way of saying: "Help me. I am suffering. I don't know what to do." This is a formula I've used over and over and over—it's why I don't experience resistance. When I reframe what I'm perceiving, I see many options for how to engage with someone exhibiting these behaviors.

Here are the key ideas I want you to take away from this example of how to respond to resistance:

- Don't take what your client says or does personally—their emotions are not about you. They're about unmet needs. How you respond to their behavior is entirely within your sphere of control.

- Reflect on your behavior, beliefs, and ways of being. Your response to whatever your client does can be reactive, or based on problematic beliefs, or misdirected. You bring a dynamic to the conversation, and you can exacerbate the situation. You bring all of your needs and emotions to the situation, and these can be expressed unskillfully. In the first scenario, that's what I did. Commit to your ongoing learning and reflection practices to continue gaining self-understanding and skills to respond to what happens.
- Communicate empathy, empathy, and empathy. What you perceive as resistance is someone's suffering. This doesn't mean that their actions are justified. Activating your empathy helps you find a place from which you can see their suffering and respond with patience.
- Get their buy-in. Look and listen for the entry points, where the conversation can matter to them, and how the conversation can meet their needs.
- Stay in relationship with your client. Remember that behaviors change when beliefs change, and beliefs change when behaviors change. But change doesn't happen when there isn't trust.
- Be persistent. Just because someone responds to something you say in a way that makes you feel like they're pushing back, don't give up—if it's the right thing to be persistent about. Acknowledging, accepting, and discussing emotions are the right things to be persistent about because they are critical to making it across the chasm.
- Keep your eyes on the prize: to have a positive impact on the experience and outcomes of kids. Staying in relationship with the person in front of you is the best way to do that. Being aware of your own emotions and needs will help you do that.
- Stay grounded in who you want to be: that's what's most in your control. Draw on courage to stay aligned to your vision for yourself.
- Acknowledge, accept, and attend to emotions, and then talk about instruction, implicit bias, and meeting the needs of our students.

When Confronted with Resistance, Get Curious

When I hear a teacher say, "These kids can't . . .," I've learned to hear that what they are really saying is, "I don't think I know how to do . . .and I'm afraid." This is how we listen to emotions. This is how we listen behind the mask of resistance. This is how we learn that resistance is often fear.

There's much more to say about coaching resistance, but here are a couple final important ideas about resistance. First, when we encounter resistance in clients, the goal is not to eliminate it. Although resistance can get in the way of meeting the needs of children—when it's a resistance to changing one's behaviors, beliefs, and ways of being—resistance can also be a vital force in undermining unjust policies. I'm grateful to those who resisted segregation, and I'm grateful to those who resist policies that further marginalize underserved communities. When we encounter resistance, we must get curious and listen for unmet needs and explore emotions. When resistance is an expression of anger and grief, when it manifests because people's needs for subsistence, security, freedom, and community have been restricted, then resistance is a worthy and understandable expression of emotion. That's the resistance that we embrace.

In contrast, there is also a kind of resistance we might encounter that means that a person is *un-coachable*. This is the resistance someone expresses when there is no way they will change a behavior, there is no way they'll explore their beliefs, and when your curiosity is met with unwillingness over and over and over again. This is the kind of resistance that someone might express toward you in hurtful ways, or behind your back, or with passive-aggressive behavior. This does happen. Sometimes our curiosity and compassion cannot create space for someone else to learn and grow. If you have done extensive reflection on your own coaching practices, you've explored how your emotions and identity might be affecting this coaching relationship, and you've used every strategy I've shared with you—then there are a few things to consider:

- Reflect on the conditions in which you are coaching. What are the expectations for your client to engage in coaching?
- Be sure that your client is really saying they aren't open to coaching. Say, "I want to clarify: I'm hearing that you don't want to engage in this kind of coaching with me. Is that correct?"
- If they say yes, then you may have a responsibility to tell the person who assigned you to this client, and then you walk away, recognizing that the client is suffering, and not taking their resistance personally. Then you find someone else to coach who will be engaged in learning.

I know that many of you might feel like you're in places that are full of resistance to change and/or resistance to examining inequitable practices. I'm encouraged by this research finding: When just 10 percent of the population holds an unshakable belief, their belief will be adopted by the majority (Rensselaer Polytechnic Institute, 2011). In any process of learning and transformation, there'll be resistance. Remember that you don't need to have 100 percent of people onboard from the beginning. There is a "tipping point," and perhaps that's 10 percent, when things can and will change (Gladwell, 2000). Find the people who might be more receptive; and attend to your emotions, shore up your support systems, and be persistent.

The Connection between Emotions and Justice

Mike was suffering—and his students were suffering—because he couldn't fully experience and express his emotions. I would have been thrilled if Mike had sobbed and wailed. His fear and sadness manifested instead as anger, and that was hurting other people. I assumed that Mike didn't allow himself to experience sadness or fear or to cry because he had internalized beliefs that men don't cry. Our patriarchal culture is very clear that men don't cry or express vulnerability or weakness—that is what women do. Not heterosexual men. Mike had been socialized into this norm since birth, and he was suffering.

Stephanie had a right to her emotions. She had a right to her fear and fragility and to her tears. She had a right to express them, and she had a responsibility to explore her needs that weren't being met. She was entitled to express her emotions, and, because she had taken on the role of a teacher, she was responsible for meeting the needs of her students. Her fragility could exist at the same time that we had conversations about race, instruction, and her implicit bias. I didn't experience her fragility as resistance, and it didn't alter our course of learning. Because I simply accepted her emotions and helped her respond to them, Stephanie was better able to discuss the things we needed to discuss. Suppressing emotions is perpetuating systems of oppression.

Emotions are also an entry point to *empathy*, which itself is an emotion expressing deep care for another being. When we can feel our own emotions, we're more likely to recognize and feel another person's emotions. And when we can feel another person's emotions, and we see our commonalities, we're less likely to hurt them—to enslave, rape, or exploit them. Systems of oppression rely on us disconnecting from our own emotions (including guilt and regret) so that we don't feel the emotions of other people.

We can learn to hear the wisdom of emotions. All emotions are OK to feel: Fear can be our friend, and anger can be our friend. It's how we respond to them that matters. Fear and anger can cause harm when we allow them to take over—when anger turns into aggression, that's problematic—but aggression is what happens when we don't really listen to anger. This is why it seems like our emotions harm us or others. It's not the emotion doing the harm—the emotion simply rang the doorbell and wanted to give us information. But when we told it to get lost, or left it in the cold, or let it in and ignored it, then our emotion becomes unhealthy or counterproductive.

When you listen to your emotions, you are rebuking the patriarchy that belittles emotions as something belonging to an inferior group. When you listen to your emotions, and express them skillfully, you are rebuking colonization and white supremacy that put boundaries aligned to race around who can experience and express which emotions. When you listen to and express emotions, you are rebuking capitalism, which says that emotions are a waste of time and an obstacle to productivity and amassing wealth and power. To listen to, explore, and express emotions is a fundamental human right, and systems of oppression strive to deprive us of fundamental rights. Reclaim your right to emotions. Invite your clients to reclaim their rights to emotions. And then sit down for tea with them and learn from them.

Looking at Emotions through an Identity Lens

We see and interpret emotions—our own and those of others—through a sociopolitical lens. This is because the meaning we make of emotions is culturally constructed. All humans experience the same basic emotions—sadness, anger, joy, fear, pride, and so on. But we ascribe different meanings to those emotions, and we have different rules about how they can be expressed, based on a person's race or ethnicity, gender, age, and class. This is critical to remember when we coach across lines of difference, because we'll likely respond to people's emotions differently. Your identity markers as a coach will also likely have an impact on how your client expresses emotions depending on their identity markers. The first step toward navigating all of this complexity is to boost your own levels of awareness. Consider the following, for example:

- **Crying.** Whose crying are you more comfortable with? A woman's? A man's? What messages did you internalize about who can cry and when and where?
- **Niceness.** When we look at emotions through an identity lens, we can also see how what we perceive sometimes as niceness—especially in women—is a mask of resistance, avoidance, fear, or disagreement. Women are supposed to be the

peacemakers, the nurturers, those who deny our own needs to put the needs of others ahead. We're told to avoid conflict. Because of that, we can act "nice" when we're not really feeling kind.

As we deepen our understanding of emotions, we'll begin questioning the actions and inactions we see our clients take, as well as our own actions and inactions:

- When white people tell people of color not to be angry, or to "let something go," or to communicate in a calm tone of voice, they're perpetuating bigotry.
- When white people center their own emotional needs at the expense of those of people of color, or as a way to avoid talking about race, they are perpetuating white supremacy. This is what has been termed *white fragility* by author and teacher Robin DiAngelo in her 2019 book by the same title. This is a valuable book for many reasons, and I highly recommend it, although I find her approach to dealing with emotions to be limited and often problematic. It is a problem when white people manipulate their emotional experiences to become a means of perpetuating inequities; it is a problem when conversations don't happen because white people claim to feel uncomfortable and their discomfort is prioritized above all. However, the solution isn't to suppress and repress emotions.

One final thing we may notice as we begin paying closer attention to emotions, and looking at them through a lens of identity awareness, is that some groups of people express more discomfort in conversations about equity than others—generally, white people are more uncomfortable. This is also something that Robin DiAngelo describes in her book. Discomfort is usually a reflection of fear, anger, sadness, and/or shame, and if your client speaks about feeling "uncomfortable" a lot, it's worth unpacking this emotion. But talking about race and privilege, and talking about our nation's history and injustice, and talking about the changes we need to make to our behaviors, beliefs, and ways of being *is* uncomfortable. It's uncomfortable for me, too. Living in systems of oppression is also uncomfortable for many of us—and although white people have been shielded from some of the pain, and may not experience the degree of discomfort that some people of color do, they are also suffering in the racist societies that we live in. Transforming our schools—and creating a more just and free society—will require that we learn strategies to engage with our discomfort and the underlying emotions.

Before You Go . . .

Read the following prompts and select two or three that feel most valuable to you based on where you are in your learning journey. Spend meaningful time considering your reflection before moving on.

REFLECT ON THIS CHAPTER

- Recall a time when you felt resistant. What were you feeling? Which of your needs weren't being met? How do you think someone else perceived you?
- Recall a time when someone else was being resistant. What do you think they might have been feeling? Which of their needs weren't being met?
- Which emotions come up in you when you perceive resistance? Which of your needs aren't met when you experience someone's resistance?
- How would your life be different if you had deeper understanding of your emotions? If you accepted your emotions? If you had more resources for navigating your emotions?

TO DO

- How could you continue learning about emotions? Here are a few suggestions: Read my 2018 book, *Onward: Cultivating Emotional Resilience in Educators*, practice listening, learn more about NVC, and consider finding a therapist—all of us can benefit from working with a therapist at some point in our lives. What could be a next step for you to learn more about emotions?
- Download the reflection exercise from my website, http://brightmorningteam.com, on the Transformational Coach's Way of Being. Reflect on your own way of being and consider which of these ways of being you saw me demonstrate in this chapter and in others.
- Plan a coaching conversation with a client you've perceived as being resistant. Plan for how to better understand what they think and feel. Identify how you can get curious and stay curious regardless of what happens.

Interlude: Connection

Connection: We never lose sight of the connections between all living things. We know that the hope for our world lies in our ability to see ourselves in all living things, and to see all living things in ourselves. We refrain from binary thinking.

We've been socialized to understand that constant growth, violent competition, and the critical mass are the ways to create change. Emergence shows us that adaptation and evolution depend more upon critical, deep and authentic connections, a thread that can be tugged for support and resilience.

—adrienne maree brown, author, activist, and healer

How do you think change happens?

How have you seen change that's for the better happen?

Which connections can you tug on for support and resilience?

CHAPTER 8

What You Need to Know about Identity

*I want to ask you, as clearly as I can, to bear with patience
with all that is unresolved in your heart, and to try to love
the questions themselves . . . Don't dig for answers that
can't be given you yet: you cannot live them now.
For everything must be lived. Live the questions now,
then perhaps then, someday, you will gradually,
without noticing, live into the answer.*

—RAINER MARIA RILKE

Our sociopolitical identity is a central part of who we are and greatly influences how we move through the world. A Transformational Coach needs to understand their own identity markers and experiences, needs skills to understand a client's identity markers, and needs skills to help clients understand their own identity markers.

In Chapter 2, I offered suggestions for how to understand your identity markers. But what does it sound like to explore someone else's? How do you do this in a way that doesn't seem rude or intrusive? Many of us are fearful of exploring identity because we're afraid of talking about race and difference, or we want to pretend we don't see difference. But it's imperative that we do so. Unless we attend to our client's identity, we run the risk of making assumptions, which in turn limits the impact of our coaching.

The Social Construction of Identity

Remember that the concept of race was created to legitimize racial inequality. Although the concept of race is absurd, we live in a racialized world in which race is very, very real. The way that we understand ourselves, and the way we understand that other people understand us, has a big impact on who we are and how we show up in the world. It's useful to understand the difference between what's called an *internal identity* and an *external experience*. Your internal identity is how you see yourself and feel inside. Your external identity is how the majority of other people see you. In the United States, and in many places in the world, if you "look white" you're treated as white and granted the advantages that come with a white status. But sometimes how we identify doesn't match how other people see us.

Identity is complicated. I have a Mexican friend who looks like her indigenous ancestors—she's dark skinned and has thick black hair; in the United States, she's always perceived as a person of color. Her sister takes after their Spanish ancestors—she has green eyes and blonde hair, and in the United States, she's perceived as white. Because of this, these two sisters have had starkly different experiences in school, in the workforce, and in everyday activities like walking around in stores. While the green-eyed sister has reaped some unearned privileges from being perceived as white, she also feels like her identity is not recognized—she feels Mexican and yet she's often seen as a white person. This has created a sense of confusion, disconnect, and sadness for her.

In addition, remember that we all have intersecting social identities. Our inner sense of racial, cultural, or ethnic identity is one aspect; how we're perceived racially or culturally is another aspect; our gender is another social identity; our age is another; our class background is another. Each identity is more or less salient depending on the context. When I'm the only person of color in a group, my racial identity feels most salient. When I'm with a group of millennials, I'm most aware of my age identity in contrast to when I'm with folks from my generation, and then I forget about my age identity. When I'm the only woman in a group, my gender feels most salient. When I'm in a mixed-race and mixed-gender group of people my age who are wealthy—and who talk about golfing, vacations in the Grand Caymans, and their stock portfolios—I feel most conscious of my economic class. If your identity markers are those that are dominant or considered normative in our society, you'll likely be less aware of those when you're with others who share those markers—and you'll become conscious of them when you're with someone who doesn't share one of those markers. I don't often think about my heterosexuality and the privileges I have because of that identity marker, for example.

As we begin to see the dynamics in play around the social construction of identity, we can begin to appreciate two broad implications for us as coaches and leaders: that we need to know ourselves and how our experience of identity influences how we are in the world, including how we coach and lead, and that as we get to know a client, we need to understand how they make sense of their identities.

How to Facilitate Reflection

It can feel awkward to open a conversation about identity, so here's some language to use. Say this:

> I'm curious how you identify in terms of your sociopolitical identity markers— race, class, gender, and so on. Of your identity markers, which ones feel most important to you? Like they play the biggest role in your daily experiences?

The first time you say something like this, you might feel self-conscious, simply because we rarely ask each other these kinds of questions because they get too close to race, which many people feel is a taboo subject. Practice this conversation first, and then ask these questions anyway. It's a really important conversation to have and many people are less comfortable than you'd imagine.

Here's another way to open this conversation:

> "I don't want to make assumptions about you, so I'm curious how you identify in terms of your race or ethnicity?"

When I asked one teacher this, she said, "I look like I'm Latina, right? But I'm Native American." She often felt this aspect of her identity was unseen and was grateful that I'd asked. Asking someone about their identity can build a trust.

Asking about identity also provides you with insight into how that person shows up as a teacher and leader. When I asked an assistant principal whom I perceived as being black about her identity, she said, "I'm from the Islands [the Caribbean], so even though I'm black, I'm not African American." This was an important distinction for her, and it helped me understand her attitudes toward the African American students she worked with.

It's important to ask this question to people whom you perceive as being white. When I asked one man I perceived as being white this question, he said: "I'm white, and I know that means I have a lot of privilege. My grandparents were Irish and they faced a lot of discrimination in Ireland. I learned a lot from them about prejudice."

I've also posed this question about identity to people I perceived as being white, and they responded with surprise and said, "I'm just white." This allowed me to open a conversation about identity and white identity.

In addition to offering insights about racial identity, opening this conversation can also surface important, and otherwise invisible, insights around a client's gender identity. In recent years, as our way of thinking about gender identity expands outside of our traditional and dominant binary of male/female, I've started asking people which pronouns they use. At first this felt awkward, especially when someone would look at me blankly and say, "What do you mean?" But I realized that this created an opportunity to understand that some people don't identify with a male or female identity, and that rather than using the pronouns "he," "him," and "his" or "she," "her," and "hers," they use "they," "them," and "theirs."

Whenever I raise gender identity, it's also an authentic time for me to share that I'm just starting to understand this aspect of identity, as someone who has always identified with the sex into which I was born. Being "cis-gendered," as that's called, has afforded me the privilege of not having to question or learn about gender identity, so I can tell a client that I'm learning about this too, and that yes, sometimes I feel awkward as I struggle to find the "right" words or as I blunder around and make mistakes. As I develop an understanding of gender identity and raise this conversation with others, it's been incumbent upon me to do some learning so I know what I'm talking about. As someone who holds gender-privilege in this case (my sense of gender matches how the world sees me), I have a responsibility to learn about what it means to be non-binary so that I have these conversations responsibly. Yes, they can be uncomfortable, and we will survive (and probably learn from) discomfort.

Questions that Cultivate Reflection

Here's a process to use for a more in-depth conversation about identity. First, ask your client to list their most prominent identity markers. Explain that this could include race, ethnicity, socio-economic status, religion, gender, sexual orientation, spoken languages, nationality, physical abilities, citizenship status, income, educational background, and age. Then ask the following questions:

- Which would you say are your top three identity markers? Which specific life experiences made those so prominent?
- Which ones do you think others typically notice about you?
- Which ones do you tend to not think about?
- Which of your identity markers are reflected in dominant culture? Which aren't?
- Do your closest friends share aspects of your identity? How so?
- How do your identity markers show up in your work? When are you aware of your identity markers in the role you play?
- Have any of your identity markers felt more salient at another time in your life?
- Which of these identity markers do you prioritize when sharing about yourself?

On my website, https://brightmorningteam.com you can find a worksheet that you can give your client to work through this.

As your client shares, follow up with coaching questions to deepen your understanding of who they are and to facilitate their self-understanding. You can simply say, "Tell me more about that." This is also an important conversation in which to use active listening and to pay attention to your own body language so that you're communicating curiosity, interest, and openness.

If someone doesn't seem to want to talk about something, you might mentally note that and reflect on why that might be—but don't push. For example, I coached a teacher who never used a name or pronoun when talking about his partner. I wondered if he was gay, and given the homophobia in our society, I understood why he'd want his sexual orientation to be private. The only time when I wondered if his sexual orientation influenced his decisions as a teacher was in advance of Valentine's Day. He was at an elementary school where teachers typically had Valentine's Day parties and encouraged kids to trade cards. He asked if he "had to do that" and said he felt like it could be uncomfortable for some kids—he insinuated that perhaps not every child felt comfortable with heterosexual romantic love. He was worried that his students would be upset if everyone else had a party but they didn't. I agreed with his concern about identity-safety and we brainstormed how he could create a celebration of friendship—after all, they were fourth-grade students—and not romantic love. In this case, whether or not he was gay or aware of our heteronormative culture, his awareness of identity was an asset to him as a teacher.

In contrast, I coached a new teacher who in anticipation of the winter holidays wanted to hold a "secret Santa" gift exchange with students. There were two problems in this situation: First, she made an assumption (that was incorrect) that all of her students celebrated Christmas. Second, she taught in a low-income community where it was a burden for families to spend $5.00 on a gift for this exchange. Because we'd had a conversation about identity when we started working together, I knew that she'd been raised in an upper-middle-class, Christian community, and I was able to bring her awareness to the way in which she was acting on her own identity markers that created inequities in her class. For this teacher, her class privilege had created a blind spot in her teaching. A coach can bring awareness of blind spots and how those impact students.

We learn about our client's sense of identity for a few reasons: so we can understand how they see themselves, so we can coach them into deeper insights about themselves, and so we can coach them into greater understanding about how their identity markers show up in their teaching and leadership. Equity can be increased or undermined in the intersection between our clients and the people they serve.

What to Share with a Client about Yourself

Be intentional about what you share about your own identity markers. Share what you think might build trust. At the same time, be thoughtful about what you share, and how much you share. You might, for example, share something that you hope will connect you with your client. Perhaps, like you, your client grew up in the Pacific Northwest. This is a relevant identity marker for you to share—but don't make assumptions about what this means for your client. Perhaps although you grew up in Portland, skiing on the weekends, she grew up in a rural community in central Washington, where she experienced food insecurity. Sometimes when we share identity markers, in our enthusiasm at having a connection, we overlook important nuances and complexity.

Here's how I generally make decisions about what to share. If a client asks me something about myself, I share. If they don't ask me, I don't share. Sometimes clients are curious about you, as their coach, and they might ask if you have children or where you were born or how you identify racially. Answer them but don't talk about yourself for too long—they might just want a short answer.

Remember not to present your experiences or relationships with people of different identity markers as evidence of your cultural competence. If you're coaching a Mexican teacher, and you traveled in Mexico one summer, say that with humility. For example:

"I traveled in Michoacan last summer and loved Lake Pátzcuaro. People were so kind, and it was beautiful. I'd love to see more of Mexico and learn more about the different cultures. What is your hometown like?"

The teacher might appreciate your appreciation, as well as your recognition that you don't know much about Mexico because you were only there one summer.

I coached an older African American male principal whom I'll call Fred. We worked together for two years, and during that time, I never mentioned that my husband was African American. There was really no need to mention this, and I didn't want Fred to think that my sharing was an insinuation of a connection or of a deeper understanding of his experience. I'd seen a good number of white women talk about their black husbands in ways that made me feel uncomfortable and that served to obscure their own unexamined privilege and biases. At the end of the time I coached Fred, in thanking him, I mentioned that I would have been thrilled had my son been a student at his school—that Fred would be have been a great role model for him. Fred thanked me, but also looked confused. I hesitated and then said that my son was African American.

"You never told me that!" Fred said. We'd had a good relationship and suddenly I felt like I'd hid something from him. He continued, "I mean, I guess I never asked about your husband or son, I just assumed . . . I guess it doesn't matter. But I wish I'd known." I felt awkward and briefly explained why I'd been reluctant to share—and said that I didn't feel like it was necessary. "I get that," Fred said, "but I don't know, I wish I'd known."

I don't think there's a right answer to what we reveal or how much or when or to whom. Before I wrote books and shared all the things I now share, my inclination was to be selective and intentional if I shared anything about myself. I'm also a fairly private person. If a client didn't ask about my identity markers, I'd leave it to them to perceive me however they did. It didn't feel like it mattered. If they said something about me that wasn't true, then I corrected them, like the time a client said, "You understand, you're Mexican." You'll need to reflect on what you feel is right to reveal, and remember that this will likely differ with each client.

Addressing Racial Differences

There are times when we need to name the difference in our racial identities. The first time I met with Fred, the principal I just described, I asked him a number of questions about how he felt working with me. I said: "I want to acknowledge that I've never been a principal, and yet here I am assigned to coach you. What does that bring up for you?" His response was positive—he said that he trusted that I'd be a good listener and would help him think through how to improve instruction at his site.

Later in the conversation, I said: "I also want to acknowledge the differences in our gender, age, and race. What comes up for you as you think about our work together and these differences?"

His response was one that stuck with me for a long time. First, his eyes got big, and then he said: "Wow. Thank you for naming that. It's a relief that you've brought that up."

This is a response I've encountered innumerable times when I've said something along the lines of, "There are differences between us—and I see them. How do you feel about them?"

Fred was concerned about the difference in our age, and what that might mean for how we communicated, and for how I might judge him because of his age—and in particular, how he used or didn't use technology.

"What about our racial difference?," I asked, wanting to communicate that I was comfortable talking about race and racial difference.

"I'm used to working in a racially diverse community," he said. "But I'm glad you named it. I've experienced my share of racism, and I'll point out racism if I see it."

"I want you to know that you have permission to give me any feedback, at any time, about my racism," I said. "I think about racism like smog in the air, and I know I've breathed it in."

"Good to know," Fred said. And that day, that's where we left it. It wasn't awkward of uncomfortable for either of us.

There were many times during that coaching relationship when either Fred or I surfaced his racial identity in connection to how he was leading, or surfaced the difference in our racial identity and how that might play out in our coaching. There was a time, for example, when he was practicing the opening remarks for what he anticipated would be a tense staff meeting. I gave him feedback, suggesting that he tone down his comments and speak more invitationally to staff. He said, "I think you're asking me to tone down my blackness."

"Whoa, give me a second," I said. A surge of defensiveness, shame, and fear washed over me, and then I said: "I hear you. You're right, I think that was what I was saying." It didn't really matter whether or not I agreed with him, although I truly did—but his experience as a black man and the racism he'd experienced wasn't for me to question. "Thanks for the feedback," I said. And he resumed practicing his meeting. Yes, there was a moment of discomfort, and I thought about this for a long time afterwards, but the discomfort also passed quickly. We can survive discomfort.

Sometimes, people of color fear that their white coach won't understand them, which is a valid fear. In contrast, I don't think many white people worry that their coach of color won't understand them—and therefore won't be able to effectively coach them. Given that the experience of white people is dominant in our media, curriculum, and literature, people of color know a lot about white people. But white people don't know a lot about people of color, or what they know is distorted and inaccurate. In a difficult coaching conversation, I observed an African American teacher tell her white coach: "You wouldn't understand. You're not from here, and you're not black."

The coach responded with humility and grace and said: "You're right. I don't understand. What would you like me to know?"

The teacher said: "You need to hold off on coming to conclusions about what you see me do. Question the assumptions you're making."

The coach nodded and said "I hear you. I've got learning to do, and I'm not asking you to be my teacher, but I also want you to know that I'm open to any feedback you have for me."

The teacher seemed surprised by her response, "OK," she said. "Then when I talk about feeling like the other members of the Leadership Team, all of whom are white, don't take me seriously, you shouldn't question my reality and ask me if I'm basically making it up."

"OK," the coach said. "What else would you like me to know?"

This was a tense moment. Everyone was uncomfortable. But the discomfort passed, and the relationship between the coach and her client got stronger, and both of them learned as their work continued.

Coaching for equity requires that we manage our discomfort around discussing race and class and identity differences. As we normalize these conversations, we normalize discomfort, which makes these conversations more comfortable. I hope that by this point in this book, you've accepted that the only way to dismantle racial inequities in schools is by strengthening our ability to see race and talk about race. And that's going to involve discomfort, courage, curiosity, and compassion.

Strengthening Awareness of Identity

Our identity markers are present in our minds and emotions whether we're aware of it or not. They influence how we see, experience, and understand the world. A Transformational Coach attends to themselves—this self-awareness and self-care is a guardrail that keeps us safely on the bridge to building equitable schools. Attending to oneself includes cultivating a deep and ongoing awareness of identity and how it manifests in coaching. Here's a two-step process to deepen your reflections about the people you coach.

Step 1

List the similarities and differences that you are aware of between you and your client as they relate to identity markers. Refrain from making assumptions about what you don't know.

Step 2

Consider how identity markers show up in your interactions with this client, as well as in your thoughts and feelings about them, observations of them, and communication with them. After a coaching conversation, reflect on these questions:

- What role did my identity play in this conversation? How did my identity markers influence how I felt, thought, and acted in this conversation?
- How might my identity markers have influenced my client?
- What role did my client's identity markers have on my thoughts, feelings, and actions in this conversation? How might I have perceived or understood my client given their identity markers?
- Was there anything I said as a result of the differences or similarities in our identity markers? What impact might that have had?
- Was there anything I refrained from saying because of the differences or similarities in identity markers? What impact might that have had?
- What conclusions did I come to today about my client? Is it possible that any of those had to do with of my client's identity markers? What is the impact on how I feel about my client based on these conclusions?
- How were my emotions influenced by the similarities or differences between our identity markers? Was it harder for me to empathize with someone who has many different identity markers from my own? Did I feel more judgmental of someone who is different from or similar to me?

Over time, look for patterns in your feelings about the clients you work with. Do you find yourself feeling more or less comfortable coaching people based on their identity markers? Do you have strong preferences about who you coach? Do you find yourself triggered more often by people in one or another identity group? Use these questions to learn about yourself and for deeper insight.

Keep Learning

Learning to be a Transformational Coach who is committed to equity is a journey that will never end—and I, too, am still on this journey. It's been 10 years since I coached Stephanie (the teacher I described in Chapters 2 and 4), and I continue to question how I coached her and whether I could have done things differently that might have yielded greater impact on her students. Here are the final ideas about identity markers I want to leave you with: A coach's learning is ongoing, a coach can sometimes not have done enough learning; sometimes even when a coach has learned a ton, it's not enough; and maybe, sometimes it's not enough because navigating the complexity of our identity markers is complicated.

As I recall teachers I coached with whom I felt less effective, I wonder again how my identity markers influenced how I worked with them. I recognize situations in which my own unhealed pain manifested in unproductive ways—where I projected my anger onto teachers (white teachers and teachers of color) who may have been treating students poorly, but who did not deserve the way I treated them. I recall these moments with compassion for myself and also accepting that I had a responsibility to do my internal work so that I could effectively coach others in order to better serve children.

I recall times when even though I had a solid skill set, and I was clear on my own stuff, I still wasn't effective in creating change. Those are hard moments because I have to recognize the limits of my abilities and accept that there are times when the best thing to do is draw boundaries and walk away. When I left the school that I've referred to as Wilson Middle School (which I wrote about in *The Art of Coaching* and *The Art of Coaching Teams*), I was doing this: drawing boundaries, accepting the limitations of my skills, and walking away. Accepting my own abilities takes courage, but I recognize that I have a limited amount of energy, and that there's somewhere else where I can direct it and have greater impact.

Learning builds resilience. When we learn, we feel empowered. Regardless of what's happened and how painful it's been, see if you can find a way to metabolize it into a learning. Surface your identity experiences, recognize the impact they've had on you and on others, explore the emotions that come up, and then create new practices.

Before You Go . . .

Read the following prompts and select two or three that feel most valuable to you based on where you are in your learning journey. Spend meaningful time considering your reflection before moving on.

REFLECT ON THIS CHAPTER

- What new insights did you get into your own identity in this chapter?
- What questions came up about the identities of people you coach?
- What would be hard about exploring identity? What might be easy?

Interlude: Courage

Principles of Transformational Coaching

- Compassion
- Curiosity
- Connection
- **Courage**
- Purpose

Courage: We draw on deep sources of courage, and face our fears, and act with courage every day. We don't wait until we know everything, or have every detail worked out to do something. We take action and course-correct when necessary. We act with healthy urgency. We know that just as people created inequitable systems and just as we have adopted the mindsets from those systems, people can create new systems and can adopt new mindsets. This gives us the energy to take risks.

The truth has a strange way of following you, of coming up to you and making you listen to what it has to say.

—Sandra Cisneros, writer

- Which are the truths—related to coaching for equity—that have been following you?
- What happens to you when you don't listen to the truths that demand your attention?
- Which truths want you to listen to them?

CHAPTER 9

Surfacing Current Reality

*Caring for myself is not self-indulgence,
it is self-preservation and that is an
act of political warfare.*
—AUDRE LORDE

I want to tell you a long story about a coaching relationship, about a teacher who transformed, and about my own journey. It will take four chapters to tell this story. Along the way, I'll point to the phases of Transformational Coaching so that you can see how I used it.

A Prequel

On the first day of the new school year, just as lunch was about to start, I was wandering the halls of Excelsior Elementary. I'd been assigned to coach a young Vietnamese American man named Khai, a kindergarten teacher in his fourth year. We'd met briefly a few weeks prior, and he'd been enthusiastic about coaching. I hadn't planned on visiting his school that day—I was on an errand for the central office science department and thought I'd just walk around Excelsior and get to know it a bit. Some 650 kids attended this school, every one of them black or brown, and every one of them qualifying for free lunch. The bustle in the halls as kids headed to lunch brought back fond memories of my days teaching second and third grade and how the school year started off with such promise. Although I felt more at home teaching middle school, I appreciated the sweetness of little kids and their energy and excitement about school.

I turned a corner and stopped abruptly. I could see Khai 12 feet ahead of me, walking with his students. As he monitored their movement, his voice boomed through the hall: "Hands behind your backs! Single file! Heads up! No talking! That's how scholars walk at Excelsior." At almost 6 feet tall, Khai towered over the tiny children, whose eyes were big and wide as they marched off to their first day of lunch as kindergarteners. From behind a massive stack of boxes in the hall, I stood and watched.

And then it happened. Khai pulled three African American boys out of line. "The rest of you, stay there and wait quietly," he instructed his class. He positioned the three boys against the opposite wall and berated them: "Scholars do not touch each other when they are in the halls! We do not run! We do not talk!" I had noticed the boys had been slipping out of the single-file line to walk together, laughing and joking with each other as they did, their five-year-old bodies moving in the way that five-year-old bodies do—loose and free. Khai continued yelling at the boys, waving his finger in front of their faces, until the boys started to cry. One—the biggest of the three—crumpled to the ground, sobbing. Khai stopped. Stared at them. "I expected more from you on our first day of school," he said solemnly. "Now we're all late for lunch. Back in the line. Don't let this happen again."

I quickly turned the corner into another hallway. My hands were shaking and my breath was shallow. Tears welled in my eyes, and all I could think was, *I have to get out of here.* I felt dizzy as I made my way to my car where I sat and tried to breathe deeply to stop my body from trembling. I felt like I had just witnessed a crime. I wanted to run inside and scream at him, *How could you treat these babies like this on their first day of school?* I wanted to drive straight to my son's school and take him home. This day, this first day of school, had been my son's first day of kindergarten, in the same school district. My African American son was also perhaps walking through the halls to lunch, and he too had a wiggly little boy's body.

My phone rang. It was my manager. I answered, trying to sound calm, but I started crying. "I can't coach him," I said over and over. I trusted her, a great deal, and I told her what I wanted to do to him—and not a single part of that included listening to him, or regarding him with kindness and curiosity, or even being in the same room as him. I cursed and insisted that she reassign me. She listened. I took the afternoon off and lurked outside of my son's school until his day ended, and then I took him out for ice cream.

I'm writing this 10 years to the week from this incident. I'm surprised by two things: First, by how painful it is to remember that moment in the hallway—my hands trembled as I typed. And second, by my memory of the last time I saw Khai. That had been at his goodbye party—he and his pregnant wife were moving to Boston where he would become a principal. We stood outside of the Mexican restaurant where his friends had hosted a dinner, and he thanked me for the two years of coaching that we'd engaged in, and the subsequent two years of friendship. He handed me a card, in which he'd penned eloquent words of appreciation, and his eyes welled up as he gave me a hug.

What surprises me now is how easily I can tap into that memory of love—that's what it was. I truly cared about Khai—I had learned so much from him, and I was deeply grateful to have worked with him. But in juxtaposition to the first time I saw him with his students, in that hallway, I am surprised that I bridged that emotional chasm. I am surprised, I suppose, at my ability to grow.

And so, this story is about that journey. It's a story about my growth as a coach and the story of a man who transformed as an educator, because Khai did transform (Figure 9.1).

Figure 9.1   The Phases of Transformational Coaching.

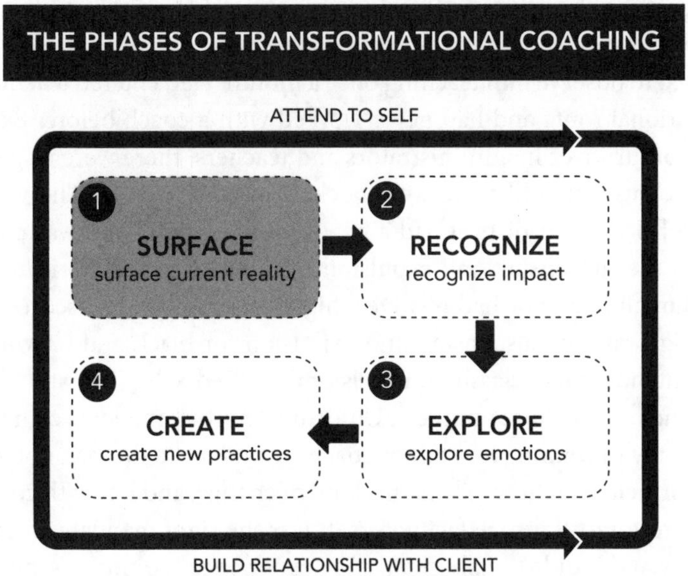

Goals in This Phase:

- Understand the client's teaching—their behaviors, beliefs, and ways of being
- Explore the client's underlying mental models
- Understand the client's organizational context
- Recognize inequitable practices and beliefs
- Build a trusting relationship

Beginning a Coaching Relationship

Meaningful coaching that changes practice only happens within a respectful relationship between a coach and client. That's where we must begin, like it or not. And I didn't like it when I started coaching Khai—I didn't want to build a relationship with him. In the first phase of Transformational Coaching, we focus on surfacing the client's current reality—we seek to understand their teaching practice, their organizational context, their mental models and beliefs, and their strengths and skills. For this to be revealed, the guardrails of a relationship need to be strong.

Khai had opted into a leadership development cohort in which all members received coaching. Everyone in this program aspired to administrative leadership roles. We were expected to meet twice a month, for 60–90 minutes each time, and I was expected to observe him teaching once a month. He'd entered teaching through a non-traditional route and had never worked with a coach before. Excelsior had high levels of turnover in administrators and teachers, there were fragments of an equity-consciousness, and there were pockets of staff toxicity. The year I started working with Khai, our district had a new superintendent who was paying closer attention to the suspension and expulsion rates of African American and Latino males. Although Excelsior had relatively high standardized-test scores, the school had very high rates of suspension and expulsion for black and brown boys. Our new superintendent had classified Excelsior as a "Red School" that had to address discipline and reduce those numbers. Unfortunately, that mandate came with nothing else—not with training for staff or coaching on *how* to do that, not with coaching for the principal on how to lead this kind of change, and not with counseling for students or restorative justice facilitators. It was the right mandate, but it created a lot of anxiety and it didn't really change the experience for kids in school.

Meeting Khai

On the day I had to meet with Khai for the first time, I woke up with a knot in my stomach. I'd prepared for the meeting for a week. I'd sketched a plan for the conversation, identified questions to get to know him, and listed information to share about coaching. But what took time and energy was preparing my internal self. Now, a decade later, when I reflect on how I responded to my own emotions—to my fear about the experience my son would have in school, and to my anger at seeing children humiliated—I recognize that my coping mechanisms at the time were limited. I suppressed many of these emotions, especially those about my own child. I pushed them away and marched on with my work. I recognize this, retrospectively, with kindness toward myself—I didn't know what else to do. My coping strategies, limited as they were, did allow me to effectively coach Khai. However, my fear and anger surfaced in various places in subsequent years, and when it did, it was sometimes unproductive. It's been a long journey to understand and process all the feelings.

Here's what I told myself, over and over, before I met Khai for the first time:

Go in with curiosity and a willingness to learn about him. Look for his strengths— everyone has them. Show up without judgment and see what you find.

That last thought was hard—I'd already cast judgment on Khai. But when you judge others, you create a barrier that declares, "You are *other*." You dehumanize them. You declare yourself to be superior, which justifies your actions. This thinking is at the root of systems of oppression and white supremacy. To engage in judgment, even with holy righteousness, is to perpetuate the systems I'm committed to dismantling. One of my commandments in coaching is, *Thou shalt not judge.* It's not my job, and I too have inflicted pain and suffering on others. I have unintentionally hurt children, including black and brown boys. Perhaps I never screamed at kindergarteners publicly on their first day of school, but I can't compare my transgressions as if some are not as bad as others. In the end, harm is harm. It's not my job to judge what kind of harm is worse. *It is not my job to judge*, I tell myself over and over.

But what, then, is my job? Isn't it to create classrooms where every child thrives every day? Aren't I responsible for the experiences and outcomes of children in school? Yes, I am. And as a Transformational Coach who leads for equity, it is my job to create a brave learning space where a client can recognize and understand the impact of their behaviors, beliefs, and ways of being; a space where they can explore their emotions. This space won't exist if I pollute it with judgment. Trust doesn't bloom in a place of judgment. My judgment came from sadness, fear, and anger. I doubted my own skills and whether I'd be able to effectively coach Khai. Casting judgment was an attempt to avoid my emotions. As I recognized my sadness, fear, grief, and insecurities, I accepted and embraced that my job was to build a trusting relationship with Khai. I tapped into my conviction that I would be able to facilitate meaningful reflection that would allow Khai to see the inequities that he perpetuated and make changes in his practice. *Trust the process,* I told myself.

Trust the Process

I walked into Excelsior at the end of the school day, chanting my mantra in my head:

Do not judge, be open, look for strengths.

This mantra was my intention for the coaching session. Intentions help me stay anchored if the waters get rough.

Khai was in his classroom, which was clean and organized, and he welcomed me warmly. I noticed that I felt icy—I had a hard time making eye contact with him when I shook his hand. I took a slow breath, and said to myself:

This is hard, I know, and you can do this. Trust the process, one step at a time. You can do this.

Self-talk is always helpful for me—sometimes it's encouraging and also firm. If I don't talk to myself, the other voices in my head get loud. And those can be destructive. They say things like:

You'll never be successful with this teacher because he's racist and you're not good enough and why don't you just go back to teaching because you're wasting your time and he'll never be open to you as a coach and you've failed so many times already.

If I don't assert myself and say what I know to be true—*Don't listen to that voice! You can do this!*—then there's little hope for success.

I opened our conversation with one of my favorite get-to-know you prompts. "I'd love to hear about what you were like at the same age as the kids you teach, as a kindergartener," I said. "It's a good way for me to start learning about someone I'm coaching."

Khai smiled. "Sure," he said, "but it's just a typical story of the kid of immigrants."

"If you're willing to share, I'd love to hear," I said, not wanting to push, but also wanting to learn about him. Who we are as teachers and how we show up in the classroom have so much to do with who we were as children and students.

Khai's parents, refugees from Vietnam, had settled in Southern California, where they ran a small restaurant. When he started kindergarten, Khai spoke only a handful of English words. He was in a school comprised predominantly of children of South East Asian descent, but instruction was entirely in English. "I picked it up quickly," he said, "I have a knack for language." He gazed out the window, remembering. "My parents were like so many immigrant parents. I mean, I guess they were like so many Asian immigrants. They expected me to study hard, be good, and get all As. They were strict." Khai stopped to drink water, but I also noticed a shift in his expression, a tightening of his facial features. "Anyway," he continued, "I was a good kid, very respectful, and I mastered everything we were taught quickly. But we were all good back then, all of my classmates were respectful and smart. I wasn't special. That was our culture."

I always take notes when I coach. I capture the words, phrases, and sentences that my clients use in part so that I refrain from interpreting in the moment. If I hear something that feels important, I'll circle or star a word. As I heard Khai describing his "culture," I wondered how he would describe his students' cultures. About half of his kids were African American and half were Latinx. He's also seemed to have made a distinction between immigrant groups when he'd said, "I guess they were like so many Asian immigrants." His Latinx students were all children of immigrants. What did he understand their culture to be? And what were his expectations for how kids behaved in school? How much of those expectations were a projection of his own experience and culture? What did respect look like to him? What did it look like and mean to be a "good kid"?

As I generated these questions, I noticed that this was curiosity bubbling up. As I recognized that emotion, I noted that I was softening toward Khai. Curiosity will do that.

"I was also shy," Khai continued, speaking slightly slower. "I really didn't have many friends in elementary school."

"That must have been hard," I said.

Khai responded: "I'll admit it was. Yes. I was lonely. I remember at lunch I'd sit alone at the end of the table. On the yard, I'd stand by myself. I was tiny—I didn't get tall until the end of high school. I was a little, shy, alone boy."

My empathy for Khai skyrocketed, because I could relate. I'd been a lonely kid in elementary school. I felt grateful to find that point of connection; I realized that I'd been wanting to find connection. "I'm so sorry to hear that," I said, and my tone communicated genuine care. *See, that wasn't so hard,* I told myself, *your heart has tremendous capacity*. It's important to acknowledge when you're fulfilling your intention.

When the moment felt right, I asked my next question: "How do you think your experience as a kindergartener influenced who you are as a kindergarten teacher?"

"That's a good question," he said, sitting up straight and leaning forward.

One of the signs of highly effective coaching is when someone says, "That's a good question," so make note of when a client says that to you. It means that your client is open to your questions in the area you're poking around in. Make sure to reflect on why you think that was a good question for your client, or even ask them what they appreciated about that question.

Khai sighed and said: "My experience affirmed that I can have high expectations for kids. I can expect that they can come to school and behave. I explain the classroom rules, and I expect them to follow them. I don't think they need to be coddled or enticed with rewards for good behavior. I didn't need that. My classmates didn't need that."

His voice was firm.

I noticed the first signs of my strong emotions being activated by the hard tone in his voice and the words "coddled" and "enticed." It felt like a steel ball expanding in my chest. I told myself: *Be curious; it's not your role to judge.* This is what it means to be aware of your emotions and engage with them: You recognize them in the moment when they come up, and then you ground yourself in an intention or commitment—which for me, in this moment, was to be present for Khai and to coach him. As I acknowledged my emotions, I saw a young man who was trying to serve his students in the way he'd been served. He was doing what had worked *for him*. He was doing what he'd seen modeled.

Khai continued: "Some teachers here let kids get away with anything. They say, 'Oh, they're poor, they're being raised by single moms who work long hours, the kids can't help this behavior.'"

He shook his head. "That's bull," Khai said. "These kids can do big things— they just need structure, routine, and discipline."

I was taking notes as fast as I could, and I took a moment to finish. In my peripheral vision, I could see Khai watching me. "Do I sound too harsh for a kindergarten teacher?" he asked.

Ah, I thought, is he opening the door to feedback? Or does he just want me to say, "No, you're not too harsh," so that he gets validation? If I don't say "no" right now, will he doubt my respect? Part of me wanted to leap at the invitation to tell him he was too harsh and to criticize him, but I also knew that this wasn't the time. I needed to focus on building relationship and trust, but I also knew I needed to be honest. I couldn't say, "No, you're not too harsh," because that would have been a lie—and we know when someone is lying. Eventually, I wanted Khai to answer that question for himself—to evaluate his behavior based on the impact he had on students and to decide for himself whether he was too harsh.

I acknowledged the sentiment he expressed. This felt honest. "I appreciate that you're asking for feedback," I said, "and that will come. Right now, I'd like to ask a follow up question, if that's OK?"

"Sure," he said.

"I'm hearing that you teach in a way that worked for you when you were a kid." I paused and Khai nodded. "And that you care about your students and want to see them succeed." I looked up for confirmation, and he nodded again. "OK, so in what ways are your students similar to the kid you were at their age, and in what ways are they different?"

Khai leaned back. "Hmm," he said, "I need to think about that." He grabbed a piece of paper, created a T-chart, and made some notes. Then he stopped, crossed his arms over his chest, and said: "I'm not really sure where you're going with this. What are you trying to get me to see?"

This was a critical moment because Khai was expressing distrust in me. He also sensed that I was trying to get him to see something—which was true. This moment became an opportunity to build or break trust. I was glad that he'd asked me what I was trying to get him to see, and I needed to address his underlying fears. "Thanks for asking that," I said, my voice softening. I put down my pen. I paused and then asked: "What's coming up for you right now? What did my question make you feel?"

"I just feel like maybe you're trying to get me to see something," he responded, "like you're trying to get a certain answer from me."

"I think that's a normal response," I said. "I think you're not sure you trust me yet—and that's fine! We just met. At any point, you are welcome to give me feedback, or say, 'back off' or share anything that's coming up." I wanted to validate whatever Khai was feeling—because all of his emotions were valid, and they all belonged—including his distrust.

He nodded. "I thought you were here to coach me on being a leader," he said.

"I am," I responded. "And who you are in the classroom, as a teacher, is who you'll be as a principal. Today I want to get to know you as a teacher." He nodded, and I could see his discomfort dissipate. Sometimes it's helpful to be transparent with your agenda.

Moments of tension in coaching conversations can be healthy. There can be tension when you ask a probing question, or when it's clear that you're not going to back away from a topic. Tension can exist along with curiosity, compassion, and firmness; tension isn't a bad thing. When tension is present, you might feel more uncomfortable than your client—because you're worrying about whether or not the tension is OK. Your client can experience the tension as productive—as an opportunity to unearth their thoughts and ways of being.

Discomfort exists along a continuum. When there's tension, acknowledge your feelings, stay calm, and pay attention to how your client responds to tension. If you are calm, this can cue them to stay calm. Discomfort can be the precipice to big learning: It's hard to take a close look at our behaviors, beliefs, and ways of being. Stand with your client, indicate that it's OK to look, communicate your confidence that they can see what is there, and trust in the coaching process.

There is such a thing as too much discomfort. When that happens, a client can freeze, flee, or fight out of self-protection. You'll know when a client shuts down—you'll experience this as pushback, resistance, or insincerity. A client who repeatedly says, "Everything is fine!" while you can see that they're not fine has shut down. This happens when you've generated too much cognitive dissonance—when someone isn't ready to look as closely at their behaviors, beliefs, and ways of being as you've wanted them to look. You'll find out how much is too much through trial and error, and you can learn to see the signs that someone is approaching their shutdown point. You'll see their body language change and become protective, and you'll hear their tone of voice either fluctuate more or settle into a low, flat register. You might notice that their talking increases or decreases. And if you pay close attention to the words they use, those will also likely give you clues.

As your coaching improves in general, and as you get to know a client, you'll see when you are approaching the territory of too much discomfort, and you'll learn how to back away and course-correct. As you do this, your client unconsciously begins to trust you more—they see that while you might lead them into scary places and let them experience healthy discomfort, you also pay close attention to when they need a break. A good sign that you left a client in healthy tension, at the right time, is that at a subsequent coaching meeting, they say: "You know, last time you asked me . . . And I've really been thinking about that." This means that you led them to a point where they could gain insight and understanding into themselves, and sensing your confidence, they looked.

When Khai said, "I'm not really sure where you're going with this," and when he expressed doubt about my line of questioning, he was giving me a cue to shift the conversation. He was letting me know that he was on the edge of too much discomfort and that he didn't want to keep going. We spent the rest of that session discussing the leadership cohort, the logistics of coaching, and his experiences as a teacher. I asked him about his strengths, and he named planning, organization, using data to drive instruction, and "running a tight ship."

When I asked him about challenges, he shrugged. "My evaluations are always excellent," he said, "I've had a few run-ins with parents—but I don't know how I could have managed those any better. We have a lot of really difficult parents here, you know that."

I didn't nod—I didn't agree with him—and focused on my notetaking. I usually keep my head still when a client is talking—I don't want to nod in agreement for 15 minutes until they say something I disagree with, and then stop nodding. It would be obvious that I disagree.

"I am always open to feedback and to improving," he said, almost as a sum of his teacher performance.

"That's great to hear!" I said enthusiastically and scribbled down his words, drawing big stars next to them. I wanted him to see that I'd heard that statement and would remember his invitation for feedback, so that when it came, he could remember that he'd given me permission.

Our time was ending. "How's this conversation been?" I asked.

"Good," he said, "different than I thought it would be."

"How so?" I asked.

"I guess I didn't expect your questions about my experience as a kindergartener. I'm going to give that more thought."

"That's great," I said. "We can pick up from there next time if you want." Always extend an invitation to your client to make choices in conversations.

He looked at me for a moment, seeming to contemplate something. Then he said, "Next time we can talk about this suspension thing? Admin is breathing down my neck, saying I have to reduce the numbers of kids that I suspend."

"Sure," I said. "Sounds good." I was glad he was raising this.

"They are putting a cap on how many kids we can suspend," he said, with an indignant expression on his face. "I mean, what are we supposed to do with the kids who can't behave here? It's absurd."

Clients often raise something important just as their session with you is ending—especially when they're starting to trust you. It's almost like they dangle an important topic in front of you to see how you'll react—will you bite right then and there? Will you remember it next time?

We didn't have time to get into a meaningful conversation about this, so I said, "Let's definitely talk about that. Would it be okay if I bring suspension data next time?" I wanted to base that conversation in data, and given what Khai had shared about his strengths, I thought he'd be receptive.

"Sure," Khai said. "And you should also observe them so you know what I'm dealing with. I mean, I know you didn't teach kindergarten so you probably don't know how hard it is, and these kids are *especially hard*." He shook his head with an air of exasperation.

I took an inaudible breath. The phrase "these kids" is particularly triggering to me. "These kids" coupled with a deficit reference is an othering strategy—every time someone says "these kids," I imagine they are pushing children away—shoving them out of sight and creating as much distance as possible between themselves and those children. But Khai had invited me in to observe. And that was good. A coach needs an invitation to enter a teacher's classroom. In that sense (and perhaps only in that sense), we're like vampires.

"I'd love to visit your classroom," I said, honestly. "It would be super helpful. How about next Tuesday?" Whenever a teacher invites you to visit, lock down a day and time right then and there.

"That's fine," said Khai. "Come after lunch if you can. That's when we do math, and they're always hyped up from all the sugar they eat. I don't know why their parents send them to school with so much candy and Hot Cheetos and junk food."

"I'll do that. Is there anything you'd like me to pay attention as far as your teacher moves? What you say or do?" When visiting teachers, I invite their input into what I'll observe—I want to know what's most important to them. I also want to indicate that I'm not there only to pay attention to the kids, as was reflected in Khai's invitation. It sounded like he wanted me to see how out-of-control his kids were, so that I would see that his behaviors (yelling at kids and suspending some of them) were justified. I wasn't going to do that. I needed to let him know.

"I don't know. I'm not sure," said Khai thoughtfully.

"Would it be helpful if I paid attention to how you respond to students who act out or break the rules? I'd be another set of eyes."

"OK, sounds good," said Khai. "But make sure you see what they do."

"Got it," I said, as I started packing up my stuff.

Walking out of Excelsior, I reflected on how the conversation had gone. I felt like I'd held my intention well—I had been curious, I'd looked for strengths, and most of the time, I'd withheld my judgment. I also thought about how much I'd learned about Khai in less than an hour. Our beliefs are formed by what we've seen, heard, and lived—and Khai's beliefs about what his students needed from a teacher emerged from his experience as a kid, and his limited understandings of his students. I felt tired as a got in my car. It took so much energy for me to be fully present as a coach, but as I drove to pick up my son from school, I realized that I felt excited to work with Khai. I sensed that I'd learn a lot, and I felt optimistic and ready for the challenge.

Planning a Coaching Conversation

The next day, I had 30 minutes to reflect on the conversation with Khai, and to plan my next conversation. I started by transferring my questions from my notebook into a Word document. For speed, I prefer to write on a computer. But when I'm with a client, I write by hand—I don't like the way an open computer makes the meeting feel, and I like to write by hand so that I can circle, star, and draw arrows in my notes.

Here are the questions I crafted:

- What does he think are the differences between Asian immigrant parents and immigrant parents from other regions?
- His "culture" was respectful. Kids worked hard. They were smart. How does he see and define the cultures of the students he's teaching?
- What were his unconscious expectations for how kids behaved in school? How much of those expectations were a project of his own experience and culture?
- What did respect look like to him?
- What did it look like and mean to be a "good kid"?
- What does he think it takes to get kids to learn something? He said he thinks they should be able to do something just because he tells them—the rules, for example. Does he understand the idea of scaffolding learning? Of assessing students' Zone of Proximal Development (ZPD), even for something like learning classroom rules?
- What's his understanding of intrinsic and extrinsic motivation?
- What does he think the purpose of education is?
- Is there a schoolwide approach to discipline? What kinds of programs have they used for classroom management?
- He says, "These kids can do big things—they just need structure, routine, and discipline." What does he aspire to see them do? What does he understand about their visions and dreams, and their parents' visions and dreams for what they want to do? What makes him feel confident in what the kids can do?

- When he asked if he sounded "too harsh," what makes him concerned about that? What is it in his own behavior that makes him worry that he's too harsh?
- Continue exploring how as a kid, he was similar to and different from his students. This question was one he didn't want to get into—so what's that about?
- What kinds of "run-ins" has he had with parents? What did he mean when he said that parents are "really difficult?" And he said he doesn't know how he could have "managed those parents better." Is he interested in learning some strategies for engaging in a healthy way with parents? Is this something he might want to work on?
- He had said, "I am always open to feedback and to improving," and he cited his high evaluation scores. But who does he want to be as a teacher? What's his vision for himself?
- Why did he get into teaching? Why does he want to be a principal?
- What kind of relationship does he have with admin?
- What does he think about the mandate to reduce suspension numbers? What are his suspension numbers?
- Why does he think kids aren't behaving?
- Is he interested in and willing to try some different classroom management strategies?
- Why does he think "these kids are *especially hard*"? Who is he comparing them to? What does he think that they need? How does he get to know students? Does he value getting to know students?

Additional Resources

Planning for an Equity-Focused Conversation is an additional resource to guide you in this process. You can find it on my website, http://brightmorningteam.com.

The Art of Coaching Workbook: Tools to Make Every Conversation Count (2020) also has many tools to guide you through planning coaching conversations.

Yes, I had a long list of questions about Khai after our first meeting, and you might be thinking, *Doesn't that take a long time to write?* And yes, it does! I love this part of coaching—it's like figuring out a puzzle. I enjoy sitting in my office and musing over who someone is, why they do what they do, and what I can say or do to bring all of that to the surface. This process pulls me farther into a state of curiosity, which feels like renewable energy for a coach.

After capturing my wonderings, I needed to craft a plan and some good questions for next time. It's generally unproductive to ask a client a question that starts with "Why," because it demands that we account for our thoughts and actions in a way that puts the person receiving the question on the defensive. Take a moment to think about this. Imagine me asking you, "Why did you say that to her?" Perhaps even close your eyes and imagine this. What feelings come up for you? You'll likely feel as if you need or want to explain yourself. There's an unhelpful adversarial undertone—because as the asker, I'm holding judgment over you. Clearly, by asking the question, I feel as if you've done something I disagree with. In general, I refrain from starting questions with "Why."

I was torn between two directions for our next conversation: between continuing getting to hear Khai's story and unpacking the suspension numbers. I often craft plans for coaching conversations as a flow chart. I plan for two or three directions that the conversation could go in, and then identify the junctures where the different paths could appear. Sometimes those junctures arise because of the mood that the client is in. For example, if a new client has had a hard day or seems tired, I might select the path of self-reflection because talking about oneself is often cathartic and energizing. However, if a client feels agitated about something that happened during the day, they may not want to share their life story or be in a reflective mood. They may want to release emotions or problem-solve about the challenge. Follow the client's lead. Go where they want to go, especially when you're building relationship and surfacing current reality. Doing so demonstrates that you aren't attached to an agenda or outcome, that you're responsive to your client's needs, and that you see and hear them. This builds trust. There are times when we need to direct the conversation, and we'll explore how to do that, but there are also times when we let the client lead.

In planning for my next meeting with Khai, my hunch was that he would want to talk about his leadership or teaching. I could probably weave-in questions about his background, but I'd need to focus on outcomes. I was learning that Khai was action-oriented, and to meet him where he was in terms of his emotions and mindset, to show him that I saw him, I'd need to facilitate conversations that felt concrete and would drive toward an outcome. I also knew that I'd be observing him and looking at data on suspensions at Excelsior before our next meeting. So, I held off on creating a plan.

The School-To-Prison Pipeline

The school-to-prison pipeline is a term to describe a process through which students are pushed out of schools and into prisons. It is the process of criminalizing youth, often set in motion by a school's disciplinary policies and practices that put students into contact with law enforcement. The key policies and practices that created and maintain the school-to-prison pipeline include the exclusion of students from schools through punitive suspensions and expulsions, the presence of police on campus (School Resource Officers—SROs), and zero-tolerance policies. A *zero-tolerance policy* means that a school has zero tolerance for any kind of misbehavior or violation of rules, no matter how minor, unintentional, or subjectively defined it may be. A student can be suspended for chewing gum, wearing their hood up, or rolling their eyes. In schools with a zero-tolerance policy, suspensions and expulsions are common ways of dealing with student misbehavior.

The presence of SROs at a school means that students have contact with law enforcement from a young age. Though their intended purpose is to ensure safety on campus, in many instances, when the police handle a disciplinary issue, nonviolent minor infractions escalate into violent, criminal incidents that have negative impacts on students. Being suspended results in student disengagement and harms a student's self-worth and belonging. Once suspended or expelled, students are less likely to complete high school and more likely to be in contact with the criminal justice system.

Analyzing Data

Before the school year started, our superintendent shared suspension data on all schools in our district. Here was the data on Excelsior:

- Number of students enrolled: 650
- Total number of suspensions: 310
- Number of students suspended: 103
- Percent of students suspended: 14.8%
- Number of African American students suspended: 57
- Percent of students suspended who are African American: 52%
- Overall population of African American students: 29%

- Number of Latino students suspended: 29
- Percentage of students suspended who are Latino: 38%
- Overall population of Latino students: 61%
- Number of suspensions for defiance: 148
- Percent suspensions for defiance: 48%
- Number of suspensions for fighting: 99
- Percent suspensions for fighting: 32%
- Lost days: 158
- Average Daily Attendance (ADA) dollar loss: $5,082.83

What first jumped out at me was the discrepancy between the number of African American children who were suspended, as compared to the number of Latinos. Latinos were 61 percent of the school, but African American children were suspended at almost twice the rate. This meant that the principal's office was full of black children. The next thing that I noticed was that a total of 103 students were suspended in one year, but the total number of suspensions was 310. That meant that many children were suspended more than once and that the principal's office was probably full of the same black children. The final glaring data point was that the overwhelming majority of students were suspended for "defiance." That word is a red flag when evaluating educational equity.

What was missing from this report was disaggregation of the data by gender and more detailed information. I wanted to know, for example, how the suspensions for fighting and defiance broke down according to race and gender. I also wanted grade-level information for suspensions—were they higher in one grade or another? But the central office didn't gather that data, and I didn't know if Excelsior's administrators did.

Planning and Processing

When I compared Excelsior's data to other elementary schools in our district that served the same community, I was aghast. Excelsior's numbers were double those of other schools. *It doesn't have to be like this,* I thought. *Children want to be in school, they love to learn; we can do better than this.* As I read the data, my chest tightened and my breathing shallowed. I got up and went for a walk. I love to walk in silence, with my thoughts; I also love walking with a friend or listening to a podcast or to music. As I walk and swing my arms and breathe fresh air, I visualize releasing the sadness that arises in my work, that drains my energy. Walking always clears my mind and replenishes my energy. It's a top self-care strategy for me.

Back at my desk, I jotted down questions to ask Khai:

- How did he make sense of this data? What story does it tell?
- What jumped out at him in this data?
- Did this data reflect his classroom? Did he suspend twice the number of African American kids as he did Latinos?
- When he suspended a kid for defiance, what exactly were the child's behaviors?
- How was defiance defined at Excelsior? What did Khai think of that definition?
- How did he understand the fact that the neighboring elementary school had only a quarter of the suspensions that Excelsior had?
- What did he think needed to happen for this data to change?

I hoped that these questions would help us gain more insight into Khai's current reality. I also suspected that as we discussed this data, we might shift into Phase 2 of Transformational Coaching, Recognizing Impact. I was aware that as I looked at the data, I was drawing on my knowledge about how white supremacy and racism manifests in schools, specifically regarding how the behavior of black and brown children is interpreted. There are a couple of concepts you'll need to understand when coaching for equity, and to make sense of the data that I've just shared with you. These are the concepts of disproportionality and defiance. Let's make sure we have shared-understandings of these terms.

Disproportionality and Defiance

Racial disparity, or *racial disproportionality*, means that racial groups are not statistically represented according to their populations. Black people make up 13.2 percent of the U.S. population—so, black people should not exceed 13.2 percent of Americans killed by the police. To be clear: *No one* should be killed by police, but if we're talking about proportional representation, this number shouldn't exceed 13 percent. Black people also shouldn't exceed 13 percent of the incarcerated population, and they should own about 13 percent of the wealth in the United States. However, African Americans own 2.7 percent of the wealth in the United States, and they make up about 40 percent of the incarcerated population. In fact, black people are five times more likely to be incarcerated than whites—this is what disproportionality means. Between 2010 and 2012, young black males were 21 times more likely to be killed by police than their white counterparts (Kendi, 2016, p. 1). And according to federal data, the median wealth of white households is 13 times the median wealth of black households (Kendi, 2016, p. 516).

Defiance is a problematic concept and term because it's entirely subjective and usually interpreted through racial bias. Almost any behavior can be (and has been) labeled defiance—repeatedly tapping a foot on the floor, chewing gum, rolling eyes, making eye contact, not making eye contact, talking in class, refusing to remove a hat, and so on. The term has been used generally for students who don't follow rules, who aren't compliant, and who express any kind of dissatisfaction or disagreement. Disproportionately, this term has been applied to students of color. As author and researcher Monique W. Morris (2016) writes, "what constitutes a threat to safety is subjective when black children are involved (p. 57)." The term *defiance* denotes aggression and suggests that a student is unpredictable, dangerous, and needs to be controlled. It's an inaccurate term that doesn't yield insight into a child's behavior, and it has permitted educators to enact severe punitive measures.

Suspension doesn't transform student behavior, and it increases the likelihood that students will leave school ("drop out") or become involved in the criminal justice system. Research has shown that suspensions and the accompanying loss of instructional time disproportionately affect students of color, particularly African Americans. In California, in 2017 and 2018, African American student suspensions represented 17 percent of total suspensions, even though African American students made up less than 6 percent of total students in the state (according to the California Department of Education). In September 2019, California passed a law prohibiting public and charter schools from suspending students in grades K-8 for disrupting school activities or "willfully defying" the authority of teachers or administrators (Agrawal, 2019).

How we perceive student behavior has everything to do with how much awareness we have of white supremacy. When we coach for equity, we draw on knowledge about bias and racism and how it shapes our beliefs and behaviors so that we can guide a client through a process of recognizing the impact their actions have on children. It doesn't work to just tell teachers to stop suspending kids for defiance; we need to help them unpack those assumptions and recognize that they interpret the behavior of black and brown children through the distortions of racism, so that they can create new beliefs and new behaviors.

A First Classroom Visit

I opened Khai's classroom door to see a large African American boy sitting in a single chair facing the door. He was flopped back, his legs sticking straight out. His eyes brightened as I stepped in, and he jumped up and said: "Hi! Are you someone's mom? Are you the PE teacher? Are you Mr. Tran's girlfriend?" This boy was one of the three boys that Khai had pulled out of line and yelled at on the first day of school; this was the kid who had crumpled to the ground in tears.

"Sit down, Jordan," Khai called from across the room. His tone was firm. "We don't talk in time-out."

I smiled at Jordan and moved into the classroom. My resolve to look for Khai's strengths felt like it had completely vanished. *I can't do this,* said a voice in my head. *Why do I have to do this? Why can't someone else coach him?* I felt angry as I perched on a table in the back.

"Scholars," Khai said, "Ms. Aguilar is a coach, and she's here to observe you today, so be on your best behavior and treat her with respect," he said. I cringed. I wasn't there to observe the kids.

The students were at their desks, which were grouped in pods of four, and they were working with manipulatives from the math program. On the screen, a graphic timer was projected that indicated when they were halfway through whatever they were doing. Students seemed engaged and remarkably focused considering that they were only four or five years old. Khai circulated and took notes on a clipboard. When Khai came over to where I was, I asked him what he was documenting.

"This week, we're working on counting to 10 and connecting numbers to objects," he responded. "I give them a number, and each person in their group represents that number with different objects. So they see that four can be four orange blocks, or four red sticks, or four tiddlywinks. Four is four. This is a kindergarten standard, so I'm taking notes on who has mastered or is approaching mastery of the standard, who is close, and who is far from mastering the standard."

I appreciated this and said that the kids seemed calm and engaged. "We'll see," he responded. I wasn't sure what to make of that response. What did he think could happen that would upset this learning environment? I didn't want to ask about Jordan—not yet. I wanted to focus on what was going well. After I'd been in the classroom for about 10 minutes, Khai went to Jordan, knelt down next to him, and said a few words that I couldn't hear, and then Jordan returned to his desk.

Things fell apart when the manipulatives had to be put away. That was when Angie, the "materials master" in Jordan's group eagerly reached for the big foam blocks that Jordan was stacking.

"Hey! I'm not done!," Jordan yelled.

"But it's clean up time!" shouted Angie.

And then Jordan was grabbing the blocks back, and Angie held on tight, and then she fell backwards onto the floor.

"That's it, Jordan!," Khai said as he strode across the room. "You're going to the office. You had three warnings today, and a time-out, and now you're fighting and pushing a classmate. That is *not* how scholars behave." He pointed at the door. "Adriana will take you to the office."

Jordan started crying. "I didn't push her," he said over and over. "I wasn't fighting," he sobbed as Adriana took a slip of paper from Khai's outstretched arm, hung the hall pass around her neck, and walked Jordan out of class.

I felt like I was in shock when Khai came over and said, "See what I'm dealing with? I told you."

If kids hadn't been in the room, I might have exploded. I didn't know what to say, and I worried that my facial expressions revealed my exasperation and anger. I said something like, "It's helpful to see examples of what you're struggling with," and then said I had to go. I just couldn't be in there any longer.

I drove to my office along one of Oakland's central corridors, a stretch that goes through some of the most marginalized communities in the Bay Area, a place where only black and brown people live. At 2:00 p.m., there were many people on the streets who were "having a hard time." That's how I'd talk to my son about the people we'd see who struggled with mental illness, or who didn't have homes, or who were intoxicated. "They are having a hard time," I'd tell my son. "We don't need to be afraid of them; once they were all little kids like you."

At a red light, I watched a young man who wore no shirt and seemed to be drunk talking incoherently to an old man on a bus bench who was definitely having a hard time (he was most certainly homeless). *Those two men,* I thought, *they were both kindergarteners once. What happened? How many teachers sent them out of class, told them they didn't belong, and stifled their curiosity and wonder?* Surely, there were many factors that contributed to the challenges in their lives—joblessness, trauma, addiction—but what role had schools and educators played? What was our responsibility to mitigate those challenges? What was the role of schools in interrupting systemic inequities? I had only questions, sadness, and anger.

Before You Go . . .

Read the following prompts and select two or three that feel most valuable to you based on where you are in your learning journey. Spend meaningful time considering your reflection before moving on.

REFLECT ON THIS CHAPTER

- What came up for you reading this chapter? Which thoughts and feelings? What connections could you make?
- How does your racial identity affect the way you read this chapter? What comes up for you when you think about this scenario through the lens of your own identity markers?
- Can you identify the moves I made to build trust with Khai? Which of those have you tried? Which could you incorporate into your coaching now?
- What kind of data did I start gathering? What other kinds of data would you be interested in seeing in this situation?

REFLECT ON YOUR PRACTICE

- Recall a time when you observed something happening to children in a school that made you feel strong emotions. What happened? How did you respond? If you could go back in time, would you do anything differently?
- Recall your own experiences as a kindergartener (or an elementary school student of another age). If I'd visited your classroom, your teacher, and you, what would I have noticed? How does it feel to recall those memories? How might those memories inform how you coach and lead now?

TO DO

- What questions do you have about the experiences and outcomes for marginalized groups in your school, organization, or district? Which groups would you like to learn more about?
- What data could you gather to gain insight into racial inequities in your school, organization, or district? What data could you gather to gain insight into inequities for other marginalized groups—for how girls experience math and science? For students with learning differences?

Interlude: Purpose

Principles of Transformational Coaching

- Compassion
- Curiosity
- Connection
- Courage
- **Purpose**

Purpose: Our purpose is to create a world characterized by justice, equity, and liberation. The journey is the destination. We can fulfill our purpose when we act with compassion, curiosity, connection, and courage.

The only legitimate use of privilege is to try and dismantle the inequalities and unfairness of privilege.

—Rebecca Solnit, writer and activist

- In which ways are you privileged?
- How have you used your privilege to dismantle the "unfairness of privilege"?

CHAPTER 10

Recognizing Impact

*Start measuring your work by the optimism
and self-sufficiency you leave behind.*
—PETER BLOCK

While I continued seeking to understand Khai, I shifted into the second phase of Transformational Coaching—into Recognize Impact. In this phase, I'd encourage Khai to explore and reflect on the unintended consequences of his behaviors and underlying mental models. I'd also coach Khai to understand the detrimental impact that systems of oppression had on everyone, including on himself. As it almost always happens, I suspected that recognizing impact would flow into exploring emotions—it's hard to see impact without having feelings. We are humans; humans have feelings (Figure 10.1).

Debriefing an Observation

In the fourth week of school, I met with Khai for our second coaching session. As soon as I sat down in his classroom, I decided to alter the plan for our coaching conversation a little bit. I think Khai was ready to recognize impact, but I still had big holes in my understanding of who he was.

Figure 10.1 The Phases of Transformational Coaching.

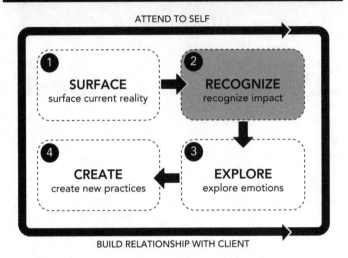

THE PHASES OF TRANSFORMATIONAL COACHING

ATTEND TO SELF

1. **SURFACE**
surface current reality

2. **RECOGNIZE**
recognize impact

4. **CREATE**
create new practices

3. **EXPLORE**
explore emotions

BUILD RELATIONSHIP WITH CLIENT

Recognize

Goals in This Phase:

- Guide a client to recognize how white supremacy and systems of oppression manifest in their classroom, teaching (or leadership) practice, beliefs, and way of being.
- Help the client identify and reflect how systemic oppression impacts students, their communities, and the teacher or leader themselves.

"Khai," I said, "could we start with about five minutes on what brought you into education? I'd love to hear that story, and then we can shift into whatever you'd like to talk about."

"Sure," he responded, "although I'm curious to hear your impressions of my teaching."

I nodded. "We can talk about that today. Is there anything else on your mind?"

Even when I have a plan, and even if a client and I have previously agreed about what we'll talk about in a session, I always invite the client's input into the conversation when I show up. I want to remind them that coaching is time for them to explore what they'd like as it relates to kids and teaching.

Khai thought, and then said, "I think just the observation you did and the suspension issue. The day I sent Jordan to the office for fighting, Mr. Langley [the principal] emailed me saying that he wants to meet about my classroom management strategies."

I jotted down these items and then continued: "Great, we can talk about all of that, but I'd like to spend five minutes hearing about how you became a teacher."

"I don't mind sharing that story." Khai shrugged, leaned back and began. "Education had saved me and many of my peers from the hard life our parents had. I was the first in my extended family to graduate from high school and go to college. My grandparents in Vietnam were rice farmers. I felt like I owed it to my community to give back."

He stopped as if signaling that the story ended there, but I wanted to know more.

"I'm curious about whether you considered teaching in the area where you grew up?" I asked.

Khai nodded. "I did, but I attended UC Berkeley, and I wanted to stay in this area after I graduated. I've come to care about the kids in Oakland. We're not all that different."

I assumed he was talking about race and ethnicity, but I wanted to clarify. "What are the similarities and differences you perceive between you and your students?"

"Well," he replied, "obviously our cultural and linguistic differences. And sometimes I think that they've had a harder time of it—the African Americans. As Vietnamese immigrants, I know we had some benefits from the government, and our parents were determined to make a good life for themselves. African Americans didn't choose to come here."

I was taking notes.

Khai continued: "As for similarities—well, I know what it's like to be on a tight budget and have parents who are always working or who are dealing with their own demons and I know what it's like to be a kid who is scared."

He paused and then finished. "But yeah, I got into teaching because I believe in the power of education, and I want to serve."

There was more I wanted to know about how Khai felt working in this community, and I could have probed into some of his responses, but I wanted to honor his desire to talk about the topics he'd named. I thanked him for sharing and asked if he wanted to shift into talking about the observation. He nodded.

"OK," I said, "tell me a bit about what you hope to hear. What are you most curious about?"

"Just what you thought," he responded.

"About what specifically?" I asked.

"I guess about Jordan."

I nodded. "I can do that," I said. "I'd really like to first hear from you about that day—what your reflections about Jordan are; what you thought about what I observed." His expression seemed to flatten. I continued: "My role as a coach is to help you think through your decisions as a teacher, to help you unpack what you say and do. If I just tell you what I think, it's not going to be as helpful as if we explore what you think."

"OK," he said. "I get very little feedback, and I want to hear your opinions, but I get what you're saying."

"I'm glad you want to improve," I said. "And I will give you feedback."

Khai's reflection on the 45 minutes I'd observed wasn't particularly insightful. He perceived himself as setting high expectations, doing the critical work of tracking students according to mastery, and of maintaining a focused learning environment. He didn't question his decisions or behaviors about instruction or how he engaged with students. Jordan, he explained, broke the rules daily. And this, I learned, was Jordan's second year in kindergarten. He'd been retained the previous year by a different teacher. "So, he should know the rules," Khai said. Khai felt he needed to make sure his class was a safe place for every child and that Jordan's behavior often made it feel unsafe for other kids.

I asked some follow-up questions. I hoped to provoke deeper reflection and analysis of the decisions Khai had made. These included:

- Can you help me understand how you made that decision to send Jordan out?
- I wonder what that moment was like for Jordan. What do you suspect he felt and thought right then?
- What could have been some alternate ways to respond to Jordan in that moment?
- What kind of safety do you think Jordan might need?

Khai responded to these questions in a brisk and perfunctory manner, and I felt as if he had an impenetrable barrier around him that my questions bounced off of. I recognized that Khai's defenses were up, so I backed off from asking questions about Jordan and the class I'd observed. Sometimes a client gets more defensive if you persist in probing when they aren't ready.

I asked him, "What would be helpful for us to talk about right now?" This is a great question to ask if you feel a stalemate coming on. It's an invitation to your client to have agency and lead the conversation to where it might be useful.

"What did you think of what you saw?" Khai said.

"Let me think for a second," I said, pressing my favorite purple Uni-Ball pen into the side of my cheek and gazing out the window. I didn't think that Khai honestly wanted to hear what I thought. I wondered if he hoped I'd validate his decision to send Jordan to the office and whether this was a test of my confidence in him as a teacher. I was tempted to ask why he wanted to hear my opinion—but I feared that would seem like I was avoiding his repeated request for feedback. And I was worried about being vague or ambiguous. I felt stuck. Then my mantra, *be curious and compassionate,* went through my mind.

"OK, Khai, here's what I noticed," I said. "You were suffering—you seemed frustrated with Jordan, and I know how committed you are to your students. I assume you are also committed to serving Jordan, so I imagine it was hard to send him out. I hear that you were trying to create a safe space for kids, and we could explore more ways to do that so that Jordan can also be there."

Khai was nodding, but I wasn't sure what he felt.

"Because," I continued, "I imagine it was hard for Jordan to miss instructional time and be sent to the office. He seemed very upset. I know you're a skilled teacher, and I hope Jordan can benefit."

"What do you think I should have done when he started fighting with Angie?" Khai asked, his voice rising a bit. "She's very sensitive around aggressive boys."

I've trained myself to listen for the positive. I was hearing, again, that Khai was committed to creating a safe learning space—but his notion of safety was limited to physical safety, and I questioned how he interpreted the behaviors of boys, and how that interpretation was clouded by racism. There was no doubt that he responded to the behavior of black boys more severely than he did others.

I asked, "What have you tried with Jordan?"

"I talk to him quietly and give him warnings," Khai said. "I send him to the timeout chair so that he can calm down. I've tried calling his mom, but she never answers."

"Tell me more about the behaviors that he gets in trouble for," I requested. I wanted to shift the focus from the actions that teachers take to manage students to how we interpret and perceive their actions.

Khai responded: "You should come and watch him again. He's constantly moving—and he's a big kid, you saw that. He bumps into other kids, he pushes kids, when we're on the rug, he's squirming all over. If I ask the class a question, he'll jump out of his chair and shout something out. He runs in the halls. He just has so much energy."

Yes, kindergarteners have a lot of energy, I thought. That was the grade I was most afraid of teaching—I'll take 200 sixth graders over 20 kindergarteners any day. I told Khai that I empathized with him—that little kids have a lot of energy. I wondered whether he had considered teaching older grades. But I suspected he was unconsciously reacting to the fact that Jordan was a black male. Many of the other kindergarteners squirmed and wiggled just as much as Jordan. But he was a large black male.

I considered whether this was the time to unpack Khai's unconscious (and conscious) biases. I could have opened up that line of inquiry. I'm not afraid of having that conversation, but this was only the second time we'd met. I suspected that in order to have a meaningful conversation about his biases, we'd need a little more trust and relationship. I recalled my experience as a teacher: even with a coach whom I trusted from day one, I would have been uncomfortable, and perhaps even defensive, had she raised my bias in our second meeting.

Our biases prevent us from seeing someone in their entirety—we see them through a distorted lens; in this case, through the distortions of white supremacy. Without awareness, and especially if we aren't black, we might see a black male and our implicit bias tells us that he's a danger, even if he's five years old. Or our bias tells us that he wants to be a basketball player. Or that he listens to rap. We don't see someone's full humanity. I wanted Khai to see Jordan's full humanity.

"What do you know about Jordan?" I asked. "What are his strengths? What does he like?"

It turned out that Khai knew a lot about Jordan's homelife, he knew his birth date, and he knew that he ate all his lunch, every day. He knew that Jordan liked music and animals and that he had strong verbal skills. Every time Khai started listing Jordan's shortcomings or areas for growth, I'd gently nudge him to focus on the positive. At one point, Khai said, "He seems to get patterns quickly, in contrast to his number recognition and letter identification and his ability to draw basic figures." I interrupted Khai (something I do with discretion) before he could go down a negative rabbit hole and asked a follow up question about patterns. I wanted to fan the flames of Khai's curiosity about Jordan.

Then I changed the subject and asked, "Does he have any pets at home?" Khai didn't know the answer, but said he'd ask Jordan. That was a good sign that his curiosity was strengthening. Khai was like a shopping cart with a wayward wheel—every time he veered off in the direction of deficits, I'd gently redirect the conversation to help him see Jordan more expansively.

Khai spoke animatedly about a lesson he'd done the previous week on properties of water during which Jordan was focused and attentive. "I think what really helped Jordan was that he had a partner," Khai reflected, and he does OK when he works with a partner. When he works with his whole group, he has a harder time. I guess I could try to pair him up more often, but I also think the content of the lesson was engaging and he *is* a curious kid.

As I had hoped would happen, Khai was arriving at insights into what worked for Jordan. I could hear that his understanding of Jordan was expanding and his reflective skills were strengthening.

As he realized our time was ending, Khai said, "This went by fast."

I smiled. "I'm glad to hear you found it useful. What specifically are you taking away from our time today?"

"I'm not sure," he said. "I guess I have a couple of ideas about how I might deal with Jordan, and I think it was useful to talk about him a bit—maybe I haven't been fair to him all the time." He paused and adjusted his glasses. I waited, not wanting to jump in, wanting to give Khai time to think and continue if he wanted.

He took a short breath. "It's easy to talk to you," he said. "It can be hard for me to open up to people, but I feel pretty comfortable with you."

"Thank you," I said. "I'm glad to hear that."

"But next time, could you give me some direct feedback and suggestions for how I can get Jordan to behave? He can't keep hijacking class. I want to see all of my students do well this year."

"I really appreciate your commitment to all your students, Jordan included, and yes, we can get specific next time," I said, noting that in my notebook.

A Pause to Look Inward

Sometimes when I'm coaching, I distance myself from my some of my experiences so I can be present for my client. I am not there as Elena, a child who often wasn't served in school; I'm not there as Elena, a former teacher; I'm not there as Elena, a mother. When the coaching session is over, then I take time to acknowledge the parts of myself that stood on the side during the session—parts that want attention or are unhealed. I acknowledge my feelings and explore them. If I don't, those emotions slip out unproductively at other times.

After that second conversation with Khai, I journaled when I got home. Sometimes to explore my emotions, I start with the words, "I feel . . .," and then I finish the sentence and start another with the same words. So, I wrote:

> I feel sad because Jordan has to be in that classroom tomorrow. I feel frustrated that coaching can be slow. I feel angry that there aren't more teachers who are skilled at working with black and brown kids. I feel scared because I don't know if my kid's teacher sees him as a full human being. I feel angry that there's so much racism in this world.

And I wrote and wrote, which for me is a cathartic release.

Especially when we coach for equity, we must process our emotions—this is simply because we're more likely to experience strong emotions. Processing feelings means exploring, understanding, and learning from them. We can do this alone or with a friend or colleague. We can also use artistic expressions to explore our feelings, or do so while engaging in physical activity. How and with whom we process can vary, but processing includes a few key steps. First, we acknowledge and name our feelings. The Core Emotions table in Appendix E is an invaluable resource to build emotional awareness. It can help us build a robust vocabulary to describe feelings. Next, we accept the emotions that we're aware of. We often want to push feelings away or make ourselves wrong for having them. Acceptance creates space for curiosity. We can wonder where an emotion came from, which of our life experiences were involved in its formation, and what the feeling is trying to tell us. Finally, part of processing emotions is to direct kindness to ourselves. We talk to ourselves the way we would to a dear friend. After that second conversation with Khai, I said to myself: "It's OK to feel sad and scared and angry. You're doing hard work. This is a challenging situation and you're doing the best you can." Treating yourself kindly can help you move through the intensity of an emotion.

As I reflected on my coaching with Khai, I noticed a particularly sharp feeling of anger that came from an assumption that I'd made about him. I realized that I'd expected more from him, that I'd assumed that because he was a man of color, who I was sure had experienced racism in this country, that he'd be more aware of his biases. I had seen plenty of white educators treat black boys more severely than others, but I had thought—or hoped—that a Vietnamese-American man would be immune from that toxicity. As I recognized this, I almost laughed at myself—I didn't believe *I* was immune from the toxicity of white supremacy. Why had I thought Khai would be? I also noticed sadness. I wanted to believe that people of color would have each other's backs, that we'd be on the same team. I was angry, I realized, at racism—not at Khai. I also wondered what his experience was with racism and bigotry.

Coaching is hard work. It's likely that we'll often experience uncomfortable feelings. When we explore them, we can learn from them and they won't weigh us down and negatively influence our coaching relationships. They're only a problem when they're suppressed or ignored.

Fostering Patience

Sometimes, I feel impatient in Phase 1 of Transformational Coaching. I know I need to focus on building relationship and understanding current reality, but I often feel antsy to get to the real stuff. I see indicators of inequitable teaching quickly, and I want to discuss them right away. But that doesn't usually work: I haven't seen enough of the whole puzzle yet, and I still need to build trust.

During the first fall that I worked with Khai, I navigated my impatience, urgency, sadness, and anger while I got to know him. It took me longer to prepare for his coaching sessions than for other clients. After our meetings, I'd write and talk to colleagues—and walk and cry and curse sometimes too—as a way to process my emotions. But when I was present with Khai, I felt calm and curious. He worked hard, and I knew he cared for his students—even though I suspected that his students didn't experience him as caring.

As I sensed a deepening commitment to coaching Khai, and as I felt like I'd gathered a good amount of information about Khai's teaching and context, I suspected I could shift into Recognizing Impact, the second phase of Transformational Coaching. In this phase, I would gather data to identify the impact of the Khai's beliefs and behavior on students, community, and himself. This would enable us to examine the underlying mental models from which Khai's beliefs and behavior emerged. Then we could explore the consequences of Khai's behaviors on his students.

Analyzing and Interpreting Data

One day in mid-October, I arrived at Khai's classroom to find the door plastered in student test data from a recent reading assessment. Construction paper covered the door: the top third was green, the middle third was orange, and the bottom was red. Students' names were written in black markers on cardstock balloons, below their name was a number between 1 and 30, and the circle was taped onto different areas. Some names were at eye level, solidly in the green zone, while some were almost at the bottom of the door. Jordan's name was by my knee, deep in the red zone. I noticed that the majority of the African American boys were down at the bottom of the door, in the red. My stomach lurched as I quickly took note of their names. What would it feel like to be a kid and walk into class every day seeing that you are in the red? What would it feel like to be a mother and bring your child to this classroom every day? I felt paralyzed standing there, not wanting to go in.

At that moment, the principal walked up and greeted me. When he asked how I was, I said I wondered whether it was ethical to publicly display data for young children. He replied: "This data is an indictment of the system that produces these results. The shame is not on the child, it's on a society that allows this data to be what it is. We display data so that we stay motivated to work harder, all of us—kids, teachers, and parents. This is our way of taking collective responsibility for our kids."

"Is shame and humiliation motivating for adults or kids?" I asked.

"It can compel people to take action," he said.

"Sure, it may produce compliance in some, but is compliance what you want?" I felt comfortable speaking directly with this principal. I'd known him for a long time.

"This data has to be public," he said, shaking his head.

"But how does Jordan feel when he gets here every day? How does he make sense of this?"

Before the principal could respond, Khai opened the door. "I'll let you two get to work," the principal said as he left.

A school leader sets the tone for a school. In a hierarchical system, we feel compelled to follow the modeling of the positional leader. Khai's principal was not a leader who centered or even acknowledged the social and emotional needs of children or adults. I felt a deeper understanding of how Khai led in his own classroom and of what he centered—and didn't center.

Khai and I were set to talk about data in that session. He had first asked to discuss it a month earlier, but since then, he had avoided the subject when we met. Although he'd agreed to look at it during this meeting, I suspected he was anxious. I wondered whether Khai had displayed the data on the door to counter the data on suspensions—as a way to round out the picture of what he was "dealing with."

The reading data suggested that many students were in the green; however, many of the boys—and in particular, the African American boys—were struggling.

In preparation for this meeting, I'd gathered Khai's suspension data from the previous two years. It mirrored the schoolwide data and indicated that he suspended more students than any of the other kindergarten teachers. And I'd learned that Jordan had been suspended three times the previous year—twice for defiance, and once for fighting.

A Simple Three Step Data Discussion Protocol

1. **Observation:** What facts or patterns you see in this data? Refrain from interpreting or judging the data. Just stick to descriptive observations.
2. **Interpretation:** How do you make sense of this data? [Encourage many interpretations and ask probing questions to surface underlying beliefs about students.]
3. **Conclusion:** What does this data suggest we need to do or do differently? [Encourage generative thinking and many ideas.]

I started by spreading out the data sets on the table, including the schoolwide suspension data. I handed Khai a highlighter pen and invited him to read through the data and see what he noticed. He took about 20 minutes to read, making notes here and there, shaking his head, and making sounds of disapproval or distress. His expression quickly looked tired and distressed.

After we'd reviewed the numbers and identified patterns in the data, I asked, "How do you make sense of the fact that African American children here are suspended at nearly double the rate of Latinos?"

Now, what you can't hear in this written text is my tone of voice—and having an awareness of tone of voice and body language is critical. Our way of being is communicated through our tone and nonverbals. You could read that question with a challenging and accusatorial tone, imagining my leaning back in my chair, arms folded across my chest. Or you could read it, as I asked it, with a tone infused with wonder and with an invitation to explore, my body slightly leaning forward. My tone wasn't fearful and apprehensive—it was authoritative and confident, but also kind and open.

When I asked that question, Khai took off his glasses and rubbed his eyes, which was what I noticed he did whenever it seemed like he was deeply contemplating something. We sat in silence for what felt like a long time but was probably less than a minute. It's good to train yourself to feel comfortable with silence. When he answered, he spoke much more slowly than he usually did. "I don't know," he said. "I think there's more trauma in the black community and so kids act out more, but . . ." His voice trailed off. I let the silence return, subduing my urge to ask a follow-up question.

After a few minutes, he continued. "Sometimes I've thought that I need to be the firm adult in charge," Khai said. "The one who pushes kids and holds them accountable and believes that they can rise above the dysfunction in their homes and neighborhoods. I've thought they need clear rules and structure and order. They don't have that at home."

He paused again. I let the silence be. "I guess I just don't know what else to do," he said, his voice lower and quieter than I'd ever heard.

I always feel relieved when a client says, "I don't know what to do." Those words are like the castle doors being flung open and the plank lowering over the moat. The client recognizes that they have reached the limits of their knowledge and skill set, and that they might be receptive to a coach's support, help, or partnership. This is a prime opportunity in coaching.

When a client says, "I don't know what to do," I say:

> Thank you so much for your honesty. It's brave to recognize that you've reached the limits of your skill set. I would love to help you figure out what else you could do. I have a few ideas, and I think that together we can find additional ones. How does that sound?

When I said that to Khai, his response was similar to what most clients say: "Sure. That sounds good."

It's important to recognize what happened in this exchange. Khai had acknowledged that there was something problematic about the fact that he suspended twice the number of black kindergarteners than Latinos—and that black students were one-third of the number of Latinos. He took responsibility for this data. He wasn't blaming the children. I decided to push the conversation in a direction where we could surface his underlying beliefs; I wanted to talk about race more explicitly.

"Khai," I said, "do you think that the way you respond to your African American children might be more severe and punitive than the way you respond to others?"

Khai's froze. Slowly, he put on his glasses, looked at me, and said, "I don't know what you're talking about," in a tone that was flat. I let the silence linger. Before I could speak, Khai added, "I don't know what you're insinuating, but you're wrong."

"OK," I said, noting Khai's defensiveness rise up. I wasn't going to get into a debate about right and wrong—that's a losing battle for a coach. At some point, we would tease out Khai's implicit bias and racism—because his underlying beliefs about his African American students drove his response to their behavior, his instructional approaches, the way he built relationships with their parents, how he developed a classroom community, and much more. But on this day, I didn't think this conversation would be productive. Instead, I engaged Khai in the Legacy Conversation that I use with almost everyone I coach at some point, and which sets us up for a conversation about race. At the end of this chapter, I'll return to this question about how a coach can decide when to talk about race.

Coaching a Way of Being: The Legacy Question

I suggested to Khai, "Let's go in another direction, OK?" Khai nodded.

"I want you to imagine something. I want you to imagine that it's 12 years from now, and you get an email from Jordan." I paused. And he writes this:

> I don't know if you'll remember me, Mr. Tran, but you were my kindergarten teacher at Excelsior—my second kindergarten teacher because I was retained. And I'm graduating from high school next month, and I wanted to invite you. I know you're probably super busy and maybe you have bad memories of me, but I'd be honored if you were there.

I paused, letting that sink in. "And then," I continued, "you decide at the last minute that you'll go, and when you get there, you end up sitting right behind his family. When Jordan crosses the stage, looking so mature in that cap and gown, and when he looks at his family—they're cheering and screaming his name—he also sees you. And a huge smile spreads across his face."

I paused again, letting this image develop further in Khai's mind. "Now," I said, speaking a little more slowly, "when he goes back to his seat, and after the ceremony is over, what do you want him to say to his friends about you? About how he remembers you as his kindergarten teacher?"

I paused, for just a second. "How do you want him to remember you?"

Khai usually made steady eye contact, but he looked away and his jaw seemed to tighten. Half a minute passed.

"I want him to say that I cared about him," Khai said, his voice constrained with emotion. "That I was strict but that he learned a lot and felt ready for first grade and that I set him on a path of success." He stopped again. "I want him to say that he knew that I cared about him," Khai said, his voice lowering almost to a whisper.

"What would it feel like to attend his graduation?" I asked.

"Amazing. Incredible. That's why I'm here—I want my kids to graduate from high school and go to college or do whatever they want with their lives. That's why I became a teacher. I dream about going to their graduations."

I was nodding and smiling. "Yeah," I said, "it's truly the best thing to get an invitation to a former student's graduation."

"I bet," Khai said.

"So, let's see how we can be sure that Jordan is on that path," I said. "Let's see what you can do so that Jordan feels that he belongs and that he can be successful." Khai was nodding. "And so that Jordan knows that you care for him."

Online Resource

You can download "A Cloze Script for the Legacy Question" from my website, http://brightmorningteam.com. Of all the coaching strategies I use, this is one that I engage almost every client with at some point in our work together because it's so powerful.

Determining Next Steps

When I ask teachers how they want a particular student (with whom they're struggling) to remember them, they almost uniformly say a version of two things: "that I cared about him/her/them," and "that he/she/they learned with me." In articulating this, they define the goal—they define good teaching. As a coach, your role is to guide them to meet that goal. It is critical that *the client names the goal*—as opposed to having the coach or principal name that goal. So many teachers feel chronically disempowered—like administrators, the school board, their department chairs, and a host of other people outside of the classroom are telling them what to do. When a client identifies their goal, they are more likely to own it. And when asked the Legacy Question, teachers identify their goal as having a social-emotional component ("I cared about him") and an academic element ("He learned"), thereby defining quality teaching. When teachers determine their own goals, and when they emerge from a deep desire to feel purposeful, resistance diminishes and commitment skyrockets.

When you coach a way of being, and someone identifies *how* they want to be, you need to follow up—ideally within the same conversation—with a discussion of what the client might do in order to be this person they want to be. You need to collaboratively start backwards-planning and identifying the steps that your client will take so that the student senses the teacher's care, and so that the student learns. In this discussion, you'll focus on two things: The student's needs (and how to find out more about them), and the teacher's areas for growth (or gaps). It's important to end the conversation with some immediate next steps that you and the teacher will take. You'll probably need to prioritize this list, which could be long, because you want the teacher to feel hopeful and optimistic about their capacity to change, not overwhelmed. And you want them to see the map that leads to their change.

To determine steps, guide your client to explore their beliefs—in this case, beliefs about how care is expressed and received. These questions can surface their beliefs:

- As a child, how did you know that a teacher cared about you? What did they do to demonstrate their care?
- Was the way you experienced feeling cared for reflected in how folks in your home culture demonstrated caring?
- What do you know about what your students need to feel cared for?
- How could you learn more about how your students experience a sense of being cared for? What could you ask? Whom could you ask?

These questions help a client unpack their definition of caring and recognize that it is a personal one (based on childhood experiences) and also one that's socially and culturally constructed. As we surface and examine beliefs about care, we pay attention to the data and knowledge on which the client has built a belief. This helps us gain insight into how their beliefs developed and helps us expand empathy for our client. As we see that their behaviors are a product of their experiences, we can more clearly understand their actions.

Here's what emerged from Khai's reflections on the preceding questions: He had felt cared for as a student when there was a great deal of structure and routine, when his classroom was quiet, and when expectations were laid out firmly and students were held accountable. In his home culture, he felt cared for when people had high expectations for him, although I got the sense that he didn't want me to probe into his home culture as those inquiries were answered superficially.

When I asked Khai what he knew about what his students needed in order to feel cared for, and specifically, what he knew about what Jordan needed, he was perplexed by the question. This question, (*What do you know about what your students need to feel cared for?*) assumes that there might be a difference between what the teacher needed as a child, and what the teacher's students need. Often, we assume that what worked for us will work for our students—and that is not always the case. We generated a short plan for Khai to learn more about what his kids needed to feel cared for, which included asking them to talk about one person in their life—friend, family, or other—whom they knew cared about them, and how they knew.

During this conversation, I wrote the following in the margins of my notebook: "Doesn't really understand psychological safety and learning." I'd recognized in Khai, as I'd recognized in many educators, some basic knowledge gaps about what kids need in order to feel cared for and to learn. Human beings can't learn when we're afraid—a conclusion that scores of reputable neuroscientists in prestigious universities have proven. Sometimes coaches need to fill in knowledge gaps. I'd collected short readings on a number of topics, including this one, which I could offer clients when I spotted a knowledge gap. I'd say: "I came across this article that I thought might be helpful for you. Let me know if you want to discuss it." And usually, as long as the text wasn't too long or theoretical, they'd read it.

Khai and I had begun to unpack his beliefs about how students experienced caring from a teacher, and although I wanted to backwards-plan the second part of this conversation—how Jordan would learn from him—I recognized that Khai was exhausted. We agreed to start our next meeting with exploring how to meet Jordan's learning needs.

As we stood by his door saying goodbye, Khai said: "Coaching isn't what I thought it would be. I really thought you'd just give me straightforward feedback on my teaching. These conversations are hard, but I guess I'll learn from them. What doesn't kill you makes you stronger right?"

I smiled. "I'm glad to hear you're learning," I said. "I'm enjoying working with you," and as I said that, I felt how true it was.

When to Talk about Race

Let's rewind to the moment when I asked Khai if he thought that the way he responded to his African American students might be more severe and punitive than the way he responded to the behavior of other students. I wanted to lead us into a conversation where we'd deeply and explicitly explore race, racism, and white supremacy. Khai responded defensively, and I chose to shift into his legacy. I want you to understand this decision and provide some guidelines around when to talk about race.

Let me clarify: When I say we need to figure out *when* to talk about race, I mean when we're going to push forward with a conversation that digs into race, identity, and white supremacy. The decision isn't *will we* or *should we* talk about race, which we must—the decision is about *when* to have a conversation that focuses on race. It's unlikely that there will ever be a "right time" for this conversation, but there are times that are better than others. To make this decision about when to talk about race, we need to back up and talk about how to make decisions in a coaching conversation.

How to Decide What to Talk about in a Coaching Conversation

As discussed in Chapter 1, there are three goals in any coaching conversation: to increase the client's emotional resilience, strengthen the client's reflective abilities, and build the client's skills. In coaching toward these three goals, we are coaching ways of being, beliefs, and behaviors. This is what defines Transformational Coaching. So how do you decide where to go in a conversation and what to talk about?

Start by considering emotions. Our emotional state either primes us for learning or undermines our cognitive capacities. If our client is emotionally fragile, then coaching toward resilience is a necessary starting point. Resilience increases when we acknowledge and explore emotions; deepen self-knowledge and self-awareness; tap into positive emotions including hope, purpose, curiosity, and empathy; focus on our sphere of influence and control; and feel like we're learning. When I sit down to meet with a client, if their emotional resilience seems low—if they look exhausted or tell me they're having a hard time or say that they're feeling hopeless, for example—I begin the session by coaching toward resilience. The goal isn't to resolve all of their emotional distress; it is to get to a point where they have more awareness of their emotions and they've processed them a little.

Once a client's emotional state has settled, we shift into coaching behaviors and beliefs, which are tightly connected. For example, let's say a teacher expresses frustration with getting students' attention when she gives instructions and wants coaching on this skill. Most likely, we need to review the routines she uses and refine them or teach her new routines—perhaps she addresses the whole class while some students talk to each other, and they've learned bad habits; maybe she talks too much and for too long. Before we focus on those skills, however, we might ask a question like, "What are your thoughts about why kids aren't quiet when you're giving instructions?" This is a question that invites reflection. It's one that can surface underlying beliefs. Perhaps she responds by saying, "I think they don't respect me." This is an assumption to unpack. Otherwise, we might teach her a new routine to get student attention, and if students continue to talk over her, her belief that students don't respect her will strengthen. As a result, she might institute additional disciplinary measures in her class, issuing warnings for disrespect and so on. As we coach to build new skills, we coach to strengthen reflective capacities, surface underlying beliefs, and connect those beliefs with the decisions that teachers make. In Chapter 11, I'll offer more guidance on how to decide which behaviors to prioritize.

So, When Do We Talk about Race?

We should talk about race whenever we can, as soon as we can in a coaching relationship, and whenever it comes up. If we talk about race regularly, it won't feel like a big scary conversation. Here are a few examples of what this can sound like:

- When getting to know a new client, say, "I use a model of coaching called Transformational Coaching, which is different from other coaching approaches because we talk about emotions, race, identity, and racism."
- When getting to know someone ask, "What were the racial demographics of the community that you grew up in?"
- Muse, "I wonder what role race plays in this situation?"
- Ask, "What role do you think your racial identity plays in this situation?"

When we need to have a brave, courageous, healing, or difficult conversation—one where we put race on the table—there are a set of questions to ask ourselves to assess the timing. It could be that midway into a conversation, we realize we need to open up the conversation then and there, or we could intentionally plan for a conversation in which we'll raise race. These questions in Table 10.1 help make that decision and as do the correlating assumptions.

When I asked Khai if he thought that the way he responded to his African American students was more punitive than the way he responded to the behavior of other students, and he got defensive, it was the third set of questions in Table 10.1 that helped me understand why that moment wasn't the right time. Khai was tired—we'd been analyzing data for a while, and it was hard data to look at. I felt ready for the conversation to dig deep into race—I had plenty of data, I'd processed my emotions, and I knew that there was enough trust in our relationship. But I could see that Khai was mentally and emotionally drained. One of the reasons I made the decision to ask the Legacy Question was because that line of questioning

Table 10.1 When Do We Talk about Race?

Questions for coaches to ask themselves	Assumptions
• Am I ready *enough* for this conversation? • Have I done some preparation and practice? • Do I know what I'm talking about? • Have I explored and processed some of the emotions that I have around this?	There will never be a perfect time; fear will make me think I'm not ready or that I need to prepare more. Most important to be ready is to process some of my emotions. If I'm not ready right now, I commit to taking action today to get ready.
• How can I evaluate my client's trust in me? • What makes me think there's enough trust so that this could be a meaningful conversation? • If there isn't enough trust, what can I do to strengthen trust?	Discussing identity, race, and white supremacy requires a trusting coaching relationship. If I don't think there's enough trust, I commit to strengthening trust today.
• How is my client feeling right now? • Do they have enough cognitive bandwidth for this conversation? • Do they have the energy required for this conversation? • If they aren't ready right now, how can I coach toward resilience so that they can get ready?	People need to be in a relatively calm emotional state to access the cognition needed for a meaningful conversation about race. If our energy is depleted, we're likely to shut down. If a client is not emotionally grounded enough for a conversation right now, I will coach toward resilience to get them there.
• What could be possible for kids if I have a conversation about race and identity? • What are the consequences for kids if I don't have this conversation? • What do the kids in the class/school need me to say and do? Who do they need me to be?	A Transformational Coach has a responsibility to take risks on behalf of children. Schools exist to serve children. As an adult, I have tremendous privilege. It's my moral obligation to draw on my courage and have conversations about race and identity.

often energizes clients. I also knew that I'd been paving the way, for a while now, for a bigger and deeper conversation about race.

On the Role of Courage

A Transformational Coach accesses courage and takes risks. We will not cross the chasm that separates where we are now and where we want to be without courage. More often than not, we wait too long to talk about race—perhaps because we're afraid, we don't feel prepared, or it's uncomfortable and we avoid discomfort. But the cost of avoiding discomfort is great—for ourselves, for our communities, and for children.

Courage is an emotion that can become a way of being. We all have it within us, and we cultivate it by taking one tiny risk after another. Each time we feel vulnerable, there's an opportunity to build courage. Courage is a compelling emotion—the more we feel it and strengthen it, the more we want it. It makes us feel strong, powerful, and capable.

To build courage, sit down and look at your fear. Get to know it. Fear often withers when we look at it closely. And then anchor in your purpose—in the legacy you want to leave. As your sense of purpose deepens and becomes more robust, there's a greater likelihood that you'll cultivate courage. Your purpose will draw you away from your fear. Finally, for inspiration and to fuel your imagination, study the courageous. We are surrounded by people who take risks—they are within our families and communities, and in history and literature—find them.

Before You Go . . .

Reflect on this chapter, take action, and take away these coaching tips.

REFLECT ON THIS CHAPTER

- How did you feel reading the description of visualizing legacy? What came to your mind?
- What legacy do you want to have as a coach? As a leader? As a teacher?
- How have you used data in your work as a coach? How have you seen data used in schools you've worked in? In which ways has data been used as a tool of oppression, and in which ways has it been used as a tool for liberation?

- When does impatience come up for you in your work? How do you understand it and respond to it?
- Who do you talk to when you need to debrief an experience you had at work, or when you need to plan for a conversation? How could that person, or your professional community, support you even more? What could you ask of them? How could you support them also?

TO DO

Identify an upcoming coaching conversation in which you want to cultivate self-awareness. During the session, discretely jot down notes about which emotions came up for you. Then immediately after the session, respond to these questions:

- Which emotions did I feel during the coaching session and now reflecting on it?
- Where did I notice those feelings in my body?
- What do I need to know or say to myself to accept those emotions? (You can always try: *I'm a human being, and human beings have emotions.*)
- What are these emotions trying to tell me? What can I learn from listening to them?
- What part of me is unhealed that might be connected to the emotions that came up?
- Which of my identity markers was I most aware of? What did those parts of me experience? What do those parts of me need?
- What can I do to nurture myself right now?

Interlude: Compassion

Principles of Transformational Coaching

- **Compassion**
- Curiosity
- Connection
- Courage
- Purpose

Compassion: We relentlessly strive to center the humanity of others. We preserve people's honor and dignity above all. We know that kindness is our greatest power. We practice self-compassion, which includes taking care of ourselves. We know that the journey toward liberation will be long, so we rest and attend to our minds, bodies, hearts, and spirits.

Caring for myself is not self-indulgence, it is self-preservation and that is an act of political warfare.

—Audre Lorde

- What does self-care mean to you? How do you care for yourself?
- What makes it hard for you to care for yourself?
- How do you think your identity markers (your gender identity, class background, and race/ethnicity) affect how you feel about taking care of yourself?
- Which of your universal human needs (listed in Chapter 7) are feeling met right now? Which are feeling unmet? How might you get some of those needs met?

CHAPTER 11

Exploring Emotions

*When I dare to be powerful, to use my strength in the service of my
vision, then it becomes less and less important whether I am afraid.*
—AUDRE LORDE

When we shift into the Explore Phase, we guide our client to explore their emotions while we continue to recognize impact. Phase 2 and 3 are often tightly connected as we shift between the data that helps the client recognize impact and the emotions that arise. As we coach in this phase, we remember that coaches need to attend to our emotional selves before, during, and after a coaching conversation (Figure 11.1).

When Anger and Doubt Arise

The last time I saw Khai, we'd explored the legacy he wanted to leave as a teacher, and he'd declared that he wanted Jordan to remember him as a teacher who cared and taught him a lot. I'd felt hopeful that Khai would change the way he treated Jordan. But the next time I observed Khai, in late November, I walked into his classroom to see Jordan sitting in the time out chair again, right next to the door. The symbolism of having a time out chair right next to a door (something I'd

Figure 11.1 The Phases of Transformational Coaching.

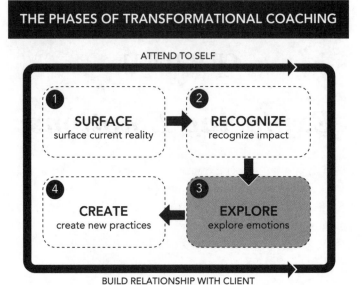

> ## Explore
>
> Goals in This Phase:
>
> - Guide the client to surface, acknowledge, accept, explore, understand, process, and release emotions.
> - Coach client to take responsibility for their feelings.
> - Solidify commitment to change.

seen in many classrooms) rattled me. That chair said to the child seated in it: *You do not belong, you are not wanted.* How could Khai think this would communicate care?

I felt angry and disappointed, and I doubted my capacities as a coach. Maybe I'd said and done the wrong thing. Maybe I should have called Khai out and told him that his suspension data was unacceptable, that he was perpetuating the school-to-prison pipeline, and that he had to change. How long did we need to wait for him to change? Jordan couldn't wait for Khai to have an epiphany about how he was perpetuating white supremacy. This was Jordan's second time in kindergarten—and there was plenty of data on the long-term, negative impact of retaining kindergarteners. I questioned my coaching strategies and felt frustrated with myself. I wanted to scoop Jordan onto my lap, read him books, and listen to his rambling five-year-old stories (which he shared whenever he saw me; he'd decided I was a friend). My heart ached and my anger surged. I wanted to shame Khai. But I'd tried using data to shame teachers before, and it had backfired.

Reflecting on Past Failures

There was one teacher, Bess, who sensed what I was up to right away when I started coaching her—from the beginning, I was horrified by her data and what I observed—and I more or less made that clear when we met. She became the most resistant teacher I ever coached. She canceled every other coaching session, stormed out of meetings I led, and organized a campaign to get me fired. I think her teaching got worse during the time I coached her, as she got more entrenched in her inequitable practices, wanting to prove that I couldn't change her. And then there was Margaret. When I'd walk down the halls to meet with her, she'd turn off her lights and hide behind her desk. These teachers were ineffective, but they had reason to avoid me—my intention was to humiliate them. You can read more about how I struggled with these teachers in my books, *The Art of Coaching* and *The Art of Coaching Teams*.

As I acknowledged that my coaching was ineffective, I began coaching in different ways, with greater self-awareness, and from a different way of being. To do this, I had to explore my own anger, sadness, and fear—but I was more committed to serving kids than I was to coaching in a way that didn't work. My sense of purpose provided the courage I needed to reflect on my practices and make changes.

Acknowledging Feelings

I was disappointed to see Jordan in the time out chair by the door, and a wave of feelings came over me. I named them—anger, sadness, and fear—and took a couple of slow, deep, intentional breaths as I moved through the classroom to sit on the side. I told myself: *Be patient. Change takes time. Trust the process—change can happen faster than we think. Be patient.*

As I sat down and pulled out my notebook and pen, I noticed that my hands were trembling with the intensity of emotions. My cortisol and adrenaline had shot up, as they do whenever we feel anger or fear, and although my mind had shifted, my body was still reacting.

I took another couple of deep breaths, and again acknowledged the emotions—anger, sadness, and fear. As I named them, I told myself: *It's okay to have these feelings. There's nothing wrong with having them. You're not a bad coach because you have them. They, too, belong. And later today, you can explore and tend to your feelings.* Those thoughts—ones I've trained my mind to cycle through—are always a relief. They remind me that the feelings are OK, that there's nothing pathological about them, and that I will have time to explore them. Within just a few minutes, I felt competent and clear-thinking again. I continued documenting my observations of the lesson, had a couple quick and positive interactions with Khai, and then left just as the class was going to lunch, letting Khai know that I'd see him the following week for our meeting.

Gathering Student Experience Data

When I met with Khai after my late-November observation when Jordan had been in the time out chair by the door, I had one goal: for Khai to agree to gather data on how students experienced him. When I proposed doing this, Khai agreed easily. It made sense given our conversation about legacy and his hope that Jordan would remember him as a teacher who cared.

We decided that I'd interview students individually and record their responses on a flip camera. There were two questions I would ask. The first question invited students to compare Khai to an animal—we wanted to explore how Khai's students felt about him through symbolism. Eliciting a metaphor from a kindergartener can be hard, but animals are often easy to connect with. However, it's important to be mindful of asking students to describe teachers of color as animals—there's a disturbing and lengthy history of people of color being compared to animals. Students can also be invited to compare their teacher to a weather pattern, a force of nature, a mythological character, or another symbol. Khai and I had planned this interview together, and he decided he wanted to ask his students to compare him to an animal. The second question I'd ask was about how students experience caring: "What kind of things do people do that make you cared for?" I'd ask follow up questions about how they felt cared for by Khai and what they'd like to him to do more or less of so that they felt cared for.

Jordan was eager and willing to accompany me to a resource room in the school where I was set up, asking if we could hold hands while we walked. I'd held his plump and sweaty little hand and listened to him chatter away as we walked down the halls.

As we settled in, I began by saying, "Jordan, Mr. Tran wants to be an even better teacher, and he asked me to help him do this. I have some questions for you, and I really want to hear your honest ideas. Mr. Tran is going to watch this video also. I think you can be very helpful."

Jordan beamed and straightened up in his seat. I hit Record.

"OK, here's the first question. I want you to close your eyes and think about Mr. Tran. Just think about him." I paused. "Now, what kind of animal is Mr. Tran like?"

Jordan's eyes opened wide and in a loud voice he said: "A Pinscher! He's like the Doberman Pinscher that lives across the street from me! A growling, scary, *mean* Pinscher!" Jordan jumped out of his seat and started barking and snapping and lunging forward at me. "The Pinscher at my street is *mean*, and spit comes out of his mouth when he barks, and it falls in long strings," Jordan flung his arms in snapping motions. "He gets so angry just 'cuz I walk by, and *he mean* that dog, growling and barking *mean*."

"That sounds really scary," I said, my heart aching.

Jordon continued: "I don't know why no one controls that dog!" He's always outside the house, and sometimes I get so scared that the gate is going to open because he looks like he just about to rip out my throat."

"I'm so sorry you feel afraid on your street," I said. "How is Mr. Tran like the Pinscher?"

"Because Mr. Tran is *mean*. Mean, mean, *mean*. I don't know why he so mean to me. He jumps out and growls at me for no reasons. I ain't even doing nothing wrong and he mean."

"Can you think of a time when Mr. Tran treated you in a caring way?" I asked.

Jordan sat back in his chair and tapped his index finger on his lips. After what felt like a long time, he leaned forward and looked straight at me. "No," he said definitively. "How come he doesn't like me?" he asked.

I felt unprepared for this and very sad. "I think he does like you, Jordan," I said. "But I think he's not great at showing you, and clearly he also does things that make you feel scared."

"I know I get in trouble sometimes, and he likes good students, but he don't have to be so mean." Jordan growled and snapped, pretending to be a Pinscher again.

"No, you're right, Jordan," I said. "He doesn't have to be mean."

I walked Jordan back to class, opened the door slightly to let him in, avoided eye contact with Khai, and went to the staff bathroom where I burst into tears. I was tempted to violate the prime rule of coaching—confidentiality—and run to the principal or the superintendent and show them the video and demand that Khai be removed from the classroom. It felt so wrong, so absolutely wrong that a six-year-old child should spend day after day with someone he was terrified of.

Debriefing the Data

After I'd recorded all the students, I did a quick analysis of the data. I grouped the animals that students had named into animals that had a neutral presence, a warm and fuzzy presence, and an aggressive or scary presence. The majority of the students had named scary animals such as sharks, lions, cheetahs, and snakes. One student insisted that he was like a T. rex. The videos were hard to watch. I decided I'd start by showing Jordan's video to Khai. I worried that watching one video after another would be overwhelming. And I felt that Jordan's words were powerful enough on their own. Depending on what happened in our conversation, I'd decide whether to show him the rest or just summarize the data.

What happened in our next conversation was one of the most intense conversations I've had in a coaching session. First, you need to know that we'd worked together for five months. I had put a great deal of effort into building trust with Khai, as I hope you've seen. He'd just completed a midyear survey about coaching and had identified himself (which was optional), and his feedback was overwhelmingly positive.

This conversation happened after school. Khai looked nervous as I sat down and pulled out my computer onto which I'd loaded the video of Jordan. I explained that I thought we should focus on Jordan as a way to gain deeper understanding of one student's experience.

"Am I going to hate this?" Khai asked.

"I don't know how you'll react," I said. "But it's important information, and I believe it will help you become a better teacher."

The video was only about three minutes long. When it ended, Khai barely moved. His face was drained of color and shimmering with perspiration. I held back from jumping in with a question. After about a minute, in a barely audible voice, he said, "I have become my father." His jaw was locked and his eyes watered. "I am my father." I let the silence be present.

"What do you need right now, Khai?" I spoke in a soft but authoritative voice.

"I don't know," he responded. "I am disgusted with myself. I should not be around children." He dropped his head into his hands.

I asked, "What are you feeling?"

"Shame," he said. "So much shame. And anger."

There was so much I wanted to say, so many thoughts going through my head as I wondered what was the "right" thing to say, but I stayed quiet.

Khai continued: "My father was a tyrant. We'd never know when he was going to lose it and beat us, and when he did, he was like a vicious animal. He didn't even drink. It just seemed like his rage was who he was. And now I've become him."

I started feeling afraid of where the conversation was going. There's a clear line between what a coach does and what a therapist does. Coaches might help a client surface and name emotions, and recognize the impact that they're having, but we're very careful about not digging into the roots of emotional responses. That's what therapists do. I could see that Khai was confronting childhood trauma and was anxious about my responsibility in opening up painful memories.

With a firm, confident voice, I said: "Khai, I really care about you and I want to make sure you get the support you need and deserve. I'm not a therapist and don't have that skill set to help you with this trauma. Is this something you've sought professional support for? Or that you'd want to do?"

He shook his head. "In my culture, it's frowned upon to go to a shrink." He paused. "My girlfriend has been suggesting that I should. Maybe it's time."

"How do you think your childhood with your father has impacted you?" I asked.

Khai exhaled loudly and then responded: "I live with the impact every single day. I know I'm tightly wound. I work so hard to control it. I've never hit anyone, but I know I can be mean in a fight with a significant other. I'm surprised Vanessa hasn't left me yet."

I was aware, again, of my own discomfort. I worried about veering too far into personal terrain, but I also recognized that this happens sometimes. When we do Transformational Coaching, clients can make connections between their professional behaviors, beliefs, and ways of being, and their personal ones. At this moment, the biggest danger was probably my response to my discomfort. I told myself: *Discomfort won't kill me, discomfort will pass.* and I reminded myself that I could manage the conversation wherever it went.

I responded: "Khai, it sounds like you're clear on the impact, and that it's hard to live with it. A therapist could help you gain deeper understanding and build additional coping strategies for dealing with anger."

Khai nodded and sighed again. His head was still resting in his palms.

"Khai," I said, "I feel responsible to name that your anger has an impact on kids, as you heard from Jordan."

He mumbled: "I know. My first instinct was to say that he is overreacting, that he's exaggerating, and to remind you that he's a difficult kid, but even as I had those thoughts, I knew that he was speaking the truth. That's exactly how I felt as a kid about my dad—that he was a wild animal."

"That must have been hard to hear," I said.

"It was brutal. Maybe the hardest feedback I've ever received," his voice trailed off. "That was never my intention as a teacher." Khai sat up and looked at me.

"It takes a lot of courage to hear that feedback," I said. He nodded. "And there's a difference between intention and impact," I added.

After a moment, he said, "I'm exhausted. I think I need to end now. I need to process this and talk to Vanessa and probably find a therapist. But I need to wrap up for today."

"Of course," I said. "I'm glad you can name that need."

"Next time, can we talk about what I can do with Jordan? Either I need to quit, or I need to do something else with him because I can't do this to a child."

"Yes, of course," I said.

My heart felt achy and tender as I drove home. I wondered whether I'd over-stepped my boundaries as a coach, and I questioned my responses, but I also tried to calm the self-critical chatter in my mind. I'd done the best I could, I told myself. I'd acted with compassion for Khai and done what I needed to do for Jordan. But I worried about whether Khai would be OK that evening, so I texted him an hour or so later to make sure that he'd gotten home to his girlfriend, and he had.

Confronting Bias

The first thing Khai said the next time we met was, "I don't know what to do with Jordan. Can we please focus on concrete things I can do when he acts out?"

"Yes," I said. "We can."

I was relieved that Khai wanted to talk about how he interacted with Jordan. However, I suspected we'd need to surface his underlying racial biases for him to make transformational changes. These biases caused Khai to see Jordan's behaviors, those of a black male child, in a different way than he saw the behaviors of children with other racial identity markers. I'd gathered heaps of observational notes that indicated patterns in Khai's racially biased responses to students. A black student would trip and stumble on the way to recess, and Khai would issue a warning for unsafe hallway behavior, whereas I'd witnessed three Latina students skipping to lunch, arm in arm, bumping into other students, and Khai said nothing. The black boys were routinely told they were too aggressive, that they moved too fast, that they talked too loud, that they were dominating group projects and needed to give others a turn, that they weren't following the rules, and that they weren't focused. I sometimes felt like I was cataloguing all the most common stereotypes of African American men—essentially, that they were dangerous and needed to be controlled. And yes, I cataloged them—I took notes and documented my observations. This was so that I could see patterns in the data, and so I could share them with Khai at some point.

Khai's problem wasn't Jordan—it was how Khai *perceived* African American males, and how he *responded* to them. I knew that if he interpreted the challenges he encountered with Jordan as being specific to that individual child, he'd miss the opportunity to uncover his biases. And he'd have another Jordan next year, and the year after, and so on. The problem was Khai's racism, not Jordan, and not Khai's lack of classroom management strategies.

"Khai," I said, "we can definitely identify some next steps with Jordan, but I think it would also be worth figuring out why you're so triggered by him."

"I really want Jordan to know I care about him," Khai said. He described how he'd been reflecting on what Jordan said in the video and that he'd made a commitment to change his behavior and he'd started seeing a therapist to work on his anger. "I'm hoping that today we can turn this commitment into a plan," Khai said. "I really need a plan so I can see the pathway and stay focused."

I questioned myself at this point. I had planned a conversation to unpack Khai's unconscious and conscious biases. I was ready to explore how white supremacy shows up in our assumptions about black and brown children and how we "manage" them. It felt urgent that we have this conversation. Khai seemed calm and energized, I knew he trusted me, I was ready, and I knew students needed me to have a conversation with Khai about race. And yet, Khai wanted to make a plan. He was animated and wanted to create a spreadsheet and checklists to capture his plans. I decided to follow his energy, to go through the door he'd swung open—one that could lead us to a conversation about racial bias, but wasn't as direct as what I hoped. I didn't know if this was the right thing to do and I felt uncomfortable. I decided that if we were going to pursue this path of how Khai could communicate care, I'd think about how it could connect with the next conversation we had—in which we'd talk about race explicitly.

One reason I followed Khai's lead was that he was brimming with enthusiasm about getting to know Jordan better. As part of this conversation, we talked about how to respond to off-task or other behaviors in a caring way. Khai knew about many of these—quiet and private (as opposed to public) redirection, proximity, positive narration, and so on—but he was hesitant to use them with Jordan.

"Why not?" I asked.

"Because I think he needs me to be firmer and clearer with him, and some of those strategies seem indirect."

Ah, I thought, *that could be implicit bias about black males—that they need authoritative control.* While we would discuss his implicit bias, I also knew he'd need to immediately change some of his daily behaviors in order for things to change for Jordan. Khai often skipped steps when responding to Jordan's behavior. He'd jump to harsher and more punitive measures, and he had very few positive or even neutral interactions with Jordan. Khai needed to see that strategies for responding to behavior in a caring way *would* work with Jordan—part of the problem was that he hadn't used them consistently, in the way they were intended to be used.

I said: "Can I suggest that you try these strategies, consistently, with complete fidelity, for a couple of weeks and see what happens? You know how to respond to off-task behaviors in a caring way. What you've been doing hasn't worked, so try those strategies with Jordan. Give them a chance."

Khai agreed.

Lunch with Jordan

One of the items on the plan that Khai created was to have lunch with Jordan in an effort to get to know him better. I thought it would be unfair to ask Jordan to be alone with Khai, given the child's fears, so I invited myself, figuring that if I was present, I could also do some subtle in-the-moment coaching of Khai.

I brought a veggie pizza, and we sat in the tiny kindergarten chairs in his classroom and told each other stories about our favorite toys, music, food, and people. Jordan talked about his Auntie Lucy who took him out on Sundays after church every week. Khai shared a story about his favorite aunt who used to take him to the beach as a kid. In extensive detail, Jordan described the noodles at the Chinese restaurant he'd gone to for his birthday, which prompted Khai to share stories of his mother's noodles. Jordan's stories were vividly embellished and entertaining, he ate and talked at the same time, and he had an amusing sense of humor. When I saw Khai laugh, genuinely, at a comment Jordan made about how mushrooms were like "slimy ocean things that swim in your mouth and then dive into your belly," I felt relieved. They were making a human connection with each other.

At the end of lunch, as we were cleaning up, Jordan—standing next to the trash can, tomato sauce dribbling down the front of his shirt—said, "Mr. Tran. Why you pick me to have lunch with you and Ms. Elena? Why me?" His pudgy hands were perched on his hips.

Khai sat on a chair in front of him and said: "I'm glad you asked, Jordan," he said. "I wanted to get to know you better. I think I've been unkind to you. I think sometimes I get too angry with you, and I shouldn't. It's not right. I care about you."

"You *are* kind of mean but sometimes you're a good teacher," Jordan said, a hesitant smile spreading across his face. Jordan was a kind kid—there were aspects of Khai's teaching that I suspected Jordan did appreciate.

"I'm working on being nicer," Khai said. "Can you give me a chance to do better?" He looked into the child's eyes.

"Yeah, sure!" Jordan said, as he flung his arms around Khai's head and pressed a big glob of tomato sauce onto Khai's light-blue button-down shirt. Khai flinched, but then put his arms lightly around Jordan. And then the bell rang.

I was moved by Khai's vulnerability. I hadn't expected this—you have to understand that with his students, Khai often seemed emotionally detached, firm in his role as a professional, and clad every day in dark slacks and a pressed shirt. He rarely laughed with his students. He had the persona of an old-school algebra teacher or a philosophy professor, not a kindergarten teacher. When I'd once asked him why he had chosen kindergarten, he told me that he hadn't wanted to teach K, he'd asked for an upper grade, but that he appreciated being the first teacher students would have. He felt it was a powerful opportunity to set them on the right path.

We Need to Talk about Race

Khai and I met the week after we had lunch with Jordan. I'd planned a conversation in which I'd put racial bias directly on the table, and I was ready. And nervous.

"Khai," I said, after a quick check-in, "We need to talk about race." I paused. Khai was biting his lower lip and nodding almost imperceptibly. "We need to talk about what it means that Jordan is black, and that you're not, and about the way you treat your black boys differently—more harshly—than you treat other students."

I exhaled loudly, louder than I'd meant to. "I felt nervous saying that," I said. Khai looked at me, surprised. Sometimes, being honest humanizes you and builds connection. I continued: "My intention in this conversation is to support your development as a leader, and your commitment to be an excellent teacher." I paused again. It's helpful to state your intentions when you open a conversation like this. It reveals your agenda and also makes you accountable to yourself to hold it. "What do you think?"

"No more elephant in the room, I guess," Khai said. "I knew you'd get to this at some point. You must be so disappointed in me," he continued. "After all, here I am—a person of color—and I'm acting like a racist."

I could relate to this feeling. It's a unique shame, I think, when you're a person of color and you see that you've perpetuated the same harm you've suffered under. This happens for several reasons. There's internalized oppression—the idea that people of color unconsciously buyinto white supremacy and inadvertently, when we haven't healed from our own pain, perpetuate it. And it happens for other reasons, because even though Khai, and I, and Jordan were people of color, we also belong to different races or ethnicities. And different races or ethnicities can hold prejudices about each other.

At that moment, I tumbled into my own memories of the shame I'd felt as a teacher when three African American male students complained to our principal that I treated them more severely than other kids. This principal, whom I trusted tremendously and who trusted me, asked me to meet with her and the boys—although she didn't alert me to what the meeting was about. As they expressed their fears and anger, I listened. I felt deep remorse and also tremendous gratitude for the boys and appreciation for their courage. I apologized; I thanked them for speaking up; I said I believed them and that I'd be doing some serious reflection on how I responded to their behavior. The fact that I, as a person of color and as the mother of a black boy, had done this felt shameful. I did shift the way I responded to them, and this was another time when I looked deeply at my unconscious bias.

Emerging from my memories, I wasn't sure what to say to Khai. Sometimes when I don't know what to say in a coaching conversation, I tell myself: *Be human. What's the human thing to say?* So I said, "I've been there. We all have. And I know, it feels awful."

His eyes got big. "You've been prejudiced?"

"Yes, Khai. We live in a world where white supremacy is instilled in us from the day we are born. It takes diligent awareness not to act on it. Most of us do, at some point."

"Wow, I just thought . . . I mean, you always seem so . . . I don't know. What happened? You don't have to tell me, I guess I just didn't think you'd ever . . ." It was unusual for him to be flabbergasted.

Sometimes it's helpful to reference your experiences, as I'd done—and then to shift back to your client. It can feel tempting to process our experiences with our clients, especially when we like them and trust them. But it's not appropriate to do so in part because we need to stay focused on our clients' learning needs and it's not their role to help us process.

"Khai," I said, "where do you think we should start in this conversation about race?"

"I don't know," he said. "You tell me."

"Let's start with what you notice about your interactions with African American students. Tell me anything that comes to mind."

Khai leaned back in his seat, looking out the window. "I'm really not sure it's just with them that I have a problem. I mean, I think I'm hard on all the boys." My memory of his office-referral data came to mind. It was so stark—his punishment of black boys was so much more severe.

"Really?" I asked, an intentional tone of disbelief in my voice.

"I guess you think I am much harsher with them," he said.

"I do," I said. "And that's what the data says. Would it be helpful for me to share notes from my observations? I've gathered a ton of them." I wanted to let Khai know I was going to challenge him to confront the truth.

Khai blanched. "No. I don't doubt you. I'm just embarrassed."

"Tell me more," I said.

"It's just not who I am," Khai said. "Or I guess not who I want to be."

Right, I thought, thinking about the concept of moral identity and how we want to see ourselves as good people. The problem was that Khai couldn't see himself as a good person who also perpetuated white supremacy and racism. I contemplated how to help him accept that he had acted unfairly and unjustly, and accept that he could change this behavior.

We all have stories of how we came to recognize and understand our own race or ethnicity, and how we learned about people of other races. I'd asked Khai about his identity markers before, but I hadn't asked him about how he'd become aware of other people's identity markers. I decided to go in that direction.

"Khai, how do you remember learning about black people? What are your earliest memories of them?"

Khai was leaning forward, his elbows resting on his knees. "As a kid, my community was pretty much all Vietnamese refugees. I don't remember the first black person I met or saw." He paused. "As I think about it though," Khai said, "I have these vague memories of being a little kid and hearing my parents talk about black people. They'd escaped from Saigon at the end of the war, and they talked about the American soldiers—and not in a good way. My parents don't like to talk about Vietnam or the war, but I have this vague memory of them expressing fear of black soldiers."

Khai stopped talking for a moment, seeming lost in thought. "Wow, I didn't know that would come up," he said.

"That's a powerful early memory," I said. I held silence. "What else do you remember learning about black people?"

"I guess stuff from TV. Basketball. Rappers. I remember the riots in L.A. after the verdict on the police who beat Rodney King. And my dad used to watch all those reality shows about cops."

"And what else?" I knew Khai could make the connections that he needed to make: that those representations dehumanize black people and create fear of black men.

"I know," Khai said. "Those are messed up first impressions. It's like how Americans think that all Vietnamese people are good at math."

"Yeah, stereotyping people is harmful. I guess the difference—just with that example—is that if Vietnamese people are stereotyped as good at math, you're likely to end up in an honors class. If black men are stereotyped as prone to violence, they might end up in the office, or in jail, or dead."

"Fuck," Khai said, shaking his head. "You don't hold back."

I laughed. It released a little tension.

"I guess you're right though. Fuck, I'm such an asshole." Khai rarely cursed. I wasn't sure what to make of this.

"OK, I'll be more coach-y," I said. Khai had recently chided me and said that when I used paraphrasing, I was being "coach-y." "I'm hearing that you don't want to be an asshole anymore, is that right?"

Khai nodded, the beginning of a grin spreading across his face. "Yeah, make sure you write that down in your notes: 'Khai doesn't want to be a racist asshole anymore.'" I smiled.

"Let me reframe that," I said, my tone returning to a serious register. "I'm hearing that you don't want to keep doing what you've been doing, that you don't want to act on distorted, racist beliefs about African American males. Right?"

"Right." Khai said.

"That you don't want to perpetuate white supremacy and racism, right?" I wanted to echo what I believed Khai was expressing with direct language. Khai nodded.

"OK," I said. "I'm going to capture this in my notes: 'Khai is committed to changing his practices so that he doesn't perpetuate racism and white supremacy.' Is that right?"

"Right," Khai said. "And to tell you the truth, I'm glad you're making me talk about this. I'm not going to lie—I've noticed that I get more worked up by how the black boys act, but I've been in denial because I've been so embarrassed."

I felt grateful for Khai's trust in that moment. "I'm really honored to be working with you, Khai. Your vulnerability and willingness to look at yourself and your teaching are inspiring."

He dropped his head and mumbled, "Thanks." And then he looked up at me and asked, "So what can I do to stop being racist? I just want to stop."

Khai often wanted to jump to action—to make spreadsheets and checklists, and plans, and we'd get there, but not before we unpacked how white supremacy manifested in the classroom a little more. In this conversation, we talked mostly about how racist beliefs shaped how we "managed" children and the kinds of relationships we built. In future conversations, we explored how racism influenced decisions about curriculum, instruction, and assessment, and relationships with parents. The conversation that I've just related allowed me to integrate discussion of race, identity markers, and racism into every conversation we had. Each time, there was a little less discomfort.

If You Doubt Your Skills

You might be reading this thinking: *This sounds too easy. I could never get Mr. X/ Ms. Z to say this.* Perhaps you are confident in the data you've gathered and what you've observed, and you know that Mr. X/Ms. Z act on their biases about students. But you're doubting your skills or whether this approach would work in your context. So, let me coach you. Here are the questions I'd ask you:

- Tell me more about your doubt. Where is it coming from? What's it about?
- Tell me about your fear (fear lives beneath doubt). Where is it coming from? What are you afraid of?
- When in your life has someone shared direct feedback with you that were able to hear? What happened? What was your relationship like with that person?
- If your roles were switched—if you were the teacher you're thinking about who would be resistant to this kind of conversation, and that teacher was the coach—what would need to be true in order for you to feel receptive to this kind of a direct conversation about your biases and racism?
- What are all the things that could go wrong in this conversation? What are all the things that the other person could say? How could you respond to their

reactions in a way that would preserve your relationship and move the conversation forward?

- What might be possible for children if you have this conversation? What do kids need you to say and do? What's at stake if you don't have the conversation?
- What would you say to this teacher if you could see the future and see that you were successful in this conversation?
- How would you feel if the conversation went poorly? What conclusion would you come to about yourself as a coach and about the other person? What would it mean about who you are?
- On a scale of 1 to 10, how willing are you to take the risk and try this conversation? What's affecting your level of willingness? What would need to be true for you to be one digit higher on this willingness scale?

Part of what would happen in this conversation is that by the end of it, you'd be willing to give it a try. You'd be willing to live with your doubts, fear, and discomfort; and the possibility that you could fail; and the potential of success—and you'd be willing to give it a try. I'm very persistent. Eventually, you'd say you'll give it a try. And then we'd practice the conversation so that you'd feel confident, and then you'd go and have it.

Accepting Regret

When I reflected on the conversation that I'd had with Khai about his biases, I felt proud of how I'd showed up and hopeful about how it had gone. It wasn't as hard as I'd worried it would be; Khai was far more receptive than I anticipated; and I was optimistic about how Khai's teaching would change. However, I hadn't anticipated the onslaught of regret I'd feel—regret over all the conversations that I hadn't had with teachers about their biases; regret about the times when I hadn't been courageous. It felt like a massive ball of guilt settled in my stomach as I thought about the students whom I'd let down. All those times I couldn't find the words to say something about the biases I witnessed. I felt angry with myself.

I sat with these feelings for a little bit. I literally closed my eyes and sensed the heaviness and sadness and noticed where in my body I felt these emotions. I didn't tell myself I was wrong for having them; I didn't ignore them or tell myself that now that I knew better, I'd do better—not yet. I accepted them, which meant that I said to myself over and over: *I'm angry with myself, I'm sad, I feel guilty—and these feelings belong.*

It didn't take long for the intensity of these emotions to loosen up a little, just enough for me to get curious about them. I recognized that these feelings came from a commitment to children and a belief that I am alive to contribute to healing our world. I hadn't been living up to my own values or sense of purpose. This sense of purpose and my values are a source of strength and courage. I wanted to feel anchored in my courage every day. These thoughts felt nourishing and brought relief. I was angry with myself because I wasn't being who I wanted to be. But I *could* be more of myself—that was within my sphere of control. I could act on my commitment and values more often, more consistently. It felt comforting to connect with my own power.

One reason why learning is uncomfortable is because we'll feel regret. But we can learn how to experience discomfort, and guilt and sadness and anger, and not let those emotions keep us from looking at what we need to look at. We won't transform our schools and create equitable organizations without attending to emotions—because we are humans and humans have emotions—and emotions can be our friends and partners on this journey. Even the hard ones, even anger and regret and sadness. Because they can remind us of who we want to be, and how we want to be treated, and of the hope we have for our world.

Before You Go . . .

Read the following prompts and select two or three that feel most valuable to you based on where you are in your learning journey. Spend meaningful time considering your reflection before moving on.

REFLECT ON THIS CHAPTER

- What emotions did the story about Jordan bring up for you?
- How might you have responded in this situation?
- When you've witnessed something similar—a situation in which a child is afraid and being treated unfairly—how have you responded?
- What insights did you get into your own coaching skills in this chapter?
- What might you try with someone you coach based on your learning ein this chapter?

Interlude: Courage

Principles of Transformational Coaching

- Compassion
- **Curiosity**
- Connection
- **Courage**
- Purpose

Courage: We draw on deepsources of courage, and face our fears, and act with courage every day. Wedon't wait until we know everything, or have every detail worked out to dosomething. We take action and course-correct when necessary. We act with healthyurgency. We know that just as people createdinequitable systems and just as we have adopted the mindsets from thosesystems, people can create new systems and can adopt new mindsets. This givesus the energy to take risks.

Without courage we cannot practice any other virtue with consistency. We can't be kind, true, merciful, generous, or honest.

—Maya Angelou

- When and where is courage hardest for you to access within yourself?
- What helps you uncover and engage with your courage?
- How have you felt when you've acted courageously?
- How does your courage help you be kind, true, merciful, generous, and honest?

CHAPTER 12

Creating New Practices

*I've learned that people will forget what you said, people will forget what
you did, but people will never forget how you made them feel.*
—MAYA ANGELOU

In Phase 4 of Transformational Coaching, we create new behaviors on top of new
beliefs—beliefs that are not polluted with white supremacy. As new beliefs and
behaviors are formed, our commitment to healing and transformation is strengthened. As Khai examined his beliefs and the mental models that informed how he
taught, and who he was as a teacher, and as he explored the emotions that surfaced
in connection to those insights, I saw that Khai was ready to move into Phase 4,
into creating new practices (Figure 12.1).

Explore

Goals in This Phase:

- Create new behaviors, beliefs, and ways of being.
- Deepen will and commitment to healing and transformation.

Recall the metaphor of Transformational Coaching as a bridge with many
lanes. In Phase 4, I shifted into the instructional coaching lane of the bridge and

Figure 12.1   The Phases of Transformational Coaching

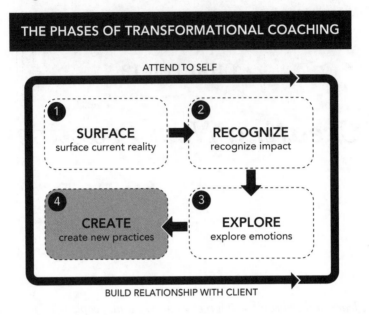

coached Khai on the rigor of instruction, how he gave directions, and how he gathered data, among other skills. Understanding that beliefs change when behaviors change, I integrated opportunities for reflection so that Khai could see how his beliefs shifted. In this chapter, I'll share a few snapshots of what this coaching looked and sounded like, I'll continue to describe the ups and downs of Khai's learning journey, and I'll suggest some ways to recognize a client's growth.

Developing New Behaviors

Khai wanted his students' behaviors to change; I hoped he'd change his own. We began looking at student behavior through the lens of developmental appropriateness. While Khai proudly held "high expectations," there were times when I knew that these were developmentally inappropriate; for example, an expectation for kindergarteners to sit still on the rug for 45 minutes. As we learned together about developmental appropriateness for kindergarteners, Khai modified learning routines. In an attempt to better understand student off-task behavior, we examined the quality of tasks that Khai assigned. While his lessons were standards-based, sometimes tasks didn't engage students' higher-order thinking skills as they could have, or the tasks seemed irrelevant. As we examined the tasks themselves, Khai's understanding of student behavior deepened. He saw their "off-task" behavior through a different lens—as a result of the level of rigor and relevance of the task he'd created. This led us to deeper exploration of what "rigor" and "high expectations" meant for kindergarteners. We visited the classrooms of other kindergartener teachers in our district, we read, and we paid close attention to what Khai's students needed.

Khai also wanted to incorporate small group structures into his lessons but was worried about how to "manage students" and ensure that they met a lesson's objectives. After observing other kindergarten teachers successfully running small groups, Khai began implementing new structures. This was something he wouldn't have done had he not examined and shifted his beliefs, because previously he didn't believe that his students were capable of learning in less-structured environments. As his belief shifted, and as he implemented new learning routines, he was surprised by how quickly his students adjusted and by how much they learned.

After one successful lesson, Khai said, "I realize they can handle much more freedom than I thought." Then he paused, looked at me, and said: "Freedom. What's the opposite of freedom? What did I think before? That they needed me to control them . . . like they were what?" He shook his head. "They thrive with freedom. Don't we all? What was I thinking?"

Scaffolding Learning for Adults

One morning, I observed Khai introduce students to rubrics. He described what they were and how we use them, and then in a whirlwind of instructions, he told students they were going to create a rubric, assess themselves with it, and then assess each other. I watched as his kindergarteners, almost every single one of them, looked up at him with a glazed and confused look on their faces. He'd given far too many instructions at once, he hadn't modeled the process, and he hadn't offered exemplars, and he didn't check for procedural understanding. After he released students to begin creating the rubrics, it wasn't more than a couple minutes before many were off task. They were confused and frustrated.

When we debriefed this lesson, I found myself referencing concepts that felt like basic teacher knowledge—the gradual release of responsibility, scaffolding learning, and knowledge of the Zone of Proximal Development (ZPD—what a learner can do with assistance). Scaffolding moves a learner out of the ZPD and into independence). Khai remembered these ideas and recognized why his lesson on rubrics had flopped, and we spent our session redesigning the lesson. This was a good example of a coaching session in which I was taking us along the instructional coaching lane of the Transformational Coaching bridge.

That afternoon, as I reflected on this coaching session and the lesson on rubrics that I'd observed, I had an epiphany about my coaching. There had been times when I'd suggested that Khai do something new—and he'd done it poorly. I'd then questioned his will, cultural competence, or emotional intelligence, but what I realized was that *I hadn't scaffolded his learning*. I hadn't recognized his ZPD accurately, and I had released him to take action before being sure that he could independently do what I was suggesting he do.

Two weeks previous to this, I had encouraged Khai to call parents to share positive updates about their children. I said little more than that—"Call them, tell them something good about their kid." But the next time I saw Khai, he was frustrated. He'd made a few calls, and they hadn't gone well. Before telling me what happened, Khai was ascending the Ladder of Inference (discussed in Chapter 6) and was saying: "See? I tried to reach out to parents, and it backfired. I don't understand why they are so disrespectful to me." I also sensed that Khai was angry with me—I'd suggested he make these calls, and they hadn't gone well. He may have unconsciously blamed me for his lack of success.

"Slow down, Khai," I said. "You're jumping to a conclusion about how parents feel about you. Can we back up? I would like to hear what happened."

In this moment, I was *also* ascending the Ladder of Inference. I was frustrated with Khai and took the conclusion he'd jumped to about parents as more evidence of his lack of cultural competence.

"Tell me exactly what happened," I said. "Pretend I'm a parent. What did you say?"

"I said: 'Hi. This is your child's teacher and I hope you can spare a few minutes to talk about your child's behavior. I think we need to have more communication.'" Khai's tone of voice was tense and lacked warmth. The parents that Khai had called responded defensively, and their conversations ended quickly.

Khai and I debriefed what had happened, and I made a few suggestions for what he could try differently. But after I saw him deliver the lesson on rubrics, and on the day when I realized he hadn't used a gradual release model with his students—and I realized that I hadn't used a gradual release model with him either. I realized that when I told him to call parents, I had made assumptions about his skills. I hadn't modeled for him, I hadn't asked him to practice, and I hadn't given him feedback before he went off alone to try.

The next time we met, I said: "In our last coaching session, we talked about how you need to remember to be aware of your students' ZPD and to use a gradual release of responsibility when you've introduced a new skill or concept."

Khai nodded.

I continued: "But what I realized is that I haven't done that with you. I'm sorry. When I suggested you call parents, I didn't guide you through a gradual release process, and I didn't take your ZPD into account. I let you down."

Khai looked shocked. "Wow," he said. "I didn't expect that. It's not your fault that I don't know how to talk to parents. But my ZPD? I've never thought about that."

I continued: "I should be thinking about it. I'm your coach." I paused. "It's my responsibility to guide you in a process of learning. It was my responsibility to understand that you didn't know how to talk to parents before sending you off to do so. So how about we try a re-do?"

Khai smiled. "Sure," he said.

"Let me start with modeling," I said. "Here's how you make this call. When someone answers, you say, with authentic enthusiasm in your voice: 'Hi! I have great news about _____ [student's name] that I want to share. Are you a parent or guardian? I'm calling from school.' "

"Say that *before* you introduce yourself, and after that, say only positive comments about the kid. The call should be short—one or two minutes—and close with: 'You've got a great kid. I'm lucky to know ___ [student's name]. Have a wonderful evening.' "

Khai practiced, and I offered feedback. The next day, he texted me to say that he'd called seven parents with great success. "I actually enjoyed that," he wrote. "Good job, coach."

There were many ways in which Khai was a competent teacher and perhaps because of that, I often wasn't clear on his ZPD. Identifying what a teacher knows and can do independently takes observation as well as questioning. You can get a clearer picture of someone's ZPD by asking them to describe in detail the skill set you're working on, and how they'd go about implementing it, and then you can follow up with questions to explore unanticipated possibilities. On many occasions, it will be your expertise as a teacher that allows you to hear or see a skill or knowledge gap. A teacher might describe, for example, how they plan to begin literature circles, and how they'll create groups and then pass out the books, and you'll visualize this, and recall your own time in the classroom, and you'll remember that a student might ask if they can be in a different literature circle. And you'll realize that the teacher you're coaching doesn't have a plan for what to do if students ask this question—and you'll see this gap. As you identify gaps, you'll get clearer on a teacher's

ZPD which allows you to create a scaffolded learning sequence. Just as we do with children, we must design a gradual release of responsibility when coaching teachers to implement new skills, routines, and structures.

Data That Reveals Beliefs and Ways of Being

In the first year I coached him, Khai's goals were to increase instructional rigor, while being developmentally appropriate; to release control of students and allow them to take more ownership of their learning; to ensure that all students were at grade level in reading and writing by the end of the year; and finally, to reduce the number of complaints from parents and administrators about how he treated kids. In particular, he wanted to heed his principal's admonishment to reduce the number of students he sent to the office—not, it seemed, because he bought into this mandate, but because he wanted to comply with his supervisor's request. To help Khai reach these goals, I gathered a variety of data.

Data can be anxiety-producing for educators. In many schools, data means only test scores, and test scores have been used to punish and humiliate children and teachers. Our definition of what constitutes meaningful data needs to expand, and we need to find ways to use it meaningfully. A Transformational Coach also needs to attend to the emotions that come up with looking at data. But we do need to gather data to support a client to meet their goals. We need data to establish a baseline in the beginning, along the way so you can evaluate progress, and at the end to celebrate growth.

There was a variety of data that I gathered and helped Khai analyze during our work together. This included parent surveys, video, and records of teacher-to-student interactions. These are three of the most useful forms of data to collect when coaching teachers, as well as when coaching administrators and coaches. Because they are data points that reveal a person's beliefs and ways of being, they are essential data sets in a Transformational Coaching model. In the following sections, I discuss these forms of data, how to collect them, and how to use them in coaching.

Parent Surveys

Although Khai was defensive about parent complaints, he was willing to reflect on his relationship with parents and wanted to improve it. One of the first steps on his action plan was to increase the amount of communication he had with parents, and to elicit their feedback. Together we created an anonymous survey that parents could do online or by hand to provide feedback. The survey asked parents to rate Khai's levels of friendliness and approachability on a scale of 1 to 5 and their sense that he cared for their child. He also asked questions about how they'd like to be involved in school, how they wanted to communicate with Khai, and what they wished Khai knew about them and their children. This survey was translated into Spanish and was sent to parents every month.

Khai was surprised by how many parents filled out the survey, and by their feedback, which he found useful and actionable. Each month, as we reviewed the survey responses, I provided Khai with an opportunity to reflect on how his beliefs about parents, and parent participation, were changing. After about five months, Khai said: "I'm really ashamed of this, but I just never believed that parents could be my partners—that they could be helpful."

I appreciated his honesty and asked him why he might have held that belief. He replied: "I'm ashamed again, but I think I thought that because they are poor, most are uneducated, and many don't even speak English, they wouldn't be helpful. It kills me to realize that I held those views—that's exactly what teachers probably thought about my parents when I was a kid."

"What are you coming to believe about parents?" I asked.

"That they are invaluable," Khai said. "That they are partners."

"If you act from that belief, how will you talk to them when they knock on your door at the end of the day?" One of the recurrent complaints about Khai was that he seemed bothered when parents showed up and he was curt and unfriendly.

"I'll be delighted to see them. I'll warmly welcome them in," Khai said.

"How will you remember that this is the belief you want to act from?" I asked. Sometimes when we're developing a new belief, it can be hard to remember it.

"I don't know," Khai said. "What do you suggest?"

"You could post a note above your door that says 'Guests are friends.' The kids wouldn't think that was strange, and it would be a cue when you see someone walk in."

"I could do that," Khai said, and then added: "I feel kind of silly needing that, but I hear what you're saying. I can see how I'll just resort to being irritated when a parent shows up at the end of the day if I don't remember that they are invaluable."

I suggested he try this and see what happens. And what happened was that often, this cue was useful and as interactions with parents improved, complaints decreased.

Video

Video is an invaluable tool in coaching. It provides what is called a "third point" in coaching—your client is the first point, you are the second point—and is often experienced as a neutral, objective form of data (surveys, student work, and other forms of data are also "third points"). It's one of the most powerful ways to help a teacher (or leader or coach) literally see themselves with more clarity. If you're interested in using video as a part of coaching, read Jim Knight's *Focus on Teaching: Using Video for High-Impact Instruction.* You'll find everything you need to incorporate video into coaching.

I hoped video would help Khai see the quality of his interactions with students—and it did, but there was also a great deal that Khai learned from watching himself. He learned about how he gave instructions and checked for understanding, taught reading, and worked with small groups. Initially, I operated the camera, and after a while, Khai recorded himself. Before we watched and debriefed the video, Khai would generate a question he wanted to hold. Some examples of these questions were:

- When I checked for understanding, did I check every single child's understanding?
- How can I assess student engagement during that reading lesson?
- What is the quality of my interactions with students—and did I interact with students equitably?
- Or did I treat groups of students differently?

I regularly nudged Khai to ask himself the final questions on this list. Having determined the questions to focus on, Khai and I would watch the video together and share our observations.

Early in our incorporation of video, Khai noticed his tone of his voice and the words he used when he redirected African American boys. During one lesson that he'd recorded, two students (one Latinx and the other African American) had tumbled out of their chairs because they were playing with manipulatives. To the Latinx girl, Khai said: "I really need you to pick up all that you dropped and then get on back into your seat and please try to stay focused." To the African American boy, Khai said: "Pick those up and sit down. Now."

When Khai watched this, he was shocked by his responses. "I can't believe what I'm hearing," he said to me. "I'm really like this?" His face was pale, and he twisted his hands together nervously.

"Like what?" I said.

"I guess, prejudiced," he said. "I mean, both students did the same thing." He shook his head.

Khai came to this awareness in Phase 2 of Transformational Coaching—when I was coaching him to recognize the impact he had on students. This was one of a number of data points that I put in front of him in an effort to help him see how his biases were showing up in his teaching. Khai had arrived at this awareness because he heard and saw himself—not because anyone else told him he spoke more harshly. In watching the video, Khai experienced healthy cognitive dissonance. Who he thought he was (a fair teacher) was not who he observed. Because he came to this awareness himself, he felt invested in changing this behavior.

He asked: "OK, so what do I do about this? How can I stop doing this?"

Before we talked about new behaviors, I nudged Khai to explore the underlying beliefs that led him to treat his African American students more severely. He echoed what he'd said before: "I think I believe that they need more discipline. That if I don't talk to them like that, they won't really understand." Khai's eyes filled with tears in at this point—it was one of the few times I saw him cry. I handed him a tissue box, and we continued talking about his beliefs and how he could shift his behaviors.

"I'm going to do better," Khai said as we ended our session that day.

"I know you can," I said. "I believe you will."

Teacher-to-Student Interactions

Psychologists have found that there's a "magic ratio" of positive to negative interactions between two people in order for them to have a healthy relationship, one characterized by psychological safety. This ratio is 5 to 1—five positive interactions for every negative interaction (neutral interactions can exist as well, but most important is the ratio of positive to negative interactions). This research holds true in the classroom as well. For kids to learn, they must feel emotionally safe with their peers and their teacher. Psychological safety can be evaluated in how a teacher interacts with individual students and the whole class on a moment-to-moment basis.

Exhibit 12.1 is an example of a tool that I created and use often to gather data on the relational dynamic between a teacher and students (you can download a blank one from my website, brightmorningteam.com). As you might gather, the challenge is that *positive* and *negative* are subjective categories, and we can feel judged if someone determines that something we say or do is positive or negative. That said, it's a really powerful tool that yields invaluable data.

Exhibit 12.1 Teacher-to-Student Interaction Tracking Tool

Teacher: Mr. G	Subject/period: Science/5th	Date and time: May 11, 2019 12:37–1:00
Total number of students: 24	**Number of male students:** 8 **Racial breakdown:** African American (AA)—3 Latino (L)—4 Asian (A)—1	**Number of female students:** 16 **Racial breakdown:** African American (AA)—3 Latina (L) —12 Asian (A)—1

Interaction	Time	Positive*	Negative*	Neutral	Gender	Ethnicity	Notes
1	12:37			X	F	AA	*Whatever's in your mouth, just get rid of it.*
2	12:38			X	F	L	*B, you're going home.*
3	12:39	X			F	L	*Bye. Have a great weekend.*
4	12:39	X			M	AA	*Thank you, have a seat.*
5	12:40			X	M	AA	*Pass the papers.*
6	12:41			X	F	L	*Put pencil down, J.*
7	12:42			X	F	AA	*5, 4, 3, 2, 1* (redirect).
8	12:45	X			F	AA	*G, go ahead.*
9	12:46			X	F	AA	*Yes, OK.*
10	12:47	X			M	A	*Please read, D.*
11	12:48			X	M	AA	*Come in quickly, please.*
12	12:48	X			F	AA	*Go ahead, S. Excellent.*
13	12:48	X			F	AA	*D, thank you.*

Interaction	Time	Positive*	Negative*	Neutral	Gender	Ethnicity	Notes
14	12:49			X	M	AA	*Into back table, please.*
15	12:49			X	M	A	*D, yes?*
16	12:50			X	M	AA	*Please, keep going.*
17	12:50	X?			F	AA	*D, (redirect—"if that happens again you're going to go in the book").*
18	12:51			X	M	AA	*L, do you have a question?*
19	12:52	X			F	AA	*Yes, please, G.*
20	12:52	X			F	AA	*Good suggestion.*
21	12:52	X			F	L	*Please, ask your question.*
22	12:53	X			M	A	*Yes, D, yes.*
23	12:53			X	F	AA	*Yes, S.*
24	12:54			X	F	AA	*Yes, D.*
25	12:55			X	M	AA	*L?*
26	12:55		X?		F	AA	*G (redirect).*
28	12:57			X	F	AA	*G, attention here.*
29	12:59	X			F	AA	*Excellent, D.*
TOTAL:		11	2	16	F: 18 M: 11	L: 4 AA: 21 A: 4	

*Interactions can be classified as "positive" or "negative" based on the specific words, the tone of voice as well as pitch and pace and volume, and any nonverbal communication that accompanies the interaction.

This is one situation in which you don't want to reveal to your client in advance that you're going to categorize their interactions with students as positive or negative, as that will likely skew the data. So, here's the process I use when I want to gather this data:

1. First, I say:
   "Thank you for inviting me to observe your classroom. I'd like to look at the dynamics, and I have a tool I use to gather that data. I'll come in a few times, and then afterwards, I'll share what I've learned with you and show you the tool and data. Would that be okay?"
2. Use the tracking tool three to five times, for 15 to 20 minutes each time.
3. Analyze the data yourself before sharing it with the client so that you can see trends and patterns and so that you can prepare for the debrief conversation.
4. When you share the data with the client, invite them to sort it into categories of "positive" and "negative" themselves—to see if there's a discrepancy between how you see things.

This tool has the greatest impact when it's used with a client who trusts you. Don't use it in the first few weeks of working with a new client, or if you feel that trust is fragile.

Although this is ideal in a live observation, you can also use this tool when watching a video of a teacher.

I used this tool with Khai and Stephanie several times during the school year. This allowed both of them to see their growth as teachers. Stephanie noticed that in the beginning of the year, she had many positive interactions with students, but that she interacted much less with her male students. Khai noticed the same trends that he saw in other data: His interactions with African American males were more punitive than those with other students. Although it was hard for him to repeatedly see these trends, it was also important that he recognize the patterns as it increased his motivation to change.

Practice, Practice, Practice

Practice plays a critical role in behavioral change. Khai had knowledge gaps, and one thing he did to close those was to read Lisa Delpit's and Gloria Ladson-Billings's books on teaching African American children. This learning helped closed some knowledge gaps, but knowledge acquisition doesn't automatically translate to skill development or new behaviors.

In their book, *Practice Perfect*, Doug Lemov and his colleagues offer 42 rules for "getting better at getting better." Over and over, they remind readers that we might learn new behaviors, and we might want to enact them, but without practice and feedback on those efforts, we won't effectively implement those new behaviors. Most often, in a professional development session, "teachers listen, reflect, discuss, and debate, but they do not practice" (Lemov, Woolway, & Yezzi, 2012, p. 8).

Malcolm Gladwell's *Outliers* is a brilliant exploration of what it takes to be a master at something. Gladwell cites research on the 10,000 hours of practice it takes to become a master. However, the authors of *Practice Perfect* challenge Gladwell's conclusion that it just takes 10,000 to be a master. You can practice something incorrectly for 10,000 hours, they remind us, and you won't be a master at it. We need to practice doing things effectively, and to do that, we need someone to observe us practicing and to offer corrective feedback quickly, before we practice and internalize an ineffective skill. This is exactly why we need coaches—coaches who cultivate trusting relationships—who can observe behavior and give feedback.

Role-Play Practice

Role-playing is a particularly effective way to practice and build new skills. When we role-play a scenario, our brain experiences the event as real. When a teacher role-plays and builds skills that are likely to be more effective when they're in the classroom, their brain builds neural pathways that contain those new, more effective strategies. The next time they're in a real situation that resembles the one they role-played, they'll be more likely to say the things they said and do the things they did during role-play, because those neural networks exist. Many people feel vulnerable and anxious about role-playing, but it's really powerful.

Khai and I did lots of role-playing. He'd practice introducing new concepts or explaining procedures for an activity. Frequently, I played a student who was off-task or ignoring directions or disrupting other students, and Khai practiced redirecting my behavior. It was fun, I'll admit, when I got to push his buttons (which we'd agreed that I should do). Then we'd reverse roles and I'd be the teacher. I'd model de-escalating a situation or redirecting students, or how to get the whole class's attention and check for readiness to listen to directions. Each time we role-played, Khai and I could both see how he was developing new skills right away.

Once, Khai was acting like a challenging student, and I intentionally diverged from modeling good teaching practices and screamed: "Get in your seat, close your mouth, and listen! This *is not* the way scholars behave in this classroom! If that's how you're choosing to behave today, then *you do not belong* in this class. I expect more from my students!"

My tone was harsh. While I didn't want Khai to feel like I was trying to shame him, I did wonder if it would help him empathize with his students.

"Whoa," Khai said, stopping the role play. "That was brutal," he said. "You were imitating me, right?"

"Tell me more," I said.

"Am I really that mean?" he asked. "Be honest."

"That's exactly what you said when I was here last week and Mikaela was wandering around after putting the art supplies away."

He was quiet for a few minutes and then said: "I guess you'd think I would have stopped acting like that by now." (It was early spring of our first year working together.) "It's not the first time I've seen how scary I can be."

"Change takes time, Khai," I said. "You're working on shifting behaviors you've witnessed since you were born, that you internalized, and that you've practiced for a long time. Now you need to practice alternate responses to frustration."

"I feel like I should have a timeout chair in my room that kids can send me to when I'm being mean," Khai said. "Or maybe one of those charts where you have color cards—like the green, orange, and red—and when I'm getting mean, they can change my card and put me on red."

"It sounds like you want to invite your students to give you more feedback. Is that right?" I asked.

"Yeah, I would," Khai answered. "I want them to know that I want to change, and I want to know when they feel like I'm not being nice."

I added: "And you want them to tell you when you *are* being nice. Remember to pay attention to positive behavior."

"Right," Khai said.

Evidence of Deepening Will and Commitment

The following Friday, when I arrived to meet with Khai, he was sorting through a stack of index cards. Each card had a red, an orange, or a green crayon circle drawn on it.

"They gave me feedback," he said. "This is my report for today on how nice or mean I was. I've been doing this all week." He looked proud and content. "Today I got 16 green cards, 5 orange, and 1 red. Not bad!"

"Khai, I love that you're asking for feedback from your kindergarteners."

"And look at this," he said as he got up and returned with a piece of poster paper. "We're graphing my results." Sure enough, a simple line graph showed his "niceness" levels for 5 days. "It's anonymous, of course. They color a circle, and then they drop it in an envelope as they leave. They think it's fun."

"I bet they do," I said. "And it's a beautiful way of giving them a voice."

"Sometimes they get annoying. All morning, Zion kept saying, 'Ima give you a red today if you don't let me sit with Tayshaun.' And then when they went to recess, he was chanting down the hall, 'red, red, red.' "

I couldn't read Khai's expression. I couldn't tell how upset he genuinely was about this. So, I asked: "How did you experience this? I can't read your expression."

Khai waved his hand dismissively. "They're kids. I get it. It stings a little—I realized how much I want their approval. But it's OK."

"I'm really moved by this," I told Khai. "People often think kindergarteners are too young to provide feedback, but clearly they aren't."

"It's making me want to do better for them. I want them to think I'm nice!"

"That's honest. What does 'nice' mean to you?" I asked.

"Nice means caring. I want them to know I care about them," Khai said.

"I can't wait to hear how this develops. I think there's a lot of potential in this activity—empowering your kids, getting feedback, and strengthening your commitment and will to create new practices."

Khai's students continued giving him a daily report for the rest of the year. Overall, the graph climbed higher and higher, and on more days than not, he got mostly greens and very few reds.

The Many Indicators of Growth

There were many data points indicating that Khai was making progress toward becoming a teacher who met the needs of every student. When I observed Khai, he used strategies that we'd talked about to calm his frustration at the moment it started to spike. I could see him taking deep breaths (I wondered if the students noticed too) and counting to 10 under his breath when he was getting angry. Sometimes an African American student would say or do something, and I could see Khai pause before he responded—and usually his response was no different from the way I imagined he'd respond to a Latinx student. Khai had almost completely stopped sending students to the office, and no one had been suspended since October. The classroom felt more relaxed and more like a typical kindergarten. Finally, by February, Jordan's reading skills shot up, and Khai hadn't sent him to the office in months.

One day in late March, I found Khai sitting on the rug reading a picture book to his students. Usually he was perched on a chair above them. Jordan was rolling around under the table, but clearly—based on his laughter and running commentary—he was listening to the story. When Khai finished reading, Jordan he saw me and bounced up to say hello. "Mr. Tran lets me go under the table when he reads now! I get to do what I want, as long as everyone can hear the story! And when I roll around, I can listen so much better!" Khai smiled at me from across the room.

Later that month, a new chart titled "A9 Superheroes!" (A9 was the classroom) was plastered on the outside of the classroom door. Each student's photo was posted on a chart that identified superhero powers. Each child was ranked "Top of the class!" Jordan's super power was "The Ability to Energize Anyone!" Each child was celebrated.

Another week that spring, on my way to meet with Khai, I found Jordan alone on the yard, 10 minutes after recess had ended, crying. My heart raced as I wondered what had happened. "Angie was teasing me! She said I was fat and stupid!" I asked if he'd told Mr. Tran, and he said no because he didn't want to be seen crying. I led him back to class. When I opened the door, I saw Khai look up and register Jordan, and then I noticed an irritated look pass over Khai's face. Seeing me, Khai took a deep breath, relaxed his face, and approached us. I stepped back, but stood within earshot, and watched Jordan explain what had happened. As Jordan's tears continued to fall, Khai's face softened into one of the kindest expressions I'd seen on him.

Khai said: "Class, we need to gather for a community meeting. One of our friends is feeling very sad and we need to talk about this."

Jordan looked apprehensive. "Nah, it's all good," he said, "I don't care what she said."

Khai looked uncertain. He'd just started a math lesson.

"No," Khai said, "I feel very sad that you're sad. Everyone belongs in our community. We need to talk." The class sat down, and Khai lead a conversation about community agreements and kindness. Afterwards, as students returned to their tables, Jordan ran up to Khai, wrapped his arms around Khai's legs, and gave him a tight squeeze. No words were exchanged, and when Jordan sat in his seat, he looked attentive and ready to learn.

A week later, Khai began a coaching session by saying, "I was a racist asshole today." I laughed.

"Tell me more," I said, using my favorite coaching sentence stem.

Khai described a student-directed small group activity that he'd set up for the day. When it had come to grouping students and assigning them a part of the activity, he realized that he'd grouped many of the black boys together and assigned them a low-rigor task that didn't involve them talking to each other. "I realized while they were working on this activity that I'd put them together in that station because I feared they wouldn't be able to control themselves in other stations."

"OK," I said, "tell me what it means to you to call yourself a 'racist asshole?' " I wondered if that was necessary.

Khai responded: "You're thinking that's not really racist. It's just my unconscious bias. But the thing is, if I'd acted on that, it would have been perpetuating racism—not giving them a chance to do the meaningful and real learning that other kids did. And I think they might have gotten bored and started acting out. So, just after they started and I realized this, I changed the task and the grouping. And they did fine. They were great. Jordan was focused and brilliant. When I call myself a racist asshole, it makes me want to step up and be better."

"OK, if that's what works for you," I said. "But I think you're wanting to remember this commitment to treat students equitably, right?"

"Yes, that sounds right, I also have so much to atone for," Khai said.

"Do you want to explore those emotions? If you've got shame coming up, we should extract it." We'd talked a great deal about how destructive shame was.

"Nah, I'm good," Khai said. "I just need you to keep me on my toes. Call me on my stuff—the unconscious bias."

"I will, but it seems like you're doing well monitoring yourself, Khai," I said.

The Ups and Downs of Learning

In early June, Jordan started acting out. I observed him refusing to follow directions, taking off running down the hallways on the way to lunch, throwing the trashcan across the room, and shouting "No!" a dozen times when Khai asked him to get ready for dismissal. I also observed Khai's patience wearing thin. He used strategies we'd practiced. He met with Jordan at lunch. He called Jordan's home— although no one answered or returned his calls. "I feel like he's testing me to see if I'll send him to the office," Khai said, "but I don't know what to do."

Khai and I were meeting after school when Jordan's mother walked in. "My son says you're going to make him repeat kindergarten again," she said, her voice booming. "You are violating his rights if you do that."

Khai stood, and they were eye to eye. "Ma'am," he said, "You don't need to yell. We can sit and talk about this like civilized adults." I cringed at his choice of words.

Jordan's mom shouted: "What are you saying? That I'm not civilized?" She dropped her purse on a table, and I noticed Khai flinch and take a step back. "Oh, are you afraid of me?" Jordan's mom asked. "You think I want to fight you?"

"No," Khai said. His face was turning red. "Can we sit down? There's no need for this kind of anger." I cringed, again.

"I can be angry if I want!" Jordan's mom said.

One of the most challenging decisions for a coach is when to intervene in a situation and when to stay out of it and let your client manage whatever is going on. Most of the time, I stay out of things. I don't want my client to think that I don't trust them or their abilities. In this situation, I saw how flustered Khai was, I saw Jordan's mom's distress, and it felt like the right thing to intervene.

I stood up, stretched out my hand, and warmly introduced myself: "I work with Mr. Tran, and we've really been talking about how to support Jordan this year. He's a wonderful kid—I always appreciate his energy and enthusiasm. And he's so perceptive. I'd love to hear more about any changes you've noticed in him this year."

"Well, I'm glad you're interested," Jordan's mom said, looking directly at me. "I wish his teacher showed more interest. Why isn't he asking me this question?"

Out of the corner of my eye, I could see Khai frown.

"I've tried to call you many times, Ms. Jackson," Khai said. "You never return my calls."

Ms. Jackson ignored Khai. "Why is he going to be retained again? You can't do that to a child. Three years in kindergarten? That's inhumane," she said, looking only at me.

"You're right—that would be inhumane," I said. "But I'm afraid you might have inaccurate information. I don't believe Jordan is being considered for retention." I turned to Khai. "Mr. Tran, could you clarify—is Jordan at risk of retention?"

"No, not at all," Khai said. "He's done well this year. I've said that on his progress reports. Have you seen those?" Khai's tone was frustrated.

"Why does my son say he's being kept back then?" Ms. Jackson said. I noticed tears pooling in her eyes.

"I really don't know," Khai said. "I'm glad you came in to talk, though. I've wanted to talk to you," he added.

Ms. Jackson hadn't been making eye contact with Khai, but now she was addressing him. "Mostly my son tells me about how you send him to the office and pick on him." Ms. Jackson's voice was restrained. "I'm sick and tired of teachers treating my children this way. His older brothers were also singled out by teachers here. Why should I want to talk to you?"

Khai took a deep breath. I was anxious about how he would respond and felt tempted to jump in and defuse the tension. But I didn't. I wanted to give Khai this opportunity. I reminded myself that discomfort can be OK, but I felt simultaneously protective of Khai and empathetic toward Jordan's mom.

Khai was silent for what felt like a second too long. Then he said:

> Ms. Jackson, I'm sorry. What I meant to say was that I'd hoped to *listen* to you this year, not to *talk to you*. I'd hoped we could work together to support Jordan. I'd hoped to learn more about him from you. I apologize for not communicating that.

"Well, then what you should know is that my son is scared of you. He just says you're mean." Ms. Jackson paused and looked directly at Khai. "Maybe you shouldn't be teaching kindergarten. Maybe you shouldn't teach black kids."

I scrutinized Khai's expression. I knew him so well, and I could see that he was working on controlling his facial reactions; however, he also appeared emotionally detached. I ached to jump in and say something—to save Khai, to save Ms. Jackson. *Stay out,* I told myself. *Give Khai this opportunity to grow and be successful.*

"Ms. Jackson," Khai said, "I am very sorry to hear that Jordan is scared of me. I understand why you think I shouldn't be teaching." Khai stopped. He turned to me. "Elena, could you help? I'm stuck. I don't know what to say." His voice trembled.

I was taken aback, and my mind went blank for a moment. *Be honest, be human,* an inner voice told me.

"Ms. Jackson," I said. "Thank you for your honesty and your willingness to have this conversation. As a mother, I can connect to your anger and fear about what your kids have experienced in school." I then explained what my role was as a coach, and that Khai and I had been working together on many things, including on how he related to his African American students. As she listened, Jordan's mom slowly started nodding her head. She pulled out a chair and sat down. Khai and I sat also.

"Well," she said after a long pause, "it's about time you teachers started looking at your racist ways," she said to both of us.

"I agree," Khai said. "And this year I've learned that I'm a racist asshole," he said.

I froze. I was in shock that he'd use profanity in front of a parent, and I braced myself for what would come. But Ms. Jackson burst out laughing. "Add that to your resume," she said. "And next time you have a black mother come in to talk to you, don't tell her she's uncivilized or angry. That's being a racist asshole."

Khai nodded. "I have a lot of learning to do. I appreciate your feedback. I'm sorry."

I left Khai to talk with Ms. Jackson and went to find Jordan in the afterschool program. We wanted him join us to explain why the thought he was going to be retained. When Khai asked him, he said: "Because I'm stupid. Everyone says so." He cried. Ms. Jackson cried. Khai's eyes filled with tears.

"No, Jordan," Khai said firmly but kindly. "You *are not* stupid. You are brilliant, and you are going to first grade without any question."

Jordan wiped his nose on his sleeve and looked at Khai. "Can you come?"

"Where?" Khai asked.

Jordan replied: "To first grade. Can you be my teacher?" Ms. Jackson raised her eyebrows. Jordan went on to say: "You're the best teacher I ever had. I don't want to go to first grade. I want to stay in kindergarten with you." Now tears filled my eyes.

"Oh, Jordan," Khai said, looking again at a loss for words. Ms. Jackson grabbed her son's arm and pulled him into a tight embrace. "Baby," she said, "You're ready for first grade. Mr. Tran's still going to be here, and you can come visit him." She looked to Khai for confirmation, and he nodded. "Your next teacher is going to be good, I just know it," she said.

Khai cleared his throat. "Your mom is right. You're ready for first grade, and you can visit me any time." I wanted him to assure Jordan that his next teacher would be good, but sadly, I knew he couldn't make that promise.

Jordan wiggled out of his mother's arms. "I am confused." he said, his hands balled up in fists. "I wanna go to first grade and I don't wanna go. I'm scared, momma," he said.

"I know, baby, I know. But you are a king, and kings are so brave. You're going to shine in first grade."

Reflection

I felt exhausted after the meeting with Khai, Jordan, and Jordan's mom. I wanted to assure everyone that everything would be OK, but I was afraid. I worried about who Jordan's first grade teacher would be, I worried about whether Khai could be the teacher his students needed him to be, and I worried about my skills as a coach. Was Khai really growing through coaching, or were the changes I saw superficial? What could I have done this year to make Khai change faster? Should I have been more directive? Should I have called Khai out on his racism earlier? Had I allowed Jordan to be in an unsafe classroom? What else could I have done so that Jordan felt more confident? I wondered (not for the first time) whether coaching was the right path for me be in—surely there must be some faster way I could create change. And I worried, always, about my own son. The underlying fear I felt about what he experienced in school, about his own developing identity as a student, and about how he was perceived by teachers—that never dissipated.

The following week, Khai and I debriefed the meeting with Ms. Jackson. Khai was initially defensive. "I felt like she wasn't fair. She was angry at me because of things that had happened to her other kids."

I said, "Maybe," but I challenged Khai to take responsibility for the assumptions that he'd made about Jordan's mom. I directed Khai to reflect on how he'd shown up in that conversation: for the ways he'd regulated his strong emotions, and for the vulnerability he'd shown and the risks he'd taken. I wanted him to see his growth and to feel proud of the way he'd navigated that interaction. I wanted him to recognize his learnings and consider the implications for how he'd interact with parents next year.

"There's just so much for me to learn," Khai said, "but every time something like that happens, I now feel more energized to learn."

As I left Excelsior that day, I wondered how teachers could partner with parents. What if teachers shared their professional goals with parents? What if parents provided feedback to teachers on how they perpetuated white supremacy or acted on unconscious bias? Or on the inclusivity and diversity in the curriculum? Or on the range of depiction of people of color in the curriculum? Or on how the strengths and beauty of a community were included, highlighted, and celebrated? What if we listened to parents talk about their own experiences as children in schools? What if we listened to parents' anger and sadness? What if we—all of us who work in or with schools—took collective responsibility for the crimes and transgressions of our educator-ancestors, even those with whom we disagree? What if we apologized and sought forgiveness on their behalf? While we may have deep disagreements with what some of these earlier educators did, we have chosen to work in institutions that closely resemble those earlier ones. We are a part of systems that hurt people. How do we heal from that history?

A few weeks later, Excelsior held a "promotion" ceremony for kindergarteners. I happened to be there and saw Jordan proudly march across the stage and receive his certificate from the principal. In the audience, his mother, father, grandparents, and three older brothers cheered. My chest felt tight and achy as I wondered what would happen to Jordan.

Celebrating Growth

Khai returned to Excelsior after a good summer in which he had started an administrative credentialing program and had gotten engaged to his girlfriend. He showed me photos of his proposal on the Golden Gate Bridge. He had also started seeing a therapist who specialized in trauma. "It's been really hard and really necessary," Khai said. He was excited that we had another year of coaching and had drafted two professional goals for the year:

- Students will know their brilliance. They'll know how they're doing, without feeling shamed. They'll feel proud of their growth and success, and they'll know how to make the growth they need to make.
- Our classroom will be a safe space for every child. I will model psychological safety in every interaction, every day. I will teach students to create a psychologically safe space for each other.

Khai's overarching growth as a teacher was reflected in these goals. He'd shifted out of the deficit mindset he'd held about his students and took responsibility for what happened in the classroom. That meant he didn't blame his kindergarteners when something didn't go well in class—instead, he'd reflect on what he had done and needed to do differently. Furthermore, as was reflected in his goals, he prioritized psychological safety.

As I heard Khai talk about his goals, I thought back to our first meetings the previous year. In those, he'd talked about his beliefs that children needed structure, order and rules, and to be held accountable to high expectations. He'd talked about children as objects that needed to be controlled. Khai was now talking about children's social and emotional needs just as often as he talked about their academic needs.

"Those sounds like powerful goals," I said. "And did you accomplish your goal of not being a 'racist asshole' anymore? Is that why it's not there?" My tone was facetious.

Khai smiled. "I'm not going to talk about myself that way anymore," he said. "My therapist is trying to get me to be kinder to myself, and talking to myself like my dad talked to me isn't useful."

I felt momentarily embarrassed—like I should have coached him out of using that language last year—but also grateful. "I'm so glad to hear that," I said.

Khai began to explain his process: "I am holding myself accountable for the biases and racism that I act on. I'm just thinking about that differently. Rather than telling myself, *don't be this* or *don't do that*, I'm thinking about *what* I want to be—*who* I want to be. When I think about it that way, it's easy—I want to be kind."

Khai paused. We sat in silence for a moment or two. Then Khai continued: "But I realized that to be kind, I need to be conscious of my internalized oppression and the biases I have about black people and poor people of color. I also realized that I have some attitudes about gay people that I'm not proud of, and also people who are disabled. So, I'm working on that."

"Wow," I said, at a loss for words. "That's incredible. I'm really . . . I don't know, I'm proud of you, I guess."

"Don't praise me," Khai said. "That feels awkward. Like 'yay! You're a tiny bit less racist!'"

"I'm inspired," I said. "It takes a lot of courage to look at yourself as closely as you have."

In that second year we worked together, Khai continued making steady growth as a teacher and leader—he was now the grade-level chair and part of the leadership team. I still coached him on his teaching practices, so on the bridge of Transformational Coaching, we were often in the instructional coaching lane, or the equity lane, or the resilience lane. But I also focused on his leadership skills— which is another lane on the bridge of Transformational Coaching. As in any learning journey, there were bumpy moments for both of us—moments when Khai was unkind, when he acted on his biases, or when he said something that triggered me and I was caught off guard. But these were few and far between.

What stood out to me as I observed him that year was how much more relaxed and comfortable Khai seemed in his classroom. He would regularly sit on the floor with students, still wearing pressed button-down shirts and shiny shoes, but he looked at ease. He'd hug students—something I'd rarely seen him do the previous year. He'd laugh with their parents at drop-off. And he didn't suspend a single child that year. Nor did he use a "timeout chair." A few children were sent to the office, but Khai would use a restorative practice to reintegrate those students back into the classroom. When we looked at a range of data points, we saw no patterns that reflected racial or gender biases, and we saw evidence of a psychologically safe classroom.

Once in a while, I'd have a flashback to the first time I saw Khai, when I observed him shaming kindergarteners on their first day of school. I'd remember seeing Jordan crumpled on the floor crying, and my heart would race. I'd wonder whether Khai had truly changed and whether I was overlooking things that Khai was still doing that were biased or cruel. I worried that because I had come to truly care about him and to enjoy coaching him, I was ignoring problems. But no, I'd realize as I reflected on my fears and what I observed: Khai had changed.

One spring morning, I observed Khai teach a science lesson. I walked around the classroom, appreciating the rigor and relevance of the activities, listening to the excited banter of the kids. I watched Khai check in with each child about their observations and watched him take notes on his clipboard. He kindly redirected a boy who had a great deal of energy and was attempting to balance a bucket of water on his head. I felt so much joy in that classroom, and so happy for the children, and a thought zipped through my head: *I wish my son could have Khai as a teacher*. As I registered this thought, my throat constricted. To wish that my son could be in Khai's class was the truest indication of my feelings about how much Khai had changed.

As I drove back to my office, I reflected on my growth as a coach. I remembered the first time I'd observed Khai in the hallway, screaming at those three black boys. I remembered calling my manager and telling her, over and over, "I can't coach him!" I remembered the temptation I'd felt a few times early on to shame him for the way he treated children. I remembered the day I'd sobbed in the bathroom after Jordan had described Khai as a "mean, mean Pinscher." Alongside these memories, I recalled what I had done so that I could effectively coach Khai. I remembered the hours I'd spent writing out plans for coaching conversations and reflecting on my notes. I remembered the many calls with colleagues to practice conversations I needed to have and to get feedback on the assumptions I held. I acknowledged the commitment I'd made to my meditation practice and recognized how critical that had been in helping me navigate my emotions. I remembered the times I'd sat with my fear about my son's experiences in school and the intention I'd set to be mindful that I didn't project those fears onto Khai. These reflections were energizing and draining—it had felt like a long journey—but looking back at the growth that I had made, I felt stronger, more whole, and more authentic than I'd been when I started working with Khai.

After five years as a teacher, the final two being the ones when we worked together, Khai became an assistant principal in our district. After two years in that role, he and his wife moved to Boston, where he became the principal of a K-8 school in a predominantly black and brown community. The card he gave me outside of the restaurant where I said goodbye to him is among my most treasured gifts. It reminds me of the impact that a coach can have on a teacher and on students; it reminds me of the impact that a client can have on a coach; and it reminds me of my capacity to learn—and of the joy and healing that is growth.

Jordan is on track to graduate from high school in 2022. Khai and I both plan to be at his graduation.

Before You Go . . .

Read the following prompts and select two or three that feel most valuable to you based on where you are in your learning journey. Spend meaningful time considering your reflection before moving on.

REFLECT ON THIS CHAPTER

- Which feelings did this chapter bring up in you? Which memories of your own experiences as a coach or teacher surfaced?
- What feelings come up for you reading this story about Jordan's mother? In your experiences as a coach, how were students' parent(s)/caregivers treated by your teachers? Which identity markers of the parent(s)/caregivers impacted the way that the students' teachers treated them?
- As a teacher, what did you find easy and challenging about building relationships with students' parent(s)/caregivers? If you could go back again and start over as a teacher, what would you do differently to build relationships with parent(s)/caregivers?

REFLECT ON YOUR PRACTICE

- How might you gather more data on student experience? How could you get a teacher invested in gathering more data?
- How do you evaluate your impact on the people you coach? How do you capture their growth?
- How do you evaluate your own growth as a coach or leader?

TO DO

- Imagine it's 10 years in the future. Write a letter to yourself from one of the people you coach and describe the impact of your coaching. Say anything—you don't have to show this to anyone else—and explore the sweet spot between humility and arrogance.
- What would it feel like to get a letter like this one? What action could you take to lead toward this outcome?

Principles of Transformational Coaching

- Compassion
- Curiosity
- Connection
- Courage
- **Purpose**

Purpose: Our purpose is to create a world characterized by justice, equity, and liberation. The journey is the destination. We can fulfill our purpose when we act with compassion, curiosity, connection, and courage.

It's not up to you to finish the work, but neither are you free not to take it up.

—The Talmud

- What does this passage mean to you?
- What are the implications from this passage on what you do?

CONCLUSION

Towards Liberty and Justice for All

In reading this book, you've completed a journey. Perhaps you've bridged knowledge gaps and acquired new skills, and maybe you've had insights into who you are and who you want to be. How are you feeling as you reach these final pages? Who are you on this side of this book?

In any coaching conversation, I have three goals: to cultivate emotional resilience, strengthen reflective abilities, and build skills. These are my goals in any workshop or talk that I deliver, and through the words I write. Let me pull back the curtain one more time and reveal what I hope you're *feeling* and *thinking* at the end of this book.

Compassionate

I hope you are feeling more compassionate towards others and towards yourself. I hope you have found deeper appreciation for who you are. I hope you have strengthened a commitment to take care of yourself and recognized where to set boundaries so that you can feel safe and at ease. I hope your heart has softened to your colleagues and supervisors and to all those in the community you serve. I hope that your compassion has reminded you that we are all on a learning journey together. I hope you are feeling more convinced than ever that other people *can* and *want to* change, and I hope you remember that other people can change more than you think they will. I hope that as your heart has opened, you have recognized that we all ache for freedom, community, and deep, authentic, safe, and joyful connection with each other. We all long to be free.

Curious

I hope you are feeling more curious about what you can do next, about who you can be, about who we can be, and about what we can create if we come together in healthy community. I hope you are curious about your own vulnerability, courage, and compassion. I hope you are curious about what you might do today and tomorrow to create more justice and liberation in the world. I hope you are thinking about how you can transfer the frameworks I've shared in this book to any area where bigotry shows up, be that gender discrimination, homophobia, class discrimination, and so on. I hope you are thinking about the places in your community where someone's social status, or lack of status, correlates to the respect and privilege that they're granted—and I hope you're curious about how to create more justice in those places. I hope you are curious about how to expand your social circles to include more diversity—racial, class, gender, sexual orientation, religious, and linguistic diversity. I hope you're curious about what books you might read next. I hope that your curiosity results in actions that will deepen your learning.

Connected

I hope you are feeling a deeper connection to all those in your community and outside of your community. I hope that your awareness of the interconnectedness of all living things has sharpened. I hope that you have sensed the power and potential of connection—with others and with yourself. I hope that you feel more connected to your own strength, courage, and power to be an agent of change. I hope you are feeling emboldened and equipped to dismantle systems of oppression, to rebuke ideologies that dehumanize people, and to recognize that your liberation is bound up in that of all others. I hope you have connected to the truth that things don't have to be this way, that another way of being and doing is possible. I hope you have connected to hope.

Courageous

I hope that you are feeling more courageous. I hope that the discomfort you've experienced while reading this book has offered you insight and opportunities for learning. I hope that you've practiced being uncomfortable and that you've learned that you can tolerate it, and that you can grow stronger through discomfort. I hope that has contributed to your ability to take risks, to be vulnerable, and to have conversations that need to be had. I hope you are feeling a new appreciation for courage and are recognizing previously untapped depths of courage in yourself. I hope that you have seen the courage in others, in our ancestors, and in our children. I hope that you've come to appreciate courage and to be curious about how to cultivate it even more.

Purposeful

I hope you are feeling clearer on your purpose to transform schools into places where every child gets what they need and deserve every day. I hope you are more committed to making every conversation count. I hope you are more committed to creating spaces of liberation for our children and for ourselves. I hope you are feeling hopeful at the end of this book: hopeful about your abilities to learn and grow, and hopeful about what coaching is and can be. I hope you have more trust in the coaching process—that you can see its potential, and you can see how to build the bridge and cross the chasm. I hope you are feeling anchored in a collective, shared purpose: to heal and transform our world.

I hope that in the final pages of this book, you recognize that the pillars that hold you up—your compassion, curiosity, connection, courage, and purpose—are the same pillars that support a collective effort to transform schools. We create what we are. If we are compassionate, curious, connected, courageous, and purposeful, we will create a reality that is compassionate, curious, connected, courageous, and purposeful. The process matters. The journey is the destination. Who we are and how we are in every moment is who we become. And we have choice about who we are and how we are.

Take one more look with me across the chasm to see the reality we could create—a reality characterized by justice *and* liberation. In that space, we've recognized that systems of oppression have hurt everyone—the perpetrators and the victims—because we are all connected. We know that every human being deserves freedom and healing from white supremacy, and patriarchy, and all forms of oppression, and we are learning new ways (and remembering ancient ways) to heal in community. We have embraced the magnificent creativity that we all possess and have found ways to heal from our pain.

While crossing the bridge, we've tended to the wounds of our past: We've returned stolen land, delivered 40 acres and a mule, and atoned for the harm that our ancestors did. We have listened to each other with open hearts and minds, we have told stories and truths that were suppressed for too long, and we have reached for each other—through the pain and across the divides, we have not stopped reaching for each other. As we glimpse the beauty that we can create, we shift, expand, and transform our ways of being.

Thank you for being with me on this journey. Now go forth and transform yourself, your schools, and your communities into places of liberty and justice *for all.*

APPENDIX A

The Phases
of Transformational Coaching

Surface: Surface Current Reality

PURPOSE
See the lay of the land: the client's teaching or leadership practice, their beliefs, their way of being, and the context in which they work. Build a trusting relationship with client.

Actions	Resources, Tools, and Strategies*
Attend to (Coach) Self • What am I feeling? • What do these feelings want to tell me? • How can I anchor in Transformational Coach ways of being? • How do I anticipate the role that my own identity will play in my ability to coach? • Who can support me in this process? Who can I talk to? Who can listen to me? Who can give me feedback?	• Transformational Coaching Rubric 2.0 • The Core Emotions

(continued)

Actions	Resources, Tools, and Strategies*
Observe and Understand • Observe the client's behaviors, and surface underlying beliefs and ways of being. • Look and listen for indicators of inequitable practices: implicit bias, deficit mindset, microaggressions, stereotyping, etc. Identify how white supremacy is manifesting in the classroom. • Understand the client's teaching practice and organizational context. • Explore the client's mental models.	• The Equity Rubric • Mind the Gap • Coaching stances (see *Art of Coaching*) • Listening strategies • Teacher to Student Interaction Tracker • Surveys
Build Relationship with the Client • Practice deep listening. • Pay attention to nonverbal communication. • Actively build trust. • Take the supportive and cathartic stances.	• Strength-Based Coaching • *The Art of Coaching*

*Some of these resources are provided on my website, http://brightmorningteam.com, or are described in my other books.

Recognize: Recognize Impact

PURPOSE
Help the client see how their behaviors, beliefs, and ways of being perpetuate systemic oppression. Engage the client in learning about how systems of oppression manifest in behaviors, beliefs, and ways of being.

Actions	Resources, Tools, and Strategies*
Attend to (Coach) Self • What am I feeling? • What do these feelings want to tell me? • How can I anchor in Transformational Coach ways of being? • What do I need to successfully be able to coach my client? • How can I continue to expand my knowledge about systems of oppression? • What new insights am I gaining about my own practices? • Who am I reaching out to for support? Am I getting what I need and want from them? If not, how might I let them know what I need? Who else could I reach out to?	• Transformational Coaching Rubric 2.0 • The Core Emotions

Actions	Resources, Tools, and Strategies[*]
Connect and Reflect • Gather and organize data to explore the impact of the client's beliefs and behavior on students, community, and self. • Name the underlying mental models, ideologies, and systems of oppression from which the client's beliefs and behavior emerge. • Explore and reflect on unintended consequences of the client's behaviors and underlying mental models. • Understand the detrimental impact of white supremacy and patriarchy on everyone, including the client.	• Video • Student data • Surveys • Classroom Observation Tool • Teacher to Student Interactions • Coaching Lenses (see *Art of Coaching*) • Informative texts • Confrontational, cathartic, and catalytic stances (see *Art of Coaching*) • Listening strategies
Build Relationship with the Client • Practice a range of listening strategies. • Actively build trust. • Ask for feedback on your coaching.	• Surveys about coach/coaching • All coaching strategies

*Some of these resources are provided on my website, http://brightmorningteam.com, or are described in my other books.

Explore: Explore Emotions

PURPOSE
Guide the client to surface, acknowledge, accept, explore, understand, process and release emotions.

Actions	Resources, Tools, and Strategies[*]
Attend to (Coach) Self • Who am I being? • What am I feeling? • What do these feelings want to tell me? • How can I anchor in the Transformational Coach ways of being? • How can this process—with my client— support my healing and transformation? • Who am I reaching out to for support? Am I getting what I need and want from them? If not, how might I let them know what I need?	• Transformational Coaching Rubric 2.0 • The Core Emotions

(continued)

Actions	Resources, Tools, and Strategies*
Explore Emotions • Hold space for emotions, including anger and grief, and instigate emotional breakthrough. • Consider the universal human needs that are/aren't being met. • Coach the client to take responsibility for behaviors, beliefs, and ways of being. • Solidify commitment to change.	• Cathartic, catalytic, and confrontational stance (see *Art of Coaching*) • Core values activity • Legacy and purpose questioning • Sphere of Influence • Universal Human Needs
Build Relationship with the Client • Stay humble and compassionate. • Remain calm and grounded when strong emotions are expressed. • Use deep listening.	• All coaching strategies

*Some of these resources are provided on my website, http://brightmorningteam.com, or are described in my other books.

Create: Build New Practices

PURPOSE
Create new behaviors, beliefs, and ways of being.

Actions	Resources, Tools, and Strategies*
Attend to (Coach) Self • What am I feeling? • What do these feelings want to tell me? • Which of the Transformational Coach ways of being is most relevant now? • What do I need to know now to successfully coach my client? • How have I grown and changed through working with this client? • Which of my coaching skill sets has most expanded? • Who has helped me in my coaching journey? How have they helped me? How can I acknowledge and appreciate their contributions?	• Transformational Coaching Rubric 2.0 • The Core Emotions

Actions	Resources, Tools, and Strategies*
Build New Practices • Develop and refine new behaviors. • Construct new mental models and beliefs. • Create new identities and ways of being. • Augment knowledge. • Deepen will and commitment to healing and transformation.	• Co-plan. • Model practices. • Observe others together. • Gather and analyze data together. • Provide real-time feedback. • Use the Ladder of Inference. • Ask legacy questions and invite creation of a vision. • Use all coaching strategies. • Scaffold learning. • Gradually release responsibility.
Build Relationship with the Client • Celebrate the client's growth and positive impact on students. • Communicate appreciation for the client. • Invite feedback on coaching.	• Supportive and instructive stances • *The Art of Coaching*

*Some of these resources are provided on my website, http://brightmorningteam.com, or are described in my other books.

APPENDIX B

The Equity Rubric

The Rubric

- This tool names indicators of equitable *inputs*. Many of these indicators address *teacher behavior*.
- The true indicator of equity is revealed in the *impact* that a teacher and school have on students, and what students gain from being in that classroom and school, which includes skills, abilities, knowledge, thoughts, feelings, a sense of belonging, and a sense of potential.

Overview of the Equity Rubric

Rubric Domain	Content
I. Teacher Beliefs	The teacher is aware of their biases and privileges.
II. Relationships and Culture	The teacher's ability to form positive relationships with students and to create a classroom that is safe, affirmative, and student-centered.
III. Class Environment	The teacher utilizes identity-affirming strategies to create a healthy community of learners.

(continued)

Rubric Domain	Content
IV. Rigor and Expectations	The teacher creates intellectually challenging work for students, holds them to high expectations, and communicates confidence in their ability to be successful.
V. Access and Participation	The teacher uses a wide range of strategies to ensure that every child has access to the content and that every child can learn.
VI. Student Performance	Every student is successful.
VII. Curriculum and Instruction	Curriculum and instructional practices are relevant, diverse, inclusive, affirming of many identities, and student-centered.
VIII. Family and Community Partnership	Parents are seen as valued partners and participate in their children's education in a variety of ways.
IX. School Culture	School staff intentionally build trusting, mutually respectful, and caring relationships with each other, and with students and their families.
X. Institutional and Organizational	The school's core policies and practices indicate a prioritization of equity.

How to Use This Rubric

- This rubric is a tool for reflection and ongoing development—and it's intended to push the conversation about equity.
- Engage with this tool in bite-sized chunks: Reflect on one domain at a time. Following the Rubric is a tool to support your reflection.
- Use this tool in community: with a Professional Learning Community (PLC), or a coach, mentor, or trusted administrator.
- Pay attention to the emotions that surface when using this tool, and explore what you can learn from them.

Two Key Definitions

- **Equity:** Educational equity means that (a) each child receives whatever they need to develop to their full academic and social potential, and (b) each child is successful in school.

- **Success:** Success must be defined by the local school community so that a definition of success is inclusive of student, parent, teacher, and larger community voices. This will allow the definition of success to take into account the local context and values, and will situate success in a larger system of access and opportunity.

I. Teacher Beliefs	Strong Evidence of Equity	Some Evidence of Equity	No Evidence/ Inconclusive	Evidence of Inequity	Evidence: Observed Examples
Indicator of Equity					
1. The teacher understands how their own identity markers (including race, class, and gender) impact how they teach.	O	O	O	O	
2. The teacher is aware of their implicit bias and how it influences their teaching and is committed to not acting from it.	O	O	O	O	
3. The teacher is aware of the privileges granted by their identity markers (including their race, ethnicity, religion, culture, gender, sexual orientation, socioeconomic status, language, physical, and neurotypical abilities).	O	O	O	O	
4. The teacher is aware of their own internalized oppression (if they belong to a historically marginalized group) and is committed to not acting from it.	O	O	O	O	

(continued)

I. Teacher Beliefs	Strong Evidence of Equity	Some Evidence of Equity	No Evidence/ Inconclusive	Evidence of Inequity	Evidence: Observed Examples
5. The teacher is aware of the unique ways that they can contribute to their students.	○	○	○	○	

Indicator of Inequity

6. The teacher uses the phrase "these kids" coupled with a negative or deficit reference.

7. The teacher talks disparagingly about students grouped by their ethnicity, religion, language, race, gender, sexual orientation, or abilities (or a combination of identity markers).

II. Relationships and Culture	Strong Evidence of Equity	Some Evidence of Equity	No Evidence/ Inconclusive	Evidence of Inequity	Evidence: Observed Examples
Indicator of Equity					
1. Teacher communicates care, warmth, and personal regard for all students.	○	○	○	○	

II. Relationships and Culture	Strong Evidence of Equity	Some Evidence of Equity	No Evidence/ Inconclusive	Evidence of Inequity	Evidence: Observed Examples
2. The teacher knows each child's preferred name and pronoun, and correctly pronounces their names; the teacher ensures that students know each other's names and pronouns and that they correctly pronounce names.	O	O	O	O	
3. Praise and words of affirmation are extended to all students for their contributions, ideas, effort, kindness, perseverance, and so on. A ratio of five positive interactions for every one negative interaction is evident.	O	O	O	O	
4. The teacher consistently makes many efforts to get to know all students, and to surface and highlight each student's strengths, skills, and unique contributions.	O	O	O	O	
5. The teacher communicates warmth and care, and also holds children to high expectations.	O	O	O	O	
6. The teacher works to reduce students' stress from microaggressions.	O	O	O	O	

(continued)

II. Relationships and Culture	Strong Evidence of Equity	Some Evidence of Equity	No Evidence/ Inconclusive	Evidence of Inequity	Evidence: Observed Examples
7. The teacher creates an environment that is intellectually and socially safe for learning.	O	O	O	O	
8. The teacher creates space for student agency, autonomy, and voice.	O	O	O	O	
9. Students are oriented toward themselves and each other, not just to the teacher.	O	O	O	O	
10. Every child is encouraged to take leadership and helper roles in the classroom. These roles are distributed based on a child's skills, ability, and interest, and there is room for them to explore new roles to uncover new interests.	O	O	O	O	
11. Seating arrangements in the classroom ensure that all students are a part of the community.	O	O	O	O	

II. Relationships and Culture	Strong Evidence of Equity	Some Evidence of Equity	No Evidence/ Inconclusive	Evidence of Inequity	Evidence: Observed Examples

Indicator of Inequity

12. Some groups of students grouped along gender, race, and linguistic ability clearly have more or less status in the class (e.g., boys are praised for being smart, girls are praised for being helpful, black boys are always in trouble).

13. The teacher's interactions with students, when examined along lines of gender and race/ethnicity, are disproportionate when categorized as positive or negative.

14. Students are isolated, either temporarily or on a long-term basis, and often those students fall along lines of marginalized groups (e.g., they are black or brown males).

III. Classroom Environment	Strong Evidence of Equity	Some Evidence of Equity	No Evidence/ Inconclusive	Evidence of Inequity	Evidence: Observed Examples
Indicator of Equity					
1. The teacher uses multiple strategies to gain every child's attention and to ensure that every student understands directions.	O	O	O	O	
2. When students do not follow behavioral expectations, the teacher has a set of routines to use, of which students are aware, which are consistently used.	O	O	O	O	
3. The teacher makes expectations clear, uses physical proximity with students, and uses a warm and direct tone of voice.	O	O	O	O	
4. Principles of restorative justice are used to redirect challenging behavior, manage conflict, and repair harm when rules are broken.	O	O	O	O	
5. The emphasis in classroom management and student behavior is on how to be a positive member of a community (not on compliance and regulations).	O	O	O	O	

III. Classroom Environment	Strong Evidence of Equity	Some Evidence of Equity	No Evidence/ Inconclusive	Evidence of Inequity	Evidence: Observed Examples
Indicator of Inequity					
6. Students of color are disproportionately disciplined for nonspecific, subjective offenses such as "defiance" or "disrespect."					
7. Students of color, especially African American and Latinx males, spend disproportional time in the office or in time-out.					
8. Children's bodies are heavily regulated: there is a great emphasis on walking silently, sitting straight, and so on.					

IV. Rigor and Expectations	Strong Evidence of Equity	Some Evidence of Equity	No Evidence/ Inconclusive	Evidence of Inequity	Evidence: Observed Examples
Indicator of Equity					
1. All students have the opportunity to develop their higher-order thinking skills.	O	O	O	O	

(continued)

IV. Rigor and Expectations	Strong Evidence of Equity	Some Evidence of Equity	No Evidence/ Inconclusive	Evidence of Inequity	Evidence: Observed Examples
2. Students from marginalized communities and from low-income communities, and English Language Learners are offered many opportunities to develop cognitive skills and habits of mind that prepare them for advanced academic tasks.	O	O	O	O	
3. Teachers communicate confidence that all students are capable of engaging in intellectually challenging work.	O	O	O	O	
4. The teacher consistently communicates high expectations and offers the support and guidance to ensure all students meet expectations.	O	O	O	O	
5. The teacher supports students to take ownership of their learning.	O	O	O	O	
6. The teacher guides students to be metacognitive about their learning and to learn how to learn.	O	O	O	O	

Indicator of inequity

7. Teachers rely heavily on lecture, rote memorization, and "the basics."

V. Access and Participation	Strong Evidence of equity	Some Evidence of equity	No Evidence/ Inconclusive	Evidence of Inequity	Evidence: Observed Examples
Indicator of Equity					
1. There is evidence that every child is engaged with their learning, and is participating, at all times.	O	O	O	O	
2. Children from marginalized communities—including English Language Learners, girls, and gender non-conforming children—participate in whole-class discussions and in small-group discussions comparable to their male, cis-gendered, and native English-speaking counterparts.	O	O	O	O	
3. In whole-class discussions, the teacher calls on students equitably, using strategies to vary participation.	O	O	O	O	
4. The teacher consistently uses wait time.	O	O	O	O	
5. The teacher makes time and space to honor student questions.	O	O	O	O	
6. When a student makes a mistake, the teacher responds in a clear and affirming way.	O	O	O	O	

(continued)

V. Access and Participation	Strong Evidence of equity	Some Evidence of equity	No Evidence/ Inconclusive	Evidence of Inequity	Evidence: Observed Examples
7. In general, the teacher talks less than students talk.	O	O	O	O	
8. The teacher considers the needs of her students' families when making decisions about requesting they buy and bring their own supplies to school for projects, holiday gift exchanges, or any other occasion.	O	O	O	O	
9. If the curriculum is not inclusive of neuro-divergent thinkers, the teacher modifies instruction to meet their needs.	O	O	O	O	
10. The teacher employs trauma-informed practices when necessary and/or brings in people who can.	O	O	O	O	

Indicator of Inequity

11. The teacher shames students publicly and/or privately.

VI. Student Performance	Strong Evidence of Equity	Some Evidence of Equity	No Evidence/ Inconclusive	Evidence of Inequity	Evidence: Observed Examples
Indicator of Equity					
1. Different ways of knowing and expressing knowledge are valued and rewarded. Success is defined and measured in many ways.	○	○	○	○	
2. Every student is successful in class.	○	○	○	○	
3. Students are recognized for being positive contributors of a community.	○	○	○	○	
Indicator of Inequity					
4. Testing data is prioritized and emphasized; success in tests is messaged as the ultimate goal and is valued above all else.					
5. Performance data is publicly displayed and shared (even when student names have been removed) for the purpose of shaming or "creating urgency."					
6. There are notable discrepancies that run along lines of race/ethnicity and gender in performance data (e.g., English Language Learners perform poorly on writing assessments).					

VII. Curriculum and Instruction	Strong Evidence of Equity	Some Evidence of Equity	No Evidence/ Inconclusive	Evidence of Inequity	Evidence: Observed Examples
Indicator of Equity					
1. The teacher is a facilitator of learning, guiding students toward discovery, providing content expertise at times, and creating structures that facilitate student-directed learning.	O	O	O	O	
2. Students' knowledge, experience, wisdom, and background are valued and seen as resources for learning.	O	O	O	O	
3. Students' knowledge, experience, wisdom, and background are accessed, centralized, and incorporated authentically into learning.	O	O	O	O	
4. Teachers use students' real-life experiences to help students connect with and make meaning of in-school learning.	O	O	O	O	
5. Teachers offer students authentic opportunities to process content in a variety of ways.	O	O	O	O	
6. Students can process new content using methods from oral traditions.	O	O	O	O	

VII. Curriculum and Instruction	Strong Evidence of Equity	Some Evidence of Equity	No Evidence/ Inconclusive	Evidence of Inequity	Evidence: Observed Examples
7. The curriculum—or at the very least, instruction— emphasizes higher-order thinking skills, an inquiry approach, and student ownership over learning.	O	O	O	O	
8. The experiences and stories of historically marginalized groups are integrated into and centralized in the curriculum. They are not relegated to a unit or month.	O	O	O	O	
9. The experiences of historically underserved groups are not reduced and limited to their experiences of suffering. People of color do not appear in literature simply to talk about their experiences of oppression.	O	O	O	O	
10. Whenever possible, the teacher includes literature by authors whose racial and cultural background reflects that of their students.	O	O	O	O	

(continued)

VII. Curriculum and Instruction	Strong Evidence of Equity	Some Evidence of Equity	No Evidence/ Inconclusive	Evidence of Inequity	Evidence: Observed Examples
11. The voices and experiences of people who have been historically marginalized are prioritized—even if members of those groups are not among the student population.	O	O	O	O	
12. The teacher connects new content to culturally relevant examples and metaphors from students' communities and everyday lives.	O	O	O	O	
13. The teacher encourages multiple perspectives (from multiple ways to solve a math problem, to multiple interpretations of a poem, to multiple perspectives on current and historical events).	O	O	O	O	

Indicator of Inequity

14. Students are seen as vessels to fill with information.

VIII. Family and Community Partnership	Strong Evidence of Equity	Some Evidence of Equity	No Evidence/ Inconclusive	Evidence of Inequity	Evidence: Observed Examples
Indicator of Equity					
1. Parents and families are viewed as partners in the education of students.	O	O	O	O	
2. Parents' and families' knowledge and wisdom of their children and community are tapped into.	O	O	O	O	
3. There is dialogue with parents about the issues that are important to them, and these issues are included in classroom curriculum and activities.	O	O	O	O	
4. Parents are warmly invited into the classroom, their input is welcomed, and they are listened to.	O	O	O	O	
5. The teacher makes every possible effort to communicate with parents across linguistic differences, seeking out interpreters and making efforts to cross language barriers with nonverbal communication.	O	O	O	O	
6. The teacher uses a variety of structures to communicate with parents and to get their input, perspective, and feedback.	O	O	O	O	

(continued)

VIII. Family and Community Partnership	Strong Evidence of Equity	Some Evidence of Equity	No Evidence/ Inconclusive	Evidence of Inequity	Evidence: Observed Examples
7. There are no patterns of disparity between which groups of parents the teacher contacts with concerns (e.g., parents of African American males are not contacted more often than other groups). There are also no differences in the quality of those contacts.	O	O	O	O	

IX. School Culture	Strong Evidence of Equity	Some Evidence of Equity	No Evidence/ Inconclusive	Evidence of Inequity	Evidence: Observed Examples
Indicator of Equity					
1. Every staff member contributes to building a culture that emphasizes trust, connection, and support.	O	O	O	O	
2. Every staff member communicates warmth, care, and high expectations.	O	O	O	O	
3. Teachers and administrators speak about children and families with respect, curiosity, and compassion. No one is shamed, ever.	O	O	O	O	

IX. School Culture	Strong Evidence of Equity	Some Evidence of Equity	No Evidence/ Inconclusive	Evidence of Inequity	Evidence: Observed Examples
4. Teachers and administrators acknowledge each other's as well as students' and families' unique cultural perspectives and assets.	O	O	O	O	
5. Teachers and administrators listen with curiosity to each other, to families, and to students.	O	O	O	O	
6. Teachers, coaches, and administrators seek to understand family and student experiences and perspectives.	O	O	O	O	
7. The school has a shared positive culture that is inclusive and intentionally cultivated. Every adult, child, and family member who are part of the school have regular opportunities to reflect on shared values and to offer the school feedback.	O	O	O	O	
8. The school's approach to culture-building is inclusive of multiple viewpoints.	O	O	O	O	
9. The school's approach to discipline builds understanding, empathy, and self-awareness.	O	O	O	O	

(continued)

IX. School Culture	Strong Evidence of Equity	Some Evidence of Equity	No Evidence/ Inconclusive	Evidence of Inequity	Evidence: Observed Examples
10. When consequences are issued, they emphasize repairing harm, rebuilding relationships, and strengthening community.	O	O	O	O	
11. Teachers, coaches, and administrators employ multiple channels to seek out parent perspectives and input and do so consistently and regularly.	O	O	O	O	
12. Teachers, coaches, and administrators recognize the contributions of all children and have ways to publicly acknowledge those contributions.	O	O	O	O	
13. Teachers, coaches, and administrators intentionally build trusting, mutually respectful, and caring relationships with students and families.	O	O	O	O	

X. Institutional and Organizational	Strong Evidence of Equity	Some Evidence of Equity	No Evidence/ Inconclusive	Evidence of Inequity	Evidence: Observed Examples

Indicator of Equity

1. Teachers and leaders reflect the racial and ethnic/cultural composition of their students.	O	O	O	O	
2. The school's mission and vision explicitly include a commitment to equity.	O	O	O	O	
3. Strategic plans, goals, and initiatives reflect a prioritized commitment to equity. Equity is not approached as an add-on initiative, but is integrated into every facet of teaching, learning, and leading.	O	O	O	O	
4. Financial resources are allocated for the school's equity plans, goals, and initiatives. A school's budget reflects the prioritization of this commitment.	O	O	O	O	
5. Teachers, coaches, and administrators disaggregate data according to race, ethnicity, home language, gender, and ability in order to see evidence of disproportionality and to determine where to allocate energy and resources.	O	O	O	O	

(continued)

X. Institutional and Organizational	Strong Evidence of Equity	Some Evidence of Equity	No Evidence/ Inconclusive	Evidence of Inequity	Evidence: Observed Examples
6. Performance data, graduation data, number of students in Advanced Placement (AP) classes, and so on do not reflect the status quo; that data indicates an interruption of inequitable patterns.	O	O	O	O	
7. The school ensures that students are aware of prerequisite courses for college and that these courses are available to all students.	O	O	O	O	
8. The school does not have homogenous grouping (tracking) or the school is actively de-tracking.	O	O	O	O	
9. Small groups, tutors, mentors, instructional assistants, and counselors support students individually and in small groups.	O	O	O	O	

X. Institutional and Organizational	Strong Evidence of Equity	Some Evidence of Equity	No Evidence/ Inconclusive	Evidence of Inequity	Evidence: Observed Examples
10. The school has a comprehensive and inclusive hiring process conducive to hiring teachers who are highly trained and experienced, who have deep pedagogical content knowledge, who are knowledgeable about systemic oppression, who have reflected on their own unconscious bias and their identity in relation to power and privilege, and who have shown commitment to equitable practices.	O	O	O	O	
11. The school invests in high-quality, ongoing professional development (PD), including coaching, so teachers have the deep pedagogical content knowledge and cultural competence to support student learning, especially if children are not successful or below grade-level.	O	O	O	O	
12. The school prioritizes professional learning (including coaching) for every member of staff, and on every item on this rubric.	O	O	O	O	

Reflect

- Which domains and indicators on this rubric are my strengths?
- How did I develop those skills and dispositions?
- Which domains and indicators do I want to prioritize developing?
- Which observable student behaviors would be evidence of my growth in those domains and indicators?
- What's the first step I could take to make growth in my prioritized areas for development?

APPENDIX C

*Transformational Coaching Rubric (TCR) 2.0**

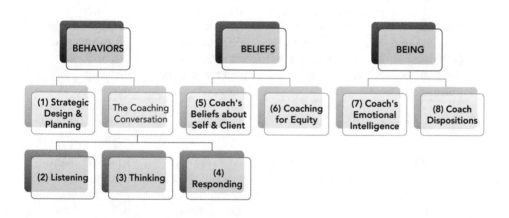

**The Art of Coaching* (Aguilar, 2013) includes a rubric called the Transformational Coaching Rubric. Therefore, this rubric is called the TCR 2.0.

Domain 1: Strategic Design and Planning

Indicator	Foundational	Intermediate	Advanced
a. Conversation Planning	May occasionally plan for a coaching conversation.	Writes up plans for coaching conversations.	Plans for coaching conversations using multiple planning tools.
b. Work Plans	May create work plans for some clients but does not engage in a rigorous goal-setting process.	Creates work plans based on SMARTE goals.	Plans conversations in support of work plans. Work plans align to school and/or district vision and larger context.
c. Zone of Proximal Development (ZPD) & Gradual Release	Understands the concept of a ZPD as it relates to coaching and its importance.	Attempts to work within client's ZPD but cannot yet articulate a plan for gradual release.	Intentionally scaffolds learning for clients and can articulate decision-making to gradually release responsibility to client.
d. Use of Data	Uses some data to inform coaching.	Uses various forms of data to inform work plan and coaching sessions. Engages client in gathering data to inform coaching.	Engages client in analyzing and responding to data (student work, surveys, test scores, and so on). Reflects on all conversations and uses reflection to inform subsequent coaching.

Indicator	Foundational	Intermediate	Advanced
e. Feedback on Coaching	Invites feedback from client and welcomes survey/ anonymous feedback.	Uses feedback from client to adjust coaching practice. Practices in advance of coaching sessions with prompting.	Gathers direct feedback and feels able to gather indirect feedback in a number of ways; uses feedback as a learning opportunity. Practices some coaching sessions in advance and can identify those that must be practiced.
f. Sense of Impact	Is unsure of the impact of coaching on client; questions whether coaching is doing anything.	Points to some evidence of the impact of coaching, but impact may feel haphazard and unpredictable.	Knows how to gather evidence to indicate the impact of coaching and can present a variety of data to prove positive impact.

Domain 2: Listening

Indicator	Foundational	Intermediate	Advanced
a. Active Listening	Occasionally uses active listening; feels somewhat comfortable using it.	Uses active listening during the first 10 minutes of the conversation.	Uses active listening throughout to identify high-leverage access points to deepen the conversation.

(continued)

Indicator	Foundational	Intermediate	Advanced
b. Use of Silence		Allows for pauses in the conversation. Speaks for less than a third of the conversation.	Holds silence comfortably.
c. Listening to Own Listening	In the moment, may be unaware that their listening is wavering; may be aware afterward.	Often notices when their listening wavers and is able to redirect self. In reflection, aware of how they listen, their mental journeys.	Listens deeply for extended periods. In refection, aware of how they listen, their mental journeys, and the impact their listening has on the client and conversation.
d. Client's Nonverbals	Pays attention to client's nonverbal cues as evidences by reflection after the conversation.	Pays attention to client's nonverbal cues as evidenced by decisions during the conversation.	
e. Coach's Nonverbals	Is aware of own nonverbal cues as well as tone of voice, pitch, pace, and volume.	Regulates own nonverbal cues as well as tone, pitch, pace, and volume.	Uses own nonverbal cues as well as tone, pitch, pace, and volume to deepen trust, facilitate learning, and strengthen the coaching process.

Domain 3: Thinking

Foundational	Intermediate	Advanced
		Frameworks clearly evident in the conversation, and used spontaneously and adaptively.
	Frameworks evident in planning, but less obvious in the conversation itself.	

Foundational	Intermediate	Advanced
Mind the Gap Approaches problems of change as problems of learning. Is grounded in a developmental approach.	**Ladder of Inference** Used during the planning process.	**Ladder of Inference** Used spontaneously during coaching.
Spheres of Influence	**Coaching Lenses** • Adult Learning (*awareness*) • Inquiry • Compassion • Emotional Intelligence (*awareness*)	**Coaching Lenses** • Adult Learning (*strategic use*) • Emotional Intelligence (*strategic use*). Seeks to cultivate client's emotional intelligence. • Change Management • Systems Thinking • Systemic Oppression
Strength-Based Coaching. Recognizes client's strengths and cultivates client's awareness of those.	**Strength-Based Coaching.** Uses client's strengths as a way to explore areas for growth.	**Personality Types** (*strategic use*)
	Personality Types (*awareness*)	

Coach develops skill in a range of frameworks to analyze the client's practice and plan a strategic approach to meet the client's explicit goals and implicit learning needs.

Domain 4: Responding

Indicator	Foundational	Intermediate	Advanced
a. Coach's Role vis-à-vis Client	May belief their role is to facilitate learning at some points and direct it at others.	Believes they have the greatest impact when they facilitate, rather than direct, learning.	Maintains a facilitative approach as much as possible and strategically directs client to maximize learning.
b. Varied Approaches	Uses a variety of coaching stems.	Moves between the different coaching stances.	Moves intentionally between the different coaching stances.
c. Coaching Stances	Comfortably uses supportive and cathartic stances.	Uses the cathartic, supportive, and catalytic stances.	Is comfortable and confident using the confrontational stance. Is intentional and selective about when and why to use prescriptive and informative stances.
d. Fluency in Coaching	May experience conversations as unpredictable and sometimes uncomfortable.	Articulates their thinking and rationale during a conversation that leads them in a particular coaching direction.	Identifies every decision in a coaching conversation and explains their reasoning for making that decision.

Indicator	Foundational	Intermediate	Advanced
e. Facilitative Activities	Supports client to identify needs, then access resources and build relationships to address those needs.	Uses a range of facilitative activities: • Role-playing • Videotaping • Surveys • Metaphorical thinking • Visualization & guided imagery • Writing & storytelling • Positive self-talk • Visual & artistic activities	Uses a diverse repertoire of facilitative and directive coaching activities strategically and spontaneously, even when not planned in advance.
f. Directive Activities	Plans for a limited range of coaching activities but may not successfully integrate them into the coaching conversation or does so in a very directive manner (e.g., leading the co-planning process).	Uses a range of directive activities: • Observation tools • Giving feedback • Modeling • Elbow teaching • Co-planning • Real-time coaching • Field trips • Shared reading • Looking at data	

Domain 5: Coach's Beliefs About Self and Client

Indicator	Foundational	Intermediate	Advanced
a. Coaching from Vision	Names core values and how they impact coaching work and relationships.	Has a coaching mission or vision statement that may guide their work.	Points to evidence in every conversation of being anchored in their coaching manifesto, vision, or mission statement.
b. Power of Conversation	Believes that every conversation counts.	Believes that listening is the core practice of a transformational coach.	Every conversation results in client feeling empowered and able to do something new or different.
c. Own Role in the Impact of Coaching	Believes that who they are and how they show up in a conversation matters.	Believes that their presence and way of being is the essential element in a coaching conversation.	Uses their way of being to positively impact the conversation.
d. Client's Core Values	Is aware of client's core values.	Uses awareness of client's core values to enroll client in the work and in a conversation.	
e. Fixed vs. Growth Mindset	Knows the distinction between fixed and growth mindset.	Identifies a client's fixed mindsets and has some tools for addressing them.	Is aware of client's mindsets—fixed or growth—and can facilitate the development of a growth mindset.

Indicator	Foundational	Intermediate	Advanced
f. Adult Learning Principles	Believes that *all* adults can learn given the right conditions.	Identifies the presence or absence of conditions that foster adult learning. Believes that learning is sometimes messy, unpredictable, and inconsistent.	Creates the conditions that foster adult learning.
g. School Transformation	Believes that transformational change in schools is necessary.	Believes that transformational change in schools is possible.	Consistently conveys hope and possibility.

Domain 6: Coaching for Equity

Indicator	Foundational	Intermediate	Advanced
a. Identifying and Shifting Limiting Beliefs	Notices when a client is expressing a biased belief.	Takes action to explore and shift a client's biased beliefs; some strategies are effective while others are not.	Quickly recognizes when a client is harboring a biased belief and can make decisions about when and how to do so. Persistently and effectively unpacks biased beliefs across the course of a coaching relationship using a range of strategies.

(continued)

Indicator	Foundational	Intermediate	Advanced
b. Coach's Socio-Political Consciousness	Is aware of historical and contemporary systems of oppression. Is aware of own identity development, privilege, internalized oppression, and conscious/unconscious bias. Recognizes power dynamics at play.	Is aware of how historical systems of oppression (including white supremacy, patriarchy and capitalism) manifest in schools, classrooms, and the behaviors of educators. Has some strategies to maneuver through power dynamics. Believes that in order to interrupt inequities, they must continuously engage in their own learning about systems of oppression.	Conversations and coaching actions lead to the disruption of inequitable practices and systems. Recognizes high leverage entry points to interrupt inequities. Is aware that even with a heightened socio-political consciousness, coach may still have biases; recognizes that coaching for equity is an opportunity for continued learning.

Indicator	Foundational	Intermediate	Advanced
c. Fostering Others' Socio-Political Consciousness		Guides client to increased awareness about systemic oppression, including about white supremacy, patriarchy and capitalism. Has some strategies to help client become aware of their identity development, privilege, internalized oppression, and conscious/ unconscious bias. Guides client to recognize power dynamics at play in a classroom and school.	Guides client to increased awareness about how historical systems of oppression manifest in schools, classrooms, and educators' behaviors. Guides client to interrupt the power dynamics in a classroom and school that uphold systemic oppression. Inspires clients to continuously reflect on their biases. Understands the role that empathy plays in interrupting inequities and cultivates empathy in clients.

(continued)

Indicator	Foundational	Intermediate	Advanced
d. Cultural Competence	May struggle with coaching clients across lines of difference.	Effectively coach some clients across lines of difference.	Perceives and adapts coaching to communication styles that differ across identity markers including culture and age. Demonstrates the ability to effectively coach across differences including race, ethnicity, gender, class, sexual orientation, age, and language.
e. Coaching for Systems Change	Believes their role is to interrupt systemic oppression in schools. Recognizes the power dynamics at play in an institution that uphold systems of oppression.	Has some strategies to address systems and structures that perpetuate oppression. Maintains commitment to interrupting inequities and oppressive systems and to creating schools that serve every child, every day. Recognizes the power dynamics at play in a system and has some strategies to navigate those.	Builds trusting relationships with a wide variety of educators within a system to collaborate on interrupting inequities. Uses coaching strategies to engage in productive conversations with colleagues and supervisors across the system. Navigates power dynamics in a system. Identifies high leverage entry points for change in systems, structures, and institutions.

Indicator	Foundational	Intermediate	Advanced
f. Coach's Emotional Intelligence (when addressing inequities)	May be triggered by a client's beliefs. May or may not be aware of the role that systemic oppression has played in their emotional experiences as an educator.	Has some strategies to respond to the ways that inequities affect their emotions.	Effectively uses a variety of strategies to respond to own emotions while coaching for equity; use of these strategies allows coach to effectively interrupt inequities. Has conversations about equity without judging the client and with compassion for the client, while also communicating an expectation that the client can change.

Domain 7: Coach's Emotional Intelligence

Indicator	Foundational	Intermediate	Advanced
a. Self-Awareness	Notices some emotions, particularly upon reflection. May be triggered occasionally. May feel defensive about some feedback received. May take things personally.	Is aware of a range of emotions in the moment. Is aware of triggers, understands their origins, and manages them. Generally accepting of feedback but may not know what to do with it.	Notices emotions in the moment and, upon reflection, has insight into them. Is rarely triggered. Is grateful for any and all feedback from clients; doesn't need feedback in order to feel affirmed.
b. Self-Management	Has some strategies to manage their own emotions when coaching is challenging. Sets intentions before coaching sessions.	Manages their own emotions. Apologizes and takes responsibility for how they show up with a client.	Often appears calm and grounded. Sets intentions before coaching and reflects on them afterward. Feels confident and able to coach anyone; finds great joy and satisfaction in coaching.
c. Social Awareness	Is aware of how their emotions impact clients.	Accesses positive emotions in themselves to positively impact clients.	Identifies coaching moves that create a safe learning environment for clients. Has empathy for clients.

Indicator	Foundational	Intermediate	Advanced
d. Relationship Management	Has some strategies for building trust, but doesn't consistently build trust. Trust-building is not intentional and is contingent upon relationship dynamics, personalities, and conditions.	Intentionally builds trust with most clients. Rebuilds trust when it is broken or weak.	Readily and easily builds trust with almost any client. Feels confident and able to coach anyone; finds great joy and satisfaction in coaching. Recognizes when client needs to release emotions in order to fully engage and has strategies to confidently facilitate that release.
e. Cultivating Emotional Resilience	Understands what emotional resilience is and why it's important to intentionally cultivate it in educators.	Has strategies to cultivate emotional resilience in others; uses these strategies when a client is struggling.	Finds opportunities in every conversation to cultivate resilience.

Domain 8: Coach's Dispositions

Indicator	Foundational	Intermediate	Advanced
a. Compassion	Has compassion for those they find easy to relate to.	Has compassion for all within their immediate circle.	Demonstrates unwavering compassion and positive regard for all.
b. Curiosity	Is genuinely curious.	Is firmly grounded in an inquiry stance and is constantly curious.	Is insatiably curious about others, what is possible, and one's self. Is hopeful about what is possible.
c. Trust in the Coaching Process	Often feels impatient. Questions whether coaching can actually have an impact on someone.	Manages impatience. Recognizes the many factors that play a role in transformation.	Remembers that there may be times when we don't see evidence of change in a conversation, but that doesn't mean that change won't happen. Is open to possibility and refrains from acting on urgency in an unproductive way. Understands that we might lay seeds of transformation that sprout in another season.

Indicator	Foundational	Intermediate	Advanced
d. Humility & Mutuality	May feel they can only be effective with certain people.	Feels moderately effective with most people and may have preferences.	Is aware of and appreciates the reciprocal nature of learning and the potential for their own improvement through the process.
e. Learner Orientation	Continues to build knowledge of the disciplines in which they work (literacy, math, leadership, classroom culture, management, school transformation, and so on) Seeks out professional learning opportunities and consultations; stays informed about current research on best practices.	Solicits feedback, both formal and informal, and takes action based on feedback. Collaborates effectively with colleagues to support their professional growth.	Consistently reflects on their own learning and development and actively seeks out ways to develop and augment skill, knowledge, and/or capacity. Identifies professional areas of strength and growth; feels inspired and energized to continue developing.

(continued)

Indicator	Foundational	Intermediate	Advanced
f. Courage	Finds moments when they can speak and act with courage.	Feels more often able to speak and act with courage; navigates some of the fear related to accessing courage.	Feels consistently anchored in their own courage and connected to the courage of others; frequently takes risks in what they say and do.

APPENDIX D

Advocating for Systems Change

A Transformational Coach advocates for systems change. This includes addressing policies and structures that preserve institutionalized racism. This appendix describes the four areas in which coaches and school leaders can advocate for change—areas in which we'd see a tremendous positive impact on our students if policy changes were made.

Area 1: Hire and Retain a Diverse Teaching Force

According to the National Center for Education Statistics, in 2015–2016, about 80 percent of public-school teachers were white, 9 percent were Latinx, 7 percent were black, and 2 percent were Asian. This same study showed that about 77 percent of public-school teachers were female and 23 percent were male.

Research has shown that white teachers have lower expectations of students of color, which affects student success, while teachers of color have higher expectations of students of color. When black and Latinx students have teachers who match their race or ethnicity, they have better attendance, fewer suspensions, more positive attitudes, and higher test scores, graduation rates, and college attendance (Gershenson and Papageorge, 2018). However, when children of color have teachers of color, the chances are higher that they will be identified as gifted. School districts must commit to hiring teachers of color—this is a moral mandate.

But just getting teachers of color to walk in the door isn't enough. School leaders must retain teachers of color and to do so, they'll need to allocate resources to support teachers of color and to create staff cultures that are addressing their own biases. You can't hire a black teacher and expect them to thrive and want to stay in a school where racism is rampant.

Teachers of color, particularly those who work in marginalized communities, need and deserve intensive support to become effective teachers, build resilience, and deal with the explicit and implicit biases that they will encounter. Teachers of color often experience a double, or even triple, burden in our schools—taking on the challenge of teaching and working in staff cultures and organizations that are often biased, and needing to attend to their (our) own pain, trauma, and healing from the oppression we've experienced.

Research has found that the primary reason that teachers of color leave the profession is because they find themselves in places where they feel unwelcome, isolated, and undervalued—because of the biases they encounter in their workplaces every day. Teachers of color also take on more responsibilities than others—many of which they are asked to take on because they are a person of color (translating for parents, leading professional development, and disciplining students)—for which they aren't recognized or compensated. They may be the first in their families to graduate from college and the fact that teacher salaries are low may contribute to their decision to leave the profession (Teach Plus and Education Trust).

But in this research, teacher pay is not the top reason that teachers of color leave teaching—the top reasons have to do with staff culture. This is something that can be changed. Schools can become places that value and affirm teachers of color, where the school's mission and vision centralizes a commitment to racial equity. Efforts can be made to reduce isolation, and teachers of color can be given coaches—ideally, people of color or white people with cultural competence and an ability to coach across lines of racial difference. Staff culture *can* be changed—and if this is the top reason why teachers of color leave schools, we can do something about that.

Area 2: Provide Professional Development

If school leaders are committed to dismantling systemic oppression, then coaching and professional development (PD) must be provided to all staff. We cannot transform schools without learning. Transformational Coaching, as I hope you've seen, is an impactful model through which to learn. Staff must be trained and coached in cultural competency, to see and interrupt inequities, and to build just and liberated classrooms. Teachers and leaders must develop cultural competency when they work with students who don't share their racial and ethnic backgrounds.

I challenge schools, districts, and organizations to reflect on how their funds are spent. How much of a budget is allocated to professional development, and specifically to PD that focuses on addressing equity? An organization's priorities are reflected in the budget. If equity, cultural competence, and diversity are priorities, and if they mean more than just a phrase in a mission statement, then the budget will reflect this. It's time to stop making excuses for not having the funding or time to focus on addressing equity.

Area 3: Integrate Schools

In the United States, racial segregation in public education has been illegal since 1954. Yet American public schools remain largely separate and unequal. This has profound consequences for students, especially students of color. Today, more than half of all schoolchildren in the United States are in racially concentrated districts in which 75 percent of students are either white or nonwhite. In addition, school districts are often segregated by income. The nexus of racial and economic segregation has intensified educational gaps between rich and poor students, and between white students and students of color.

School segregation is a result of how districts are drawn. This has a lot to do with gerrymandering—a practice of manipulating boundaries to establish advantages for a group. In the United States, redlining and gerrymandering created racial and economic segregation. Not recognizing this manipulation leads to perpetuating the myth of meritocracy and to enforcing deficit mindsets about marginalized communities. It may be harder to remedy housing segregation in our country, but we can redraw lines around districts to equalize inherent disparities.

One of the greatest predictors of how much overt and unconscious racial bias a person will have is how diverse their community is during their childhood. Children recognize racial difference, and understand status and privilege, as young as three years old. It's time to integrate our communities. Furthermore, in the United States, the greatest successes in closing the "achievement" gap—the opportunity gap—have been in places where schools have been integrated. It's time we take on the challenge of integrating our schools. The inequities in our country today were designed. We can design something different.

Area 4: Fund Public Schools

We have got to change the way schools are funded. In 2016, school districts that predominantly serve students of color received *$23 billion less* in funding than mostly white school districts in the United States, despite serving the same number of students (EdBuild, 2019). School funding is closely connected to how districts are drawn, so to increase the funding of schools, we'll also need to talk about redrawing districts and integrating schools. Here's why: Schools rely heavily on local taxes, so small, wealthy communities have drawn borders to protect the interests of a small group, and in doing so, have concentrated resources. Our school system is inherently inequitable because our education system relies heavily on funding from community wealth.

Let's look at some numbers. In California during the 2018–2019 school year, 58 percent of funds for schools came from the state, 22 percent came from property taxes, 10 percent came from other local sources, and 9 percent came from the federal government. So let's compare two neighboring districts: one predominantly white small district—one with a student population of about 1,500, and the other made up of almost 95 percent students of color and with approximately 12,000 students. Because of contributions from local property taxes, the district with the 12,000 students of color ends up with about 20 percent less funding than its neighboring counterpart.

What does this mean for the students? In the small, white district, a student is likely to have higher paid teachers, which means they'll likely have more experience and receive more training; In addition, it's more likely that the school administration is stable and experienced. The students are likely to have more options for courses to take, including advanced and AP courses; more opportunities to participate in extracurricular activities, a wide range of athletics, and art and music classes; school buildings that are well maintained; smaller class sizes; technology and science supplies; access to mental health and college counselors; and much more.

The structural lack of access that so many low-income children of color have to what their counterparts in small, wealthy, white districts have is inequitable and unconscionable. Lack of access results in lack of opportunities, which results in disproportionate, adverse outcomes for people of color. And then those people of color are blamed for their "laziness," or their "irresponsibility," or their "broken homes." Blaming the victims obscures the truth of the structural racism in our country.

We live in a country where the gaps are created by an inherently unequal distribution of wealth, and we need to challenge this. But it doesn't have to be this way.

We can vote for changes in tax laws that redistribute wealth. We can mobilize to change the ways that districts are drawn. We can vote for local, state, and national politicians who prioritize funding schools. We can also use our coaching skills to talk to our families, neighbors, and community members to encourage them to vote for the people who will fund our schools and dismantle the institutions that uphold systems of oppression.

APPENDIX E

The Core Emotions

Core Emotion	Fear	Anger	Sadness	Shame
Common labels for this emotion	Agitated	Aggravated	Alienated	Besmirched
	Alarmed	Agitated	Anguished	Chagrined
	Anxious	Annoyed	Bored	Contemptuous
	Apprehensive	Antagonized	Crushed	(of self)
	Concerned	Bitter	Defeated	Contrite
	Desperate	Contemptuous	Dejected	Culpable
	Dismayed	(other	Depressed	Debased
	Dread	than for self)	Despairing	Degraded
	Fearful	Contentious	Despondent	Disapproving
	Frightened	Contrary	Disappointed	Disdainful
	Horrified	Cranky	Discouraged	Disgraced
	Hysterical	Cruel	Disheartened	Disgusted
	Impatient	Destructive	Dismayed	(at self)
	Jumpy	Displeased	Dispirited	Dishonored
	Nervous	Enraged	Displeased	Disreputable
	Panicked	Exasperated	Distraught	Embarrassed
	Scared	Explosive	Down	Guilty
	Shocked	Frustrated	Dreary	Hateful
	Shy	Furious	Forlorn	Humbled

(continued)

Core Emotion	Fear	Anger	Sadness	Shame
	Tense	Hateful	Gloomy	Humiliated
	Terrified	Hostile	Grief-stricken	Improper
	Timid	Impatient	Hopeless	Infamous
	Uncertain	Indignant	Hurt	Invalidated
	Uneasy	Insulated	Insecure	Mortified
	Worried	Irate	Isolated	Regretful
		Irritable	Lonely	Remorseful
		Irritated	Melancholic	Repentant
		Mad	Miserable	Reproachful
		Mean	Mopey	Rueful
		Outraged	Morose	Scandalized
		Resentful	Neglected	Scornful
		Scornful	Oppressed	Sinful
		Spiteful	Pessimistic	Stigmatized
		Urgent	Pitiful	
		Vengeful	Rejected	
			Somber	
			Sorrowful	
			Tragic	
			Unhappy	

Core Emotion	Jealousy	Disgust	Happiness	Love
Common labels for this emotion	Competitive	Appalled	Agreeable	Acceptance
	Covetous	Dislike	Amused	Admiration
	Deprived	Grossed out	Blissful	Adoring
	Distrustful	Insulted	Bubbly	Affectionate
	Envious	Intolerant	Cheerful	Allegiance
	Greedy	Nauseated	Content	Attached
	Grudging	Offended	Delighted	Attraction
	Jealous	Put off	Eager	Belonging
	Overprotective	Repelled	Ease	Caring
	Petty	Repulsed	Elated	Compassionate
	Possessive	Revolted	Engaged	Connected
	Resentful	Revulsion	Enjoyment	Dependent
	Rivalrous	Shocked	Enthusiastic	Desire
		Sickened	Euphoric	Devoted
		Turned off	Excited	Empathic

Core Emotion	Jealousy	Disgust	Happiness	Love
			Exhilarated	Faithful
			Flow	Friendship
			Glad	Interested
			Gleeful	Kind
			Glowing	Liking
			Gratified	Passionate
			Harmonious	Protective
			Hopeful	Respectful
			Interested	Sympathetic
			Joyful	Tender
			Jubilant	Trusting
			Lighthearted	Vulnerable
			Meaningful	Warm
			Merry	
			Optimistic	
			Peaceful	
			Pleasure	
			Pride	
			Proud	
			Relieved	
			Satisfied	
			Thrilled	
			Triumphant	

Source: Adapted from Erin Olivo, *Wise Mind Living* (Louisville, CO: Sounds True, 2014). This document is available for download from my website, https://brightmorningteam.com

APPENDIX F

Resources for Further Learning

This list contains resources from an array of authors, artists, activists, organizations, and change-makers who have influenced and inspired me. I strived to center the authorship of people of color and historically marginalized groups. This list is just a sampling of all the brilliant sources in the world from people working towards our collective liberation and healing. On my website (brightmorningteam.com), you'll find an annotated and more expansive list of resources including recommendations for podcasts, online resources, and trainings.

Here are my top recommendations for what to read next, if you haven't read them:

When you want to read prose that will break your heart open in a way for which you'll be forever grateful, read these:
- *Heavy,* by Kiese Laymon
- *On Earth We're Briefly Gorgeous,* by Ocean Vuong
- *There There,* by Tommy Orange
- *Between the World and Me,* by Ta-Nehisi Coetes
- *Ceremony,* by Leslie Marmon Silko

For white folks who seek greater self-understanding:
- *White Supremacy and Me,* by Layla Saad
- *White Fragility,* by Robin DiAngelo

For inspiration on how we can heal and transform our world, read these two (very different from each other but complimentary) books:

- *The Racial Healing Handbook,* by Anneliese Singh
- *Emergent Strategy,* by adrienne maree brown

To boost your emotional resilience and help you muster the strength and courage that it'll take to transform our world, read my previous book, *Onward.*

History

Bonilla-Silva, Eduardo. *Racism without Racists: Color-Blind Racism and the Persistence of Racial Inequality in the United States.* Rowman & Littlefield Publishers. 5th edition, 2017.

Coates, Ta-Nehisi. "The Case for Reparations." *The Best American Magazine Writing 2015,* 2015, pp. 1–50.

Dunbar-Ortiz, Roxanne. *An Indigenous Peoples' History of the United States.* Beacon Press, 2015.

Hannah-Jones, Nikole. "The 1619 Project." *The New York Times,* 14 Aug. 2019.

Hilliard, Asa G. *The Maroon Within Us: Selected Essays on African American Community Socialization.* Black Classic Press, 1995.

Kendi, Ibram X. *Stamped from the Beginning.* Reprint edition. Bold Type Books, 2017.

Reséndez Andrés. *The Other Slavery: The Uncovered Story of Indian Enslavement in America.* Reprint edition. Mariner, 2017.

Rothstein, Richard. *The Color of Law: A Forgotten History of How Our Government Segregated America.* Reprint edition. Liveright, 2018.

Race and Racism

Alexander, Michelle. *New Jim Crow: Mass Incarceration in the Age of Colorblindness.* Anniversary edition. The New Press, 2020.

DeWolf, Thomas Norman, and Sharon Leslie Morgan. *Gather at the Table: The Healing Journey of a Daughter of Slavery and a Son of the Slave Trade.* Beacon Press, 2012.

Groeger, Lena, Annie Waldman, and David Eads. "Miseducation: Is There Racial Inequality at Your School?" *ProPublica,* 16 Oct. 2018, projects.propublica.org/miseducation.

Jones, Kenneth, and Tema Okun. "White Supremacy Culture." dRworks. Dismantlingracism.org.

Kendi, Ibram X. *How to Be an Antiracist*. New York: One World, 2019.

Menakem, Resmaa. *My Grandmother's Hands: Racialized Trauma and the Pathway to Mending Our Hearts and Bodies*. Central Recovery Press, 2017.

Metzl, Jonathan M. *Dying of Whiteness: How the Politics of Racial Resentment Is Killing Americas Heartland*. Basic Books, 2019.

Morris, Monique. *Pushout: The Criminalization of Black Girls in Schools*. The New Press, 2016

Oluo, Ijeoma. *So You Want to Talk About Race*. Seal Press, 2018.

Perry, Theresa, Claude Steele, and Asa G. Hilliard III. *Young, Gifted, and Black: Promoting High Achievement Among African-American Students*. Beacon Press, 2003.

Saad, Layla F. *Me and White Supremacy: Combat Racism, Change the World, and Become a Good Ancestor*. Naperville, IL: Sourcebooks, 2020.

Singh, Anneliese A. *The Racial Healing Handbook: Practical Activities to Help You Challenge Privilege, Confront Systemic Racism & Engage in Collective Healing*. New Harbinger Publications, 2019.

Sue, Derald Wing. *Microaggressions in Everyday Life: Race, Gender, and Sexual rientation*. Wiley, 2010.

Tatum, Beverly Daniel. *Why Are All the Black Children Sitting Together in the Cafeteria?* And *Other Conversations About Race*. 20th Anniversary Edition. Basic Books, 2017.

West, Cornel. *Race Matters*. Beacon Press, 2018.

Whiteness and White Supremacy

Battalora, Jacqueline M. *Birth of a White Nation: The Invention of White People and Its Relevance Today*. Strategic Book Publishing, 2013.

DiAngelo, Robin. *White Fragility: Why It's so Hard for White People to Talk About Racism*. Beacon Press, 2018.

Emdin, Christopher. *For White Folks Who Teach in the Hood . . . and the Rest of Y'all Too: Reality Pedagogy and Urban Education*. Beacon Press, 2017.

Helms, Janet E. *A Race Is a Nice Thing to Have: A Guide to Being a White Person or Understanding the White Persons in Your Life*. Cognella Academic Publishing, 2019.

Irving, Debby. *Waking Up White, and Finding Myself in the Story of Race*. Elephant Room Press, 2014.

Kivel, Paul. *Uprooting Racism* - 4th Edition: *How White People Can Work for Racial Justice*. New Society Publishers, 2017.

Michael, Ali. *Raising Race Questions: Whiteness and Inquiry in Education (Practitioner Inquiry)*. Teachers College Press, 2015.

Moore Jr., Eddie, Ali Michael, and Marguerite W. Penick-Parks. *The Guide for White Women Who Teach Black Boys*. Corwin Press, 2017.

Rothenberg, Paula S. *White Privilege* (Anthology). 5th Edition. Worth Publishers, 2015.

Tochluk, Shelly. *Witnessing Whiteness: The Need to Talk About Race and How to Do It*. 2nd Edition. R&L Education, 2010.

Wise, Tim. *White Like Me: Reflections on Race from a Privileged Son*. Soft Skull Press, 2011.

Intersectionality

Collins, Patricia Hill. *Black Feminist Thought: Knowledge, Consciousness, and the Politics of Empowerment*. Routledge, 2015.

Crenshaw, Kimberle (1989). "Demarginalizing the Intersection of Race and Sex: A Black Feminist Critique of Antidiscrimination Doctrine, Feminist Theory and Antiracist Politics." *University of Chicago Legal Forum*, Vol. 1989, Article 8.

Davis, Angela Y. *Women, Race, & Class* (1st Vintage Books edition). Vintage, 1983.

Gay, Roxane. *Bad Feminist: Essays*. HarperCollins, 2017.

hooks, bell. *Feminism Is for Everybody: Passionate Politics*. Routledge, 2015.

Lorde, Audre. *Sister Outsider Essays and Speeches* (Reprint Edition). Crossing Press, 2007.

Mock, Janet. *Redefining Realness: My Path to Womanhood, Identity, Love & So Much More*. Atria Books, 2014.

O'Toole, Corbett Joan. *Fading Scars: My Queer Disability History*. Autonomous Press, 2015.

Pedagogy

Delpit, Lisa. *Other People's Children: Cultural Conflict in the Classroom*. The New Press, 2006.

Freire, Paulo. *Pedagogy of the Oppressed*. 30th Anniversary Edition. Continuum, 2000.

Gay, Geneva. *Culturally Responsive Teaching: Theory, Research, and Practice*. 3rd Edition, Teachers College Press, 2018.

Germán, Lorena. *The Antiracist Teacher Reading Instruction Workbook*. The Multicultural Classroom, 2019.

Hammond, Zaretta L. *Culturally Responsive Teaching and The Brain: Promoting Authentic Engagement and Rigor Among Culturally and Linguistically Diverse Students*. Corwin Press, 2014.

hooks, bell. *Teaching to Transgress: Education as the Practice of Freedom*. Routledge, 1994.

Howard, Gary. *We Can't Teach What We Don't Know: White Teachers, Multiracial Schools*. 3rd Edition, Teachers College Press, 2016.

Nieto, Sonia. *The Light in Their Eyes Creating Multicultural Learning Communities: 10th Anniversary Edition*. Teachers College Press, 2009.

Noguera, Pedro A. *The Trouble with Black Boys: . . . And Other Reflections on Race, Equity, and the Future of Public Education*. Jossey-Bass, 2009.

Decolonization and Indigeneity

Dunbar-Ortiz, Roxanne. *An Indigenous Peoples' History of the United States*. Beacon Press, 2015.

Fanon, Frantz. *Black Skin, White Masks*. Revised edition. Grove Press, 2008.

LaDuke, Winona. *Recovering the Sacred: The Power of Naming and Claiming*. 2nd Edition. Haymarket Books, 2016.

Steinem, Gloria, and Wilma Mankiller. *Every Day Is a Good Day: Reflections by Contemporary Indigenous Women*. Fulcrum Publishing, 2011.

Literature

Adichie, Chimamanda Ngozi. *Americanah*. Knopf, 2013.

Akhtar, Ayad. *American Dervish: A Novel*. Reprint edition. Back Bay Books, 2012.

Chin, Justin. *98 Wounds*. Manic D Press, 2011.

Cisneros, Sandra. *The House on Mango Street*. Vintage Press, 25th anniversary edition, 2009.

Erdrich, Louise. *The Round House: A Novel*. Reprint edition. Harper Perennial, 2013.

Giovanni, Nikki. *The Collected Poetry of Nikki Giovanni: 1968–1998*. HarperCollins Publishers, 2007.

Gyasi, Yaa. *Homegoing*. Reprint edition. Vintage, 2017.

Harjo, Joy. *An American Sunrise: Poems*. W. W. Norton & Company, 2020.

Henríquez, Cristina. *The Book of Unknown Americans*. Reprint edition. Vintage, 2015.

Hughes, Langston. *The Collected Works of Langston Hughes*, edited by Arnold Rampersad. Vintage Classics edited edition, Vintage, 1995.

Hurston, Zora Neale. *Their Eyes Were Watching God*. 75th Anniversary edition. Amistad, 2006.

Marmon Silko, Leslie. *Ceremony*. Penguin Classics Deluxe Edition, 2006.

Morrison, Toni. *Beloved*. Knopf Doubleday Publishing Group, 2004. (And everything else by Toni Morrison)

Orange, Tommy. *There There*. Reprint edition. Vintage, 2019.

Otsuka, Julie. *The Buddha in the Attic*. Penguin, 2013.

Petry, Ann. *The Street*. Houghton Mifflin, 1946.

Purdy, John Lloyd., and James Ruppert. Nothing but the Truth: An Anthology of Native American Literature. Pearson, 2000.

Rankine, Claudia. *Citizen: An American Lyric*. Graywolf Press, 2014.

Vuong, Ocean. *On Earth We're Briefly Gorgeous: A Novel*. Penguin Press, 2019.

Nonfiction and Memoirs

Angelou, Maya. *I Know Why the Caged Bird Sings*. Random House, 2009.

Baldwin, James, *The Fire Next Time*. Vintage, 1992.

Boyle, Gregory. *Tattoos on the Heart: The Power of Boundless Compassion*. Free Press, 2011.

Coates, Ta-Nehisi. *Between the World and Me*. Random House, 2015.

Dubois, W.E.B. *The Souls of Black Folk*. Reprint edition. Oxford University Press, 2009.

King, Martin Luther, and Coretta Scott King. *Strength to Love*. Beacon Press, 2019.

Laymon, Kiese. *Heavy: An American Memoir*. Reprint edition. Scribner, 2019.

Lorde, Audre. *Zami: A New Spelling of My Name: A Biomythography*. Crossing Press, 1982.

Malcom, X., and Alex Haley. *The Autobiography of Malcolm X*. Ballantine, 1999.

Moraga, Cherríe. *Native Country of the Heart: A Memoir*. Picador, 2020.

Miranda, Deborah A. *Bad Indians: A Tribal Memoir*. Heyday, 2013.

Ward, Jesmyn. *Men We Reaped: A Memoir*. Bloomsbury Publishing, 2018.

Wilkerson, Isabel. *The Warmth of Other Suns: The Epic Story of America's Great Migration*. Reprint edition. Vintage, 2011.

On Change, Organizing, and Action

brown, adrienne maree. *Emergent Strategy: Shaping Change, Changing Worlds*. Reprint edition. AK Press, 2017.

Chugh, Dolly. *The Person You Mean to Be: How Good People Fight Bias*. Harper Collins, 2018.

hooks, bell. *All About Love: New Visions*. Harper Perennial, 2018.

Horton, Myles, and Paulo Freire. *We Make the Road by Walking: Conversations on Education and Social Change*. Reprint edition. Temple University Press, 1991.

Love, Bettina. *We Want to Do More Than Survive: Abolitionist Teaching and the Pursuit of Educational Freedom*. Reprint edition. Beacon Press, 2020.

Powell, john a. *Racing to Justice: Transforming Our Conceptions of Self and Other to Build an Inclusive Society*. Reprint edition. Indiana University Press, 2015.

Wheatley, Margaret J. *Turning to One Another: Simple Conversations to Restore Hope to the Future*. 2nd edition. Berrett-Koehler Publishers, 2009.

Mindfulness

Brach, Tara. *Radical Acceptance: Embracing Your Life With the Heart of a Buddha*. Reprint edition. Bantam, 2004,

Brach, Tara. *Radical Compassion: Learning to Love Yourself and Your World with the Practice of RAIN*. Rider, 2020.

Magee, Rhonda V. *The Inner Work of Racial Justice: Healing Ourselves and Transforming Our Communities Through Mindfulness*. TarcherPerigee, 2019.

Sofer, Oren Jay. *Say What You Mean: A Mindful Approach to Nonviolent Communication*. Shambhala, 2018.

Williams, Rev. angel Kyodo, et al. *Radical Dharma: Talking Race, Love, and Liberation*. North Atlantic Books, 2016.

Films and Television

12 Years a Slave [Film]. Steve McQueen (Director). 20th Century Fox, 2013.

13th [Television Documentary]. Ava Duvernay (Director). Netflix, 2016.

Bread and Roses [Film]. Ken Loach (Director). 2000.

Fruitvale Station [Film]. Ryan Coogler (Director). Significant Productions, 2013.

Hidden Figures [Film]. Theodore Melfi (Director). 20th Century Fox, 2017.

Incident at Oglala [Documentary Film]. Michael Apted (Director). Miramax, 1992.

Matewan [Film]. John Sayles (Director). Cinecom Pictures, 1987.

Milk [Film]. Gus Van Sant (Director). Focus Features, 2008.

Moonlight [Film]. Barry Jenkins (Director). A24, Plan B Entertainment, 2016.

Hannah Gadsby: Nanette [Television]. Madeleine Perry and Jon Olb (Directors). Netflix, 2018.

Pride [Film]. Matthew Warchus (Director). BBC Films, 2014.

Selma [Film]. Ava DuVernay (Director). Paramount Pictures, 2014.

Watchmen [Television]. Nicole Kassell (Director). HBO, 2019.

When They See Us [Television]. Ava DuVernay (Director). Netflix, 2019.

GLOSSARY

Agency: One's capacity or ability to navigate systems and leverage power.

Ally: A member of a different group who works to end a form of discrimination for a particular individual or designated group.

Asset-based (strength-based) coaching: Focusing on strengths, talents, competencies, and what someone is doing well to support lasting change.

Assimilation: The full adoption (by an individual or a group, forced or voluntary) of cultural values and patterns of a different social, linguistic, or religious ethos, resulting in diminished or eliminated attitudes and behaviors of the original cultural group.

Bias: An inclination or preference either for or against an individual or group that interferes with impartial judgment.

Bigotry: Judging a group of people based on their identity markers, and feeling and expressing intolerance of them.

Binary thinking: Placing things in terms of two options that are mutually exclusive, often leading to oversimplifications of complex or nuanced ideas and identifying markers. Examples include gender binaries and modes of thinking (either/or) that underscore systems of white supremacy.

Catalytic coaching stance: A stance to help another person reflect, work through feelings and thoughts, and learn for themselves. From this stance, the coach elicits self-discovery and problem-solving, encouraging the client to take responsibility for their learning and further actions.

Cathartic coaching stance: A stance to help the client release and express emotions. From this stance, the coach helps the client release the emotions that block progress.

Cisgender: A person who identifies as the gender they were assigned at birth.

Classism: Prejudiced thoughts and discriminatory actions based on a difference in socio-economic status, income, class, usually perpetuated by wealthier/upper classes.

Coachability: The willingness and ability to be present and open to exploration, to examine assumptions, to generate creative solutions, and to take the risk of trying new things; the general ability to be an open and receptive learner at that particular time.

Cognitive dissonance: The discomfort that results when one's beliefs run counter to their behaviors and/or new information that is presented. People want to have consistency between their attitudes and perceptions, so when something they hold true is challenged, they will change something—a belief or behavior—to reduce the dissonance.

Colonialism: The establishment, exploitation, maintenance, acquisition, and expansion of colonies in one territory by people from another territory.

Color blindness (and the problem with it): The belief in treating everyone "equally" by treating everyone the same and not seeing color; based on the problematic presumption that differences are bad to acknowledge, and therefore ignored.

Colorism: A socially constructed hierarchy that favors lighter-skinned people over darker-skinned people.

Confrontational coaching stance: An interrupting stance to raise awareness, challenge the client's assumptions, or stimulate awareness of behavior, beliefs, or being; it also helps clients see the consequences of an action or boost the client's confidence by affirming success. The coach uses this stance to mediate a behavior, mind frame, belief, or way of being to generate a little cognitive dissonance.

Cultural appropriation: The action of taking or misusing elements of peoples' culture without having authentic relationships with the people or the culture and/or without their permission. Often (but not always) this is in order to financially profit. This often occurs without any real understanding of why the original culture took part in these activities. It also includes, converting culturally significant artifacts, practices, and beliefs into popular culture or giving them a significance that is completely different/less nuanced than they would originally have had. Examples include Halloween costumes based on a person/group's culture.

Deficit thinking: A perspective that attributes failures such as lack of achievement, learning, or success to a personal lack of effort or deficiency in the individual, rather than to failures or limitations of a system. Typically applied to students of color, low-income students/families, and immigrant students.

Discrimination: Unfair treatment of one person or a group of people because of their identity (race, religion, gender, ability, etc.). Discrimination is an action that can come from prejudice.

Disproportionality: A group's representation in a particular category that exceeds expectations for that group, or differs substantially from the representation of others in that category (e.g., overrepresentation of black male students in Special Education classes, and black and brown student suspension rates).

Dominant culture: The cultural values, beliefs, and practices that are assumed to be the most common and influential within a given society.

Drop outs (also known as "push outs"): When the long-term structures and systems explicitly or implicitly, through policies and actions, slowly push students out of school.

Equity: Every child gets what they need in our schools—regardless of where they come from, what they look like, who their parents are, what their temperament is, or what they show up knowing or not knowing. Every child gets what he, she, or they need every day in order to have all the skills and tools to pursue whatever they want after leaving our schools, to live a fulfilling life. Equity is about outcomes and experiences—for *every child, every day.*

Ethnicity: A group of people who share a common or distinct ancestry and cultural practices, generally according to a geographic region and often with psychological attachment.

Ethnocentrism: Seeing things from the point of view of one's own ethnic group, which can lead to an attitude that views one's own culture as superior.

Eurocentrism: The inclination to consider European culture as normative. While the term does not imply an attitude of superiority, many align this term with the awareness of the historic oppressiveness of Eurocentric tendencies in U.S and European society.

Genocide: The act or intent to deliberately and systematically annihilate an entire religious, racial, national, or cultural group.

Hate crime: A criminal act directed at a person or group because of the victim's real or perceived race, gender, sexual orientation, ethnicity, national origin, religion, or ability.

Heterosexism: The presumption that everyone is, and should be, heterosexual.

Hierarchy of oppression: No single form of oppression is more important or dominant than another.

Homophobia: The fear or hatred of homosexuality (and other non-heterosexual identities) and persons perceived to be gay or lesbian.

Implicit (unconscious) bias: An unconsciously held set of associations about a social group. Can result in the attribution of particular qualities to all individuals from that group, also known as stereotyping. Implicit biases are the product of learned associations and social conditioning. They usually begin at a young age, and these biases do not necessarily align with personal identity. It's possible to unconsciously associate positive *or* negative traits with one's own race, gender, or another identity marker.

Instructive coaching stance: Coaching that focuses on changing behaviors. Also called *directive coaching.*

Institutionalized racism: Racism perpetrated by social and political institutions such as schools, the courts, and the military. Also referred to as systemic racism, it has the power to negatively affect the bulk of people belonging to a racial group. Institutional racism can be seen in areas of wealth and income, criminal justice, employment, health care, housing, education, and politics.

Internalized racism/oppression: The process whereby individuals in the target group make racist/oppressive beliefs and attitudes internal and personal by coming to believe that the lies, prejudices, and stereotypes about them are true. Internalized racism/oppression can create low self-esteem, self-doubt, and even self-loathing. It can also be projected outward as fear, criticism, and distrust of members of one's target group.

Intersectionality: A term coined by critical race theorist Kimberlé Crenshaw that means that prejudice stems from the intersection of racist ideas and other forms of bigotry including sexism, classism, ethnocentrism, and homophobia. When examining equity in schools, it's essential to explore the intersection of identities and oppression. There is no hierarchy of oppressions. Each identity intersects with another to generate a more complex worldview than the one that would exist if any of us walked through life with a singular identity.

Islamophobia: The fear, hatred of, or prejudice against the Islamic religion or Muslim peoples generally, usually leading to discrimination and stereotypes.

Justice: The full and equal participation of all groups in a society that is shaped to meet their needs, distribute resources equitably, and where all members feel psychologically and physically safe and secure.

Latinx: A person of Latin American origin or descent (used as a gender-neutral or nonbinary alternative to Latino or Latina).

Liberation: The efforts to effect lasting change and freedom from systems of oppression with the ultimate goal of self-determination the right to opportunity, thought, expression, and action.

Minority: Racial, ethnic, religious, or social subdivisions of a society that is subordinate to the dominant group in political, financial, or social power without regard to the size of these groups.

Normative culture/White-dominant culture: Defines what is considered "normal" by creating the standard for judging values, privileging individuals over groups, and assigning a higher value to some ways of behaving and knowing than others without considering the broad social-cultural differences that exist across communities and identifying markers. For example, white dominant culture presupposes that the thoughts, beliefs, and actions of white people are superior to people of color.

Patriarchy: The norms, values, beliefs, structures, and systems that grant power, privilege, and superiority to men, and therefore marginalize and subordinate women.

Power: The ability to influence others and impose one's beliefs. All power is relational.

Prejudice: Judging or forming an idea about someone or a group of people before you actually know them. Prejudice is often directed toward people in a certain identity group.

Prescriptive coaching stance: A stance that gives directions, recommendations, or advice to direct behavior. This stance is used when the client is open to hearing it, and when it is caring, candid, practical, wise, and well-timed.

Privilege: Refers to gaining benefits, advantages, and rights by default at the expense of others, because one belongs to the perceived "us," "normal," or "natural" state of the "mainstream" or dominant culture. Privilege allows for active, persistent exclusion and devaluation of "them," those who are "othered" or "marginalized."

Race: A socially constructed phenomenon, based on the erroneous assumption that physical differences such as skin color, hair color and texture, and facial (or other physical) features are related to intellectual, moral, and cultural superiority. Although race is a socially constructed concept, it has significant impact on the lives of people of color.

Racial profiling: The use of race or ethnicity as grounds for suspecting someone has committed an offense.

Racism: A system of oppression that emerges from beliefs that one race is superior to another based on biological characteristics. Racism is fueled by the ideology of white supremacy, which designates white people as superior to people of color. In racist systems, white and light-skinned people are granted unearned privileges or advantages by society just because of their race. Social attitudes, actions, and structures that oppress, exclude, limit, and discriminate against individuals and groups.

Redlining: The systematic denial of various services by federal government agencies, local governments, and the private sector to residents of specific, most notably black, neighborhoods or communities. Examples of redlining include the denial of loans, insurance, and health care.

Reparations: Anything paid or done to make up for a wrongdoing, or the act of making up for a wrongdoing. In the context of the United States, reparations indicates that compensation should be provided to the descendants of slaves from the Atlantic slave trade, ranging from individual monetary payments to land-based compensation.

Scapegoating: Blaming a person or a group of people for something when the fault lies elsewhere. Scapegoating includes hostile words or actions that can lead to physical violence; a person or group is blamed for something because of some aspect of their identity, but they usually lack the power or opportunity to fight back.

Sexism: The cultural, institutional, and individual set of beliefs and practices that privilege men, subordinate women, and devalue ways of being that are associated with women.

Stereotype: The false idea that all members of a group are the same and think and behave in the same way.

Supportive coaching stance: This stance offers the client confirmation, encouragement, and help so they can maintain focus and motivation. The coach helps clients notice and experience moments of success (macro and micro) and encourages risk-taking to promote further learning.

Transgender: An umbrella term for people whose gender identity differs from the sex they were assigned at birth. This term is not indicative of gender expression, sexual orientation, hormonal makeup, physical anatomy, or how one is perceived in daily life.

White fragility: Behaviors (often manifesting in discomfort and defensiveness) on the part of a white person when confronted by information about racism, racial inequality, and injustice.

Whiteness: A social construction that has created a racial hierarchy that has shaped all the social, cultural, political, educational, and economic institutions of society. Whiteness is linked to domination and is a form of race privilege invisible to white people who are not conscious of its power.

White privilege: Unearned, and largely unacknowledged, advantages based on race, which can be observed both systemically and individually. Peggy McIntosh coined the term and described it as "an invisible weightless knapsack of special provisions, assurances, tools, maps, guides, codebooks, passports, visas, clothes, compass, emergency gear, and blank checks." We can also have unearned privilege related to class, religion, ethnicity, sexual orientation, age, or ability.

White supremacy: The belief system that underlies the concept of whiteness—a historically based, institutionally perpetuated system of exploitation and oppression of continents, nations, and individuals of color by white individuals and nations of the European continent for the purpose of maintaining and defending a system of wealth, power, and privilege.

Xenophobia: The attitudes, prejudices, and behaviors that reject, exclude, and vilify people based on the perceptions that they are outsiders or foreigners to a community, society, or national identity. A fear or hatred of foreigners or strangers and their customs and cultures.

REFERENCES

Accapadi, M. M. (2007). When White Women Cry: How White Women's Tears Oppress Women of Color. *The College Student Affairs Journal, 26*(2), 208–215.

Adichie, C. N. (2009). The Danger of a Single Story. *TED Global.* Retrieved from http://www.ted.com/talks/chimamanda_adichie_the_danger_of_a_single_story

Agrawal, N. (2019, September 10). California Expands Ban on 'Willful Defiance' Suspensions in Schools. *The Los Angeles Times.* Retrieved from https://www.latimes.com/california/story/2019-09-10/school-suspension-willfuldefiance-california

Aguilar, E. (2013). *The Art of Coaching: Effective Strategies for School Transformation.* San Francisco, CA: Jossey-Bass.

Aguilar, E. (2016). *The Art of Coaching Teams.* San Francisco, CA: Jossey-Bass.

Aguilar, E. (2018a). *Onward: Cultivating Emotional Resilience in Educators.* San Francisco, CA: Jossey-Bass.

Aguilar, E. (2018b). *The Onward Workbook: Daily Activities to Cultivate Your Emotional Resilience and Thrive.* San Francisco, CA: Jossey-Bass.

Aguilar, E. (2019). Getting Mindful About Race in Schools. *Educational Leadership, 76*(7), 62–67.

Aguilar, E. (2020). *The Art of Coaching Workbook: Tools to Make Every Conversation Count.* San Francisco, CA: Jossey-Bass.

Alliance for Excellent Education. (2014). On the Path to Equity: Improving the Effectiveness of Beginning Teachers. Retrieved from https://all4ed.org/press/teacher-attrition-costs-united-states-up-to-2–2-billion-annually-says-new-alliance-report

American Psychiatric Association. (1971). Zung Instrument for Anxiety. *Psychosomatics, 8,* 371–379.

Bambara, T. (1987, June 1). Interview by K. Bonetti. Audiocasette. Amer Audio Prose Library Inc.

Bartlett, M. Y., & DeSteno, D. (2006). Gratitude and Prosocial Behavior: Helping When It Costs You. *Psychological Science, 17*(4), 319–325.

Blackmon, D. A. (2008). *Slavery by Another Name: The Re-Enslavement of Black Americans from the Civil War to World War II.* New York: Anchor Books.

Bohan, S., & Kleffman, S. (2009, December 2). Day I: Three East Bay ZIP Codes, Life-and-Death Disparities. *East Bay Times*. Retrieved from https://www.eastbaytimes.com/2009/12/02/day-i-three-east-bay-zip-codes-life-and-death-disparities/

Bowman, B., Comer, J. & Johns, D. (2018). Addressing the African American Achievement Gap: Three Leading Educators Issue a Call to Action. *Young Children, 73*(2).

brown, a.m. (2017). *Emergent Strategy: Shaping Change, Changing Worlds* (Vol. 14). Chico, CA: AK Press.

Brown, B. (2018). *Dare to Lead: Brave Work. Tough Conversations. Whole Hearts* (Vol. 4). New York, NY: Random House.

Carter, P., Skiba, R., Arredondo, M. & Pollock, M. (2017). "You Can't Fix What You Don't Look At: Acknowledging Race in Addressing Racial Discipline Disparities." *Urban Education, 52*(2).

Characteristics of Public School Teachers. (2018, April). *National Center for Education Statistics*. Retrieved from https://nces.ed.gov/programs/coe/indicator_clr.asp

Chetty, R., Hendren, N., Jones, M., & Porter, S. (2018, March). Race and Economic Opportunity in the United States: An Intergenerational Perspective. Retrieved from http://www.equality-of-opportunity.org/assets/documents/race_paper.pdf

Chugh, D. (2019). *The Person You Mean to Be: How Good People Fight Bias*. New York, NY: Harper Collins.

Coates, T. (2014, June). The Case for Reparations. *The Atlantic. 313*(5).

Cox, D., Navarro-Rivera, J., & Jones, R. (2016). *Race, Religion, and Political Affiliation of American's Core Social Networks*. Washington, D.C: Public Religion Research Institute.

Crenshaw, K. (1989). Demarginalizing the Intersection of Race and Sex: A Black Feminist Critique of Antidiscrimination Doctrine, Feminist Theory and Antiracist Politics. *Feminism in the Law: Theory, Practice and Criticism*. Students at the University of Chicago Law School.

Cubberley, E. P. (1916). Public School Administration. quoted in *The 'Business' of Reforming American Schools. Education Week*, 30 September 1998.

Cullors, P., Ross, R., & Tippet, K. (2016, February 18). The Spiritual Work of Black Lives Matter. *On Being* Podcast. Retrieved from https://onbeing.org/programs/patrisse-cullors-and-robert-ross-the-spiritual-work-of-black-lives-matter-may2017

Delpit, L. (1995). *Other People's Children: Cultural Conflict in the Classroom*. New York, NY: W.W. Norton & Company.

DiAngelo, R. (2018). *White Fragility: Why It's So Hard for White People to Talk about Racism*. Boston, MA: Beacon Press.

Devine, P. (1989). Stereotypes and Prejudice: Their Automatic and Controlled Components. *Journal of Personality and Social Psychology, 56*, 5–18.

East Bay Times. (2009). https://www.eastbaytimes.com/2009/12/02/day-i-three-east-bay-zip-codes-life-and-death-disparities

Echeverría, R., & Olalla, J. (1993). *The Art of Ontological Coaching*. Boulder, CO: Newfield Network.

Edbuild.org. "Nonwhite School Districts Get $23 Billion Less than White Districts Despite Serving the Same Number of Students." 18 Mar 2020. Retrieved from https://edbuild.org/content/23-billion

Estes, C. P. (2008). You Were Made for This. http://Awakin.org. Retrieved from https://www.awakin.org/read/view.php?tid=548

Freire, P. (1968). *Pedagogy of the Oppressed*. New York, NY: Seabury Press.

Gershenson, S., & Papageorge, N. (2018). The Power of Teacher Expectations. *Education Next*. Winter, *18 (1)*.

Ginott, H. (1993). *Teacher and Child: A Book for Parents and Teachers*. New York, NY: Scribner.

Gladwell, M. (2000). *The Tipping Point*. New York, NY: Little Brown.

Gladwell, M. (2011). *Outliers: The Story of Success*. New York, NY: Back Bay Books.

Goldhaber, D., et al. (2015). Uneven Playing Field? Assessing the Teacher Quality Gap Between Advantaged and Disadvantaged Students. *Educational Researcher, 44*(5), 1.

Goleman, D. (2001). *Emotional Intelligence: Perspectives on a Theory of Performance*. In C. Cherniss & D. Goleman (Eds.), *The Emotionally Intelligent Workplace*. San Francisco, CA: Jossey-Bass.

Grissom, J. A., & Redding, C. (2016, January 18). Discretion and Disproportionality: Explaining the Underrepresentation of High-Achieving Students of Color in Gifted Programs. *AERA Open*.

"If You Listen, We Will Stay: Why Teachers of Color Leave and How to Disrupt Teacher Turnover." Teach Plus. 25 Sept 2019. Retrieved from https://teachplus.org/DisruptTeacherTurnover

Javdani, S. (2019). Policing Education: An Empirical Review of the Challenges and Impact of the Work of School Police Officers. *American Journal of Community Psychology, 63*(3–4), 253–269.

Jefferson, T. Multiple sources: https://famguardian.org/Subjects/Politics/thomasjefferson/jeff1350.htm

Joyce, B., & Showers, B. (1982). The Coaching of Teaching. *Educational Leadership, 40*, 4–10.

Kendi, I. X. (2016). *Stamped from the Beginning: The Definitive History of Racist Ideas in America*. New York, NY: Nation Books.

Kendi, I. X. (2019). *How to Be an Antiracist*. New York, NY: Penguin Random House.

Kivel, P. (1996). *Uprooting Racism: How White People Can Work for Racial Justice* (1st ed., pp. 19). Gabriola Island, BC, Canada: New Society Publishers.

Klopfenstein, K. (2004). Advanced Placement: Do Minorities Have Equal Opportunity? *Economics of Education Review, 23*(2), 115–131.

Knight, J. (2014). *Focus on Teaching: Using Video for High-Impact Instruction*. Thousand Oaks, CA: Corwin.

Ladson-Billings, G. (2006). From the Achievement Gap to the Education Debt: Understanding Achievement in U.S. Schools. *Educational Researcher, 35*(7), 3–12.

Lemov, D., Woolway, E., & Yezzi, K. (2012). *Practice Perfect: 42 Rules for Getting Better at Getting Better* (Vol. 8). San Francisco, CA: Jossey-Bass.

Losen, D., & Skiba, R. (2010). "Suspended Education: Urban Middle Schools in Crisis." White Paper for The Civil Rights Project.

Magee, R. V. (2019). *The Inner Work of Racial Justice: Healing Ourselves and Transforming Our Communities through Mindfulness.* New York, NY: Tarcher Perigee.

Menakem, R. (2017). *My Grandmother's Hands: Racialized Trauma and the Pathway to Mending our Hearts and Bodies.* Las Vegas, NV: Central Recovery Press, LLC.

Miles, R. (1989). *The Women's History of the World.* New York, NY: Harper Collins.

Morris, M. (2016). *Pushout: The Criminalization of Black Girls in Schools.* New York, NY: The New Press.

Neville, H., & Cross, W., Jr. (2017). Racial Awakening: Epiphanies and Encounters in Black Racial Identity. *Cultural Diversity and Ethnic Minority Psychology, 23*(1), 102–110.

Olivo, E. (2014). *Wise Mind Living.* Louisville, CO: Sounds True.

OnBeing (2017). Retrieved from https://onbeing.org/programs/patrisse-cullors-and-robert-ross-the-spiritual-work-of-black-lives-matter-may2017.

powell, j. a. (2015). *Racing to Justice: Transforming Our Conceptions of Self and Other to Build an Inclusive Society.* Bloomington, IA: Indiana University Press.

Raufu, A. (2017). School-to-Prison Pipeline: Impact of School Discipline on African American Students. *Journal of Education & Social Policy, 7*(1).

Rensselaer Polytechnic Institute. (2011, July 25). Retrieved from https://news.rpi.edu/luwakkey/2902

Rocque, M., & Paternoster, R. (2011). Understanding the Antecedents of the 'School to Jail' Link: The Relationship between Race and School Discipline. *The Journal of Criminal Law and Criminology, 1010*(2), 633–666.

Senge, P. (1994). *The Fifth Discipline Fieldbook: Strategies and Tools for Building a Learning Organization* (Vol. 243). New York, NY: Doubleday.

Shlain, L. (1998). *The Alphabet Versus the Goddess: The Conflict Between Word and Image.* New York, NY: Penguin.

Smith, E. J., & Harper, S. R. (2015). Disproportionate Impact of K-12 School Suspension and Expulsion on Black Students in Southern States. University of Pennsylvania Center for the Study of Race and Equity in Education.

Suspension Data. (2019, December 12). California Department of Education. http://Cde.ca.gov. Retrieved from www.cde.ca.gov/ds/sd/sd/filessd.asp

Tatum, B. (1999). *Why Are All the Black Children Sitting Together in the Cafeteria? And Other Conversations about Race* (Vol. 6). New York, NY: Basic Books.

Teach Plus. (2019, September 25). "If You Listen, We Will Stay: Why Teachers of Color Leave and How to Disrupt Teacher Turnover." Retrieved from https://teachplus.org/DisruptTeacherTurnover

The Equality Institute, (n.d.) www.equalityinstitute.org

Thomas Jefferson on Politics & Government. (2009, August 15). http://Famguardian .org. Retrieved from https://famguardian.org/Subjects/Politics/thomasjefferson/ jeff1350.htm

Todd, A. R., et al. (2016). Does Seeing Faces of Young Black Boys Facilitate the Identification of Threatening Stimuli? *Psychological Science, 27*(3).

Trujillo, T., et al. (2017). *Responding to Educational Inequality.* Haas Institute Policy Brief.

U.S. Census Bureau. (2018, March 13). Older People Projected to Outnumber Children for First Time in U.S. History. Retrieved from https://www.census.gov/newsroom/ press-releases/2018/cb18-41-population-projections.html

U.S. Department of Education Office for Civil Rights. (2014, March). Data Snapshot: School Discipline. *Civil Rights Data Collection.*

Zinn, H. (1980). *A People's History of the United States.* New York, NY: Harper Collins.

INDEX

NOTE: Page references in *italics* refer to figures and tables.

Carlson, Frank (Skolnik), 79

case study (Khai), 211–233, 235–256, 257–274, 275–300

background, 211–213

coaching and looking inward, 241–243, 257–260

coaching relationship inception, 214–223

commitment to behavioral change, 288–296

confronting bias, 264–273

data used in, 243–247, 260–264, 280–286, *284–285*

debriefing of observation, 235–241

developing new student behaviors, 276–277

discussing race, 250–254, *253*

legacy question used in, 247–250

observation of classroom, 229–231

planning of coaching conversation, 223–229

practice and behavioral change, 286–288

scaffolding learning for adults, 277–280

Transformational Coaching phases, overview, *213,* 214, *236,* 236–237, 258, *258,* 275–276, *276*

Chugh, Dolly, 123

cis-gendered, defined, 202

Cisneros, Sandra, 210

clients

assessing readiness to discuss race with, 250–254, *253*

decision making by, 105–106

identity markers of, 199–210

resistance by, 175–176, 186–193, 259

trust between coach and, 107, 219–223

working with clients who dispute their gaps, 136 (*See also* Mind the Gaps Framework)

See also data; observation; Transformational Coaching

"A Cloze Script for the Legacy Question" (Bright Morning Team), 248

coaches

abilities needed by, 3, 10, *11–12*

assessing readiness to discuss race with clients, 250–254, *253*

assumptions about coaching process, 31

clients' resistance to, 175–176, 186–193, 259

coaching, defined, 32–34, 53

emotions of, 63–69, 257–260

goals for coaching conversations, 251–252

identity markers of, 14–15

Mind the Gaps for coaches as learners, 139–141, *140* (*See also* Mind the Gaps Framework)

ongoing learning of, 209

patience of, 243

personal offense felt by, 190

self-disclosure by, 204–209, 267–271

video used by, 260–262, 282–283

See also self-care; Transformational Coaching; Transformational Coaching Rubric (TCR) 2.0